Palgrave Modern Legal History

This series provides a forum for the publication of high-quality monographs that take innovative, contextual, and inter- or multi-disciplinary approaches to legal history. It brings legal history to a wider audience by exploring the history of law as part of a broader social, intellectual, cultural, literary, or economic context. Its focus is on modern British and Imperial legal history (post 1750), but within that time frame engages with the widest possible range of subject areas.

Laura Cahillane • Donal K. Coffey
Editors

The Centenary of the Irish Free State Constitution

Constituting a Polity?

palgrave
macmillan

Editors
Laura Cahillane
School of Law
University of Limerick
Limerick, Ireland

Donal K. Coffey
Maynooth University
Maynooth, Ireland

Max Planck Institute for Legal History
and Legal Theory
Frankfurt am Main, Germany

ISSN 2947-6186 ISSN 2947-6194 (electronic)
Palgrave Modern Legal History
ISBN 978-3-031-46180-4 ISBN 978-3-031-46181-1 (eBook)
https://doi.org/10.1007/978-3-031-46181-1

This Palgrave Macmillan imprint is published by the registered company Springer Nature Switzerland AG.
The registered company address is: Gewerbestrasse 11, 6330 Cham, Switzerland

Paper in this product is recyclable.

Foreword

Before I offer some thoughts on the end product of their deliberations, I would like to sincerely congratulate both Laura Cahillane and Donal K. Coffey on the organisation of such an impressive conference on the topic of the 1922 Constitution. The conference played host to many insightful contributions on fascinating topics which have been developed in the chapters in this book.

It is right, perhaps, to start with the question of why it is important to commemorate a constitution that existed for only 15 years, and which was acknowledged to have flaws, and to have carried within it the seeds of its own destruction.

The 1920s were undoubtedly an era of enthusiastic constitutionalism, but subsequent decades were very turbulent waters for those constitutional vessels constructed in the immediate aftermath of the First World War. The 1922 Free State Constitution was not immune to this turbulence:

1. It was weighed down from the outset by the inclusion of certain provisions from the Treaty, such as the Oath of Allegiance, which were almost universally unpopular in Ireland;
2. It was drafted by theorists, but put in the hands of legislators, administrators, and—to a large extent—a legal community which did not always appreciate its possibilities, or indeed, its values;
3. The drafters, although themselves people of substance (three, for example, would become judges of the Supreme Court) did not go on to take a public role in the politics of the State such as to capture

the imagination of subsequent generations in the way, for example, that the drafters of the US Federal Constitution did; and

4. In any event, as we know, the Constitution carried a hairline fracture below the waterline in the provisions of Article 50 permitting its amendment by ordinary legislation, and which would in due course sink the Constitution.

And so, after 15 years, having been eviscerated by a process of amendment permitted by Article 50, it was revoked and replaced by Bunreacht na hÉireann, which (in significantly amended form) remains our basic law. So why consider the 1922 Constitution today?

In my view, the continuing value of the 1922 Constitution lies, at least in part, precisely in what occurred in 1937 when a new Constitution was drafted by an administration comprising those who had opposed the Treaty settlement, and indeed, the Constitution that followed it. While significant changes were made and innovations introduced, what was striking was that the essential structure established in 1922 was retained. That was, I think, because, leaving aside the features of the Treaty which were required to be contained in the Constitution, and some experimental innovations which did not take root, the essential structure of the 1922 Constitution was at its heart, a very modern document. This was partly due to the extensive study the committee made of the existing constitutions of the world, and in particular those emerging in the aftermath of the First World War. This infusion of modern secular and democratic optimism had a significant influence on the text—an achievement which should not be underestimated when you consider the visible piety of members of the committee such as Hugh Kennedy and Alfred O'Rahilly. It succeeded in establishing something that only became the norm in the period following the Second World War: a state based on the separation of powers in which the institutions of state were created and defined by law, limited by a constitution providing for fundamental rights and where those limitations and rights could and would be enforced by actions in the courts, and, perhaps as importantly, that the decisions of those courts would be, and have been, complied with by the other branches of government.

I would like to touch very briefly on this last feature of the Constitution: i.e., the provision for judicial review contained in Article 66 of the Irish Free State Constitution and continued in Article 34.3.2° of the 1937 Constitution.

I remember being fascinated by the 1922 Constitution when I first encountered it. I think part of that was the fact that it was clearly the product of idealism, both international and national. It was also arguably the last opportunity to avoid the division that led to the Civil War, which would scar Irish affairs in the succeeding 100 years, and perhaps one of the last points in which the business being conducted was approached on an all-Ireland basis. Partition had not yet taken root, and accordingly, at least three of the participants in the drafting of the Constitution had strong connections with what is now Northern Ireland. The tone of the deliberations was one of openness and generosity to the Unionist and largely Protestant minority in the new state. It was a glimpse of a different possible Ireland—without partition, without the Civil War.

The provisions for judicial review contained in Article 66 were described later by Professor John Kelly as "potentially crucial"[1] and are certainly central to those aspects of the 1922 and 1937 Constitutions which involve the courts.

When I first encountered the Constitution, it was said generally that the inspiration for this came from the United States. Thus, for example, Hugh O'Flaherty in his book of essays *Justice, Liberty and the Courts*[2] could confidently say of our Constitution that judicial review "came to our present Constitution via the Constitution of the Irish Free State, from the Constitution of the United States of America". It was said, by the standard texts, that the inspiration for Article 66 was either Kevin O'Sheil—one of the northerners I mentioned—who, it was said had written a book about the US Constitution, "*The Making of a Republic*"[3] published in 1920, or it could be traced to the influence of C.J. France, an American member of the committee who had met James Douglas while being active in the work of the Irish White Cross. Thus, Akenson and Fallin[4] in their interesting series of articles in *Éire-Ireland* 1970 could say:

> He [France] was a useful addition because he possessed a familiarity with the structural advantages and disadvantages of the American Constitution.

[1] J.M. Kelly, 'Grafting Judicial Review onto a System Founded on Parliamentary Supremacy: The Irish Experience' quoted in Laura Cahillane, *Drafting the Irish Free State Constitution* (Manchester University Press 2016).

[2] Hugh O'Flaherty, *Justice, Liberty and the Courts* (Round Hall Sweet & Maxwell 1999).

[3] Kevin O'Sheil, *The Making of a Republic* (The Talbot Press 1920).

[4] D.H. Akenson and F.P. Fallin, 'The Irish Civil War and the Drafting of the Irish Constitution' (1970) V (1) Éire-Ireland 10.

Taking each of these in turn, I remember acquiring a copy of *The Making of the Republic* and opening it with some excitement, but discovering that it did not contain any account of the American Constitution, or American constitutional law. Instead, it was an account of the American Revolution of 1776, rather than the Federal Constitution of 13 years later. Furthermore, we know Kevin O'Sheil did not attend many of the meetings, of the committee and did not consider himself in a position to sign any of the drafts of the Constitution. While he was a significant and interesting figure and left a fascinating account of his life, nothing in his background or subsequent career suggests to me he was particularly interested in US constitutional law, or indeed, the theory of judicial review.

C.J. France from Seattle was another intriguing member of the committee. He was initially a much-valued member of the committee, being associated with James Douglas, himself an important and influential member of the group. But C.J. France seems an entirely unlikely enthusiast for *Marbury v. Madison*.[5] It seems clear from the papers of the committee that his involvement was principally directed towards the question of establishing the ownership by Ireland of its natural resources. We also know that during the progress of the committee, Douglas was warned by some of the American contacts against C.J. France. Brian Farrell records a letter to Douglas which he passed to Collins which stated that:-

> We have no knowledge, of course, of what Mr. France's ideas or sentiments regarding the Constitutional Provisions are. He may reflect our sentiments and he may correctly reflect predominant American sentiment, but we do not know and therefore our concern can be readily understood, especially as his brother came out of Russia recently with ideas and opinions regarding the establishment of a Government there that shocked and astounded the great majority of thinking Americans.[6]

Subsequently, Douglas appears to have concluded that, on the face value of the correspondence, France looks "a pure adventurer". It seems probable that France did share his brother's shocking ideas, which must have been of a socialist, if not communist, variety. This was a period when the International Workers of the World, were particularly active, especially in the North-western states of the United States. E.V. Debs, a socialist

[5] *Marbury v. Madison* 5 U.S. 137 (1803).

[6] Brian Farrell, 'The Drafting of the Irish Free State Constitution: II' (1970) 5(2) The Irish Jurist 343.

candidate for president, won nearly one million votes in 1920. One interesting indicator of the view of France can be found, I think, in a fascinating speech delivered by Hugh Kennedy to the semi-centennial meeting of the American Bar Association in 1928. It is entitled "Character and Sources of Constitution of the Irish Free State"[7] and refers to the influences of the written constitutions of the United States, Germany, and Switzerland, but nowhere addresses the question of Article 66 of the Free State Constitution or draws any parallel with the United States.

Hugh Kennedy is an interesting and complex character. Thomas Mohr has done very valuable work on the Kennedy papers and it would, I think, be particularly valuable to have a fully rounded picture of this talented, complex and sometimes difficult man, and the first occupant of the office I now hold. He undoubtedly could be both passionate and eloquent. The speech concludes:

> To adapt the poet's modest claim, it may be a poor thing, but it is all our own, and as such we assert its authority and claim upon our people. This boast at least we may make without fear of challenge, that under the institutions as we have made them there is no room for ascendency of class or religion, and the upgrowing youth of our state will compete, with equality of opportunity, in a free country ....

During the speech, Kennedy gave quite a detailed account of the drafting of the Constitution, and described, but did not identify by name, the members of the committee, drawing attention for example, to the US connections of James Murnaghan. But he made no reference at all to the US lawyer who was a member of the committee. This is all the more striking because the conference was being held in Seattle, France's hometown. It seems that Kennedy may have been warned, or perhaps had already come to the conclusion, that reference to C.J. France in the United States would not be welcome among US lawyers.

The picture of France which we can glimpse is one which makes him a very unlikely enthusiast for judicial review. After all, in the United States *Lochner v. New York*[8] was only 17 years old, *Plessey v. Ferguson*[9] had been

[7] Hugh Kennedy, 'Character and Sources of Constitution of the Irish Free State' (1928) 14(8) American Bar Association Journal 437.

[8] *Lochner v. New York* 198 U.S. 45 (1905).

[9] *Plessey v. Ferguson* 163 U.S. 537 (1896).

decided 24 years earlier, and *Dred Scott*[10] was still vividly remembered. It is very unlikely that somebody on the left of the spectrum in the United States would have considered that giving a power of judicial review to the courts would be a good idea.

All of this is more interesting, and perhaps striking, because as we know, draft C, which was produced by Alfred O'Rahilly but also signed by someone of the significance of James Murnaghan, only contemplated the possibility of review of the validity of acts of the executive, but specifically excluded that possibility in the case of the legislature. This was because he considered that the influence of the US Supreme Court had been unhelpful, particularly in its development of substantive due process in the *Lochner* era, and the manner in which it constrained progressive legislatures.

Unfortunately, perhaps because draft C only became available late in the day, there does not appear to be much extensive debate about this, and so the thinking behind the provisions of Article 66 remains something of a mystery.

But it may be that we have been looking at this wrongly, through modern eyes, and starting from the proposition that since judicial review was anathema to the common law system in the Westminster model and looking for some decisive counterbalance to that by reference to the United States.

It may be that the story is more nuanced. I have previously discussed the impact of the debates over the three Home Rule Bills and in particular, the Home Rule Bill of 1893 and had occasion to consider the history in the context of preparing for *Maguire v. Ardagh*.[11] The reason why it was necessary to consider that history was that one of the issues to be decided was whether the power to conduct the inquiry was one that was inherent in legislatures. This led to a consideration of the Privy Council case of *Kielley v. Carson*[12] in 1842, which decided that unlike the Imperial Parliament, colonial legislatures had no inherent power to punish for contempt. It may, I think, be a mistake to think of judicial review *per se*, as anathema to the common law, and the British Empire. In fact, judicial review was commonplace in that context. Most, if not all of the provisions for self-government of dominions or colonies required legislation establishing the division of functions and powers between the Imperial

[10] *Dred Scott v. Sandford* 60 U.S. 393 (1856).

[11] *Maguire v. Ardagh* [2002] IESC 21, [2002] 1 I.R. 385.

[12] *Kielley v. Carson* (1842) 13 ER 225.

Parliament and the newly established colonial or dominion legislatures, and furthermore, that that division must be capable of enforcement by courts. As the recent case in the United Kingdom Supreme Court on Scottish devolution has shown, this is, in itself, important constitutional law. The Government of Ireland Act, 1920 is a very good example. Sir Frederick Pollock[13] quoted Kent's commentaries to the effect that "the judicial department is the proper power in the government to determine whether a statute be or be not constitutional", and stated further that "[t]his is the view most natural to minds trained in English legal and political tradition", was established in the law of the United States and "has been accepted by British publicists and lawyers as applicable to the decision of causes involving constitutional questions throughout the British Empire".

Looked at in this way, what was unusual about the Irish Free State Constitution was not so much that the validity of acts of the newly established legislature could be reviewed and decided by courts, but rather that the Constitution, by reference to which those acts could be reviewed, contained a particularly expansive statement of fundamental rights.

The fact that the Irish Free State Constitution contains at its very outset, this expansive statement of fundamental rights, most of which made their way into the 1937 Constitution almost unchanged, was perhaps one element of good luck in what was otherwise an unhappy story. The history of the Home Rule Bills suggests strongly that the British side may have wanted to protect the minority in the new State, and the Irish side wished perhaps to emphasise the independence of the State, and its difference from the prior legal order. If so, and if this led to the delimitation of fundamental rights, and the provisions of Article 66 of the Constitution, then that is something to be grateful for. All of this illustrates the fact that we still lack knowledge as to the influence that led to the adoption of the 1922 Constitution, but also that the text remains, overall, of real current relevance, and perhaps most importantly, that there remains work to be done. This book is a welcome, and very substantial, contribution to that work.

Chief Justice of Ireland Donal O'Donnell

[13] Frederick Pollock, 'The Judicial Committee and the Interpretation of the New Constitution' in J.H. Morgan (ed) *The New Irish Constitution: An Exposition and Some Arguments* (Hodder & Stoughton 1912).

References

Akenson, D.H. and F.P. Fallin. "The Irish Civil War and the Drafting of the Irish Constitution." *Éire-Ireland* V, no. 1 (1970): 10.

Farrell, Brian. "The Drafting of the Irish Free State Constitution: II." *The Irish Jurist* 5, no. 2 (1970): 343.

Kelly, J.M. "Grafting Judicial Review onto a System Founded on Parliamentary Supremacy: The Irish Experience." In Laura Cahillane. *Drafting the Irish Free State Constitution.* Manchester University Press, 2016.

Kennedy, Hugh. "Character and Sources of Constitution of the Irish Free State." American Bar Association Journal 14, no. 8 (1928) 437.

O'Flaherty, Hugh. *Justice, Liberty and the Courts.* Round Hall Sweet & Maxwell, 1999.

O'Sheil, Kevin. *The Making of a Republic.* The Talbot Press, 1920.

Pollock, Frederick. "The Judicial Committee and the Interpretation of the New Constitution." In *The New Irish Constitution: An Exposition and Some Arguments,* edited by J.H. Morgan, Hodder & Stoughton 1912.

CONTENTS

1 **Introduction** 1
Laura Cahillane and Donal K. Coffey

2 **Constituting a Polity** 9
Laura Cahillane

3 **The Partition of Ireland and the 1922 Constitution** 25
C. R. G. Murray

4 **'The Supreme Legislative Authority Speaking as the Mouthpiece of the People': Constituent Power and the Irish Free State** 47
Alan Greene

5 **Opposition to the Constitution of the Irish Free State in 1922** 73
Thomas Mohr

6 **The Representative of the Crown and the Governor-General of the Irish Free State: Text and Context** 91
Graham Butler

7 **The National Language and Article 4 of the 1922 Constitution** 113
Róisín Á. Costello BL

8 **A New Constitution; a New Language? How the New Courts Talked About the Free State Constitution 1922** 135
Maurice Collins

9 **'Environmental Stewardship' and Article 11 of the 1922 Constitution** 153
Jamie McLoughlin

10 **The 1922 Constitution as a Failed Attempt to Break with Westminster Tradition** 175
David Kenny

11 **Property Rights and Democratic Decision-Making: Lessons from the 1922 Constitution** 197
Rachael Walsh

12 **The Civil War, the Constitution and the Collapse of the Rule of Law** 217
Seán Enright

13 **Revisiting the Legacy of the Amendment Procedure** 233
William Quill

14 **What the Drafters Learnt in 1937 from the 1922 Experience** 253
Gerard Hogan

15 **The Afterlife of the Constitution of the Irish Free State: Constitutional Echoes in South Asia** 271
Donal K. Coffey

Index 287

Notes on Contributors

Graham Butler is a full Professor of Law, University of Southern Denmark, Odense, Denmark.

Laura Cahillane is an Associate Professor in the School of Law, University of Limerick. Her research interests lie in the areas of constitutional law, legal history and judicial studies. She is editor-in-chief of the Irish Judicial Studies Journal.

Donal K. Coffey is an Assistant Professor, Maynooth University, and Affiliate Researcher, Max Planck Institute for Legal History and Legal Theory, Frankfurt am Main.

Maurice Collins is a judge of the Supreme Court.

Róisín Á. Costello BL is an Assistant Professor in the Law School at Trinity College Dublin and a practicing barrister. She is the author and editor of volumes published by Hart, Bloomsbury and Edinburgh University Press. Róisín is currently undertaking research funded by the AHRC on courtroom interpretation for minority language users in Ireland, and Wales and has previously undertaken research on minority language rights in Ireland funded by the Irish Research Council and the Department of Foreign Affairs.

Seán Enright is a Legal historian and Circuit Judge.

Alan Greene is a Reader in Constitutional Law and Human Rights at Birmingham Law School, UK. He is the author of Permanent States of Emergency and the Rule of Law: Constitutions in an Age of Crisis (Hart

Publishing, 2018) and Emergency Powers in a Time of Pandemic (Bristol University Press, 2020).

Gerard Hogan is a judge of the Supreme Court. He was previously an Advocate General of the Court of Justice of the European Union.

David Kenny is Professor in Law and Fellow at Trinity College Dublin, where he researches and teaches Irish and comparative constitutional law and law and literature.

Jamie McLoughlin BCL (NUI), BCL (Oxon), is a PhD candidate and Irish Research Council Graduate Research Scholar at the Sutherland School of Law, University College Dublin. His research interests are in the areas of Irish and comparative constitutional law and international and comparative human rights law, with a particular focus on economic, social, and environmental human rights.

Thomas Mohr is an associate professor at the School of Law, University College Dublin. He is vice president of the Irish Legal History Society and book review editor of the Irish Jurist, Ireland's oldest law journal. His publications on Irish legal history range from medieval Gaelic law to the law of the independent Irish state in the twentieth century. His latest books are Guardian of the Treaty – The Privy Council Appeal and Irish Sovereignty (2016) and Law and the Idea of Liberty in Ireland – From Magna Carta to the Present (2023).

C. R. G. Murray is Professor of Law and Democracy at Newcastle Law School, with his research encompassing devolution, the right to vote, imperialism's impact on the UK Constitution and the human rights implications of counter-terrorism powers.

William Quill studied at Trinity College Dublin where he received a a BA in History and an MSc in Comparative European Politics. He studied at the King's Inns and was called to the bar in 2016. He practised at the bar from 2016 to 2023. William is an investigator for the Office of the Commissioner for Environmental Information.

Rachael Walsh is an Associate Professor at the School of Law, Trinity College Dublin, and a Fellow of TCD. She is author of Property Rights and Social Justice: Progressive Property in Action (Cambridge University Press, 2021) and co-author of Kelly: The Irish Constitution (Bloomsbury, 2018).

CHAPTER 1

Introduction

Laura Cahillane and Donal K. Coffey

The year 1922 was meant to be the calm after the storm. The Articles of Agreement for a Treaty between British and Irish delegates signed in December 1921 provoked some visceral protest, but the possibility existed that a constitutional formula could yet be found that would allow all sides to take part in the new State. It was in this context that the drafting of the Irish Free State Constitution began.

During a period of about six weeks in early 1922, the Constitution was written. Sequestered in the Shelbourne hotel, five lawyers (including one American lawyer), two professors, a writer, and a businessman, aided by three secretaries, drafted the document which provided the framework for the modern Irish State. Their key task, according to their

L. Cahillane (✉)
School of Law, University of Limerick, Limerick, Ireland
e-mail: laura.cahillane@ul.ie

D. K. Coffey
Maynooth University, Maynooth, Ireland

Max Planck Institute for Legal History and Legal Theory,
Frankfurt am Main, Germany
e-mail: Donal.Coffey@mu.ie

L. Cahillane, D. K. Coffey (eds.), *The Centenary of the Irish Free State Constitution*, Palgrave Modern Legal History,
https://doi.org/10.1007/978-3-031-46181-1_1

Chairman—Michael Collins—was to create "a free democratic constitution." One of the principal drafters—Hugh Kennedy—has written that they aimed to "respond to the guidance of Irish history and existing Irish conditions and, on the other hand, borrow from the experience of the constituted democracies of the world." When the Constitution passed through the Irish Constituent Assembly, Minister for Home Affairs—Kevin O'Higgins—explained that the document gave the Irish people "the making and moulding, the amending or repealing of their own laws. It gives them full fiscal control; it gives them power to develop in peace and reconstruction towards the fullness of National life." Unfortunately, those involved have largely been forgotten by history and the document they created has been over-shadowed by the political developments of the period.

This was not inevitable, as while a bitter Civil War broke out, the victors in the military conflict were the proponents of the Constitution. The ultimate political triumph was to belong, however, to the losers in that conflict, who went on to found the most successful political grouping in the history of the State, Fianna Fáil, who ascended into high political office within a decade of the end of the Civil War. The Constitution that was enacted in 1937 was associated with this party, and has naturally been the focus of consideration since its enactment.

The 1922 Constitution received less scholarly consideration as a result. It should be noted that some excellent contemporaneous scholarship existed, notable examples being the works of Leo Kohn and a young Nicholas Mansergh. More recently, there has been a renewed scholarly interest in the period, best found in the works of authors in this volume such as Thomas Mohr and Laura Cahillane.

In early 2022, we discussed the possibility of putting together a conference to mark the centenary of the 1922 Constitution. It seemed to us that this was an opportune time to consider the state of the art of the research in relation to the Constitution of the Irish Free State. The result was a conference held in the Shelbourne hotel on 5 December 2022. We gratefully acknowledge here the support we received from the University of Limerick, the Courts Service, the Maynooth University Social Sciences Institute, and the Shelbourne hotel. We should also like to record our thanks to all of the speakers and chairs at the original conference, both those whose work is published here and those whose presentations helped inform the research community more broadly. The interest in the conference fortified our belief that there was a desire in the scholarly community and amongst the general public for greater insights into this period of our national life; this edited collection is our attempt to satiate that interest.

Opening the conference to mark the centenary of the 1922 Irish Free State Constitution, Attorney General Paul Gallagher commented that the document was "a remarkable achievement" and it set the new state "on a democratic trajectory from which it has never deviated." Continuing that theme, in Chap. 2, Laura considers the document in its attempt to construct a new polity and notes the fact that due to the turbulent circumstances surrounding the creation of the document and its subsequent demise, it has generally been looked upon in a negative light. She asks however if whether that portrayal of the Constitution is a fair and accurate one. This chapter argues that scholarship on the Constitution should look beyond the "failure" and the controversial elements to discover the true impact and lasting legacies of the document.

In Chap. 3, Colin Murray reflects upon the missing elements of the 1922 Constitution which were nonetheless central to understanding the transformation in Ireland's governance arrangements at this juncture. In December 1922, Northern Ireland refused to join the Irish Free State's new constitutional order, as everyone involved in the process foresaw. But the uncertainty around partition meant that the Constitution did not engage with the legal process of creating (and mitigating) a border on the island of Ireland. The border itself would not be regarded as settled until the Agreement to set aside the Boundary Commission Report in late 1925. It is argued that the 1922 Constitution, for good and ill, therefore neglected some of the defining aspects of the new constitutional dispensations on the island. This chapter explores how these measures and interactions affected the relationship between Ireland's new constitutional orders at the time and in the subsequent decades.

Next, in Chap. 4, Alan Greene argues that constituent power—the power to create a constitution that in Ireland is usually considered to be vested in "the people"—is an overlooked concept in Irish constitutional thought. He writes in this chapter that this is evident from key moments in the history of the Irish Free State: in particular, the seminal case of the *State (Ryan) v Lennon*. This chapter further argues that there is a proto-understanding of constituent power as vested in the people latent in the famous dissenting judgement of Kennedy CJ, although this has been overshadowed by the aspects of his judgment focusing on natural law. This is most clearly identifiable in regard to the competing perspectives in the judgments as to the role of the people both in the exercise of constituent power that created the Free State Constitution and within the constituted order. The chapter concludes with a brief discussion of how a better understanding of constituent power may influence and shape constitutional debates on the island of Ireland today.

Thomas Mohr in Chap. 5 then provides a snapshot of the opposition to the Free State Constitution in the year 1922 before opinions were influenced by the course of subsequent events and the benefit of hindsight. It outlines why some Irish people felt that they could not support the new Constitution and how they expressed their opposition to it. The most obvious group that opposed the 1922 Constitution were those that had also opposed the Anglo-Irish Treaty signed in 1921. This chapter also examines the legal arguments used by this group to challenge the validity of the 1922 Constitution, Unionist objections, and the position of those who felt that they could support the Treaty but had serious reservations concerning the Constitution.

In Chap. 6, Graham Butler looks at the office of the Governor-General. He writes that the centenary of the Constitution provides for the opportunity to revisit the text and context of the Treaty and Constitution to understand the nature of the representative of the Crown as emboldened in the office of the Governor-General, which in turn laid the foundation for what subsequently became the office of the President of Ireland in the Constitution of 1937.

The National language is the subject of Chap. 7 as Róisín Á Costello looks at Article 4 of the Constitution. She notes that Irish is only mentioned twice in the document—elevating the language to a first and official tongue but providing little practical support for the language's continued use or revival in public spaces. The result of this framing of Irish was, it is argued, to relegate the language to a position of demonstrative symbolism. It was a position which, whether it was intentional or not, continued to characterise the official view of the language for much of the jurisdiction's first 100 years. The constitutional status of Irish, from the outset, was as a language whose existence was both highly visible and under-determined. This chapter examines the drafting and development of the language protections in the 1922 text, and how they came to frame national commitments through judicial interpretation in the first decades of the new state—and the twentieth century.

Next, echoing the theory versus reality theme from Chap. 2, and in a different take on language, Maurice Collins in Chap. 8 discusses how the Irish Courts spoke about the Constitution during its lifetime and explores whether the language used by the courts suggests an enthusiastic embrace of it as "the fundamental instrument of the new State" constituting an entirely new legal order or whether the courts effectively approached the Constitution from a positivistic perspective. In truth, we are told, the position revealed by a review of the *Irish Reports* is untidy: the data-set is small and Article 50 throws a long shadow over what is there. The reality according to this chapter, at least as regards judicial review, is that the 1922 Constitution was largely still-born, with an ever-increasing gap between constitutional rhetoric and constitutional reality.

In Chap. 9, Jamie McLoughlin considers the idea of "environmental stewardship" and Article 11 of the Constitution. He argues that Article 11—and the successor provision it inspired in Bunreacht na hÉireann—can be understood as creating a State duty of environmental stewardship. This duty entails managing the country's natural resources to respond to the current climate and biodiversity crises.

In Chap. 10, David Kenny re-examines a dominant popular narrative about the 1922 Constitution: that it largely followed and replicated, without great change, the Westminster model of parliamentary and executive governance. He opines that if this were the case, it would be surprising given the revolutionary zeal of the Irish independence movement and its critiques of the operation of the Westminster parliament. Contrary to this narrative, however, the 1922 Constitution in fact represents a fascinating but failed attempt to radically break with the Westminster tradition. The Constitution's oft-overlooked experimental elements—functional/vocational councils, external ministers, direct democracy, etc.—envisaged a stark break with the Westminster reality of executive dominance, empowering parliament and the people, and limiting the influence of cabinet governance. This experiment failed for various complex reasons, and perhaps was always destined to fail in the circumstances in which the new state found itself. Nevertheless, as David reminds us, it is important to remember the 1922 Constitution as the radical experiment in governance that it was.

Rachael Walsh in Chap. 11 then analyses the lessons that can be taken from the drafting of the 1922 Constitution for current-day constitutional property dilemmas. In particular, this chapter examines alternative strategies for mediating between property rights protection and democratic decision-making that are highlighted by the 1922 experience and which signal different constitutional pathways for addressing contemporary housing and environmental challenges.

The collapse of the rule of law in the context of the Civil War is the subject of Chap. 12 by Seán Enright. He notes that the autumn of 1922 witnessed two momentous and contradictory events. The first was the creation of the Irish Free State Constitution, which guaranteed liberty, freedom of religion, expression, and association. It also guaranteed what we now recognise as the rule of law: universal suffrage, separation of powers between the judiciary and government, and trial by due process of law. The second event was the implementation of the execution policy which would result in 83 executions for carrying arms and/or attacking the National Army. The policy was not the product of legislation or other process of law, and after the war, the government passed an Act of Indemnity to protect those who had taken part in military courts. It did not render legal what was done but it prevented any prosecutions and litigation. A century later, an attempt is made in this chapter to re-assess and reconcile those two events.

William Quill then considers how the amendment process of the 1922 Constitution shaped the politics of the new State in Chap. 13. He argues that although the process of amendment proved a weakness in the stability of the Constitution, these circumstances shaped the development of the nascent Irish state. He points out that had the original strict thresholds been applied, several of the amendments might not have been enacted, or might have been enacted only after a delay. Elements of direct participatory democracy such as the initiative and referendum on legislation would have remained as tools of opponents of government, while the state would have had less freedom to respond swiftly to the changing relationship with the United Kingdom in the 1930s. William observes that the Constitution of Ireland in place since 1937 was built on the framework of its predecessor, including what was learned during this transitional period.

In the penultimate chapter (Chap. 14), Gerard Hogan examines what the drafters of the 1937 Constitution learnt from the 1922 experience. He contends that, with the benefit of hindsight, it was clear that the 1922 Constitution was doomed from the start. This was in part because the Constitution was shackled to the Anglo-Irish Treaty of December 1921—itself the cause of the Civil War 1922–1923—but also because a last-minute drafting change allowed that Constitution to be amended by ordinary legislation. This proved to be the undoing of that Constitution. This, he says, was the principal lesson learnt by the drafters in 1937 inasmuch save for a short transitional period, the Constitution could henceforth be amended only by way of referendum. In addition, we are told, the organisation and drafting of the 1937 Constitution was better and much that was novel and new in 1937—enhanced judicial review, an extended catalogue of fundamental rights, provisions dealing with international law and the office of the Presidency—has weathered well. The chapter also argues that that the 1937 Constitution reflected more faithfully the Irish nationalist and Catholic Zeitgeist of the period in a way that was not true of the Constitution of the Irish Free State but that now in 2023 we now have a document which at every turn reinforces democracy, the rule of law, fundamental rights, effective judicial protection, and the ultimate *Grundnorm* of popular sovereignty.

Finally, Donal K. Coffey in Chap. 15 looks at the influence of the Irish Free State Constitution outside the borders of the State. The chapter examines the way in which constitutional theorists outside Ireland adapted and adopted the provisions of the Constitution for their own constitutional experiments. This can be most clearly seen in South Asia, and the chapter looks at the particular influence of the 1922 Constitution in India and Ceylon/Sri Lanka. The chapter also considers a particularly critical view of the Irish Free State Constitution that can be found in the Northern Ireland Legal Quarterly and analyses if the criticism was warranted. It concludes by looking at the influence of South Asian constitutional theory on a recent development in Irish constitutional jurisprudence.

We hope that this collection will inspire further interest and scholarship in this fascinating document and this keystone moment in Irish legal history.

On a personal note, we would like to thank our families, whose love and support made the conference and edited collection possible.

26 June 2023

CHAPTER 2

Constituting a Polity

Laura Cahillane

The creation of a new state and construction of a new constitution is often a very divisive moment in a state's history—fraught with difficulties related to the desires and plans for building something new and moving away from existing ways of doing things. The creation of the Irish Free State and the drafting of the 1922 Constitution is no different, as Thomas Mohr has outlined in his chapter in this collection.[1] It was a very turbulent period of Irish history with many parts of the population refusing to accept the new status quo. Many others were also disappointed that the status which had been achieved was less than what had been desired but pragmatically felt that it would be better to work within the new polity to try to achieve more. The 1922 Irish Free State Constitution is therefore understandably

[1] See Chap. 5, Thomas Mohr, "Opposition to the Constitution of the Irish Free State in 1922".

L. Cahillane (✉)
School of Law, University of Limerick, Limerick, Ireland
e-mail: Laura.Cahillane@ul.ie

L. Cahillane, D. K. Coffey (eds.), *The Centenary of the Irish Free State Constitution*, Palgrave Modern Legal History,
https://doi.org/10.1007/978-3-031-46181-1_2

always viewed within the context of that division. In addition to that, there is a tendency to point to the fact that it lasted only 15 years as evidence of failure. This is despite the fact that 15 years is about the average life span for a constitution.[2] The over-riding attitude surrounding the 1922 Constitution has primarily been negative.

However, on the 100th anniversary of the document it is only right to ask whether that portrayal of the constitution is a fair and accurate one. While the project did indeed end in failure with many of the novelties and experimental provisions being removed or nullified and with the Constitution itself being replaced having been ravaged with amendments more generally, the reasons behind this are multifaceted and only a few relate to the document itself—most are attributable to the wider context of the time. The Constitution itself is somewhat of a paradox in that it presented a particular vision of a new state but the reality which followed did not fulfil this vision. Instead, the *realpolitik* of the time ensured that the vision could never emerge.[3] But in order to fully appreciate and assess the Constitution in its entirety, as well as consider its legacy, it is necessary to reflect, not just on the end result, but also on what was originally intended and how that may have had impacts which are less obvious but which may still have echoes today.

Vision and Identity

I have written in the past about the Committee which drafted the 1922 Constitution and about their approach to this momentous task[4]—it is no exaggeration to say that there was great hope and enthusiasm amongst the Committee members that what could be built was a modern, liberal, democratic polity based on ideals such as popular sovereignty, democracy, participation, and shared values and which would take its inspiration from

[2] See Tom Ginsburg, James Melton & Zachary Elkins, *The Endurance of National Constitutions,* (Cambridge: Cambridge University Press, 2009).

[3] See Laura Cahillane, "The Origins of Popular Sovereignty in Ireland: Theory and Reality", in Maria Cahill, Colm Ó Cinnéide, Seán Ó Conaill, Conor O'Mahony (eds) *Constitutional Change and Popular Sovereignty: Populism, Politics and the Law in Ireland* (Oxford: Routledge 2021).

[4] For details on the drafting, see Laura Cahillane, *Drafting the Irish Free State Constitution* (Manchester: Manchester University Press 2016); on the Committee in particular, see Chap. 1. See also Laura Cahillane, "An Insight into the Irish Free State Constitution", American Journal of Legal History, Volume 54, Issue 1, (2014): 1–38.

both ancient Ireland and from modern democracies. It would have been so much simpler to write a basic constitution, following Dominion models, using the mechanisms which already existed under the British regime, but there was a feeling amongst Committee members that in order to ensure that the Constitution would be accepted and embraced by the people, during such a turbulent period, that there had to be a great effort to demonstrate to the people that this new state was going to be different and better. Many Irish people were not interested in the details of politics—in fact for many, Irish independence simply meant being left alone,[5] but the Committee evidently felt that by proving to the Irish people that this was their Constitution—they held the sovereign power and ownership over it and that they could be actively involved in governance—that this might lead to a change. There were many devices and provisions in the Constitution designed to bring law and politics closer to the people.

Sovereignty and Democracy

The central and related themes of the Constitution, as originally drafted, were ideas based on giving the people ownership of the Constitution and moving away from Westminster-style politics. First, the foundation stone of the Constitution was the principle of popular sovereignty. This is enunciated in Article 2:

> All powers of government and all authority, legislative, executive, and judicial, in Ireland are derived from the people of Ireland, and the same shall be exercised in the Irish Free State (Saorstát Eireann) through the organisations established by or under, and in accord with, this Constitution.

It had originally been set in an even stronger form using the words of Pádraig Pearse, but these were toned down during negotiations in London.[6] However, the principle that all power derives from the people was retained and became the cornerstone of the document. This was important because it suited the narrative that the Irish people had always

[5] See Wilfred Ewart, *A Journey in Ireland* (London: G.P. Putnam, 1922), Tom Garvin, *The Evolution of Irish Nationalist Politics* (Dublin: Gill and Macmillan, 1981), and Tom Garvin *1922: The Birth of Irish Democracy* (Dublin: Gill and Macmillan, 2005).

[6] The British took issue with a number of the more independent or experimental provisions. Many which were seen as 'Republican' or even 'Bolshevik' were removed at the insistence of the British team. See Cahillane (n 4), 47–64.

remained sovereign just as Ireland had always remained a nation[7] and it also matched the sentiments in the post-war European constitutions, based on Rousseau's conception of sovereignty, which provided inspiration for the 1922 Drafting Committee.[8] The ideal of popular sovereignty could also be associated with the ancient Gaelic State[9]—a further source of inspiration—as well as the 1916 and 1919 declarations.

The inclusion of the doctrine of popular sovereignty was essential in order to gain the trust of the people for the new system, particularly one which had not yet freed itself completely from the shackles of the British Crown. Crown, Parliament and politics were traditionally regarded with suspicion in Ireland. However, if the people were to hold the power in their own hands, then perhaps the evils of the previous system could be avoided. It was a way of trying to ensure an autochthonous constitution. The declaration of popular sovereignty was also seen by the people as a republican aspect of the Constitution—a sign that the Irish Free State was not going to be controlled by the Crown. No doubt, many felt comforted by the fact that their rights would be protected in a system in which it was the people who were declared to be sovereign. As proof that the declaration was not just rhetoric, many devices were included in the Constitution in order to invest the idea with 'concrete reality'.[10]

One of the experiments included to further these goals was the idea of direct democracy. This idea was to involve the people directly in governance and in legislating. It was hoped that this would be achieved by the devices of the referendum and initiative. Article 47 introduced the device of referendum for ordinary legislation, which was in effect a veto on legislation:

> Any Bill passed or deemed to have been passed by both Houses may be suspended for a period of ninety days on the written demand of two-fifths of

[7] The Committee was influenced by the ideas contained in the writings of those such as Wolfe Tone, James Fintan Lalor, John Mitchel and Thomas Davis, who espoused similar ideas.

[8] Agnes Headlam-Morley, *The New Democratic Constitutions of Europe; A Comparative Study of Post-War European Constitutions with Special Reference to Germany, Czechoslovakia, Poland, Finland, The Kingdom of the Serbs, Croats & Slovenes and the Baltic States* (Oxford: Oxford University Press 1928), 89–90.

[9] See Darrell Figgis, *The Gaelic State in the Past and Future* (Dublin: Maunsel 1917).

[10] Kohn's phraseology. Leo Kohn, *The Constitution of the Irish Free State* (London: George Allen & Unwin Ltd. 1932) 116.

> the members of Dáil Eireann or of a majority of the members of Seanad Eireann presented to the President of the Executive Council not later than seven days from the day on which such Bill shall have been so passed or deemed to have been so passed. Such a Bill shall in accordance with regulations to be made by the Oireachtas be submitted by Referendum to the decision of the people if demanded before the expiration of the ninety days either by a resolution of Seanad Eireann assented to by three-fifths of the members of Seanad Eireann, or by a petition signed by not less than one-twentieth of the voters then on the register of voters, and the decision of the people by a majority of the votes recorded on such Referendum shall be conclusive. These provisions shall not apply to Money Bills or to such Bills as shall be declared by both Houses to be necessary for the immediate preservation of the public peace, health or safety.

So not only was there a requirement that the people would decide on amendments to the Constitution by way of referendum but also if certain legislation which had passed through the Oireachtas was not agreeable to the people, then the people could, before the measure would be signed into law, bring a petition demanding a referendum on the issue. Kevin O'Higgins explained the purpose of the provision when introducing it in the Constituent Assembly:

> [P]ersonal, actual contact between the people and the laws by which they are governed is advisable in a country where the traditional attitude of the people is to be against the law and against the Government. The referendum, we consider, will be a stimulus to the political thought and the political education of the people.[11]

The referendum was intended to be (and arguably is today under the 1937 Constitution) the primary manifestation of the expression of sovereignty in Irish constitutional law.

Article 48 then provided for the establishment of the initiative which, almost as a corollary to Article 47, was a method by which the people could propose their own laws or constitutional amendments. The Drafting Committee was greatly influenced in this regard by the Swiss Constitution, which is famous for its emphasis on democratic ideals, and also the Constitutions of the post-war European States, which were all infused with ideas of popular sovereignty and democracy. The intention was that

[11] Dáil Deb 5 October 1922 vol 1 col. 1211 (Kevin O'Higgins, Minister for Home Affairs).

the people would be interested in governance because they would have a real voice and control over their own destiny. Both provisions were highly experimental and it is questionable as to whether they would have been workable in this jurisdiction, but an opportunity to test the provisions never arose as they were abolished by the government in 1928 due to fears that they would be used to undermine the treaty settlement and potentially destabilise relations with Britain.[12]

A Fair and Democratic Political System

As part of this desire to make the people the true masters of the state, there was also a scheme to eliminate political party-style politics in Ireland. This was because it was felt that political parties were blighted by corruption and the Committee wished to create a new kind of political system which would allow for independent thought, would be above party-politics, and would move away from traditional British-style politics.[13] One element of this was the external ministers scheme. This was an idea conceived by James Douglas, one of the members of the Constitution Committee. The theory behind this scheme was that a new form of executive could be created which would be above party politics and which would function simply for the good of the state. Douglas suggested the creation of a two-tier executive: the first group would be responsible for policy and would comprise the President of the Executive Council and ministers responsible for defence, state, finance, and foreign affairs. The second group would be composed of a number of non-parliamentarians, appointed on the basis of their technical expertise. They would have responsibility for matters such as agriculture, education and justice. They were to be expert outsiders, who would not necessarily be politicians and

[12] The Fianna Fáil Party had decided to petition for the setting up of the initiative, as a means to remove the parliamentary Oath from the Constitution. The petition was signed by 96,000 voters and was submitted to the Dáil on 3 May 1928. However, Article 48 did not set out the procedure to be followed when a petition was brought before the Dáil and this led to a debate as to the correct procedure to be adopted. Eventually, the Dáil decided to postpone the issue until the proper procedure had been decided on. Apparently, it was intended to establish a Joint Committee to consider the procedure. However, before this ever happened, the government introduced a bill, which had been incubating for some time, which provided for the abolition of the need for referendum and the initiative.

[13] See, for example, Andrew E Malone, "Party Government in the Irish Free State" *Political Science Quarterly*, 44, no 3, (1929) 363. See also David Kenny's chapter in this volume.

indeed would have to resign their seats if they had been elected to one of the Houses (thus ensuring a more complete separation of powers), but the main aim is that they would be experts in the particular area they would be appointed to.

The scheme, originally based on similar provisions of the Swiss constitution,[14] changed a number of times before its final insertion into the Constitution. During the debates in the Constituent Assembly, many deputies were unsure of the scheme and so a watered-down version was eventually approved.[15] Nevertheless, the ideals behind the scheme remained the same. The problem is that the scheme was never really put into practice.

The first government elected under the Constitution included three external ministers, who were all pro-Treaty Sinn Féin deputies. (Deputy P.J. Hogan was elected as Minister for Agriculture, Deputy J.J. Walsh as Postmaster-General and Deputy Fionán Lynch as Minister of Fisheries.) In the following election the same ministers were re-elected except for one addition: this time there were four external ministries, Local Government being added. In 1925, the Amendments to the Constitution Committee recommended amending the external ministers provision to give a choice to the President of the Executive Council whether or not to appoint any external ministers and after that time no further external ministers were appointed.[16]

And so the scheme failed and while there were various contributing factors, the true downfall of the scheme was that there were never any actual external ministers appointed. Thus, the scheme was never given a chance to function as intended.[17] The idea was that experts, who were not necessarily politicians, could be appointed and that these ministers would be above politics. However, all of the actual appointees were members of the government party and there does not seem to have been any attempt to ensure that the appointees were actually experts in the area. Thus, the crucial element in the scheme was ignored.

[14] Letter to the Provisional Government from the signatories of Draft B, 8 March 1922, file 2, Papers of EM Stephens, MSS 4235, Trinity College Dublin Archives.

[15] See National Archives of Ireland, Department of the Taoiseach S8953.

[16] See Patrick Fay, "The Amendments to the Constitution Committee, 1926", *Administration* 26 no 3 (1978), 331–351.

[17] See Alan J Ward, "Challenging the British Constitution", *Parliamentary History* 9 (1990), 116 at 125.

A related experiment was the idea of functional or vocational councils.[18] This was another device intended to involve ordinary people in politics by setting up groups based on trade and aspects of national life and using these as advisory groups for the Oireachtas. Article 45 specified: "The Oireachtas may provide for the establishment of Functional or Vocational Councils representing branches of the social and economic life of the Nation." It was also envisaged that once they were up and running, these groups could elect external ministers.[19] It is another example of an experiment which was never initiated and even though this particular provision was retained in a slightly different form in 1937, nothing ever came of it.[20]

There were more aspects to the anti-party theme, such as the idea of PR-STV (proportional representation with the single transferrable vote), which was intended to create a multiplicity of parties in the Dáil and prevent the advent of a dual-party system. It was envisaged that groups would come together to vote on particular issues but that independent thought would flourish in a system not restrained by the demands of parties. It was also hoped that such a system would mean that the government would truly be answerable to the Dáil as no party would hold an overall majority. However, the Civil War split and its effect on politics in Ireland meant that this did not transpire.

The original Seanad, or Upper House, was also to form part of this theme. It was envisaged that the second House would comprise senatorial persons of high integrity and Article 30 provided that citizens should be proposed "on the grounds that they have done honour to the Nation by reason of useful public service or that, because of special qualifications or attainments, they represent important aspects of the Nation's life". There were no organised political parties in the early Seanad, and in the beginning, it did function as a forum for independent debate and discussion. As evidence of this, Donal O'Sullivan wrote of the first Seanad:

> This new Senate was in a position to realize, in microcosm, [Thomas] Davis's dream of a united Ireland wherein all men of goodwill would work together in a self-respecting, self-governing motherland: and, given the conditions, a spirit of co-operation there engendered and fostered might in time infuse the whole polity.[21]

[18] See further Cahillane (n 4), 138–145.

[19] Article 56.

[20] Article 15.3 Bunreacht na hÉireann 1937.

[21] Donal O'Sullivan, The Irish Free State and Its Senate (London: Faber, 1940), 116.

He also mentioned the election of Lord Glenavy as chairman of the House when, despite the fact that he had been "Edward Carson's right-hand man in the campaign of opposition to Home Rule", the Nationalists "made it clear that these things belonged to the dead past".[22] However, with the entry of Fianna Fáil into politics and into the Seanad as a political party, political lines hardened and party politics entered the Seanad also. So none of these idealistic provisions succeeded in their original aims.

Judicial Review

However, one experiment which did succeed, although it took many years, is judicial review of legislation. The judicial review provision in Article 65 of the Constitution has been described as "the most arresting provision in the Irish Free State Constitution".[23] The reason being that it constituted a massive break with the British tradition whereby parliament was supreme and judges could not question the actions of parliament. Popular sovereignty had already been proclaimed in Article 2, but this was an even further extension of that. Nothing like this had ever been seen in a Dominion constitution. However, judicial review did not flourish in this period partly due to the lack of entrenchment but also due to the legal profession; the lawyers and judges had all trained in the British tradition of parliamentary sovereignty and so were unused to the idea of the courts questioning the actions of parliament. The Irish judiciary had an opportunity to ignite the judicial review provision and to create entrenchment in the case of *State (Ryan) v Lennon*.[24] However, besides Chief Justice Kennedy the dissentient, all of the judges took a positivist and excessively literalist approach in their interpretation of the Constitution and the chance was lost.

This particular episode, which is also discussed by Alan Greene in his chapter,[25] could have signalled the beginning of the major period of judicial review which was to occur some 30 years later, but the judiciary was simply not ready for this innovative, unfamiliar power. However, the provision was maintained and went on to become one of the most significant

[22] Ibid.

[23] Letter from Professor Felix Frankfurter from Harvard University to Lionel Curtis, 10 August 1922, as cited by Gerard Hogan, Development of Judicial Review of Legislation and Irish Constitutional Law 1929–1941 (unpublished PhD thesis, Trinity College Dublin, 2001).

[24] [1935] IR 170.

[25] See Chap. 4, Alan Greene, "'The Supreme Legislative Authority Speaking as the Mouthpiece of the People': Constituent Power and the Irish Free State".

aspects of the current Irish Constitution. Thus, a device which seemed a surprising inclusion in 1922 and which failed to have much of an impact for a number of decades became a defining feature in modern times.

The idea of power for the people and a fair and independent political system was the leitmotif which runs through the entire 1922 document and there were many other aspects which flow from those themes. While Kohn has suggested that the primary inference drawn from popular sovereignty in the Constitution was the institution of a distinctive Irish citizenship,[26] other aspects, including the name of the state[27] and the declaration of the Irish language in Article 4 as an official language, were all linked to the affirmation of popular sovereignty in Article 2. (For a discussion on Article 4 and the Irish language, see Róisín Á Costello's chapter.)[28]

However, the contradiction at the heart of the 1922 Constitution now becomes clear—the vision was obvious: popular sovereignty was intended to empower the people; the referendum and initiative were designed to provide mechanisms for the people to exercise that power;[29] the functional councils[30] were intended to give an extra voice to the people in choosing the government; wide franchise and PR-STV was expected to provide for a broader spread of representation in voting; the external ministers scheme[31] was designed to provide non-political expertise in government, a more strict separation of powers and therefore more legislative oversight of government, judicial review and the independence of the judiciary[32] was supposed to ensure the people had recourse to the courts if parliament over-stepped its role; and originally, entrenchment would have ensured that the document would be difficult to amend in order to protect the people from arbitrary actions.[33] However, the dream never became a reality and while the reasons are more complicated than we have time to con-

26 Kohn (n 10), 116.

27 See Cahillane (n 4), 106–107.

28 See Chap. 7, Róisín Á Costello, "The National Language and Article 4 of the 1922 Constitution".

29 Articles 47 and 48.

30 Article 45.

31 Article 55.

32 Articles 65 and 69.

33 Originally, the Draft Constitution did not contain any period of grace in relation to constitutional amendments. All amendments were to be submitted to the people. Of course this was changed during debates in the Constituent Assembly and the new amendment procedure was eventually used to remove the experimental provisions and many other provisions and so render the document dilapidated.

sider in this brief chapter,[34] a simple drafting mistake which made the Constitution easy to amend by a parliamentary majority without being time-limited,[35] combined with the Civil War context, poor decision-making, and the interpretation given by the Court in the *State (Ryan v Lennon)* case, all led to the sinking of the constitutional project.

Re-assessment; Appreciation, Identity and Legacy

So why does all this matter given that the Constitution failed to live up to what it had initially promised?

Up until fairly recently, the 1922 Constitution had been relatively ignored by legal scholars.[36] It had been explored from historical and political science perspectives, but the legal analysis was often missing. For this and for other reasons, Irish lawyers and students of Irish law generally know very little of the document, other than the commonly perpetuated myths and the controversial elements which caused opposition to the document. However, since this is the document which founded the modern Irish State, the lack of more general knowledge of the document, particularly amongst lawyers, is most unusual and a situation which needs to be addressed. In order to fully appreciate and understand the 1922 document, it is necessary to go beyond the basic historical facts.

The 1922 Drafting Committee was inspired by the ideals of popular sovereignty and democracy and enthusiastically (some may say naively) believed that they could draft a Constitution based on those ideals. Within the space of six weeks, they had drafted a document which is still the foundation of the modern Irish State.[37] While the decision was taken to draft a completely new constitution in the mid-1930s, most of the spine of the

[34] For a detailed consideration, see Cahillane (n 4) 154–185.

[35] See Chap. 13, William Quill, "Revisiting the Legacy of the Amendment Procedure" for an alternative view of the amendment provision.

[36] Kohn's work (n 10) is a major exception of course, but until the last 15 years or so the principal works considering the Constitution had all been from a historical or political science perspective. See, for example, Brian Farrell, "The Drafting of the Irish Free State Constitution", *The Irish Jurist*, 5(1) (1970).

DH Akenson & FP Fallin, "The Irish Civil War and the Drafting of the Irish Constitution" *Éire-Ireland* Vol V (1) (1970) 10, Vol V (2) 42, Vol V (4) 28. Alan J. Ward, *The Irish Constitutional Tradition* (Washington DC: Catholic University of America Press, 1994), Nicholas Mansergh, *The Irish Free State: Its Government and Politics* (London: Allen & Unwin, 1936).

[37] For details on the drafting process, see Cahillane (n 4).

1922 Constitution was actually retained, which demonstrates the prescience of those involved in 1922. There are many aspects of the 1937 Constitution which quite probably would never have come into being if they had not been included in the 1922 Constitution. Judicial review is one such example.[38] Also, the drafters of 1937 were able to learn from the 1922 experience and this enabled a more successful result in many cases. We often also forget that the main institutions of the state that we have today were conceived in 1922, and so perhaps the document achieved more than we might realise.

We still have much to learn from the 1922 Irish Free State Constitution and, in particular, from the spirit which was originally espoused by the document; it was intended to be a document which would work for the people of the new Irish State. Unfortunately, for various reasons, that are too numerous to elaborate on here,[39] the original spirit of the Constitution evaporated and now it has been all but forgotten. As a result, myths and misunderstandings have developed about the document. For example, as David Kenny has skilfully set out in his chapter, the radical experiments on forms and mechanisms of government in the 1922 Constitution may have failed, but it is not accurate to say, as is often asserted, that the 1922 Constitution was based on the Westminster model; it may have ended up with that model in practice but the full story is much more complicated than that.[40] So it is with many aspects of the 1922 Constitution—without a detailed understanding of the document, we are often left with an impression which is not faithful to the original vision espoused by the document. When it comes to the various experiments which were included in the document, one might argue that it was not advisable to trial so many devices untested in the jurisdiction but one has to commend the drafters for their bravery and commitment to their ideals and the belief that the Constitution really could effect major change and provide the basis for a new democratic Irish State.

[38] Graham Butler also argues in his chapter that the experience of the governor general provided a strong influence on the provisions on the president in the 1937 Constitution. See Chap. 6, Graham Butler, "The Representative of the Crown and the Governor-General of the Irish Free State: Text and Context".

[39] For more detail on the aspects which led to the downfall of the Constitution, see Cahillane (n4).

[40] See Chap. 10, David Kenny, "The 1922 Constitution as a Failed Attempt to Break with Westminster Tradition". See also Laura Cahillane, "Anti-party Politics and the Irish Free State Constitution" Dublin University Law Journal, 35 (2012), 34.

One really interesting aspect of the 1922 Constitution is its clear constitutional identity. Constitutional identity as a concept has only recently emerged in Ireland and there has been little real engagement with the concept as of yet.[41] One could make the argument that the identity based around popular sovereignty and democracy in the 1922 Constitution was obvious, and in fact, this is not too far removed from the arguments made in Kennedy CJ's dissent in the famous *State (Ryan) v Lennon* case, mentioned earlier. This case could have changed the whole fate of the document—in fact, had Kennedy's views found favour with a majority, it is possible the 1937 document would not have come into being—certainly not when, and in the manner that it did.[42] For Kennedy CJ, it was all about the people:

> Our trust is for the people, our duty and responsibility to the people, and, while bowing inevitably to lawful amendment, when established to have been properly and duly made, we must be watchdogs to protect against unlawful encroachment and to maintain intact, so far as in us lies, the principles and provisions embodied in the Constitution for the protection of the liberties of the citizens in mass and individually.[43]

Kennedy CJ, arguably the principal architect of the 1922 Constitution, saw the absurdity of declaring that the Constitution could be amended by ordinary legislation, without the legislation even expressly setting out to do so, and that this situation could be allowed to continue indefinitely, despite the fact that the Constitution clearly intended the people to have not only a role but the ultimate role as sovereign. For Kennedy, therefore, allowing indefinite legislative amendments constituted a usurpation of that role. However, even judicial review as a concept was alien to the vast majority of the judiciary of the time so the idea of constitutional interpretation based on such vague terms as constitutional identity would have been a step too far. Hugh Kennedy's constitutional identity, never termed as such, may have been a slightly different creature, but it will be

[41] See Costello v Government of Ireland [2022] IESC 44. See also Seán Rainford, "Costello v Ireland and an Irish Constitutional Identity", Irish Judicial Studies Journal Vol 7(1) (2023), 70.

[42] See also Chap. 13, William Quill, "Revisiting the Legacy of the Amendment Procedure".

[43] *State (Ryan) v Lennon* [1935] IR 170, 203.

interesting to see if the idea of constitutional interpretation based on 'fundamental and immutable principles'[44] takes hold here in the future.[45]

As part of Ireland's Decade of Commemorations, we have been asking what is worth preserving or commemorating. The 1922 Irish Free State Constitution certainly should be commemorated and further investigated and studied and the aim of this collection is to do just that. The Constitution was a revolutionary project. It contained many remarkable innovations in an attempt to create a new successful Irish State, and under different circumstances, it might well have, but it was prevented from fulfilling its potential due to the complicated Civil War legacy in existence in Ireland at the time. And so, while acknowledging the failures of the Constitution, it is important also to evaluate the document in a holistic manner and to appreciate the achievements and the legacy of the Constitution.

On its 100th anniversary, perhaps now is the time to appreciate the immensity and foresight of the 1922 project.

References

Cahillane, Laura. "The Origins of Popular Sovereignty in Ireland: Theory and Reality." In *Constitutional Change and Popular Sovereignty: Populism, Politics and the Law in Ireland,* edited by Maria Cahill, Colm Ó Cinnéide, Seán Ó Conaill and Conor O'Mahony, Oxford: Routledge, 2021.

Cahillane, Laura. "An Insight into the Irish Free State Constitution." *American Journal of Legal History* 54, no. 1 (2014): 1-38.

Cahillane, Laura. "Anti-Party Politics and the Irish Free State Constitution." *Dublin University Law Journal* 35 (2012): 34.

Cahillane, Laura. *Drafting the Irish Free State Constitution.* Manchester: Manchester University Press, 2016.

Ewart, Wilfrid. *A Journey in Ireland.* London: G.P. Putnam, 1922.

Farrell, Brian. "The Drafting of the Irish Free State Constitution." *The Irish Jurist* 5, no 1. (1970).

Fay, Patrick. "The Amendments to the Constitution Committee, 1926." *Administration* 26 no. 3 (1978): 331–351.

Figgis, Darrell. *The Gaelic State in the Past and Future.* Dublin: Maunsel, 1917.

[44] Ibid., 213.

[45] It has already been mentioned in two further cases since its initial mention in the Costello case: *In the matter of The Adoption Act 2010, Sections 49(1) and 49(3) and in the matter of A (a minor) and B (a minor): Adoption Authority of Ireland v. C and D and the Attorney General* [2023] IESC 6; and *Heneghan v. Minister for Housing, Planning & Local Government & ors* [2023] IESC 7.

Garvin, Tom. *1922: The Birth of Irish Democracy.* Dublin: Gill and Macmillan, 2005.
Garvin, Tom. *The Evolution of Irish Nationalist Politics.* Dublin: Gill and Macmillan, 1981.
Ginsburg, Tom, James Melton, and Zachary Elkins. *The Endurance of National Constitutions.* Cambridge: Cambridge University Press, 2009.
Headlam-Morley, Agnes. *The New Democratic Constitutions of Europe; A Comparative Study of Post-War European Constitutions with Special Reference to Germany, Czechoslovakia, Poland, Finland, The Kingdom of the Serbs, Croats & Slovenes and the Baltic States.* Oxford: Oxford University Press, 1928.
Kohn, Leo. *The Constitution of the Irish Free State.* London: George Allen & Unwin Ltd, 1932.
Malone, Andrew. "Party Government in the Irish Free State." *Political Science Quarterly* 44, no 3. (1929): 363.
Mansergh, Nicholas. *The Irish Free State: Its Government and Politics.* London: Allen & Unwin, 1936.
O'Sullivan, Donal. *The Irish Free State and its Senate.* London: Faber, 1940.
Rainford, Seán. "Costello v Ireland and an Irish Constitutional Identity." *Irish Judicial Studies Journal* 7 no. 1 (2023): 70.
Ward, Alan. "Challenging the British Constitution." *Parliamentary History* 9, (1990): 125.
Ward, Alan. *The Irish Constitutional Tradition.* Washington DC: Catholic University of America Press, 1994.
Hogan, Gerard. "Development of Judicial Review of Legislation and Irish Constitutional Law 1929-1941." PhD thesis, Trinity College Dublin, 2001.

CHAPTER 3

The Partition of Ireland and the 1922 Constitution

C. R. G. Murray

Introduction

This chapter addresses the significance of the 'silences'[1] with regard to the partition of Ireland in the 1922 Constitution, providing one of the most significant contrasts between it and the territorial claims which would become so prominent within Articles 2 and 3 of Bunreacht na hÉireann. This lack of direct reference to partition should not be surprising. The division of Ireland might have been a reality since the Government of Ireland Act 1920 entered effect in the summer of 1921, but following the December 1921 Treaty, the new Constitution had to be adopted before Northern Ireland's Parliament was given a formal opportunity, under Article 12, to reject its place within the new Irish Free State. The Northern

[1] John Regan, "Southern Irish nationalism as a historical problem," *The Historical Journal* 50 (2007): 197, 203.

C. R. G. Murray (✉)
Newcastle University, Newcastle upon Tyne, UK
e-mail: colin.murray@newcastle.ac.uk

L. Cahillane, D. K. Coffey (eds.), *The Centenary of the Irish Free State Constitution*, Palgrave Modern Legal History,
https://doi.org/10.1007/978-3-031-46181-1_3

Ireland Parliament had to have the formal opportunity to consider the governance order it was spurning, even though all concerned knew that there was nothing in the terms of the 1922 Constitution that would make a difference to its decision.[2] The document had to be drafted in light of its application, in theory at least, to all of Ireland.

This uncertainty around partition meant that the new Constitution did not engage with the legal process of creating (and mitigating) a border on the island of Ireland. The Common Travel Area would develop very much in the background, through technocratic dealings between the Irish Free State and the United Kingdom, while the arrangements for the Free State's independent customs regime, a significant and late concession made by the Westminster Government as part of the 1921 Treaty negotiations, would not be ready to take effect until April 1923. At that time, Sir James Craig, Northern Ireland's prime minister, decried the erection of the customs border as a 'great error of judgement', and appealed to W. T. Cosgrave's Government to delay the decision.[3] But Craig had long been aware that a land border was coming, having been directly involved in the negotiations on the setting up of the new devolved institutions, and been informed of every twist in the Treaty negotiations the following year.[4] Indeed, UK Customs authorities had, from early 1922, been making detailed preparations for customs controls on the land boundary for when the Free State 'has its full constitution'.[5] As this chapter explores, Craig's attention was more upon the problems an operative border would pose for his administration, and his narrow prioritisation of 'the defence of Ulster's interests and the protection of her unionist people',[6] than a serious appeal against partition. It addresses how these constitutional silences, and the developments around partition thus being relegated to the background of the new Free State's governance order, affected the relationship between Ireland's new polities in the subsequent decades.

[2] See Thomas Mohr, "Law and the Foundation of the Irish State on 6 December 1922," *Irish Jurist* 59 (2018): 31, 43.

[3] Dennis Kennedy, *The Widening Gulf: Northern Attitudes to the Independent Irish State, 1919–49* (Belfast: Blackstaff, 1988), 160.

[4] See Patrick Buckland, "Carson, Craig and the Partition of Ireland, 1919–1921," in *Nationalism and Unionism: Conflict in Ireland, 1885–1921*, ed. Peter Collins (Belfast: QUB Inst of Irish Studies, 1994) 75, 84–86.

[5] See UK National Archives (UKNA) CUST 49/1298, Otto Niemeyer (UK Treasury) to Sir Horace Hamilton (Customs & Excise), February 23, 1922, p. 1–2.

[6] Bryan Follis, *A State Under Siege: The Establishment of Northern Ireland 1920–1925* (Oxford: OUP, 1995), 57.

Two Households, Both Alike in Dignity?

The measures concluded in the early 1920s provided for two governance orders on the island of Ireland. From the outset, they were presented as rivals. Indeed, in the chauvinistic expectations of some in Westminster, Northern Ireland's institutions would provide a beacon for good governance to guide its inevitably feckless neighbours:

> I believe that there is a chance, and more than a chance, if the Southern Legislature and the Northern Legislature eventuate, and if both function, that in time the North might give a lead to the rest of Ireland and show that Irishmen can govern themselves in an orderly and sensible fashion ...[7]

It was an expectation which played into Craig's infamous contrast of a 'Catholic State' and a 'Protestant State'.[8] But there was never a level playing field between the two entities. Article 1 of the 1921 Treaty established that the Irish Free State would enjoy the same constitutional status as the existing self-governing Dominions, with expansive powers to legislate for the 'peace, order and good Government of Ireland'. Notwithstanding prominent contemporary depictions of Northern Ireland as having something akin to Dominion status,[9] it received the very same Government of Ireland Act 1920 structures that had been so unacceptable to Sinn Féin during the war of independence.[10]

The difference in constitutional status was by no means cosmetic. In ministerial conferences between 13 and 17 October 1920, there had been 'prolonged' discussions on whether to transfer broad taxation and customs powers to the Irish Parliaments under the Government of Ireland Act, but Lloyd George remained adamant, with Craig in the room as

[7] Duke of Abercorn, HL Deb, vol. 42, col. 466, November 23, 1920.

[8] HC Deb (NI), vol. 16, p. 1095, April 24, 1934.

[9] The Dominion analogy became, for example, the basis for the Speaker's exclusion of issues devolved to Northern Ireland from Westminster debates; J. Whitley, HC Deb, vol. 163, col. 1624–1625, May 3, 1923.

[10] At one point in the Treaty negotiations Craig became so alarmed about what was being offered to the Sinn Féin delegation that he demanded Dominion status for Northern Ireland; Follis, *A State Under Siege*, n 6, 66.

Parliamentary and Financial Secretary to the Admiralty in the Coalition Government, that retaining these powers at Westminster would provide a necessary lever for control over the new polities.[11] Arthur Griffith, of all of the Sinn Féin leaders, had long been alive to the importance of control over fiscal policy and put its necessity for the development of Ireland's economic independence at the heart of his constitutional vision.[12] But this crucial issue, if not immediately exciting in terms of public discourse, remained intractable. Lloyd George came to appreciate that it would have to be part of a final settlement, on the pretext that the UK's economic weight would still enable it to assert considerable indirect control, but he did not win over a sceptical Lord Birkenhead to this concession until the Treaty negotiations were underway.[13] Although the final settlement of the 1922 Constitution's terms and subsequent debate over them within Ireland, and with it the lurch into the Civil War, came to be overshadowed by issues such as the Oath of Allegiance, Ireland's ability to chart an independent economic policy was essential to effecting a separation from the United Kingdom. When the Constitution came to be debated in Westminster, Edward Carson, sitting in the House of Lords as one of the Law Lords, denounced such window-dressing as a salve for the UK Government's vanity as the Free State broke away from the UK; 'a curtain to screen from your view the ignominy and humiliation which faces you in everything you did'.[14] The independent customs arrangements, moreover, ensured that there would be a hard edge to partition in the form of physical border infrastructure.

The contrast between the Government of Ireland Act and the 1922 Constitution in regard to public financing and control of economic policy is stark. Customs duties are the subject of only one 'transitory' provision in the new Constitution, which committed the Irish Free State to not altering a board range of taxes and duties until 1 April 1923. This suited its authorities; against the backdrop of the Civil War, it would take time to make border arrangements and to assess how best to construct a tariff

[11] UKNA CAB 23/38, Conclusions of a Conference of Ministers, October 17, 1920, para. 2.

[12] See Colum Kenny, "'A Man Who Has Both Arms': Arthur Griffith, the Economy and the Anglo-Irish Treaty Agreement 1921," *Irish Economic and Social History* (2022): Advanced Access.

[13] Winston Churchill, *The World Crisis: The Aftermath, 1918–1928* (New York: Scribner's, 1929), 301–302.

[14] HL Deb, vol. 52, col. 199, December 1, 1922.

regime which promoted domestic interests. The clear time limits set out in Article 74, however, indicated to officials in Belfast that, under the terms of Articles 9 and 15 of the Treaty, they must be 'fully prepared for complete severance on that date'.[15] For all that they fully expected the Free State Government to exercise its new powers, the Government of Ireland Act tightly constrained the Northern Ireland Government's freedom of action in response: '[T]hey shall not have power to made laws in respect of ... Trade with any place out of the part of Ireland within their jurisdiction'.[16] The lack of reference to such hard-won powers within the 1922 Constitution is significant, but it accords with its prime movers' broader constitutional thinking. As Michael Collins, fresh from his role in negotiating the 1921 Treaty, informed Hugh Kennedy, the Free State Constitution that Kennedy was drafting must be succinct and easily adaptable 'as the final stages of complete freedom were achieved'.[17] The overwriting and overshadowing of the 1922 Constitution was not a glitch, but a feature of its operation. It was to be expected that there would be no substantive provisions which would detail the administration of customs or the levying of duties, lest they provide a basis for fettering the Irish Government's freedom of action.

In contrast with the 'freedom to achieve freedom',[18] Collins' aphorism which animated the drafting of the Free State Constitution and which accorded with the developing status of the Dominions, the Northern Ireland Government found its activity strictly curtailed by the 1920 Act. Most of Northern Ireland's taxation was controlled by London, and its contribution to imperial finances had been set at an unsustainably high level.[19] This issue was compounded by the precise requirements for apportioning revenues under the 1920 Act, which added a disruptive element of bureaucracy to trade between Great Britain and Northern Ireland as the Imperial Treasury struggled to establish which goods were destined for

[15] UKNA CUST 49/1298, W. Young (Commissioner of Customs and Excise, Belfast) to A. Waterfield (UK Treasury), December 15, 1922, para. 1.

[16] Government of Ireland Act 1920 (UK), s. 4(7).

[17] UCD Archives, Hugh Kennedy Papers, P4/15 and P4/303, December, 1921.

[18] See Charles Townshend, "The meaning of Irish Freedom: Constitutionalism in the Free State," *Transactions of the Royal Historical Society* 8 (1998): 45, 55.

[19] See Arthur Quekett, *The Constitution of Northern Ireland, vol. 1* (Belfast: HMSO, 1928), 43–50.

Northern Ireland and which were being transhipped to Ireland.[20] Although, contrary to the expectations prevalent in Dublin in the early 1920s, these constraints did not make Northern Ireland unviable, the Unionist Government increasingly found itself tangled between the financial strictures of London and invidious comparisons with Dublin's exercises of its own freedom of action. It had too little revenue to effectively govern Northern Ireland because of the mistakes in the calculation of Ireland's budget surplus which were embedded in the 1920 Act.[21] It could not, moreover, take the same overt protectionist steps as Dublin by erecting tariff barriers for the benefit of certain domestic industries. Nor could it follow Cosgrave and de Valera's circumvention of the Treaty's 'public debt' obligations upon the Free State. The Unionist Government did gradually turn to goods regulations to provide for non-tariff barriers, particularly in acting to protect its own agricultural sector against competition from the Free State, but this was a marker of the extent to which its options were curtailed.[22] The 1920 Act's shortcomings did not absolve Craig's Government of responsibility for its dismal track record, but in significant areas little could have been done even if it had genuinely sought to govern in the best interest of Northern Ireland's society as a whole.[23]

In subsequent years, the London courts began to talk about each Dominion as being 'mistress in her own house'.[24] The gendered rhetoric is significant. In terms of the persistent personification of states, it connoted that the Dominions remained something less than fully fledged members of the international community, even if London could not exert direct control over their internal affairs.[25] Debates over whether the same level of latitude applied to Northern Ireland's internal governance would long persist,[26] but, for Harry Calvert, London's dominance of its finances

[20] See Colin Murray and Daniel Wincott, "Partition by degrees: Routine exceptions in border and immigration practice between the UK and Ireland, 1921–1972," *Journal of Law and Society* 47 (2020): S145.

[21] See Follis, *A State Under Siege*, n 6, 140–145.

[22] See Patrick Buckland, *The Factory of Grievances: Devolved Government in Northern Ireland, 1921–39* (Dublin: Gill and Macmillan, 1979), 89–91.

[23] Ibid., 140–144.

[24] *Edwards v Attorney-General of Canada* [1930] AC 124, 136 (Lord Sankey).

[25] See Aoife O'Donoghue, "The admixture of feminine weakness and susceptibility: gendered personifications of the state in international law," *Melbourne Journal of International Law* 19 (2018): 227.

[26] See, for example, *Attorney General v Jaffé* [1935] NI 98, 120 (Megaw J).

made 'a mockery of the Dominion analogy'.[27] Northern Ireland was thus something avowedly less; not even not-quite-a-state. And this status had a marked impact on the early years of its governance and its attitude towards the Free State.

Siege Mentality

The run in to the Treaty's 'Ulster Month' in December 1922, during which the Northern Ireland Parliament could vote on its status with regard to the new Free State, was a frenetic period for Ulster Unionism. The mid-November UK General Election, precipitated by the collapse of the Coalition Government, left legislative preparations for the creation of the Irish Free State incomplete. Craig found it difficult to engage in his preferred personal meetings in London as office holders shifted.[28] Carson, by now a peripheral figure given his judicial role, continued to ruminate darkly on the 'damnosa hereditas' which Lloyd George had bequeathed to Bonar Law's administration as the legislation relating to the Free State Constitution eventually made its way through the UK Parliament in early December.[29] Against the backdrop of the recent boycott of Northern Ireland goods and the intense sectarian violence which had continued to grip the Northern counties after the War of Independence truce, a siege mentality gripped Craig's administration. The prevailing assumption amongst the Provisional Government in Dublin, however, was that Northern Ireland was too unstable to survive, and that the Boundary Commission would deal it an inevitable blow.[30] But Craig was not to know how quickly Dublin would lose any active interest in Northern Ireland, and the development and management of the new border thus generated multiple acute problems for his government in 1922, challenges which were exacerbated by the restrictions imposed by the Government of Ireland Act 1920.

[27] Harry Calvert, *Constitutional Law in Northern Ireland: A Study in Regional Government* (London: Stevens, 1968), 66.

[28] Buckland, *The Factory of Grievances*, n 22, 16.

[29] HL Deb, vol. 52, col. 174, December 1, 1922.

[30] National Archives of Ireland (NAI) TSCH/1/1/1, Minutes of the Provisional Government, February 7, 1922. See Kennedy, *The Widening Gulf*, n 3, 108.

The Border and Security

Craig's most pressing concern in 1922 was security. The Craig/Collins talks in January and March had not curtailed the violence in Northern Ireland and the Unionist Government remained convinced that the Provisional Government was doing little to address threats which were regarded as emanating from the Free State. The previous summer, the UK Government had made extensive plans to close the land border, other than to the holders of specific travel permits, under the Restoration of Order in Ireland Regulations.[31] This work continued apace even after the July 1921 truce, and the military authorities had prepared a system that could be instituted alongside Martial Law in Southern Ireland, as defined under the 1920 Act, immediately in the event of the truce breaking down, by which, amongst other severe restrictions on movement, '[n]o person over the age of 16 years may … cross the frontier between Northern and Southern Ireland' without a military permit. Donegal, for practical reasons, was to be treated as part of Northern Ireland.[32] The following summer the Northern Ireland authorities, and particularly the Minister for Home Affairs, Sir Richard Dawson Bates, sought to revive the plans. The truce had done little to kerb violence in their jurisdiction, and even the introduction of Dawson Bates' own set of emergency powers, the Special Powers Act, and with it internment, in May 1922,[33] was yet to have appreciable impact. Dawson Bates therefore led a Cabinet Conference proposing to Craig that the border be closed, even if these ministers were always keen in correspondence to emphasise that the Northern Ireland Government should not bear the cost of the measures.[34]

This scheme was not particularly compelling in security terms, because 'much of the violence during 1922 was sectarian rather than secessionist

[31] Restoration of Order in Ireland Act 1920 (UK), Reg. 35(c).

[32] Public Record Office for Northern Ireland (PRONI) HA/32/1/408, "Military Travel Permits: Instructions for Civil Police in Ireland as to dealing with Applications for Permits," August, 1921, para. 1.

[33] Civil Authorities (Special Powers) Act (Northern Ireland) 1922, s. 1 and Reg. 23. See Laura Donohue, "Regulating Northern Ireland: The Special Powers Acts, 1922–1972," *The Historical Journal* 41 (1998): 1089, 1092.

[34] The previous summer, these efforts had gone as far as Dawson Bates insisting that identity cards be extended to Northern Ireland, but that the associated costs 'should be made from Imperial Funds'; PRONI HA/32/1/408, Sir Richard Dawson Bates (NI Home Affairs Minister) to Colonel Wickham (GHQ, Dublin), July 23, 1921, p. 1.

in nature'.[35] But Dawson Bates' Military Adviser, General Arthur Solly-Flood, fulminated that '[t]here is still traffic of individuals and goods over the frontier, amidst which the importation of arms and explosives, seditious literature, and disloyal people continues'.[36] He was therefore insistent that forces within the Free State posed an immediate threat and that the border 'should be definitely closed as far as possible' using a new regulation under the Special Powers Act.[37] Given that Craig had eagerly delegated security considerations to Dawson Bates, it fell to the Attorney General for Northern Ireland, Richard Best, to pour cold water on the plans. He emphasised that the Northern Ireland authorities did not have the same latitude in their border policy that the Imperial Government enjoyed. In particular, the Government of Ireland Act's restriction of competence on any measures that affected trade undermined the proposal, and he therefore insisted that 'the Minister could make a Regulation dealing with passenger traffic, but not with goods'.[38] The interlocking nature of goods movements, and the movements of the people carrying them, made the scheme a much more complicated proposition.

Craig was already locked in a dispute with the Colonial Office over the abolition of proportional representation under the Local Government Bill, and indeed threatened resignation in light of what he regarded as the UK Government's unjustifiable interference with that measure, given Best's certification that the controversial scheme was within the limits of the 1920 Act.[39] He was also eager to secure funding from London to bear the cost of Dawson Bates' Special Constabulary. Amid these active confrontations over the relationship between devolved and central government, Craig had to reject the border security plans. In this instance, he had chosen his battles in a way that would suit his immediate interests. A month later, the assent to the Local Government Bill would come to establish a constitutional convention limiting the operation of the UK Government's legal powers to intervene over Northern Ireland legislation

[35] Keith Ewing and Conor Gearty, *The Struggle for Civil Liberties: Political freedom and the rule of law in Britain, 1914–1945* (Oxford: OUP, 2001), 373.

[36] PRONI CAB/4/47, "Report by General Solly-Flood," June 2, 1922, p. 1.

[37] PRONI CAB/4/47, Sir Richard Dawson Bates (NI Home Affairs Minister) to Sir James Craig, June 2, 1922, p. 1.

[38] PRONI CAB/4/47, Minutes of Cabinet Conference, June 2, 1922, p. 2.

[39] See Adam Evans, "A tale as old as (devolved) time? Sewel, Stormont and the legislative consent convention," *The Political Quarterly* 91 (2020): 165, 166–167.

for almost half a century.[40] As this episode demonstrates, the restraint-of-trade provision proved to be one of the few significant live wires in the 1920 Act. Provided it stayed clear of legislating in a way which overtly flouted this requirement, the Northern Ireland Government gradually came to realise that there was little that the courts or Westminster would do to circumscribe their legislative powers. The Special Powers Acts would remain in force for the entire duration of the Northern Ireland Parliament.

The Customs Border

The imminent transfer of customs controls to the Free State brought further travails for the Northern Ireland Government. In late November and early December 1922, the Free State's North-Eastern Boundary Bureau, established 'for the purpose of collecting statistics and other information in connection with the six Northern Counties generally and the border question in particular', wrote repeatedly to the Great Northern Railway (Ireland), seeking all possible statistics on cross-border goods movements by rail.[41] In the same period, the reports circulating between Northern Ireland's departments foresaw the possibility of the Free State using its customs powers as a means of 'discrimination against Ulster goods with a view to forcing Ulster into union'.[42]

The institution of the customs border on 1 April 1923 did indeed facilitate aspects of a lingering form of boycott deep into the 1920s. Some Free State Customs authorities, for example, continued into 1924 to reject Northern Ireland goods marked 'Irish Manufacture' or 'Made in Ireland'.[43] Within the Northern Ireland Government it was concluded that there was little point in complaining to either the Free State Government or the Colonial Office in London, then responsible for Dominion affairs, indeed it was accepted that it was within Dublin's power 'to pass legislation definitely preventing such goods from entering the Free State'.[44] If that came to pass, it was suggested that it might be necessary to encourage

[40] Government of Ireland Act 1920 (UK), s. 75.

[41] PRONI CAB/8/F/1, E.M. Stephens (IFS North-Eastern Boundary Bureau) to Secretary, Great Northern Railway, November 17, 1922, p. 1.

[42] PRONI COM/23/213, Memorandum, "Customs and Excise," October 5, 1923, p. 3.

[43] PRONI CAB/9/F/25/1, W. D. Scott (Secretary, NI Ministry of Commerce) to Wilfred Spender (Cabinet Secretary, NI), July 31, 1924, p. 1.

[44] PRONI CAB/9/F/25/1, G. H. Parr (Ministry of Commerce) to Wilfred Spender (Cabinet Secretary, NI), July 8, 1924 p. 1.

manufacturers to adopt a dual labelling system, separating exports which were bound for the Free State from other export goods.[45] Craig intervened in the discussions to the effect that 'Manufactured in Ulster' would ultimately prevail as a mark of product origin, given 'the future advantages likely to accrue when the differences between the financial stability of the Irish Free State and of Northern Ireland comes to be more clearly recognised in course of time',[46] and the officials, having established that export businesses regarded this mark of origin as being received negatively in key markets, quietly let the issue drop.[47] Soon after the Customs boundary took shape Craig insisted on touring the border, in the summer of 1923, to underline his commitment to holding onto Northern Ireland's territory ahead of the Boundary Commission process.[48] The backdrop to Craig's tour saw ongoing security efforts to close off minor routes to traffic, and increasing enforcement of bureaucratic permit systems for cross-border travellers seeking to use so-called unapproved routes (those without designated customs checkpoints).[49]

The mere possibility that the border might soon change induced considerable inertia within rural officialdom. In November 1923 residents of Derrylin, a border village in Fermanagh, vigorously petitioned Craig himself that the Free State was still handling all of their postal services, and charging customs dues on what should have been internal UK post.[50] When the matter was investigated on Craig's behalf, the embarrassed Permanent Secretary to the Ministry of Commerce responded that 'owing to the additional expenditure which adjustment would entail to the Government of Northern Ireland, we cannot definitely ask that such adjustment should be affected forthwith'.[51] There was scarcely a single issue facing officials in the early years of Northern Ireland which was not met with a concern about funding, which goes some way to explaining

[45] Ibid., p. 1.

[46] PRONI CAB/9/F/25/1, Wilfred Spender (Cabinet Secretary, NI) to G. H. Parr (Ministry of Commerce), April 12, 1924, p. 1.

[47] The problem was concluded to be largely confined to Cork customs officials, and no one wanted to give it more prominence within the Free State; Scott, n 43, p. 1.

[48] PRONI CAB/4/84, Conclusions of Cabinet, July 30, 1923, para. 13.

[49] Craig largely confined his tour to meetings with the Special Constabulary, enthusing in Armagh that '[i]t was good for him to renew close touch with the backbone of the province'; "Boundary Question," *Irish Examiner*, August 1, 1923.

[50] PRONI COM/21/27, Rev. F. W. Grant to Sir James Craig, November 27, 1923, p. 1.

[51] PRONI COM/21/27, Cecil Litchfield (NI Ministry of Commerce) to Wilfred Spender (Cabinet Secretary, NI), December 7, 1923, p. 1.

Unionist reticence around the formation of the customs border[52]; it came with so many associated and up-front costs (even if the management of customs itself was a matter for the UK Government). And if rural postal services adapted too slowly for Craig's liking, HM Revenue and Customs might well have moved too fast. Amid a rush to establish new customs facilities in Derry/Londonderry in May 1923, customs officials attempting to gain the compliance of port authorities emphasised that they could hardly continue to use their old facilities, because '[t]he Moville waters are within the jurisdiction of the Irish Free State'.[53] This prompted a furious response within the Northern Ireland Government. Officials pestered Craig that an imperial official should be 'quite out of touch with the fact that the jurisdiction over these waters is in dispute',[54] seemingly oblivious to the reality that customs could not continue to be administered from Moville, almost 20 miles inside the Free State. Craig's rallying cry regarding the border might have been 'not an inch', but behind the scenes he found the reality of setting up a border proved to be rather more burdensome than he would have liked.

Reach Across

For Craig's Government one advantage of the Free State being on a distinct constitutional footing from Northern Ireland after the Treaty was that it enabled a greater degree of administrative separation between the polities on the island of Ireland than the 1920 Act had provided.[55] With regard to the cross-border issues of fisheries, railways and animal disease control, however, the Government of Ireland Act still provided for a Council of Ireland as a mechanism for enabling cooperation between Ireland's new institutions.[56] Subsequent to the 1921 Treaty the Free State enjoyed complete authority to manage these issues within its jurisdiction, but no provision was made altering how the Council of Ireland was to

[52] See Kennedy, *The Widening Gulf*, n 3, 160.

[53] PRONI COM/64/1/42, J. T. Boyd (Surveyor of Customs) to Port Sanitary Authority, May 17, 1923, p. 1.

[54] PRONI COM/64/1/42, Cecil Litchfield (NI Ministry of Commerce) to Wilfred Spender (Cabinet Secretary, NI), May 28, 1923, p. 1. Craig would subsequently raise the issue with London.

[55] John McColgan, *British Policy and the Irish Administration 1920–22* (London: George Allen, 1983), 136.

[56] Government of Ireland Act 1920 (UK), s. 10(2).

operate with regard to Northern Ireland. Unionists chaffed that Articles 12 and 13 of the Treaty 'expressly preserved the Council of Ireland and the Irish Free State representation thereon, whilst depriving the Council of any powers in that State'.[57] By late 1922 the Unionist Government was concerned with the issues this posed; copies of confidential Free State documents seeking extensive details of cross-border railway operations were being 'obtained confidentially' and were reaching Stormont Castle within days of being written.[58] The Council of Ireland was seen as a means by which the Free State could reach into important aspects of Northern Ireland's governance, and indeed 'control' the railways in Northern Ireland,[59] with the Northern Ireland Government being unable to exert comparable influence on these issues over the border.

For these reasons, a major priority for Craig's parlour diplomacy in London in late 1922 became the amendment of these elements of the 1920 Act, with Northern Ireland officials advancing a range of amendments to both enlarge and clarify the scope of Northern Ireland's authority.[60] They found, however, that they could make limited headway amid the dislocation of the November 1922 General Election campaign. Following discussions at the Colonial Office, Arthur Quekett, Belfast's lead official on the issue, anxiously reported that '[t]he U.K. Government seem to be willing to implement by legislation any suitable understanding between the parties, but otherwise will not'.[61] Dublin, in short, had to accept any change. At the last minute, amid the rush to enact the necessary legislation to give effect to the 1922 Constitution in the few weeks between the election and the anniversary of the Treaty, a provision was introduced to forestall the transfer of powers to the Council of Ireland for up to five years.[62] Cosgrave's Government agreed to this suspension because the use of these mechanisms was not on its agenda; public attitudes to all aspects of the

[57] Quekett, *The Constitution of Northern Ireland*, n 19, 58.

[58] PRONI CAB/8/F/1, Cecil Litchfield (NI Ministry of Commerce) to Wilfred Spender (Cabinet Secretary, NI), December 30, 1922.

[59] PRONI COM/23/213, NI Ministry of Commerce, "Irish Free State Bill: Amending Legislation for Northern Ireland," October 14, 1922, p. 1.

[60] The studied disinterest in the 1922 constitution in Unionist newspapers in Northern Ireland, discussed by Mohr in this volume at fn 9–14, thus belies considerable concern with these developments within Craig's administration.

[61] PRONI COM/23/213, Arthur Quekett (NI Parliamentary Draughtsman) to Wilfred Spender (Cabinet Secretary, NI), October 19, 1922, p. 2.

[62] Irish Free State Constitution Act 1922 (UK), s. 3(2).

1920 Act remained so visceral that it continued to pin its hopes in the Boundary Commission.[63] This suspension received little public attention, to the extent that there was surprise in the Dáil in June 1924 when Cosgrave, faced with questions as to why his Government did not make more of the Council of Ireland, acknowledged the deal amid a florid pseudo-apology: 'If the action of the Provisional Government in the arrangement entered into between the three Governments in November, 1922, were blamable, I accept it and accept the fullest responsibility for it'.[64] He deflected any criticism, however, by styling his approach as following Michael Collins' own dissatisfaction with the Council[65] and accusing his interrogators of 'taking the ostrich line'[66] for missing the suspensory provision which had been embedded within the UK's Irish Free State Constitution Act 1922.[67]

When the Boundary Commission expectations were thwarted, Cosgrave still had the option to fall back on Council of Ireland mechanisms applicable to Northern Ireland, an option which Stanley Baldwin, as prime minister, informed Parliament 'would be a source of great trouble'.[68] Instead, Cosgrave bargained them away, alongside acceptance of an unchanged border, for an improved financial settlement for the Free State.[69] These developments underscored partition: with no formal cooperation mechanism, there was no obligation upon Ireland's two governments to engage with each other. The confirmation of the border and dissolution of the Council of Ireland were particularly significant for Craig's Government; together they 'formed the keystone of Northern Ireland's constitutional structure'.[70] The management of shared issues, particularly fisheries,[71] went unresolved and continued to generate inter-

[63] See Hogan in this volume at fn 5.

[64] Dáil Éireann Deb, vol. 7, no. 26, June 18, 1924.

[65] Michael Hopkinson, "The Craig-Collins Pacts of 1922: Two Attempted Reforms of the Northern Ireland Government," *Irish Historical Studies* 27, no. 106 (1990): 145.

[66] Dáil Éireann Deb, vol. 7, no. 26, June 18, 1924.

[67] In the same debate, Darrell Figgis, of the 1922 Constitution Committee, sought to persuade the Dáil that the Council of Ireland was the 'one feature' of the 1920 Act 'which was judged by the negotiators of the Treaty to be worth preservation'.

[68] HC Deb, vol. 189, col. 318, December 8, 1925.

[69] Ireland (Confirmation of Agreement) Act 1925 (UK), s. 5. See Paul Murray, *The Irish Boundary Commission and Its Origins, 1886–1925* (Dublin: UCD Press, 2011), 315–317.

[70] Calvert, *Constitutional Law in Northern Ireland*, n 27, 47.

[71] See Peter Leary, *Unapproved Routes: Histories of the Irish Border, 1922–1972* (Oxford: OUP, 2016), 60–94.

mittent tensions, but both leaderships became content to largely ignore the other for decades. Craig, at least for his own purposes, was fortunate to be faced in the 1920s with an administration in Dublin that was as uninterested in affairs in Northern Ireland as he was in the governance of the Free State.

'Voting Out' of the Free State

Articles 11 and 12 of the treaty provided for the 'Ulster Month', in which Northern Ireland's institutions could decide not to take part in the new Free State. It did not begin until the Treaty was fully ratified by the Dáil and Westminster, which was only completed with the passing of the Irish Free State Constitution Act 1922.[72] Debate has since swirled about the nature of this provision; was Northern Ireland seceding from the Free State when it exercised the option included within the Ulster Month, or opting out of becoming part of it?[73] On one level, this question is unresolvable. There was no authoritative adjudicatory mechanism responsible for settling disputes over the Treaty, as the Lord Chancellor, Lord Cave, was obliged to concede to Lord Carson in 1922; 'There is, of course, no tribunal to decide a matter of that kind. Here is the Treaty. We are entitled to have it fulfilled'.[74] Lord Cave was perhaps being somewhat disingenuous; the UK Government was confident that the jurisdiction of the Judicial Committee of the Privy Council, under Article 66 of the 1922 Constitution, would encompass disputes over the Treaty.[75] He was nonetheless explicit about the control which the UK could continue to exert over the settlement because of its dominant strategic position.[76] The handling of the

[72] Irish Free State Constitution Act 1922 (UK), s. 5.

[73] See David Torrance, "Secession or opting out? Northern Ireland and Article 12 of the Anglo-Irish Treaty," in *Northern Ireland, 1921–2021: Centenary Historical Perspectives*, ed. Caoimhe Nic Dháibhéid, Marie Coleman and Paul Bew (Belfast: Ulster Historical Foundation, 2022), 52, 52–56 and Colin Murray and Aoife O'Donoghue, "Life after Brexit: operationalising the Belfast/Good Friday Agreement's principle of consent," *Dublin University Law Journal* 42 (2019): 147, 162–163.

[74] HL Deb, vol. 52, col. 181, December 1, 1922.

[75] See Thomas Mohr, "Lord Cave, The British Empire and Irish Independence—A Test of Judicial Integrity," *Oxford University Commonwealth Law Journal* 12 (2012): 229, 238.

[76] This confidence would prove misplaced, given Irish success in unpicking unpalatable elements of the arrangements, but Lord Cave himself sought to exert this sort of control using dubious legal reasoning in multiple Privy Council judgments, most controversially in *Wigg v Attorney-General for the Irish Free State* [1927] AC 674 (PC); see Martin Maguire, *The Civil Service and the Revolution in Ireland 1912–1938* (Manchester: MUP, 2008), 188–192.

Ulster Month process illustrates the extent to which interpretations of aspects of the 1922 Constitution came to depend upon the terms of the Treaty.[77]

Concerned for the potential for loss of face, and even violence, if he delayed in responding to the creation of the Free State, Craig arranged for a special sitting of the Northern Ireland Parliament to exercise the Article 12 process as quickly as possible.[78] The day after the Free State came into being, at midnight on 6 December, the Northern Ireland Parliament issued the requisite declaration under the 1921 Treaty, which was then rushed into the hands of George V as a request 'that the powers of the Parliament and Government of the Irish Free State shall no longer extend to Northern Ireland'. A week later, on 13 December, Craig reported back to the Northern Ireland Parliament that the King had accepted this declaration. This address had been subject to anguished drafting in the preceding weeks. Once again, concerned about the cross-border aspects of the Government of Ireland Act, the Northern Ireland Government's priority became to exclude any possible claim of ongoing legal powers of the Free State over Northern Ireland.[79]

The multi-facetted Arthur Quekett, the parliamentary draughtsperson responsible for crafting the address, insisted that it must explicitly state, in line with Article 12, that 'the powers of the Parliament and Government of the Irish Free State shall no longer extend to Northern Ireland', even if it offended Unionist sensibilities to imply that the Free State had ever had even *de jure* jurisdiction over Northern Ireland. He was emphatic that these words 'are inserted on the opinion of the highest available legal authority to the effect that they are legally and formally necessary to ensure the validity of the Address'.[80] He would subsequently describe this treaty term as the mechanism by which Northern Ireland could 'vote herself out

[77] See Laura Cahillane and Paul Murray, "The Treaty: An Historical and Legal Interpretation," in *The Treaty: Debating and Establishing the Irish State*, ed. Mícheál Ó Fathartaigh and Liam Weeks (Dublin: Irish Academic Press, 2018), 240.

[78] Craig did so in the face of the strong advice from the Colonial Office that there was no need for an extraordinary early summoning of the Northern Ireland Parliament 'to take Northern Ireland out of the Irish Free State'; PRONI CAB/6/76, Irish Office to Wilfred Spender (Cabinet Secretary, NI), November 28, 1922.

[79] Nicholas Manseragh, *The Unresolved Question: The Anglo-Irish Settlement and Its Undoing 1912–72* (New Haven: YUP, 1991), 218.

[80] PRONI CAB/6/76, Arthur Quekett Memorandum, December 2, 1922, para. 1(d).

of the Free State'.[81] The adoption of this form of words by the Northern Ireland Parliament, and the exercise of the Article 12 vote subsequent to the Free State's creation, were elements of the Treaty process that the UK Government accepted. Indeed, in recognition of the Treaty's impact on Ireland as a whole, Northern Ireland affairs were dealt with primarily by the Colonial Secretary in London for much of 1922 and would only be transferred to the Home Office after the Ulster Month declaration. This amounts to significant conduct with regard to the meaning of the Treaty obligations, and all weighs in favour of Northern Ireland being described as seceding from the newly created Free State. It would not be without direct consequence.

A decade later Judge George Moonan, sitting in Letterkenny Circuit Court, would have to consider, in *In re Logue*,[82] whether inhabitants of Northern Ireland at the time of the Free State's creation enjoyed citizenship and with it, the right to vote.[83] John Logue, who had been born and resided in Derry/Londonderry in his childhood, moved to Buncrana as an adult and found himself excluded from the Dáil franchise because his residence in Northern Ireland in 1922 meant that he was not 'domiciled in the area of the jurisdiction of Saorstát Éireann at the time of the coming into operation of the Constitution'.[84] The case attracted little attention in Ireland's national newspapers and would receive a scant write up in the law reports, but reshaped understandings of nationality and citizenship in Ireland and was closely followed by the local newspapers in the border region, such as the *Derry People*, *Strabane Chronicle*, and *Fermanagh Herald*, where many readers had an interest in the outcome. There are shades in the proceedings of the theory that George Moonan was one of the major influences behind the character of the barrister J.J. O'Molloy in James Joyce's *Ulysses*, once the 'cleverest fellow at the junior bar', but whose ambitions were thwarted.[85] Moonan clearly relished the opportunity to engage with these complex and significant issues. During the hearing he upbraided counsel for referring to Northern Ireland as Ulster

[81] Quekett, *The Constitution of Northern Ireland*, n 19, 57.

[82] *In re Logue* [1933] 67 ILTR 253.

[83] Constitution of the Irish Free State (Saorstát Éireann) Act 1922 (Ire), Art. 14. Electoral Act 1923 (Ire), s. 1 and 2.

[84] Constitution of the Irish Free State (Saorstát Éireann) Act 1922 (Ire), Art. 3.

[85] Vivien Igoe, *The Real People of Joyce's Ulysses: A Biographical Guide* (Dublin: UCD Press, 2016).

('There are a good many Ulster people here'),[86] and he opened his judgment with a rousing declaration that the 1921 Treaty had been between Great Britain and Ireland, 'an "Ireland" one and indivisible not any mutilated torso of a country'.[87]

The issue of whether Free State citizenship, and its attendant rights, applied to people resident in Northern Ireland in December 1922 was hotly contested. Counsel for the County Registrar raised multiple problems with recognising Logue's citizenship.[88] It might impact upon the interpretation of the area of the Free State's jurisdiction for the purposes of parliamentary university franchise, and whether this should be taken to include Queen's University Belfast.[89] It could enable the conscription of people from Sandy Row, a Loyalist area of Belfast, who entered the Free State during wartime.[90] It might even provide a pretext for a Jewish person fleeing Nazi Germany to claim Irish citizenship on the basis of a short period of residence in Belfast.[91] For Judge Moonan, however, the case turned on how he approached Articles 11 and 12 of the Treaty and their impact on the terms of the 1922 Constitution[92]:

> The phraseology of Article 11 conveys clearly to my mind that all Ireland was regarded as within the area of jurisdiction although the jurisdiction was provisionally suspended in the excluded portion. The "area" of any jurisdiction must be that over which the authority extends de jure, although for so arbitrary or provisional reason it may not in fact be exerciseable in certain districts. … The wording of Article 12 that the powers shall "no longer

[86] "Did the Saorstat ever Comprise All Ireland?," *Strabane Chronicle*, July 8, 1933.

[87] "Saorstat Citizenship," *Derry People*, October 28, 1933. The same report was reproduced in the *Fermanagh Herald*; "Saorstat Citizenship," *Fermanagh Herald*, November 4, 1933.

[88] "Did the Saorstat ever Comprise All Ireland?," *Strabane Chronicle*, July 8, 1933.

[89] Constitution of the Irish Free State (Saorstát Éireann) Act 1922 (Ire), Art. 27 and 32.

[90] This was a proposition which foreshadowed the converse conscription, as British subjects, of Irish citizens in the UK during the Second World War; *Murray v Parkes* [1942] 2 KB 123.

[91] An argument redolent of the anti-semitism in Ireland which would gain prominent affirmation a decade later in *Schlegel v Corcoran and Gross* [1942] IR 19. See Brian Girvin, *From Union to Union: Nationalism, Democracy and Religion in Ireland – Act of Union to EU* (Dublin: Gill and Macmillan, 2002), 111.

[92] He acknowledged, but attributed no direct importance to, Kennedy CJ's recognition that the constitutional status of the Saorstát dated, at the latest, to 31 March 1922; *In re Reade* [1927] IR 31, 47.

extend" indicates clearly that until the address was presented they did so extend.[93]

Moonan therefore concluded that 'all persons domiciled in Ireland on 6th December, 1922 who possess the other necessary qualifications, are citizens of the Saorstat with the power of election not to accept the citizenship given by Article 3'.[94] He buttressed this conclusion with an appeal to the 'intentions of the framers of the Constitution':

> I am convinced that they never intended to exclude from citizenship of the Saorstat, solely because they had resided beyond an artificial and generally invisible border, the thousands of their fellow countrymen in the rest of Ulster whose traditions and interests, associations and affiliations, unite them intimately and permanently with their kindred people of the rest of Ireland.[95]

The case created a lacuna in terms of people born in Northern Ireland after December 1922, but most of them could continue to claim citizenship through their parents given the short period which had elapsed, and the decision forced de Valera's Government to codify the right of those born in Northern Ireland to claim Irish citizenship in the Irish Nationality and Citizenship Act 1935. Judge Moonan's interpretation might have been more easily contestable, in line with the 'opt-out' accounts of these Treaty provisions, had it not been for the manner in which the conduct of the UK Government and the Northern Ireland Parliament sustains his explanation. Unionist paranoia over the potential cross-border reach of the Free State's legal powers thus exerted an unintended effect on the development Irish nationality law.

Conclusion

Partition's absence from the 1922 Constitution is a significant 'non event', involving an implicit acceptance of the emergence of two separate polities on the island, masked by the notional opportunity for Northern Ireland to have a place within the Free State in December 1922. By contrast, the 1937 Constitution had the virtue of at least being forthright about its

[93] "Saorstat Citizenship" *Derry People*, October 28, 1933.

[94] Ibid.

[95] Ibid.

position on Northern Ireland. It might therefore be tempting to conclude that Irish constitutional thinking, in the 1998 reworking of Articles 2 and 3, had to take a step backwards to recover a position that had pertained in 1922.[96] But the constitutional shift between 1922 and 1937 did not, in this regard, mark a deeper shift in national policy. Indeed, the hardening of the border and the increasing difficulties for Northern Ireland businesses attempting to compete in their traditional markets elsewhere on the island had developed apace from the creation of the customs border.

Northern Ireland's leadership could even be said to be happier with de Valera's constitutional project than its predecessor; there was thereafter no need to apply any veneer to their cross-border antipathy, not that the veneer had made a practical difference.[97] The tripartite agreement to set aside the Boundary Commission outcome might have said that the parties were 'united in amity' and 'resolved mutually to aid one another in a spirit of neighbourly comradeship',[98] but this did not in practice mean that there was a genuine impetus towards the Northern Ireland and Free State Governments meeting 'together as and when necessary for the purpose of considering matters of common interest'.[99] This is not to say that there was no official response from Stormont Castle to the 1937 Constitution and what one official waggishly referred to as 'the area formerly known as the Irish Free State'.[100] One immediate response to the territorial 'claiming' inherent in Bunreacht na hÉireann was a renewed push to have Northern Ireland renamed Ulster, to match Unionism's own rhetoric about the polity.[101] This drew a jaded response from the Finance Ministry, noting how important the ability to sell 'Irish Linen' was for Northern Ireland's mills, particularly in North American markets. Notwithstanding Craig's personal enthusiasm for a 'Made in Ulster' designation, he was warned by the Minister of Finance that a position 'might arise similar to that which occurred in the early days when there was a boycott of our

[96] See Luke McDonagh, "Losing Ireland, losing the Empire: Dominion status and the Irish Constitutions of 1922 and 1937," *International Journal of Constitutional Law* 17 (2019): 1192, 1207.

[97] See Buckland, *The Factory of Grievances,* n 22, 70–71.

[98] HC Deb, vol. 188, col. 2656, December 3, 1925, Agreement Preamble.

[99] Ibid, Art. 5.

[100] PRONI FIN/18/18/45, C. H. Blackmore (Clerk of the Council) to Sir Wilfred Spender (Permanent Secretary, NI Ministry of Finance), May 26, 1938, p. 1.

[101] PRONI FIN/18/18/45, Northern Ireland Cabinet Conclusions, January 27, 1938, para. 3.

linen goods', and the Northern Ireland Cabinet concluded that there should be no formal move to change the name of the polity.[102] It was not, after all, only Northern Ireland's cows that were Irish.

Acknowledgement With thanks to Laura Cahillane (Limerick), Donal K. Coffey (Maynooth) and Aoife O'Donoghue (Queen's University Belfast) for their advice and encouragement regarding this chapter. Paper last updated on 30 April 2023.

References

Buckland, Patrick. "Carson, Craig and the Partition of Ireland, 1919-1921." In *Nationalism and Unionism: Conflict in Ireland, 1885-1921*, edited by Peter Collins, 75. Belfast: QUB Inst of Irish Studies, 1994.

Buckland, Patrick. *The Factory of Grievances: Devolved Government in Northern Ireland, 1921-39*. Dublin: Gill and Macmillan, 1979.

Cahillane, Laura, and Paul Murray. "The Treaty: An Historical and Legal Interpretation." In *The Treaty: Debating and Establishing the Irish State*, edited by Mícheál Ó Fathartaigh and Liam Weeks, Dublin: Irish Academic Press, 2018.

Calvert, Harry. *Constitutional Law in Northern Ireland: A Study in Regional Government*. London: Stevens, 1968.

Churchill, Winston. *The World Crisis: The Aftermath, 1918–1928*. New York: Scribner's, 1929.

Donohue, Laura. "Regulating Northern Ireland: The Special Powers Acts, 1922–1972." *The Historical Journal* 41 (1998): 1089.

Evans, Adam. "A tale as old as (devolved) time? Sewel, Stormont and the legislative consent convention." *The Political Quarterly* 91 (2020): 165.

Ewing, Keith, and Conor Gearty. *The Struggle for Civil Liberties: Political freedom and the rule of law in Britain, 1914-1945*. Oxford: OUP, 2001.

Follis, Bryan. *A State Under Siege: The Establishment of Northern Ireland 1920-1925*. Oxford: OUP, 1995.

Girvin, Brian. *From Union to Union: Nationalism, Democracy and Religion in Ireland – Act of Union to EU*. Dublin: Gill and Macmillan, 2002.

Hopkinson, Michael. "The Craig-Collins Pacts of 1922: Two Attempted Reforms of the Northern Ireland Government." *Irish Historical Studies* 27, no. 106 (1990): 145.

Igoe, Vivien. *The Real People of Joyce's Ulysses: A Biographical Guide*. Dublin: UCD Press, 2016.

Kennedy, Dennis. *The Widening Gulf: Northern Attitudes to the Independent Irish State, 1919-49*. Belfast: Blackstaff, 1988.

[102] PRONI FIN/18/18/45, Northern Ireland Cabinet Conclusions, December 7, 1937, p. 2.

Kenny, Colum. "'A Man Who Has Both Arms': Arthur Griffith, the Economy and the Anglo-Irish Treaty Agreement 1921." *Irish Economic and Social History* (2022): Advanced Access.

Leary, Peter. *Unapproved Routes: Histories of the Irish Border, 1922-1972.* Oxford: OUP, 2016.

Maguire, Martin. *The Civil Service and the Revolution in Ireland 1912-1938.* Manchester: MUP, 2008.

Manseragh, Nicholas. *The Unresolved Question: The Anglo-Irish Settlement and Its Undoing 1912–72.* New Haven: YUP, 1991.

McColgan, John. *British Policy and the Irish Administration 1920–22.* London: George Allen, 1983.

McDonagh, Luke. "Losing Ireland, losing the Empire: Dominion status and the Irish Constitutions of 1922 and 1937." *International Journal of Constitutional Law* 17 (2019): 1192.

Mohr, Thomas. "Law and the Foundation of the Irish State on 6 December 1922." *Irish Jurist* 59 (2018): 31.

Mohr, Thomas. "Lord Cave, The British Empire and Irish Independence—A Test of Judicial Integrity." *Oxford University Commonwealth Law Journal* 12 (2012): 229.

Murray, Colin, and Aoife O'Donoghue. "Life after Brexit: operationalising the Belfast/Good Friday Agreement's principle of consent." *Dublin University Law Journal* 42 (2019): 147.

Murray, Colin, and Daniel Wincott. "Partition by degrees: Routine exceptions in border and immigration practice between the UK and Ireland, 1921–1972." *Journal of Law and Society* 47 (2020): 145.

Murray, Paul. *The Irish Boundary Commission and Its Origins, 1886-1925.* Dublin: UCD Press, 2011.

O'Donoghue, Aoife. "The admixture of feminine weakness and susceptibility: gendered personifications of the state in international law." *Melbourne Journal of International Law* 19 (2018): 227.

Quekett, Arthur. *The Constitution of Northern Ireland.* Belfast: HMSO, 1928.

Regan, John. "Southern Irish nationalism as a historical problem." *The Historical Journal* 50 (2007): 197.

Torrance, David. "Secession or opting out? Northern Ireland and Article 12 of the Anglo-Irish Treaty." In *Northern Ireland, 1921-2021: Centenary Historical Perspectives*, edited by Caoimhe Nic Dháibhéid, Marie Coleman and Paul Bew, Belfast: Ulster Historical Foundation, 2022.

Townshend, Charles. "The meaning of Irish Freedom: Constitutionalism in the Free State." *Transactions of the Royal Historical Society* 8 (1998): 45.

CHAPTER 4

'The Supreme Legislative Authority Speaking as the Mouthpiece of the People': Constituent Power and the Irish Free State

Alan Greene

Introduction

Constituent power—the power to create a constitution—is a neglected concept in Irish constitutional thought. This absence is surprising in a state founded in a moment of revolutionary upheaval, where an old unwritten constitutional order was rejected through a combination of democratic politics and violence, culminating in the enactment of a new Constitution. This surprise is further compounded by the fact that this Constitution was itself replaced by a subsequent Constitution, ratified by a plebiscite. This chapter argues that although the concept of constituent power is largely absent from the life of the Free State Constitution, a latent, prototypical understanding of a concept close to constituent power animates a key point of contestation surrounding the document in the

A. Greene (✉)
Birmingham Law School, University of Birmingham, Birmingham, UK
e-mail: a.greene@bham.ac.uk

L. Cahillane, D. K. Coffey (eds.), *The Centenary of the Irish Free State Constitution*, Palgrave Modern Legal History,
https://doi.org/10.1007/978-3-031-46181-1_4

infamous Supreme Court case of the *State (Ryan) v Lennon (*hereinafter: *Ryan v Lennon)*. This case therefore can be understood in terms of competing perspectives as to the nature of the constituent power that created the Free State Constitution and who ultimately possessed it.

Part I explains the concept of constituent power, arguing that its revolutionary connections makes it inimical to the UK constitutional order which also lacks a clear-cut moment of constitutional authorship attributable to the people. Part II argues that this ambivalence towards constituent power affects the judicial reasoning seen in the High Court and majority of the Supreme Court in *Ryan v Lennon*. That stated, this chapter further argues that there is a proto-understanding of constituent power as vested in the people latent in the dissenting judgment of Kennedy CJ in *Ryan v Lennon*. This is most clearly identifiable in regard to the competing perspectives as to the role of the people both in the exercise of constituent power that created the constitution and within the constitutional order its exercise created. The chapter concludes with a discussion of how a better understanding of constituent power may influence constitutional debates on the island of Ireland today.

Constituent Power on These Islands

Essentially, constituent power is the power to create a constitution. This simplicity, however, masks deeper, more complex questions about who possesses constituent power, how this constituent power is exercised, and the subsequent relation between constituent power and the constitutional order its exercise created. The origins of constituent power are often traced to the French Revolution and the pamphlet *Qu'est-ce que le Tiers-État? (What is the Third Estate?)*.[1] Written by Emmanuel Joseph Sieyès—the Abbé Sieyès—his concept of constituent power was designed to legitimate the destruction of the *Ancien Régime* through the Estates General called by King Louis XVI. Fundamentally, constituent power facilitated the Third Estate which consisted of the representatives of the common people passing a motion transforming itself into a National Assembly and, in effect, usurping the other two Estates of the Nobles and the Church. For Sieyès, only the Third Estate was capable of speaking for the nation as unlike the other two estates, only its representatives had been

[1] Emmanuel-Joseph Sieyès, What Is the Third Estate? [1789], <http://pages.uoregon.edu/dluebke/301ModernEurope/Sieyes3dEstate.pdf> accessed 1 April 2023.

'sent by almost the totality of the nation.'[2] Through this move, political authority was wrested from monarch who claimed a Divine Right to rule and instead vested in 'the nation.'

The authority of the people's representatives to speak for the nation reveals the normative dimension of constituent power, imbuing the concept and the constitution its exercise establishes with democratic legitimacy. However, while certain theories of constituent power assume it to be possessed by 'the people', this only serves to raise further questions as to how, if at all, the people can participate in the constitution-making process and the subsequent relation between the people as the constituent authority and the constitutional order they have created.[3] Indeed, a further motivation for Sieyès to advocate for constituent power being vested in the Third Estate was to neutralise the people's participation by channelling it through their representatives rather than involving the people more directly. Thus, Lucia Rubinelli argues that 'the idea of constituent power served to reduce the people's exercise of power to the election of ordinary and extraordinary representatives.'[4] For this reason, Sieyès is careful to vest constituent power in 'the nation' rather than 'the people' per se. Far from empowering the people, 'fear of the people' is evident in this original iteration of constituent power. This is still as a common theme in constitution-making and constitutional thought today.[5]

This fear of the people reveals constituent power's radical and destructive potential and certain conceptions of constituent power are thus motived to disempower rather than empower the people.[6] Competing perspectives on this are revealed in the discourse on the relation between constituent power and the constituted order its exercise created. The exercise of constituent power creates a fundamental dichotomy between the constituent power and the subsequently created 'constituted powers', the

[2] Lucia Rubinelli, *Constituent Power: A History* (Cambridge: Cambridge University Press, 2020), 34.

[3] This emphasis on the people as the possessors of constituent power is best conceptualised in the work of Antonio Negri, who states that 'to speak of constituent power is to speak of democracy'. See Antonio Negri, *Insurgencies: Constituent Power and the Modern State* (Maurizia Boscagli trans, Minneapolis: University of Minnesota Press, 1999), 1.

[4] Rubinelli, *Constituent Power*, 33.

[5] See Christoph Möllers, "'We are (afraid of) the people': Constituent Power in German Constitutionalism" in *The Paradox of Constitutionalism: Constituent Power and Constitutional Form*, eds, Martin Loughlin and Neil Walker (Oxford: Oxford University Press, 2007), 87.

[6] See Joel Colon-Rios, *Constituent Power and the Law:* (Oxford: Oxford University Press, 2020) Ch. 7.

latter of which are exercised through the constitution and so are legal in nature. However, constituent power also raises the question as to whether it is exhausted at the moment of the creation of the constitution or whether it can be exercised even once the constitution is established—if so, how?

On this issue of the relation between the constituent power and the resulting constitution, there are, two broad models: closed and open. Closed models of constituent power view the power as existing outside of the legal order and as the power that creates the legal order in the first place. Once this legal order is up and running, there is no longer any need for constituent power. Any subsequent exercise of state power is a form of constituted power, exercised within the parameters of the constitution.[7] This may include the constitutional amendment power itself. In contrast, open models of constituent power may also view constituent power as beyond the constitutional order but nevertheless existing alongside the constitution once it has enacted.[8] Far from being exhausted, this power can act as a catalyst for change in the constitutional order, interacting with the constituted powers and shaping how these constituted powers are exercised.

A third approach is to reject the concept of constituent power altogether. This rejection is often motived by a fear of using the concept of constituent power to understand the authority of law, owing to its 'tense and ambivalent' relationship to the constitutional order its exercise has founded and constituent power's potential to destroy the very thing it created.[9] However, according to Andrew Arato, avoiding constituent power risks adopting a Hobbesian perspective by implying that it does not matter how constitutions are made because ultimately they are based on fear.[10] Conversely, a legal order through which constituent power may be readily exercised may not be much of an order at all, as its frequent exercise, or even threat of frequent exercise, undermines the stability necessary upon which a constitutional order may be founded.

[7] Alan Greene, "Parliamentary Sovereignty and the Locus of Constituent Power in the United Kingdom," 18(4) *International Journal of Constitutional Law* (2020): 1166, 1181.

[8] Illan Rua Wall, "Notes on an Open Constituent Power," 11 *Law, Culture and Humanities* (2015): 378, 379.

[9] See David Dyzenhaus, "Constitutionalism in an Old Key: Legality and Constituent Power," 1(2) *Global Constitutionalism* (2012): 229.

[10] Andrew Arato, *Post Sovereign Constitution Making: Learning and Legitimacy* (Oxford: Oxford University Press, 2016), 3.

Thus, if we are to avoid conceding that all constitutions are ultimately based on fear, constituent power can act as a legitimating function; however, the understanding of constituent power must be rooted in democracy. This requires an analysis of how, if at all, the people possess and exercise constituent power. This necessarily entails analysis of the relation between the people and those who claim to speak on their behalf[11] and, in turn, this interrogation of how, if at all, the people can mount this challenge.[12] The vesting of constituent power cannot be taken for granted and there may exist other constitutional orders that vest constituent power elsewhere—for example, in a monarchy or oligarchy or aristocracy.[13] The normative dimension of constituent power therefore requires interrogation of where this locus of constituent power lies with the people conceptualised as the ideal possessors. Constituent power therefore has both descriptive and normative dimensions. Descriptively, it is an account of the power to create a constitution; normatively, certain theories of constituent power argue that this power *should* be vested in the people.

The debate as to the juridical status of constituent power outside of the original constitution-making process is best revealed in studies on nature of the constitutional amendment power. Competing perspectives view the amendment power as, inter alia: an expression of constituent power; or a power; or as a *sui generis* power.[14] This, in turn, raises questions as to the possibility of unconstitutional constitutional amendments—the question at the heart of *Ryan v Lennon*.

The British Neglect of Constituent Power

The French revolutionary origins of constituent power may explain, to an extent, the fact that the concept has long been eschewed by UK constitutional thought.[15] That stated, there have been some attempts at tracing the British credentials of constituent power, most notably identifying elements in the thoughts and writings of the Levellers during the English

[11] See Martin Loughlin, "The Concept of Constituent Power," 13 *European Journal of Political Theory* (2014) 218.

[12] Greene, "Parliamentary Sovereignty" 1192.

[13] See Renato Cristi, "Schmitt on Power and the Monarchical Principal," 18 *Constellations* (2011) 352.

[14] Yaniv Roznai, *Unconstitutional Constitutional Amendments: The Limits of Amendment Powers* (Oxford: Oxford University Press, 2017).

[15] See Greene "Parliamentary Sovereignty."

Civil War.[16] The lack of a codified constitution attributable to the people also explains to an extent the lack of necessity to have recourse to constituent power. Instead, the UK's constitutional order with parliamentary sovereignty as the apex norm is conceptualised as a more amorphous concept, its content evolving over time, eschewing the distinction between constitutional politics and ordinary politics seen in other jurisdictions. This legislative supremacy has thus led Martin Loughlin to conclude that constituent power serves no juristic function in the UK having been 'entirely absorbed into the doctrine of the absolute authority of the Crown-in-Parliament to speak for the British nation'.[17] This aligns closely with Alexis de Tocqueville describing Westminster as 'at once a legislative and constituent assembly'.[18] To this end, the distinction between the constituent power and the constituted but ostensibly unlimited legislative power is blurred.[19]

If the Westminster Parliament is to possess constituent power, this raises the question as to whether it can be considered to be vested in the people. There have been attempts to do so by claiming that Parliament possesses derived constituent power—a conception of constituent power that requires its exercise accord with the formal rules and procedures established by the constitution.[20] Ultimately, the people, it is claimed, possess the constituent power and they delegate this to their representatives in Parliament.[21] This derived constituent power can be contrasted with the original constituent power that created the constitution in the first place and is ultimately possessed by the people. This neat resolution of the relation between the people and their representatives has been fundamentally challenged, however, in the past decade, most notably in the context of Brexit referendum in 2016 and the resulting constitutional crisis it resulted in. Far from being merely advisory, Brexit in particular revealed deep

[16] Martin Loughlin, 'Constituent Power Subverted: From English Constitutional Argument to British Constitutional Practice in *The Paradox of Constitutionalism: Constituent Power and Constitutional Form,* eds Martin Loughlin and Neil Walker (Oxford: Oxford University Press, 2008) 27, 35–38.

[17] Loughlin, "Constituent Power Subverted."

[18] Alexis de Tocqueville, *Democracy in America* (first published 1835, New American Library, 1956) 74.

[19] Greene, Parliamentary Sovereignty 1188.

[20] Roznai, *Unconstitutional Constitutional Amendments* 110.

[21] Thomas Poole, "Devotion to Legalism: On the Brexit Case," 80 *Modern Law Review* (2017): 685.

tensions between the British people—or peoples—and those who claim to speak on their behalf.[22] Such tensions may have been foreseeable had the concept of constituent power been deployed in advance and the idea of an 'advisory' referendum more carefully interrogated. In turn, a more careful examination of constituent power would reveal the dangers of relying on representation as a conduit for the people's constituent power, as much of the literature on constituent power and constituent assemblies focuses on *delegation* rather than representation.[23]

Ultimately, constituent power in the UK constitutional order is an under-explored concept, owing largely to its usurpation and neutralisation through parliamentary sovereignty. Parliament, unbounded by any norm higher than its own sovereignty possesses radical potential but this is effectively neutralised through the electoral system, constitutional conventions and parliamentary procedure to the extent that it is questionable to what degree constituent power can be claimed to be vested in 'the people' in the UK.[24] This British avoidance of constituent power does not merely have consequences for the UK but can potentially explain legal developments in other jurisdictions with close connections to the UK, not least the Irish Free State.

Constituent Power and The Irish Free State

In contrast to the British hegemonic constitutional narrative, Ireland has experienced revolutionary rupture. The drafting of two codified constitutions in the Twentieth Century provided opportune moments for the interjecting of constituent power into Irish constitutional theory and practice; yet despite this, constituent power in Irish constitutional thought is conspicuous by its absence. The Free State Constitution was a product of negotiation between the provisional Dublin Government and the British Government in line with the terms of the 1921 Anglo-Irish treaty.[25] Following elections in 1922 in which pro-treaty parties won a majority, the Third Dáil sitting as a constituent assembly then ratified the

[22] Greene, "Parliamentary Sovereignty" 1194–1195.

[23] See William Partlett, "The American Tradition of Constituent Power" 15(4) *International Journal of Constitutional Law* (2015): 955.

[24] Greene, "Parliamentary Sovereignty" 1191–1192.

[25] For a comprehensive history and analysis of the drafting of the Free State Constitution see Laura Cahillane, *Drafting the Irish Free State Constitution* (Manchester, Manchester University Press, 2016).

constitution by a simple majority vote on 25 October 1922. This was then followed by Westminster enacting the Irish Free State Constitution Act 1922 which received royal assent on 5 December 1922. Consequently, the Free State Constitution was the product of a peace agreement between two competing sources of political legitimacy. These competing legal sources of legitimate authority were reflected by the Constitution's approval by two separate legislative organs: the Third Dáil sitting a constituent assembly, and the Westminster Parliament. 'Constructive ambiguity' as to whether this document was simply attributable to the authority of Westminster or whether it was the product of a revolutionary rupture was thus hardwired into the authority of the Free State Constitution.[26]

The identification of the possessor of constituent power in the case of the Free State Constitution therefore is deliberately ambiguous. One the one hand, one strand of Irish republican thought may claim that the Free State Constitution was enacted by the Third Dáil. A democratic connection to the people as the true possessors of constituent power could be maintained by insisting that the Third Dáil possessed *derived* constituent power delegated to it by 'the people'. That stated, such a derivation would be dependent upon the concept of representation rather than delegation. On the other hand, the British could claim that the Irish Free State was the creation of the sovereign Westminster parliament. It was the product of legislation, not revolution. Any power, be it legislative, executive, judicial, or even a *sui generis* constitutional amendment power were all exercised by bodies subordinate to the Westminster parliament. Section 4 of Irish Free State Constitution Act 1922 passed by Westminster is illustrative in this regard as it clearly restates the Imperial Parliament's 'power to make laws affecting the Irish Free State in any case where, in accordance with constitutional practice, Parliament would make laws affecting other self-governing Dominions.[27] This view may also align with anti-treaty republicans seeking to deny the legitimacy of partition and the notion that the people of the twenty-six counties as distinct from the people of the

[26] The term 'constructive ambiguity' is often attributed to former US Secretary of State Henry Kissinger. See Antoine Rayroux, "Speaking EU defence at home: Contentious discourses and constructive ambiguity" 49(2) *Cooperation and Conflict* (2014): 386, 387.

[27] Irish Free State Constitution Act 1922, section 4.

island of Ireland as a whole possessed constituent power.[28] These competing perspectives thus reveal not just the juristic potential of constituent power but also its normative dimension and different views as to the value, if any, of this normativity.

The attempt to break with the ultimate authority at the basis of the UK constitution is also reflected in the substantive content of the Free State Constitution as originally enacted. The Free State Constitution ostensibly rejected the British tradition of parliamentary sovereignty by establishing the primacy of the Constitution over the newly incepted Oireachtas, empowering the High Court to determine the validity of any law, including legislation, having regard to the provisions of the Constitution.[29] It further stipulated in Article 50 that the amendment of the Constitution could only be done by a referendum, of which two thirds of the electorate had turned out.[30] The Free State Constitution made an attempt at conceptualising the people as a source of political and therefore ultimate legal authority. In turn, this had the potential to clearly establish the Oireachtas' power as a constituted and limited legislative power, distinct from that possessed by the Westminster Parliament.

However, this compromised attempt to cement the people of the Irish Free State as the ideal and true possessors of constituent power can explain why this constitution was doomed to fail. It was fundamentally undermined by a transitory provision within Article 50 permitting it to be amended by ordinary legislation during the first eight years of the Constitution's entry into force. This time-limit was itself circumvented by the 16th Amendment of the Constitution which extended the period by which the Constitution could be amended by ordinary legislation from

[28] This idea of the exercise of constituent power in the Irish Free State—as distinct from Ireland as a whole—has been confronted by Oran Doyle who has argued that the operation of the Free State Constitution from 1922 to 1937 was fundamental in constructing the 26 counties of the Free State as a separate geographical entity from the residual six counties in Northern Ireland. Consequently, when constituent power was exercised by the people and institutions of the 26 counties to enact the 1937 Constitution, this had been legitimised by the prior existing legal system and, as such, an existing legal system can pave the way towards its own unlawful replacement. Consequently, the enactment of the 1937 Constitution was not 'a big bang event in which a constituent power willed itself into existence'. Oran Doyle, 'Populist constitutionalism and constituent power' (2019)2 20 *German Law Journal* 161, 176.

[29] Article 65.

[30] Article 50

eight to sixteen years following its introduction.[31] A constitutional challenge to what ostensibly appears to be a return to parliamentary sovereignty was rejected by the Supreme Court in the (in)famous case of *Ryan v Lennon*.[32] Yet the judgment itself reveals that despite the majority upholding the validity of the Oireachtas' claim to the constitutional amendment power; both it and the minority which rejected this validity acknowledged that there were substantive limits to the Oireachtas' legislative power. In turn, this raises questions as to where the locus of constituent power lay in relation to the Irish Free State Constitution.

Constitutional Supremacy Subverted: The State (Ryan) v Lennon

In *Ryan v Lennon*, the Appellant challenged the validity of the Constitution (Amendment No. 17) Act 1931 which inserted Article 2A into the Irish Free State Constitution. This sought to permit the establishment of military tribunals 'whenever the Executive Council is of opinion that circumstances render it expedient'.[33] It is not hyperbole to describe Article 2A as making a mockery of the protections afforded to human rights and the rule of law by the Free State Constitution. These tribunals—for to refer to them as courts would be an insult to judicial institutions—were comprised solely of military officers who did not require legal training. They could try persons for any offence, including for conduct which was not criminal at the time it was committed. They could also impose any sanction they saw fit, up to and including the death penalty.

Article 2A epitomises the deepest concerns of critics of parliamentary sovereignty and the notion of an unconstrained legislature. Leslie Stephen as quoted by AV Dicey famously remarked that such concerns as to the tyrannical potential of parliamentary sovereignty do not arise in the UK as:

> If a legislature decided that all blue-eyed babies should be murdered, the preservation of blue-eyed babies would be illegal; but legislators must go mad before they could pass such a law and subjects to be idiotic before they could submit to it.[34]

[31] See William Quill's chapter in this collection.

[32] [1935] IR 170.

[33] Constitution (Amendment No. 17) Act 1931.

[34] Mark D Walters, *AV Dicey and the Common Law Constitutional Tradition: A Legal Turn of Mind* (Cambridge: Cambridge University Press, 2020) 202–203.

While the imperial Parliament may have been reticent to persecute blue-eyed babies, the same concern cannot be said to have been held for their colonial subjects where notions of emergency and exception were often invoked to exempt these jurisdictions from the ordinary requirements of the rule of law and the traditional British liberties supposedly enjoyed by all in the empire.[35] In choosing to enact Article 2A, the Oireachtas was mirroring the Westminster Parliament, acting as if it were free from any constitutional restrictions. Even the state's lawyers in *Ryan v Lennon* were repulsed by Article 2A, opening their submissions by stating that 'they were in the unenviable and very difficult position of having to stand over an Act which was repellent to the instincts of every lawyer'.[36]

In *Ryan v Lennon t*he appellants argued that the change in the period of time during which the Free State Constitution could be amended without the need for a referendum was ultra vires. It would then follow that Article 2A was itself invalid. The Court also had to consider whether what was contemplated by Article 2A was actually an amendment or as Kennedy CJ dissenting argued, effected 'a radical alteration of the basic scheme and principles of the Constitution'.[37]

Ostensibly, one may have expected *Ryan* to have come down to a clash between maximalist and minimalist conceptions of the breadth of power afforded to the Oireachtas by the Constitution. A maximalist interpretation would tend to point towards upholding the validity of both the 16th Amendment and Article 2A. In turn, this maximalist approach may blur the distinction between the amendment power and the constituent power, raising further questions as to the possessor of this constituent power and the relation between the people and their representatives. In contrast, a minimalist interpretation, finding that both the 16th Amendment and, in turn, Article 2A were invalid would demonstrate that the Oireachtas' power was more limited. This would clearly establish the legislative power as a limited constituted power, created by the original exercise of constituent power. This would also raise further questions as to the possessor of constituent power but may point in a different direction as where this constituent power lay than the maximalist interpretation. What is striking

[35] For analysis on the role of empire in Dicey's constitutional thought see Dylan Lino, "Albert Venn Dicey and the Constitutional Theory of Empire," (36(4) *Oxford Journal of Legal Studies* (2016)L 751; Dylan Lino, "The Rule of Law and the Rule of Empire: AV Dicey in Imperial Context," 81(3) *Modern Law Review* (2018): 739.

[36] *Ryan*, 194.

[37] *Ryan*, 200.

from a constituent power perspective, however, is that the *Ryan v Lennon* judgments are more nuanced than this, eschewing such a 'maximum-minimum' analysis.

The Majority

Speaking for the majority, Fitzgibbon J rejected the contention that the 16th Amendment was unconstitutional, stating:

> I cannot accede to the argument that the Oireachtas cannot alter, modify, or repeal them [the constitutional amendment rules]. The framers of our Constitution may have intended "to bind man down from mischief by the chains of the Constitution," but if they did, they defeated their object by handing him the key of the padlock.[38]

Taken alone, this extract would suggest that the Oireachtas' power was no less limited than that of the Westminster Parliament making it similar to what Tocqueville described as 'at once a legislative and constituent assembly.' However, Fitzgibbon J also expressly rejected the state's argument that the Third Dáil transmitted its authority—described as 'supreme legislative authority'—to the Oireachtas.[39] Assuming that the Third Dáil had 'supreme legislative authority'—although it is unclear as to what he means by this—Fitzgibbon J then stressed that the exercise of this power expressly stipulated that the Constitution 'shall be construed with reference to the Articles of Agreement for a Treaty between Great Britain and Ireland' and therefore that

> if any provision of the said Constitution *or of any amendment thereof or of any law made thereunder* is in any respect repugnant to any of the provision of the Scheduled Treaty, *it shall,* to the extent only of such repugnancy, *be absolutely void and inoperative.*[40]

Fitzgibbon J thus concludes that

[38] *Ryan,* 234.

[39] *Ryan* 226. Fitzgibbon J's judgment is unclear as to whether the 'supreme legislative authority' of the Third Dáil was itself limited by the terms of the Treaty. Ultimately, this point is moot as the Constitution the Third Dáil created was subject to review and approval by the British authorities.

[40] *Ryan,* 226; emphasis in the original.

> the supreme legislative authority speaking as the mouthpiece of the people, expressly denied to the Oireachtas the power of enacting any legislation by way of amendment of the Constitution or otherwise, which might be 'in any respect repugnant to any of the provisions of the Scheduled Treaty.'[41]

Consequently, Fitzgibbon J recognises that there are limits to the Oireachtas' legislative power and that it is distinct from the 'supreme legislative authority' of the Third Dáil sitting as a constituent assembly. However, as both the 16th Amendment arrogating to the Dáil the power to amend the Constitution, and the 17th Amendment introducing military courts did not violate the Treaty provisions, the amendments were valid. Similar conclusions are reached by Murnaghan J who also found that the Constitution must be construed in accordance with the Treaty. As the amendments were not contra to the Treaty, they were valid. Murnaghan J also voiced a sceptical and revealing view of referendums:

> It must also be remembered that in this country the Referendum was an untried political experiment and it cannot be assumed that the Referendum should be incapable of alteration or removal. I feel bound by the words of Article 50, which allows amendment of the Constitution as a whole, of which Article 50 is declared to be a part.[42]

The ramification of the majority judgments is that there are provisions of the Free State Constitution that are unalterable via the mechanism of constitutional amendment stipulated. Instead, such alterations could only be completed through amendment of the Treaty, that is, with the agreement of the UK. Donal K. Coffey notes that this limit on the Oireachtas' ability to amend the Constitution initially was unclear as in the oral hearing announcing the judgment, media coverage by the Irish Press suggested that the Oireachtas had an unlimited amendment power. It was not until the judgments were published that this limitation become clear.[43] Therefore, while the state ultimately succeeded in convincing the Court as to the validity of the constitutional amendments in question; it nevertheless would have been deeply disappointed with this line of reasoning. Coffey details the lengths the state sought to go to in order to avoid this

[41] *Ryan*, 226.

[42] *Ryan*, 244.

[43] Donal K. Coffey, *Constitutionalism in Ireland, 1932–1938: National, Commonwealth and International Perspectives* (Cham: Palgrave Macmillan, 2018) 68.

outcome. A memorandum discovered by Coffey reveals that the state engaged with the issue of constituent assemblies and various theories with a view to maximising the power of the Oireachtas. This memorandum revealed that a key objective of the State was to convince the Court in *Ryan* that the Oireachtas was 'a perpetual assembly' with Article 50 giving it 'full power to amend the Constitution'.[44] The state was attempting to walk a fine line between empowering the Oireachtas while simultaneously downplaying the importance of the Treaty. It ultimately failed to do so.

Under the majority's understanding, the constitutional amendment power is a constituted power and one which the Oireachtas could arrogate to itself, notwithstanding that the exercise of constituent power which originally vested this in 'the people'. There is no need to reach for a concept such as constituent power; instead, all is explicable through pre-existing legal norms. The clearest latent rejection of the notion of constituent power in *Ryan v Lennon*, however, comes not from the majority in the Supreme Court but from the High Court judgment of Meredith J, upholding the validity of the constitutional amendments. Meredith J confronts head on the idea that the Third Dáil possessed a power superior to the legislative power possessed by the Oireachtas and delegated to it by the people:

> In particular, the one argument put up against the validity of the Constitution (Amendment No. 16) Act 1929, was the result of a raid on the law of agency. It could not be contested that the change of eight to sixteen years was in the nature of an amendment, but it was urged that it was not competent for the Oireachtas itself to enlarge the authority delegated or entrusted to it by the people. That argument asserts a legal principle, adopted in the form of a principle of constitutional law, which looks outside the four corners of the Constitution itself, and, accordingly, this Court has no authority to pay regard to it in exercising its jurisdiction under Art. 65 ... If this Court has authority to look outside the Constitution to extraneous principles of law to determine the validity of any law 'having regard to the provisions of the Constitution' it could build up a body of judge-made law standing alongside the Constitution. Art. 65 gives no such authority.[45]

The High Court and majority Supreme Court judgments therefore reveal not only a highly positivist approach to constitutional interpretation; they

[44] Coffey, 69.
[45] *Ryan*, 179.

also eschew any notion of constituent power, and particularly, any conception of constituent power vested in the people. Meridith J's judgment is particularly revealing, arguing that the striking down of the 16th Amendment would have been an extreme form of judicial supremacy rather than a means of protecting the constitutional function of the people.[46] There is therefore no understanding of the people as the true or ideal conferrers of political or legal authority; or the Third Dáil as possessing derived constituent power; or of the people as possessing any constitutional agency of their own. Instead, the default of parliamentary sovereignty is essentially reverted to. Tom Hickey thus argues that the 'Oireachtas had, it seemed, cast the essential principles of the Constitution aside and had arrogated to itself the power to amend it indefinitely'.[47] However, while the majority accorded to the Oireachtas a broad constitutional amendment power, it also simultaneously conceptualised this as a constituted and limited power—specifically by the Treaty—rather than as an expression of the constituent power.

Kennedy CJ's Dissent

In contrast to the majority, Kennedy CJ, downplays the importance of the Treaty as a limiting factor on the power of the Free State to amend its Constitution. Instead, Kennedy CJ argued that a treaty is 'simply an agreement between parties' and as such 'is not something immutable in its character as a treaty but is subject to modification or termination.'[48] A treaty also requires some further step for it to become part of the 'municipal law of either country'.[49] Kennedy CJ therefore argued that the Free State Constitution was this additional step. However, this obligation in domestic law remains only in so far as 'it remains unrepealed'.[50] This, he argued, is quite separate from 'an obligation having a sanction quite independently of the political and moral obligation of such Treaty internationally as an international agreement'.[51]

[46] *Ryan*, 179.

[47] Tom Hickey, 'Revisiting *Ryan v Lennon* to make the case against judicial supremacy (and for a new model of constitutionalism in Ireland' (2015) 53 Irish Jurist 125, 129.

[48] *Ryan*, 206.

[49] *Ryan*, 205–206.

[50] *Ryan*, 206.

[51] *Ryan*, 206.

Instead, in his famous dissent, Kennedy CJ argued that the 16th and 17th Amendments were unconstitutional. Kennedy CJ attempted to limit the Oireachtas' legislative power through several distinct arguments. Firstly, in what may be the most studied paragraph in Irish constitutional history, Kennedy CJ famously invoked natural law principles constraining positive law and the democratic branches by declaring that

> all lawful authority comes from God to the people, and it is declared by Article 2 of the Constitution that 'all powers of government and all authority, legislative, executive and judicial, in Ireland are derived from the people of Ireland …' it follows that every act, whether legislative, executive or judicial, in order to be lawful under the Constitution must be capable of being justified under the authority thereby declared to be derived from God. From this it seems clear that, if any legislation of the Oireachtas (including any purported amendment of the Constitution) were to offend against that acknowledged ultimate Source from which the legislative authority has come through the People to the Oireachtas, as for instance, if it were repugnant to the Natural Law, such legislation would be necessarily unconstitutional and invalid and it would be, therefore absolutely null and void and inoperative.[52]

In so doing, Kennedy CJ seeks to place limits on the Oireachtas without reference to the Treaty; instead he reaches for the supremacy of natural law.

While Kennedy CJ's conception of natural law has received a substantial amount of scholarly and legal attention,[53] his subsequent analysis of the relation between the Third Dáil sitting as a constituent assembly and any subsequent Oireachtas, reveals a proto-conception of constituent power struggling to assert itself without the deployment of the specific grammar of constituent power. Firstly, Kennedy CJ attempts to establish a clear distinction between the Third Dáil sitting as a Constituent Assembly and the subsequently established Oireachtas:

> … that Assembly [the Third Dáil] was a single-chamber parliament, membership of which was not restricted by, or conditioned on, any test, oath or declaration of any kind, and which did not act in combination or association with any other chamber or body or person (Lord Lieutenant or Governor-

[52] *Ryan*, 204–205.

[53] See Gerard Hogan, "A Desert Island Case set in the Silver Sea: The State (Ryan) v Lennon" in *Leading Cases of the Twentieth Century*, ed. Eoin O'Dell (Dublin: Sweet & Maxwell, 2000).

> General), and that it was the Parliament to which the then Executive or administration, including the 'Provisional Government' as it was called, was responsible.[54]

In this paragraph we see Kennedy CJ's attempt to establish a closer degree of connection between the Third Dáil and the people than any other legislature subsequently established under the Free State Constitution. Unlike the Oireachtas, the Third Dáil was unencumbered by an unelected or unrepresentative Seanad. Members were also free from the requirement to take an oath of allegiance to the British King, a prerequisite that excluded many anti-treaty TDs from the Oireachtas. Kennedy CJ thus seeks to establish a greater democratic legitimacy for the Third Dáil over the Oireachtas, using this as the normative basis upon which to establish the supremacy of the Third Dáil and by extension, the Constitution over the legislative power of the Oireachtas. Kennedy CJ then builds upon this distinction between the Constituent Assembly and the Oireachtas to argue that the former made it clear that the people's authority it claimed to represent should be maintained even after the constitution entered into effect:

> A moment's consideration will demonstrate that this clause [the time limit in Article 50] was enacted in clear realisation of the relative positions of the Constituent Assembly and the Oireachtas. Membership of the Constituent Assembly, as I have mentioned already, was not restricted by any oath or other test. The Assembly therefore felt itself entitled to speak for all the people in the territory for which it was elected, and it is very clear, on the evidence of the Constitution itself which it enacted, that the Assembly intended, and, so far as it could by constitutional provision, tried to preserve intact the overriding authority of the people.[55]

He continues:

> Thus, the Constituent Assembly, endowing the more limited Assembly, the Oireachtas, with a power of amendment of the Constitution, reserved to the people on whose behalf it was enacting that Constitution absolute control of the exercise of that power, so that in every case after the period of eight

[54] *Ryan*, 204.
[55] *Ryan*, 210.

> years the decision of the people must be obtained and, during that period, such control was secured by the right to demand a Referendum.[56]

In this manner, Kennedy CJ distinguishes the power possessed by the Third Dáil sitting as a Constituent Assembly from the legislative power of the Oireachtas. Having established this more limited legislative power, Kennedy CJ then proceeds to interpret the Free State Constitution as creating two distinct amendment powers:

> Now, the power of amendment is wholly contained in a single Article, but the donee of the power and the mode of its exercise are so varied with regard to a point of time as to make it practically two separate powers, the one limited to be exercised only during the preliminary period of eight years, the other, a wholly different and permanent power, to come into existence after the expiry of that preliminary period and so continue thereafter.[57]

This leads to a fascinating argument in which the Oireachtas' amendment power during the initial eight years of the Free State Constitution is treated as a very clear limited constituted power with an express time limit. In contrast, after this period of eight years:

> There is a prohibition, utterly unambiguous in its terms, forbidding the passing into law of any amendment which shall not have been submitted to a Referendum of the people and been approved by a specified majority of the people.[58]

The people's power to amend the Constitution beyond this period therefore is treated as something distinct. Kennedy CJ appears to suggest that this general power of amendment, although contained in the Constitution, is not necessarily a constitutional or constituted power:

> A power of amendment is not an essential part of, or provision in, or addition to, a Constitution. The Constituent Assembly which creates and grants a Constitution need not grant any power to amend it, in which case amendment can be effected only by re-convoking the Constituent Assembly for that purpose. If it should have granted a power of amendment and an

[56] *Ryan*, 211.
[57] *Ryan*, 213.
[58] *Ryan*, 214.

> amendment outside the scope of that power should be proposed, that amendment can only be effected by again convoking the Constituent Assembly to enact it, if the Assembly think fit. A power of amending a Constitution is something outside and collateral to the Constitution itself. It may be conferred on a donee other than an authority owing its existence to the Constitution, as, for instance, on the whole body of the people, on a religious or legal hierarchy, or any other person or body that might be selected for the purpose. Again, such a power may be given by the Constituent Assembly by a separate instrument and not in the instrument containing the Constitution. In the present case, Article 50 might have been enacted by the Constituent Assembly as a separate Act or it might have been enacted as a section of the Constitution Act instead of being inserted in the Schedule containing the Constitution.[59]

Is this amendment power of the people identical to the constituent power exercised by the Constituent Assembly? There are some hints at this in the above extract, suggesting that the Constituent Assembly could have placed this amendment power in a different document. This would also tie in with Kennedy CJ's suggestion that even if an amendment power had not been articulated in the Constitution, the Free State Constitution could still be amended if the Constituent Assembly was re-convened.[60] Kennedy CJ's argument therefore has echoes of a concept of derived constituent power with the original constituent power stipulating the manner and form in which the derived constituent power may be exercised. This latent understanding of constituent power in Kennedy CJ's judgment, however, struggles to assert itself clearly without the actual grammar of constituent power at his disposal.

The People of The Irish Free State as Possessors of Constituent Power

Kennedy CJ's latent concept of constituent power is not merely descriptive; instead, its democratic basis is fundamental to his understanding. His judgment makes a concerted attempt to articulate an understanding of a constitutional amendment power that empowers 'the people' while simultaneously disempowering the Oireachtas and downplaying the external limits on the Free State Constitution. However, a key weakness in Kennedy

[59] *Ryan*, 218.
[60] *Ryan*, 204.

CJ's vesting of constituent power in the Third Dáil lies in his attempt to demonstrate its closer relation to the people than any subsequent legislature. Firstly, like Westminster, Kennedy CJ relies on the concept of representation rather than delegation. Secondly, his attempt suffers from the same legitimacy decay that afflicts all entrenched constitutional norms. Even if a constitution results from a constituent process that can be attributed to 'the people', this only serves to raise the question of how long such an attribution can last. The democratic legitimacy of all laws decays over-time, not least constitutions. Thomas Jefferson famously postulated that a constitution should be renewed every generation to avoid being ruled by ghosts and to ensure that every generation can re-legitimate democratically the constitution which they ought to obey.[61] As time progresses, this justification for the superior democratic legitimacy of the Third Dáil wanes, notwithstanding the specific remarks made regarding the lack of a requirement to take the oath of allegiance. This argument would be further weakened by the Constitution (Removal of Oath) Act 1933, which removed the requirement for Oireachtas members to take the oath of allegiance.[62] That stated, Kennedy CJ's reasoning could be deployed to turn this weakness into a strength. Although the democratic legitimacy of the Third Dáil may decay over time, this only serves to prove that the vesting of the permanent amendment power in the people—the original possessors of constituent power from whom the Third Dáil derived its constituent power—was a concerted attempt to assuage these concerns regarding legitimacy decay.

Kennedy CJ's reference to the Seanad as a 'nominated or unrepresentative element' is a more compelling basis upon which to distinguish the Third Dáil's superior democratic credentials from that of any subsequent Oireachtas. However, such an argument would also dissipate in the event that the Seanad was abolished; this duly occurred with the enactment of the Constitution (Amendment No. 24) Act 1936. That stated, Kennedy CJ had to work with the factual circumstances presented to him rather than some imaginary constituent process, perfectly reflecting the will of the people. To that end, it is understandable that he sought to latch on to

[61] Letter from Thomas Jefferson to James Madison Vol 15, March 1789 to November 1789 (Princeton University Press, 1958), 392–8. < https://jeffersonpapers.princeton.edu/selected-documents/thomas-jefferson-james-madison> accessed 28 April 2023.

[62] Constitution (Removal of Oath) Act 1933.

any demarcating features between the Third Dáil and any subsequent Oireachtas.

As noted, the concept of constituent power can have normative as well as descriptive elements, with the normative element reflected in its democratic potential. An open, 'relational' conception of constituent power aligns with this democratic potential. This relational conception of constituent power as articulated by Loughlin understands that constitutional ordering is dynamic and never static.[63] Further, Loughlin argues that although constituent power is vested in the people, this does not mean that political authority is exercised by the people. Loughlin thus seeks to establish relational constituent power as a 'dialectic of right' between the rulers and the ruled such that it 'seeks constantly to irritate the institutionalised form of constitutional authority'. However, this democratic potential of constituent power is lost if the claim that the people possess constituent power is simply assumed rather than stress-tested. To that end, not only must the people be able to challenge those who speak on their behalf, the degree to which they actually can, must be interrogated.[64] Consequently, it may be the case that the people do not possess constituent power in a specific constitutional order.

When examining who possessed the constituent power that created the Free State Constitution, it is submitted that this was not possessed by one single authority. Rather, a better question to ask is where the *locus* of constituent power lies.[65] This is invariably the case for all constitutional orders as constitutional creation tends to involve multiple actors. This is clear from Sieyès' original formation of constituent power as possessed by the Third Estate by virtue of their representative connection with the people. In the case of the Free State Constitution, the locus of constituent power lay between the people, their representatives in the Third Dáil, and the British Authorities by virtue of the treaty. The majority's judgments in *Ryan v Lennon* repudiated any role for the people outside of their elected representatives. It shifted the locus of constituent power towards the British authorities through the Treaty and the Oireachtas, weakening considerably the degree to which one could claim constituent power was vested in the people.

[63] Loughlin "The Concept of Constituent Power," 227–231.

[64] Greene, "Parliamentary Sovereignty" 1192.

[65] Greene, "Parliamentary Sovereignty" 1185.

The majority's conclusions in *Ryan v Lennon* were assisted by the hyper-literal approach to constitutional interpretation they took, facilitated by conflating the constitutional amendment power with the legislative power. They therefore rejected Kennedy CJ's contention that Article 50 actually contained two separate amendment powers. This paved the way for the validity of the Constitution (Amendment No. 16) Act 1929 to be upheld. This conflation between the constitutional amendment power and the legislative power is helped by the political constitutional order that existed prior to the Irish revolution and which the Supreme Court judges were educated in and in which they had practised for most of their careers.

The majority's line of reasoning was mirrored, to an extent, by the Privy Council in *Moore and Others v Attorney General*.[66] This case concerning a fisheries dispute in the Erne estuary centred on The Constitution (Amendment No. 22) Act 1933 which was enacted to prevent cases from being heard by the Privy Council. Although appeal to the Privy Council was not expressly provided for by the Treaty, it was argued that it was implied because the Irish Free State was in the same constitutional position in relation to the Westminster parliament as Canada which retained an appeal to the Privy Council.[67] The Privy Council held:

> Thus the Treaty received the force of law, both in the United Kingdom and in Ireland by reason of the passing of an Act of the Imperial Parliament; and the Constituent Act owed its validity to the same authority.[68]

However, as the Statute of Westminster had been passed giving the Irish Free State the same powers as Canada and Australia to amend their constitutions, it followed that the State could now abolish appeal to the Privy Council. Consequently, a clear nexus of validity between the Free State Constitution and an Act of Parliament of the UK is still insisted upon. No recourse to constituent power is required.

In contrast, Kennedy CJ's dissent downplays the role of the British authorities; instead, it amplifies the role of the people, situating the locus of constituent power between the two poles of the people and the Third Dáil. Representation is then deployed as the nexus of connection between

[66] [1935] IR 170. For a detailed analysis of this case see Thomas Mohr, "Law Without Loyalty—The Abolition of the Irish Appeal to the Privy Council" 37 *Irish Jurist* (2002): 187.

[67] Donal K. Coffey, "The need for a new constitution: Irish constitutional change 1932–1935" 34 *Irish Jurist* (2012): 275, 300.

[68] *Moore* 479.

the Constituent Assembly and the people. However, Kennedy CJ's judgment also inserts God into this dynamic, insisting that 'all lawful authority comes from God to the people'. Kennedy CJ was keen to stress natural law as a limit on the amendment power, thus conceptualising it as a constituted power. This does add an additional layer of fortification to his judgment; however, it also raises the question as to whether this natural law limitation only affected the Oireachtas' power to amend the Constitution within the first eight years, or whether it also limited the permanent power to amend the Constitution which Kennedy CJ was careful to distinguish.

Conclusions: The After-Life of Constituent Power in Ireland

Kennedy CJ's natural law analysis as a limitation on the legislative power has had an afterlife, to an extent, under the 1937 Constitution through both the case law and legal analysis, most notably in the concept of unenumerated constitutional rights. Taking this argument to its logical conclusion, some suggested that it—or a form of it—could be resurrected to limit even the amendment power of the people.[69] This was ultimately rejected by the Supreme Court which, in a case challenging the constitutionality of the 14th Amendment of the Constitution Act 1992 declared:

> The People were entitled to amend the Constitution in accordance with the provisions of Article 46 of the Constitution and the Constitution as so amended by the Fourteenth Amendment is the fundamental and supreme law of the State representing as it does the will of the People.[70]

Again, there is no express engagement with the concepts of constituent or constituted power in this judgment. Consequently, despite there being

[69] While this argument was expressly rejected in *In the Matter of the reference to the court of the Regulation of Information (Services Outside the State for Termination of Pregnancies Bill 1995* [1995] 2 ILRM 81, Aileen Kavanagh has suggested that a version of it similar to the Dworkinian analysis of the concept of 'principles', could be used to curtail the amendment power. Kavanagh's interesting argument does not, however, engage with the concept of constituent power, save for a brief reference to the notion of 'pouvoir constituant'. Aileen Kavanagh, "Unconstitutional Constitutional Amendments from the Irish Free State to Irish Republic" in *The Constitution of Ireland: Perspectives and Prospects*, ed. Eoin Carolan (Dublin: Bloomsbury, 2012) 331, 338.

[70] *In re Article 26 and the Regulation of Information (Services Outside the State for Termination of Pregnancies) Bill 1995* [1995] 1 I.R. 1, 43.

numerous opportunities in Irish constitutional history to grapple with the concept of constituent power, this has not been done yet to date. This may be due to the quotidian status of referendums, illustrating Ireland's understanding of constitutional amendments as the exercise of a 'constituted power', prescribed by the Constitution and exercised through law. As such, there is no need to explore extra-legal conceptions of constituent power as a means of explaining the role of 'the people' in the Irish constitutional legal order; one merely has to consult Articles 46 and 47 of the Constitution. In this way, while Westminster has collapsed constituent power into parliamentary sovereignty, Ireland may also have collapsed constituent power into the constitutional amendment power.[71]

While there has not yet been an express juristic demonstration of a knowledge of constituent power in Ireland, it is arguably the case that a latent conception of constituent power, touched upon by Kennedy CJ has animated subsequent constitutional moments. The majority's emphasis in *Ryan v Lennon* on the supremacy of the Treaty vis-à-vis the constitution was a key reason why de Valera decided upon a new constitution.[72] The ratification of this constitution through a referendum added an additional means through which the Constitution could be attributed to the people, beyond merely representation in the Dáil and removing any role for British authorities.

Finally, it would be remiss to discuss the idea of the people of Ireland possessing constituent power without remarking on partition. While Kennedy CJ's judgment is keen to stress a role for the people, these people are, nevertheless, only 'the inhabitants of Saorstát Éireann' and not the island of Ireland as a whole. No doubt, to talk of the people in this regard would have been grating to the anti-treaty republicans. Consequently, the ratification of the Good Friday Agreement through referendums held both north and south arguably constitutes a key moment in which the people of the island of Ireland as a whole exercised their constituent power, albeit one with acute involvement by other holders of political and legal authority. On a related note, any process of achieving Irish reunification must take the concept of constituent power and the people as the ideal possessors of constituent power seriously. We would do well to heed one of the lessons from the demise of the Free State Constitution and that

[71] See Eoin Daly, "Translating Popular Sovereignty as Unfettered Constitutional Amendability" 15(4) *European Constitutional Law Review* (2019): 619.

[72] Coffey, "The need for a new constitution."

any top-down constituent process dominated by pre-existing constitutional actors runs the risk of collapsing the constituent power into the pre-existing constituted powers, diluting the creative potential of the constituent moment and resulting in a constitution that may be doomed to fail.

References

Arato, Andrew. *Post Sovereign Constitution Making: Learning and Legitimacy.* Oxford: Oxford University Press, 2016.

Cahillane, Laura. *Drafting the Irish Free State Constitution.* Manchester, Manchester University Press, 2016.

Coffey, Donal K. "The need for a new constitution: Irish constitutional change 1932-1935." *Irish Jurist* 34 (2012): 275.

Coffey, Donal K. *Constitutionalism in Ireland, 1932-1938: National, Commonwealth and International Perspectives.* Cham: Palgrave Macmillan, 2018.

Colon-Rios, Joel. *Constituent Power and the Law.* Oxford: Oxford University Press, 2020.

Cristi, Renato. "Schmitt on Power and the Monarchical Principal." *Constellations* 18 (2011).

Daly, Eoin. "Translating Popular Sovereignty as Unfettered Constitutional Amendability." *European Constitutional Law Review* 15 no. 4 (2019): 619.

de Tocqueville, Alexis. *Democracy in America.* New American Library, 1956.

Doyle, Oran. "Populist constitutionalism and constituent power." *German Law Journal* 20, no. 2 (2019): 161.

Dyzenhaus, David. "Constitutionalism in an Old Key: Legality and Constituent Power." *Global Constitutionalism* 1, no. 2 (2012): 229.

Greene, Alan. "Parliamentary Sovereignty and the Locus of Constituent Power in the United Kingdom." *International Journal of Constitutional Law* 18, no. 4 (2020): 1166.

Hickey, Tom. "Revisiting *Ryan v Lennon* to make the case against judicial supremacy (and for a new model of constitutionalism in Ireland)." *Irish Jurist* 53 (2015) 125.

Hogan, Gerard. "A Desert Island Case set in the Silver Sea: The State (Ryan) v Lennon." In *Leading Cases of the Twentieth Century,* edited by Eoin O'Dell, Dublin: Sweet & Maxwell, 2000.

Kavanagh, Aileen. "Unconstitutional Constitutional Amendments from the Irish Free State to Irish Republic." In *The Constitution of Ireland: Perspectives and Prospects,* edited by Eoin Carolan, Dublin: Bloomsbury, 2012) 331.

Lino, Dylan. "Albert Venn Dicey and the Constitutional Theory of Empire." *Oxford Journal of Legal Studies* 36, no. 4 (2016): 751.

Lino, Dylan. "The Rule of Law and the Rule of Empire: AV Dicey in Imperial Context." *Modern Law Review* 81, no. 3 (2018): 739.

Loughlin, Martin. "Constituent Power Subverted: From English Constitutional Argument to British Constitutional Practice." In *The Paradox of Constitutionalism: Constituent Power and Constitutional Form,* edited by Martin Loughlin and Neil Walker, Oxford: Oxford University Press, 2008.

Loughlin, Martin. "The Concept of Constituent Power." *European Journal of Political Theory* 13 (2014).

Mohr, Thomas "Law Without Loyalty—The Abolition of the Irish Appeal to the Privy Council." *Irish Jurist* 37 (2002): 187.

Möllers, Christoph. "We are (afraid of) the people': Constituent Power in German Constitutionalism." In *The Paradox of Constitutionalism: Constituent Power and Constitutional Form*, edited by Martin Loughlin and Neil Walker, Oxford: Oxford University Press, 2007.

Negri, Antonio. *Insurgencies: Constituent Power and the Modern State.* Maurizia Boscagli trans, Minneapolis: University of Minnesota Press, 1999.

Partlett, William. "The American Tradition of Constituent Power." *International Journal of Constitutional Law* 15, no. 4 (2015): 955.

Poole, Thomas. "Devotion to Legalism: On the Brexit Case." *Modern Law Review* 80 (2017): 685.

Rayroux, Antoine. "Speaking EU defence at home: Contentious discourses and constructive ambiguity." *Cooperation and Conflict* 49, no. 2 (2014): 386.

Roznai, Yaniv. *Unconstitutional Constitutional Amendments: The Limits of Amendment Powers.* Oxford: Oxford University Press, 2017.

Rubinelli, Lucia. *Constituent Power: A History.* Cambridge: Cambridge University Press, 2020.

Wall, Illan. "Notes on an Open Constituent Power." *Law, Culture and Humanities* 11 (2015): 378.

Walters, Mark. *AV Dicey and the Common Law Constitutional Tradition: A Legal Turn of Mind.* Cambridge: Cambridge University Press, 2020.

CHAPTER 5

Opposition to the Constitution of the Irish Free State in 1922

Thomas Mohr

Introduction

The 1922 Constitution of the Irish Free State was not universally welcomed when it came into force on 6 December 1922. This is hardly surprising as few national constitutions in genuine democracies are welcomed without some element of dissent. Yet, there can be little doubt that the Irish Constitution of 1922 proved to be one of the most bitterly contested and divisive constitutions of any democratic State in modern times.

The following chapter examines why some Irish people felt that they could not support the Free State Constitution and how they expressed their opposition to it at the time of its establishment in 1922. Much of the opposition to the Constitution reflected wider opposition to the settlement popularly known as "the Treaty" signed in London on 6 December

T. Mohr (✉)
School of Law, University College Dublin, Dublin, Ireland
e-mail: thomas.mohr@ucd.ie

L. Cahillane, D. K. Coffey (eds.), *The Centenary of the Irish Free State Constitution*, Palgrave Modern Legal History,
https://doi.org/10.1007/978-3-031-46181-1_5

1921.[1] Provisions relating to the Treaty settlement were inserted into the text of the unpublished draft Constitution at the insistence of the British government during secret negotiations that concluded in June 1922. These provisions ensured that opponents of the Treaty came out in uncompromising opposition to the Constitution and developed a number of legal arguments, which will be examined below, to contest its legitimacy.

Although the stance taken by opponents of the Treaty constituted the most serious source of hostility to the Constitution, a reality that will be reflected in this chapter, it is important to acknowledge that theirs was not the only source of opposition. For example, northern unionists firmly opposed any prospect of their own inclusion under the jurisdiction of the 1922 Constitution. It is also important to recognise that there was no unanimity in terms of attitudes towards the Constitution among supporters or opponents of the Treaty in 1920s Ireland. Some opponents of the Treaty were implacable in their hostility towards the Constitution while others adopted a more flexible stance. There was even a body of opinion in 1920s Ireland that supported the Treaty but maintained serious reservations concerning the 1922 Constitution. This chapter will attempt to reflect all these facets of opinion that greeted the Constitution of the Irish Free State at the time of its creation in 1922.

Sources of Opposition to the 1922 Constitution of the Irish Free State

(a) Opposition to Particular Provisions of the Constitution

Opposition to the Constitution, or aspects of it, stemmed from a number of different roots.

The most obvious source were the varying degrees of opposition to particular provisions of the Constitution. For example, the provisions on "extern ministers", unelected members of the executive, proved divisive.[2] There were also disputes over the rights provisions, the provisions for

[1] The official title was "Articles of Agreement for a Treaty between Great Britain and Ireland".

[2] See Leo Kohn, *The Constitution of the Irish Free State* (London: Allen and Unwin, 1932), 271–83, Laura Cahillane, "Anti-Party Politics in the Irish Free State Constitution" *Dublin University Law Journal* 35 (2012) 34, and "The 1922 Constitution; Constituting a Polity" in Chap. 2 of this volume. See also David Kenny, "The 1922 Constitution as a Failed Attempt to Break with Westminster Tradition" in Chap. 10 of this volume.

judicial review and many others. These inevitable divisions of opinion were the result of debates that might occur in the parliament and media of any true democracy. Consequently, this category of opposition to the 1922 Constitution has only been included for the sake of completeness. Opposition to particular provisions of the Constitution cannot be equated with opposition to the Constitution as a whole. Indeed, the absence of any form of dissent concerning any provision of the Constitution would have been a sure sign that the infant Irish State had lapsed into tyranny.

(b) Pro-Treaty Opposition to the Constitution

It is important to recognise that the most bitter opposition to the 1922 Constitution was based on pre-existing divisions concerning the 1921 Treaty. However, supporters of the Treaty were not a monolith in 1922. It was certainly possible to support the Treaty but object to the draft Constitution published in June 1922.

There were supporters of the Treaty who argued that the draft Constitution that had returned from the British-Irish negotiations in June 1922 fell short of what they perceived as the full degree of sovereignty offered by the terms of the Treaty. The Labour Party questioned the very necessity of having a written constitution in 1922 in the hope that this might avoid inclusion of provisions from the Treaty which they felt unsuitable for the Free State Constitution.[3] George Gavan Duffy, a former minister for foreign affairs in the Dáil cabinet, also provided forceful arguments that the Constitution had not taken full advantage of the autonomy offered by the Treaty. His arguments were enhanced by the reality that he was one of the signatories of the Treaty, albeit the last member of the Irish delegation to be persuaded to accept it. Gavan Duffy made repeated efforts to amend provisions influenced by the Treaty when the draft Constitution was being considered by the third Dáil Éireann, sitting as a constituent assembly.[4] The strength of this opposition from a Treaty signatory and former minister for foreign affairs was deeply embarrassing for the Irish provisional government.

The critical stance maintained by Gavan Duffy, the Labour Party and others cannot be equated with opposition to the Constitution as a whole.

[3] *Dáil Debates*, vol. 1, col. 361–5, 18 September 1922.

[4] See Thomas Mohr, "George Gavan Duffy and the legal consequences of the Anglo Irish Treaty, 1921–1923" *Northern Ireland Legal Quarterly* 73 (2023) 55.

When the text was finally passed by the constituent assembly all of these critical voices, including George Gavan Duffy and Labour TDs, agreed that the Constitution, while not perfect or all that they had hoped for, was still a great advance for the cause of Irish nationalism and a considerable asset for the new Irish State.[5]

(c) Unionist Opposition to the Constitution

Public expressions of unionist opposition to the Constitution were largely absent from the twenty-six counties that would form the Irish Free State in 1922. Southern unionist politicians and newspapers had overwhelmingly accepted the Treaty and welcomed the Constitution as a promise of a much-desired restoration of law, order and stability. This does not mean that southern unionists were satisfied with all aspects of the Constitution. Some openly complained that the provisions concerning the senate (which would be officially known as "Seanad Éireann") were insufficient to give a real voice to their community in the Irish Free State.[6] These included the members of an unofficial group of southern unionists, led by Lord Midleton, who attempted to negotiate with British and Irish authorities in 1921 and 1922.[7] Midleton duly declined an offer of a seat in Seanad Éireann in 1922.[8]

Northern Ireland had its origins in the Government of Ireland Act 1920 and so preceded the creation of the 1922 Constitution. Under the terms of the Treaty the parliament of Northern Ireland would be given the choice after 6 December 1922 between opting for the United Kingdom under the Government of Ireland Act 1920 or for the Irish Free State under the 1922 Constitution. Few northern unionists had any doubt as to which choice would be made. Their stance was primarily based on the background and nature of the Irish Free State rather than any legal objections to the provisions of the 1922 Constitution.

Northern unionist newspapers were deeply sceptical as to whether the 1922 Constitution could long survive in its current form. The challenge from nationalist opponents of the Treaty was all too obvious and the

[5] *Dáil Debates*, vol. 1, col. 1909–14, 25 October 1922.

[6] For example, *Irish Times*, 16 June 1922, 4 and *Church of Ireland Gazette*, 15 December 1922, 713–4. See also *Belfast News Letter*, 16 June 1922, 10 and 17 June 1922, 4.

[7] *Irish Times*, 16 June 1922, 4.

[8] *Irish Times*, 1 December 1922, 6

Belfast News Letter concluded that if the rejection of the Constitution by prominent leaders of the IRA was representative of their followers "the Constitution will be stillborn".[9] The pessimistic conclusion of the *Northern Whig* was typical of the northern unionist media in 1922:

> However admirable in theory some of the provisions of the Constitution may be, the most profoundly significant fact in relation to it is that, like the treaty, it came into being as the result of a surrender to assassins. That is a lesson which those who wish to destroy or amend it in a Republican sense have learned and can apply as well as the members of the majority, who are for the most part handicapped by their want of any real faith in those articles of the Constitution which will be the subject of the fiercest controversy.[10]

The *Belfast News Letter* argued that even if W.T. Cosgrave's public aspirations for partnership within the Commonwealth were sincere, the majority of his followers did not share these values.[11] It concluded that the pro-Treaty government in Dublin suffered from a dual personality disorder in claiming to lead a loyal part of the Empire while also seeking concessions that would enable the creation of a future Irish republic.[12] The unionist press maintained that even the restless Union of South Africa could not be compared to the Irish Free State as a Dominion. It insisted that there were significant differences between the two in terms of the origins of their Constitutions and in sentimental bond to the Commonwealth.[13] The *Belfast News Letter* voiced the suspicions of many northern unionists that "after a few years under the Irish Constitution Ireland may tail off into a declaration of independence".[14]

Few were surprised when, under terms of the Treaty, the parliament of Northern Ireland opted for the United Kingdom and the Government of Ireland Act and not the Irish Free State and its Constitution on 7 December

[9] *Belfast News Letter*, 17 June 1922, 4.

[10] *Northern Whig*, 22 June 1922, 4.

[11] *Belfast News Letter*, 7 December 1922, 4.

[12] *Belfast News Letter*, 5 December 1922, 4.

[13] For example, see *Belfast News Letter* 16 June 1922, p. 10 (citing an article in the *Morning Post*) and *Northern Whig*, 30 November 1922, p. 4. This perspective was shared by some Irish supporters of the Treaty. For example, see P.S. O'Hegarty, *The Victory of Sinn Féin* (Dublin: UCD Press, 1998), p. 141.

[14] *Belfast News Letter*, 17 December 1922, 5.

1922.[15] The Boundary Commission, envisaged under the terms of the Treaty in the event of this choice, collapsed in 1925 leaving the Irish border unchanged.[16]

(d) "Abject Surrender"—The Reaction of Opponents of the Treaty

The reaction of nationalist opponents of the Treaty to the Constitution was overwhelmingly negative when it was published in draft form in June 1922. Their opposition was exacerbated by the crushing of hopes, shared by many supporters of the Treaty, that the Constitution would offer an opportunity to expand on the autonomy of the future Irish Free State. In addition, it was hoped that the provision for extern ministers would allow opponents of the Treaty to enter a coalition government without taking the much maligned parliamentary oath.

As events transpired, the British-Irish negotiations of May and June 1922 on the draft Constitution dashed all hopes of using the Constitution as a means of healing the split over the Treaty. The British government made clear that it would not tolerate a Constitution that substantially ignored the Treaty settlement and insisted on the addition of new provisions that the original drafters had been keen to avoid. These included references to the British monarchy, the controversial parliamentary oath and the appeal to the Judicial Committee of the Privy Council. Loopholes allowing extern ministers to enter government without taking the parliamentary oath were closed.[17] These realities were revealed to the Irish public when the resulting draft Constitution was published on 16 June 1922.

The anti-Treaty press, which consisted of some established local newspapers together with a number of new publications created in early 1922, immediately made its position clear on the draft Constitution. *Poblacht na h-Éireann* dedicated most of its issue on 22 June 1922 to detailed analysis

[15] Contemporary newspapers confirm this expectation. For example, see the *Belfast News Letter*, 8 December 1922, 10 and *Northern Whig*, 8 December 1922, 4. See also the nationalist *Irish News*, 7 December 1922, 4. See also C.R.G Murray, "The Partition of Ireland and the 1922 Constitution" in Chap. 3 of this volume.

[16] *Report of the Irish Boundary Commission 1925* (Shannon: Irish University Press, 1969). See also Michael Laffan, *The Partition of Ireland, 1911–25* and Paul Murray, *The Irish Boundary Commission and its Origins, 1886–1925* (Dublin: UCD Press, 2011).

[17] Article 55 of the final text of the 1922 Constitution made clear that extern ministers would be required to take the oath.

of the Constitution under the headline "Abject Surrender".[18] Predictably, this analysis focused almost entirely on the provisions of the Constitution relating to the 1921 Treaty.[19] It described the new Constitution by using words such as "sham", "deception", "camouflage", "humbug", "shameful" and, most common of all, "surrender".[20]

The response to the draft Constitution was soon overtaken by other events. The outbreak of civil war on 28 June 1922 solidified and exacerbated existing divisions concerning the Treaty. The draft Constitution could not hope to remain aloof from this political schism. On some occasions the draft Irish Constitution was mentioned in the anti-Treaty press with either the word "Irish" or "Constitution" placed in inverted commas.[21] On other occasions, it was referred to as the "so-called 'Constitution'",[22] the "enslaving Constitution",[23] the "faked Constitution",[24] the "King-pitted Constitution",[25] as "Churchill's Constitution"[26] or even as the "British made 'Constitution'".[27] Some sources declared the Constitution to be worse than the Treaty itself.[28] Others even blamed it for the outbreak of civil war.[29]

Anti-Treaty Legal Arguments Against the 1922 Constitution

(a) Challenging the Third Dáil Éireann

Opponents of the Treaty used several arguments to challenge the legality of the 1922 Constitution. One such argument is often called "republican legitimacy" or "republican legitimism". This argument emerged in public

[18] *Poblacht na h-Éireann*, 22 June 1922, 1.

[19] *Poblacht na h-Éireann*, 22 June 1922, 1.

[20] *Poblacht na h-Éireann*, 22 June 1922.

[21] For example, see *Poblacht na h-Éireann*, 22 June 1922, 1 This example actually precedes the outbreak of civil war.

[22] *Poblacht na h-Éireann (Scottish Edition)*, 28 October 1922, 1

[23] *Poblacht na h-Éireann (Scottish Edition)*, 21 October 1922, 1

[24] *Poblacht na h-Éireann (Scottish Edition)*, 25 November 1922, 3

[25] *Poblacht na h-Éireann (Scottish Edition)*, 26 August 1922, 8.

[26] *Poblacht na h-Éireann (Scottish Edition)*, 30 September 1922, 8.

[27] *Poblacht na h-Éireann (War News)*, 6 December 1922, 1.

[28] For example, see the stance of David Kent TD in *Evening Herald*, 20 June 1922, 1 and *The Plain People*, 18 June 1922, 2.

[29] See the announcement of the IRA 4th Northern Division in *Dundalk Democrat*, 19 August 1922, 9.

discourse towards the end of 1922 as the Constitution was coming into force.[30] It focused on the contention that the second Dáil Éireann had not been validly dissolved and that, consequently, all subsequent iterations of Dáil Éireann were illegitimate.[31] There are many points that might be made concerning this argument but it is beyond the scope of this chapter to detail them all. However, it is worthy of note that the first Dáil Éireann had not been dissolved in the manner that some opponents of the Treaty argued was essential with respect to the second Dáil Éireann. In addition, an anti-Treaty IRA convention held in March 1922 saw its leadership repudiate the authority of the second Dáil Éireann, a decision defended by de Valera at the time.[32]

In 1922 some opponents of the Treaty insisted that membership of Dáil Éireann was dependant on swearing an oath to the republic and that this must apply to the third Dáil. An editorial in *Poblacht na h-Éireann,* an anti-Treaty publication edited by Erskine Childers, declared: "If the Republican Oath is not administered, the Dáil will not be the Dáil".[33] In the end no form of oath, neither the one mentioned by *Poblacht na h-Éireann* nor the oath included in Article 4 of the Treaty, was required as a precondition for any TD to attend the debates of the third Dáil, sitting as a constituent assembly. The non-attendance of TDs who opposed the Treaty was a consequence of boycott and the realities of the ongoing civil war rather than any exclusionary test.[34]

[30] For example, *Poblacht na h-Éireann (Scottish Edition),* 11 November 1922, 1 and 6.

[31] For example, see Letters 11 and 13, *Correspondence of Mr Eamon de Valera and* Others (Dublin: Stationary Office, 1922), pp. 7–9. By contrast, see the definition of the third Dáil Éireann in section 2(9), Interpretation Act 1923.

[32] *Freeman's Journal,* 27 March 1922, p. 5. See also *Irish Independent,* 23 March 1922, p. 5. Evidence that de Valera later regretted this stance is provided by correspondence intercepted during the Civil War and later published. He wrote on 13 September 1922 that "Rory O'Connor's unfortunate repudiation of the Dáil, which I was so foolish as to defend even to a straining of my own views in order to avoid the appearance of a split is now the greatest barrier that we have". Letter 20, *Correspondence of Mr Eamon de Valera and* Others (Dublin: Stationary Office, 1922), pp. 14–5. The IRA would repudiate the authority of the second Dáil again in 1925. See Earl of Longford and Thomas P. O'Neill, *Eamon de Valera – A Biography* (Boston: Houghton Mifflin, 1971), p. 240.

[33] *Poblacht na h-Éireann,* 29 June 1922, 4. The fadas on the word "Dáil" do not appear in the original text but were added by the author for the sake of consistency. See also *Poblacht na h-Éireann (Southern Edition),* 6 September 1922, 1. de Valera abandoned this argument in Letter 13, *Correspondence of Mr Eamon de Valera and* Others (Dublin: Stationary Office, 1922) p. 8.

[34] See Letter 13, *Correspondence of Mr Eamon de Valera and* Others (Dublin: Stationary Office, 1922), pp. 8–9.

Opponents of the Treaty also challenged the third Dáil by arguing that it owed its existence to British legislation in the form of the Irish Free State (Agreement) Act 1922.[35] The provisional government rejected this contention and asserted an Irish origin. Eoin MacNeill told the Dáil, "Now the source of our powers is this, and this alone, that the Irish electorate held an election, and by their intention gave that election effect, and the source of our powers is the action and intention of the Irish electorate".[36]

Opponents of the Treaty found other reasons to challenge the legitimacy of the third Dáil, and by extension the draft Constitution, in 1922. Until the Constitution and the State formally came into being on 6 December 1922 the third Dáil also described itself as the "provisional parliament". Its primary role lay in its additional identity as a "constituent assembly" that would approve an agreed text of the draft Constitution.[37] The third Dáil refrained from passing any permanent legislation until the Constitution had come into force. Anti-Treaty newspapers used this stance to support an argument that this was "an illegal, powerless provisional body whose only reason for life is to fasten upon Ireland the slave status designed by the Treaty and detailed in Churchill's Constitution".[38] After 6 December 1922 the third Dáil passed 47 statutes until an election in 1923 saw the creation of a fourth Dáil Éireann. The argument that only TDs of the second Dáil Éireann who had not in any way diluted their republican principles could be considered elected representatives of the Irish people became more and more difficult to sustain with the passage of time.

(b) The 1919 Constitution of Dáil Éireann

For the sake of completeness, the existence of the 1919 Constitution of Dáil Eireann is raised as a possible basis for challenging the legitimacy of

[35] For example, see Earl of Longford and Thomas P. O'Neill, *Eamon de Valera – A Biography* (Boston: Houghton Mifflin, 1971), p. 200. Thomas Johnson, leader of the Labour party also assumed that the legal origins of the provisional parliament lay in the Irish Free State (Agreement) Act 1922. *Dáil Debates*, vol. 1, col. 424–5, 19 September 1922.

[36] *Dáil Debates*, vol. 1, col. 428, 19 September 1922. See also Section 2(9) of the Interpretation Act 1923 that asserts an Irish origin for the 1922 election in addition to Westminster's Irish Free State (Agreement) Act 1922.

[37] The preamble to the Constitution of the Irish Free State (Saorstát Éireann) Act 1922 began with the words "DÁIL EIREANN sitting as a Constituent Assembly in this Provisional Parliament".

[38] *Poblacht na h-Éireann (Scottish Edition)*, 30 September 1922, 8 and 14 October 1922, 3. See also *The Plain People*, 18 June 1922, 2 and *Poblacht na h-Éireann*, 29 June 1922, 4 and 5.

the Constitution of the Irish Free State even though it is difficult to find clear arguments along these lines from 1922. There are a number of reasons why opponents of the Treaty were reluctant to follow this apparently obvious means of challenging the 1922 Constitution. First, the 1919 document was difficult to access in 1922 as no official publication was ever produced. It was presented to the first Dáil in the Irish language and several alternative wordings in the English language were produced.[39] It remains open to dispute which of these might be considered definitive.[40] Secondly, senior members of Sinn Féin failed to mention it in contexts where it might be expected to be mentioned as a national constitution.[41] Thirdly, the use of the 1919 document was impeded by the interpretation that it was, as its name "Bunreacht Dála Éireann" suggested, a Constitution for Dáil Éireann. In other words, it was a constitution for a parliamentary assembly and not for an Irish State.[42] Its text only consisted of five short articles that all related to the functioning of the Dáil. This argument was not unique to supporters of the Treaty. Seán McBride, who had opposed the Treaty in the 1920s, would later write that "the first Dáil adopted 'The Democratic Programme of Dáil Éireann', and a 'Provisional Constitution of Dáil Éireann'. ... Neither of these instruments purported to be a Constitution for the Republic".[43]

[39] *Dáil Debates*, vol. F, no. 1, 21 January 1919. See the differing wording provided by *The Plain People*, 23 April 1922, 2–3; Dorothy Macardle, *The Irish Republic* (London: Gollancz, 1937), pp. 959–60 and Brian Farrell, "A Note on the Dáil Constitution, 1919" *Irish Jurist* 4 (1969) 127 at 135–6.

[40] Farrell argues that the version supplied by his article was that actually used by the Dáil. Farrell, "Dáil Constitution, 1919", 130.

[41] This reality is acknowledged by Brian Farrell who provides the example of Aodh de Blacam, *What Sinn Féin Stands For* (Dublin: Cahill and Co, 1921), pp. 98–99. See Farrell, "Dáil Constitution, 1919", 127.

[42] See Section 2(7), Interpretation Act 1923.

[43] University College Cork Archives, O'Rahilly papers, U. 118, Box 6, Submission to the New Ireland Forum, 1984. See also Basil Chubb, *The Constitution of Ireland* (Dublin: Institute of Public Administration, 1966) 8 and *The Government and Politics of Ireland* (Oxford: Oxford University Press, 1974), 62–3. The claimed identity of the 1919 document as a national constitution was rejected in 1922 by a newspaper associated with the Labour Party. *Voice of Labour* insisted that "it is ridiculous to say that the Republic had or has a Constitution". *Voice of Labour*, 24 June 1922, 4. For a contrasting perspective, see Farrell, "Dáil Constitution, 1919", 127. Farrell bases his argument that the 1919 document served as a national Constitution on draft provisions that were rejected for inclusion rather than on provisions that were selected for the final text (see 130–1).

The Plain People, a short-lived anti-Treaty newspaper, provides a rare example of a publication in 1922 that was prepared to argue that the 1919 document constituted a national constitution.[44] In April 1922 it contrasted the Irish origins of the 1919 document with the alleged British origins of the future 1922 Constitution which, at this time, was still being drafted under the supervision of the provisional government. Yet, even this publication was forced to admit that the 1919 Constitution of Dáil Éireann was intended to be a provisional and temporary instrument.[45] Even if it could be argued that the 1919 document was intended to be a national Constitution, its own provisions made clear that it could be easily be amended and replaced at any opportune moment in the future.[46] A simple majority in Dáil Éireann was all that was required to amend or remove this instrument. In any case, the 1919 document never mentioned the existence of a republic in any of the alternative wordings that were produced after the first sitting of the first Dáil Éireann. These realities ensured that the 1919 document did not provide solid foundations to challenge the legal status of the 1922 Constitution of the Irish Free State.[47] Supporters of the 1922 Constitution did not view the 1919 document as constituting any kind of threat, as is evident from proposals to have it published in official collections of historic documents in the mid-1920s.[48] The 1919 provisions were not used as source material during the drafting of the 1922 Constitution of the Irish Free State or the succeeding 1937 Constitution of Ireland.

[44] *The Plain People*, 23 April 1922, 2.

[45] *The Plain People*, 23 April 1922, 2 and 18 June 1922, 2. This reality is made clear in the Dáil debate that introduced this document. *Dáil Debates*, vol. F, no. 1, 13–14.

[46] Article 5 of this instrument provided "This Constitution is provisional and is liable to alteration upon seven days written notice of motion for that specific purpose".

[47] A letter to *An Phoblacht* in the 1930s complained of the lack of attention paid to the 1919 document within the anti-Treaty press. It was described as "the first draft of a Constitution for the Republic" that was "printed and circulated for discussion and amendment". The letter noted that the 1919 document had been ignored by "the imperialist organs" but then asked "why was it boycotted by AN POBLACHT [sic]?" *An Phoblacht,* 23 April 1932, p. 6.

[48] See Thomas Mohr, "The Influence of Chief Justice Hugh Kennedy on Irish Legal Scholarship and Publishing" *Irish Jurist* 64 (2020) 97 at 128.

(c) The Treaty and Repugnancy Clause

In 1922 the Free State Constitution was often challenged on the basis of its associations with the 1921 Treaty. Opponents of the 1921 settlement rejected all arguments that it constituted any form of international treaty and occasionally placed the word "Treaty" in inverted commas.[49] From their perspective, it was a settlement signed under duress that sought to abolish the republic that members of the second Dáil had sworn by oath to support and defend. Another oath, contained in Article 4 of the Treaty and reproduced in Article 17 of the Constitution, was presented as excluding opponents of the Treaty from Irish political life.[50] As mentioned earlier, some opponents of the Treaty also seized on the incorporation of the Treaty in a British statute, the Irish Free State (Agreement) Act 1922, to argue that the settlement represented the imposition of external law.[51] In early 1922 opponents of the settlement were confident that the provisions of the Treaty would have a profound influence on the text of the unpublished Constitution. Even leaving such considerations aside, they were keen to argue that the very existence of the Constitution had its roots in the Treaty. Erskine Childers wrote "It is the "Treaty" which empowers the Free Staters to make a Constitution" while another newspaper article described the Treaty as "the very source of all the magic" underpinning the emerging constitutional order.[52]

The use of the Treaty in challenging the future Constitution often centred on a constitutional provision that was sometimes called the "Repugnancy Clause". This made clear that the provisions of the Treaty had force of law and overrode all other sources of Irish law including the provisions of the Constitution and any amendment to them.[53] Opponents

[49] For example, *Poblacht na h-Éireann*, 4 May 1922, 1 and Letter 15, *Correspondence of Mr Eamon de Valera and* Others (Dublin: Stationary Office, 1922), pp. 9–12. On other occasions the term "Treaty of Surrender" was used. For example, *Poblacht na h-Éireann (Scottish Edition)* 28 October 1922, 1 and 6 January 1923, 5.

[50] For example, see *Poblacht na h-Éireann,* 29 June 1922, 5 and *Freeman's Journal*, 28 April 1923, 7.

[51] For example, *Poblacht na h-Éireann,* 4 May 1922, 1 and 22 June 1922, 1 and *Poblacht na h-Éireann (Scottish Edition),* 28 October 1922, 1.

[52] *Poblacht na h-Éireann*, 12 April 1922, 1.

[53] Section 2, Constitution of the Irish Free State (Saorstát Éireann) Act 1922 [Irl.] and preamble to the Irish Free State Constitution Act 1922 (Session 2) [UK]. The use of the term "repugnancy clause" for these provisions was created by Leo Kohn. Kohn, *Constitution of the Irish Free State*, 98–100.

of the Treaty used these provisions to argue that the draft Constitution would not be a basic law. *Poblacht na h-Éireann* argued, "The basic law is, in fact, the 'Treaty'".[54] This newspaper and other anti-Treaty publications referred to the draft Irish Constitution with the word "Constitution" placed in inverted commas.[55] The Scottish edition of *Poblacht na h-Éireann* contended that the draft Constitution "declares that that treaty is a straight-jacket that can never give and can never be removed".[56] Opponents of the Treaty also stressed that the final word in assessing the compatibility of the draft Constitution with the Treaty would lie with the Judicial Committee of the Privy Council in London.[57] In fact, the Repugnancy Clause and the Privy Council appeal were removed in 1933 following the enactment of the Statute of Westminster Act 1931. The complicated circumstances surrounding their removal have been described elsewhere and are beyond the scope of this chapter. [58]

(d) Perceived British Legal Origins

The final legal argument used by opponents of the Treaty to invalidate the Constitution of the Irish Free State concerned the perceived origins of that document. The 1922 Constitution came into force following the enactment of parallel statutes, one passed by the Irish constituent assembly and the other by the parliament at Westminster.[59] Pro-Treaty newspapers were keen to emphasise the Irish origins of the new Constitution. For example, the *Freeman's Journal* declared on 6 December 1922, "the Irish Free State begins its life to-day under a Constitution of Irish manufacture".[60] The *Westmeath Examiner* praised "this truly Irish Constitution, prepared by Irishmen in Ireland, and adopted by an Assembly elected by the Irish people".[61]

[54] *Poblacht na h-Éireann,* 22 June 1922, p. 1 and 29 June 1922, 8.

[55] For example, see *Poblacht na h-Éireann,* 22 June 1922, 1 and *Poblacht na h-Éireann (War News),* 6 December 1922, 1.

[56] *Poblacht na h-Éireann (Scottish Edition),* 16 September 1922, 3.

[57] For example, see *Poblacht na h-Éireann,* 29 June 1922, 4.

[58] See Thomas Mohr, *Guardian of the Treaty: The council Appeal and Irish* Sovereignty (Dublin: Four Courts Press, 2016).

[59] Constitution of the Irish Free State (Saorstát Éireann) Act 1922 [Irl.] and the Irish Free State Constitution Act 1922 (Session 2) [UK]. See also Alan Greene, "'The Supreme Legislative Authority Speaking as The Mouthpiece of the People': Constituent Power and the Irish Free State" in Chap. 4 of this volume.

[60] *Freeman's Journal,* 6 December 1922, 4.

[61] *Westmeath Examiner*, 2 December 1922, 5.

By contrast, opponents of the Treaty used various means to present the Constitution as a British imposition in 1922. A good example is provided by a cartoon that appeared in the anti-Treaty newspaper *The Plain People.* This depicted the Constitution as a racehorse with Arthur Griffith as a jockey wearing union jack colours. The racehorse "Constitution" bore a crown on its head and, far from being a thoroughbred, was depicted as a knock-kneed donkey.[62] As seen earlier, some anti-Treaty sources were emphasising the alleged British origins of the Constitution long before its text was published. In May 1922 Erskine Childers wrote an article in *Poblacht na h-Éireann* entitled "A Forecast and a Warning" in which he concluded that the very existence of a statute passed at Westminster, which in British eyes would be the sole source of legal validity for the Constitution, would negate the independence of the Irish Free State. He concluded, "A free nation does not accept its Constitution from a foreign parliament".[63] The legal effect of the proposed Irish statute bringing the Constitution into force and its validity in Irish eyes were not considered.

In the years that followed, the Irish courts have confirmed that, as far as Irish law is concerned, the 1922 Constitution was the creation of an Irish constituent assembly.[64]

By contrast, British courts have stressed that this Constitution was created by legislation passed at Westminster.[65] Opponents of the Treaty chose to adhere to the British theory in 1922 and the years that followed. They maintained that the 1922 Constitution was the fruit of a British statute and attacked the Constitution on that basis. This reality ensured that the anti-Treaty press was unimpressed in the 1930s when the provisions relating to the Treaty settlement were being removed from the 1922 Constitution. They continued to refer to it with such names as "the British-made Constitution of the 'Free State'",[66] the "British-imposed Constitution"[67] and "the English-approved Constitution for Southern Ireland".[68]

[62] *The Plain People*, 25 June 1922, 1.

[63] *Poblacht na h-Éireann*, 4 May 1922, 1.

[64] *State (Ryan) v. Lennon* [1935] IR 170 and *In the Matter of the Criminal Law (Jurisdiction) Bill 1975* [1976] 109 ILTR 69 at 76.

[65] *Moore v. Attorney-General for the Irish Free State* [1935] IR 472 and [1935] AC 484.

[66] *An Phoblacht*, 23 April 1932, p. 4.

[67] *An Phoblacht*, 7 January 1933, p. 4 and 21 October 1933, p. 4.

[68] *An Phoblacht*, 7 May 1932, p. 2.

Diversity Within the Anti-Treaty Response to the Constitution

This chapter has already noted that the response of supporters of the Treaty to the 1922 Constitution was not a monolith. The same applied to opponents of that settlement. However, discovering evidence of diversity within the anti-Treaty response to the Constitution is hampered by the extent to which considerations relating to the Treaty predominated in 1922. In fact, it is difficult to find much substantive analysis of the provisions of the Constitution that were not related to the 1921 Treaty within the statements of prominent opponents of the Treaty. When Rory O'Connor saw the text of the draft Constitution on 16 June 1922 he dismissed the many provisions that were untouched by the Treaty with a joke. He concluded that the only good feature was the provision that declared the day of a general election to be a public holiday. Otherwise, O'Connor rejected the draft Constitution by declaring "The thing is too rotten to talk about".[69]

It could be argued that O'Connor's dismissive response was influenced by a crushing sense of disappointment when, as mentioned earlier, many had hoped that the Constitution might be used to extract more autonomy than was strictly offered by the provisions of the Treaty. Yet, if anything, the anti-Treaty response tended to harden after the initial shock. The most extreme response was registered by the anti-Treaty newspaper *The Plain People*, which concluded that Dáil Éireann had no legal capacity to discuss, let alone approve, the text of the "Constitution of the Slave State". It added that TDs who supported such consideration would vote themselves out of Dáil Éireann and "The Republican minority in such an eventuality would be the Dáil".[70]

These responses can be contrasted with that of Éamon de Valera who studied the draft Constitution for five days after its publication on 16 June 1922 before making any comment on it. This period of silence did not go unnoticed and was the subject of some media speculation.[71] When de Valera finally broke his silence his condemnation of the existing draft focused on claims that it would exclude opponents of the Treaty from

[69] *Irish Times*, 17 June 1922, 7 and *Belfast News Letter*, 17 June 1922, 5.

[70] *The Plain People*, 18 June 1922, 2. The "fada" on the word "Dáil" does not appear in the original text but was added by the author for the sake of consistency.

[71] For example, *Belfast News Letter*, 17 June 1922, 5, 21 June 1922, 4 and 22 June 1922, 6.

public service in the same way as the Penal Laws and related legislation had excluded Catholics in other periods of Irish history. However, de Valera did note that the published Constitution was still only a draft and was confident that Dáil Éireann would not pass it as it stood.[72] It is possible that de Valera may already have been hoping and searching for some means of working with the future Constitution or crafting it into something with which he could work. He would not find such a path until 1927 when, as leader of Fianna Fáil, he would bring his new party into the Oireachtas.

Conclusion

de Valera would prove to be the principal agent in the eventual replacement of the Constitution of the Irish Free State in 1937. In 1949 the Irish State became a republic. It should be remembered that these developments, the pace of change and a peaceful transition were not matters that could have been predicted with total confidence in 1922. In that year, the outbreak of civil war hardened pre-existing attitudes, a feature that was just as applicable to supporters of the Treaty as opponents of the settlement.

It is important to recognise that the depth of emotions that accompanied the rejection of the Constitution in 1922 was easily matched by expressions of support for it. Pro-Treaty newspapers promoted the Constitution as a symbol of Irish liberty and, as seen earlier, countered anti-Treaty claims of British imposition by repeatedly asserting Irish origins and identity. They also welcomed the Constitution as providing a much-needed return to order and stability that would, in turn, create the foundations for a better and more prosperous future.[73]

A direct plebiscite or referendum on the Constitution of the Irish Free State was not possible in the difficult circumstances of 1922. This option

[72] *Waterford News*, 23 June 1922, 6, *Poblacht na h-Éireann,* 29 June 1922, 5, *Anglo Celt*, 24 June 1922, 5 and *Belfast News Letter*, 22 June 1922, 6. de Valera's reference to a system aimed at the "the degradation of a people" might be interpreted as more scathing condemnation of the draft Constitution but this was drawn from a quote of Edmund Burke speaking of the penal laws.

[73] Irish newspapers quoted the conclusion of the London *Times* that "The Constitution … is Ireland's last chance of peace". For example, see *Evening Herald*, 24 November 1922, 2. See also *Waterford Standard*, 1 July 1922, 2, *Limerick Chronicle,* 28 October 1922, 2, *Evening Herald*, 25 November 1922, 4, *Derry Journal*, 4 December 1922, 4, *Limerick Leader*, 16 June 1922, 3 and *Westmeath Examiner*, 7 October 1922, 4.

was never seriously considered as this was not a normal procedure for enacting a constitution in this period.[74] As for the 1922 election, it is possible that opponents of the Treaty would not have allowed it to be held without the agreement known as the "Collins-de Valera Pact".[75] After the votes had been counted they refused to concede that the election of a large majority of pro-Treaty candidates constituted popular endorsement of either the Treaty or the Constitution.[76] Yet there can be little doubt what the final result would have been if a direct plebiscite on the Free State Constitution had been possible in 1922. Majority support for the Treaty, which even opponents of that settlement did not deny, combined with the failure of opponents of the Treaty to offer any realistic alternative to the 1922 Constitution would have ensured that many Irish voters would have perceived a stark choice between order and anarchy.

However, it is unlikely that a plebiscite on the 1922 Constitution would have blunted the depth of feeling against it held by many of its opponents. Opponents of the Treaty saw the 1922 Constitution as the instrument and symbol of the scrapping of the Irish republic declared during the 1916 rising and confirmed by the first Dáil in 1919.[77] For them, the association between the 1921 Treaty and the 1922 Constitution ran so deep that it remained alive in the mid-1930s when most legal links between the two documents had been severed by a series of constitutional amendments.

Yet, if the 1922 Constitution remained unacceptable for one section of the Irish electorate, acceptance of "republican legitimism" remained out of the question for the majority after 1922. The coming into force of the 1937 Constitution, following a plebiscite, rendered its central precepts even more obscure.[78] Within a few decades its very existence, outside a few extreme fringes, had largely faded from memory.

[74] See *Select Constitutions of the World* (Dublin: Stationary Office, 1924).

[75] See the views of Desmond FitzGerald quoted in Tom Garvin, *1922 – The Birth of Irish Democracy* (Dublin: Gill and Macmillan, 1996), p. 128.

[76] For example, see *Poblacht na h-Éireann (Scottish Edition)*, 26 August 1922, 2 and 23 September 1922, 2 and *Dublin News*, 16 December 1922, 1.

[77] *Poblacht na h-Éireann (Scottish Edition)*, 16 September 1922, 3 and *The Plain People*, 23 April 1922, 2.

[78] In 1938 seven surviving anti-Treaty TDs of the second Dáil Éireann, who refused to recognise the validity of all subsequent Irish parliaments, attempted to vest all powers of government in the IRA. See Thomas Mohr, "The Strange Fate of the Dáil Decrees of Revolutionary Ireland, 1919–22" *Statute Law Review* 43:1 (2022) 120 at 132.

References

Cahillane, Laura. "Anti-Party Politics in the Irish Free State Constitution." *Dublin University Law Journal* 35 (2012): 34

Chubb, Basil. *The Constitution of Ireland*. Dublin: Institute of Public Administration, 1966.

Chubb, Basil. *The Government and Politics of Ireland*. Oxford: Oxford University Press, 1974.

de Blacam, Aodh. *What Sinn Féin Stands For*. Dublin: Cahill and Co, 1921.

Earl of Longford, and Thomas P. O'Neill. *Éamon de Valera – A Biography*. Boston: Houghton Mifflin, 1971.

Farrell, Brian. "A Note on the Dáil Constitution, 1919." *Irish Jurist* 4 (1969): 127.

Garvin, Tom. *1922 – The Birth of Irish Democracy*. Dublin: Gill and Macmillan, 1996.

Kohn, Leo. *The Constitution of the Irish Free State*. London: Allen and Unwin, 1932.

Macardle, Dorothy. *The Irish Republic*. London: Gollancz, 1937.

Mohr, Thomas. "George Gavan Duffy and the legal consequences of the Anglo Irish Treaty, 1921–1923." *Northern Ireland Legal Quarterly* 73 (2023): 55.

Mohr, Thomas. "The Influence of Chief Justice Hugh Kennedy on Irish Legal Scholarship and Publishing." *Irish Jurist* 64 (2020): 97.

Mohr, Thomas. "The Strange Fate of the Dáil Decrees of Revolutionary Ireland, 1919–22." *Statute Law Review* 43, no. 1 (2022): 120.

Mohr, Thomas. *Guardian of the Treaty: The Council Appeal and Irish* Sovereignty. Dublin: Four Courts Press, 2016.

Murray, Paul. *The Irish Boundary Commission and its Origins, 1886-1925*. Dublin: UCD Press, 2011.

O'Hegarty, Patrick. *The Victory of Sinn Féin*. Dublin: UCD Press, 1998.

Select Constitutions of the World. Dublin: Stationary Office, 1924.

CHAPTER 6

The Representative of the Crown and the Governor-General of the Irish Free State: Text and Context

Graham Butler

Introduction

The Governor-General of the Irish Free State (the State), as contained in the Constitution of the Irish Free State of 1922 (the Constitution) was the representative of the Crown from 1922 to 1936. This office replaced and abolished the office of the Lord Lieutenant of Ireland before it in the United Kingdom of Great Britain and Ireland, and was succeeded afterwards, in effect, by the President of Ireland in 1937 following the entering into force of the Constitution of Ireland (*Bunreacht na hÉireann*) that same year.

Popular depictions of the Governor-General, from the establishment of the office to historical analysis thereafter for the years in which the office existed, have largely been unfavourable. Indeed, it has been accepted that

G. Butler (✉)
University of Southern Denmark, Odense, Denmark
e-mail: grbu@sam.sdu.dk

L. Cahillane, D. K. Coffey (eds.), *The Centenary of the Irish Free State Constitution*, Palgrave Modern Legal History,
https://doi.org/10.1007/978-3-031-46181-1_6

the office was politically embarrassing, given that its existence, as the representative of the Crown, did not fully remove British shackles off Ireland. After the State became Ireland in 1937, the office of the President of Ireland and its powers and functions have been explored in the text and context of the Constitution of Ireland of 1937,[1] but much less so on its predecessor office. This chapter thus anticipates closing this gap by examining the text and context of the 'representative of the Crown', as mandated by the Anglo-Irish Treaty of 1921 (the Treaty), and as included as a 'Governor-General' in the 1922 Constitution.

For the United Kingdom, a representative of the Crown was to be a safeguard of British interests in the new State. After all, upon the Constitution coming into being, the State was to be an independent state under international law,[2] and not merely a dominion of the British Empire. The place of the Governor-General in the State is consequently of particular curiosity given that all legislation passed by the Oireachtas between 1922 and 1936 bears the signature of the officeholder as the representative of the Crown. All three Governors-General during this period were Irishmen: Tim Healy,[3] James McNeill,[4] and Domhnall Ua Buachalla (Donal Buckley).[5]

Politically, the years in which the office of the Governor-General existed was a turbulent and tremulous time, with what appeared as a strained relationship to the Executive Council in particular. The initial officeholder, Governor-General Healy, fulfilled the duties expected of him by the parties to the Treaty.[6] However, Governor-General McNeill who followed,

[1] Starting with Michael McDunphy, *The President of Ireland: His Powers, Functions and Duties* (Dublin: Browne and Nolan, 1945), and all textbooks on the Constitution of Ireland and Irish constitutional law ever since.

[2] The fact that it was an independent state, with a head of state of another state (the United Kingdom) was of no significance. For example, the fact that the Irish Free State became a member of the League of Nations in 1923 was evidence and acceptance of this by the international community, both legally and politically.

[3] 1855–1931. Governor-General, 1922–28. See, Frank Callanan, *T. M. Healy* (Cork: Cork University Press, 1996).

[4] 1869–1938. Governor-General, 1928–32. See, *inter alia*, Brendan Sexton, *Ireland and the Crown 1922–1936: The Governor-Generalship of the Irish Free State* (Dublin: Irish Academic Press, 1989).

[5] 1866–1963. Governor-General, 1932–36. See, Adhamhnán O Súilleabháin, *Domhnall Ua Buachalla: Rebellious Nationalist, Reluctant Governor* (Dublin: Merrion Press, 2015).

[6] There was reaction in the international media to his initial appointment, coinciding with the State coming into being. Thomas Mohr, 'The Irish Media and the Foundation of the Irish State on 6 December 1922', *Irish Studies Review* 31, no. 2 (2023): 217–19.

tried to protect the constitutional role of the office by executing his interpretation of the role that the Governor-General was to take. His attachment to this may have been owed to his involvement in the drafting of the Constitution. The Executive Council however, under President de Valera's leadership, having only recently come into power, had an alternative interpretation to Governor-General McNeill, and towards the end of the customary term of office, Governor-General McNeill relinquished the office.[7] The final officeholder, Governor-General Ua Buachalla, was a 'retired country shopkeeper',[8] political ally of President de Valera, and exercised the formal powers of affixing his signature to legislation, and nothing more. With a plot of President de Valera to demean the office, Governor-General Ua Buachalla certainly contributed to the office's eventual elimination,[9] alongside other developments, as will be analysed in this chapter.

Legally however, much more interesting features of the office of the Governor-General come to light when the design, powers, and prerogatives of the Governor-General are considered, and the Treaty and Constitution are read side by side. This chapter concerns the arising power allocation in the Treaty and Constitution of the representative of the

[7] Note, the term formally used was that Governor-General McNeill 'relinquished' the office, which was not a 'resignation' or 'removal'. For the view that Governor-General McNeill was sacked, and necessarily resigned, see, J.J. Lee, *Ireland 1912–1985* (Cambridge: Cambridge University Press, 1989), 177. For a thoroughly detailed account of the developments leading to Governor-General McNeill's department from office, see, Anne Twomey, *The Veiled Sceptre: Reserve Powers of Heads of State in Westminster Systems*, Cambridge Studies in Constitutional Law (Cambridge: Cambridge University Press, 2018), 746–57.

[8] Peter Mair, 'The Break-up of the United Kingdom: The Irish Experience of Regime Change, 1918–1949', *Journal of Commonwealth & Comparative Politics* 16, no. 3 (1978): 296.

[9] One view is that the final officeholder was a co-conspirator in 'demeaning the office' of the Governor-General. Lee, *Ireland 1912–1985*, 177. A clear example of this was the moving of the Governor-General out of the Vice-Regal Lodge in the Phoenix Park, Dublin; and the renting of a residence for the Governor-General in the south Dublin suburb of Dún Laoghaire/Monkstown, in a house called Gortleitragh, on Sloperton Road. Whilst it was where Governor-General Ua Buachalla resided and carried out his duties from, the same residence also has another place in Irish history much later, for it was the residence of the German Minister in Ireland, Eduard Hempel, during World War II, and was the scene of where the then Taoiseach de Valera offering his condolences to the German legation on the death of Adolf Hitler in 1945.

Crown. Through this lens, the place of the representative as the Governor-General can be reflected upon, 100 years after the office's creation.

In this chapter, "The Crown, the Treaty, and the Constitution" section examines the text of the Treaty and Constitution, demonstrating the open-choice left to the State to create an office deemed worthy of being the representative of the Crown. Next, "The Powers and Terms of the Governor-General" section reflects upon the powers afforded to the Governor-General under the Constitution as per the provisions themselves. Thereafter, "The Abolition of the Governor-General" section moves onto the context of when the Governor-General operated, and how numerous British and Irish developments, both legally and politically, paved the way for the State to eventually abolish the office. The "Conclusion" section offers some reflections on how the office of the Governor-General set out, in part, a vision for how the head of state would be envisaged in a newly formed state trying to shake off the Crown.

The Crown, the Treaty, and the Constitution

The State was made possible by the Treaty. This was followed by the Constitution, which referred to the Treaty as the 'Scheduled Treaty' appended to it. As a result of this clear bridging between the two texts,[10] forming an unbreakable link (at the time of their ratification and entering into respective force), the office of the Governor-General must be understood by looking at the text of both the Treaty and the Constitution.

An even-wider net must be drawn too beyond these two texts, however. Given that the Treaty provided some shape to what became many provisions of the Constitution, which provided that the State would have 'the same constitutional status in that community of nations as … Canada, … Australia, … New Zealand, and … South Africa', examining particular aspects of the Constitution, like the office of the Governor-General, also demands an international outlook, in determining the place of a representative of the Crown in a new breakaway state from the British Empire.

A representative of the Crown was explicitly prescribed in the Treaty, and thus, had to be carried over into the Constitution of the State in some way. Article 3 of the Treaty provided that

[10] It has been stated that the two 'must be construed together'. W. P. M. Kennedy, 'Significance of the Irish Free State', *The North American Review* 218, no. 814 (1923): 320.

> [t]he representative of the Crown in Ireland shall be appointed in like manner as the Governor-General of Canada and in accordance with the practice observed in the making of such appointments.[11]

On a textual reading of the Treaty therefore, an office of a 'Governor-General' did not need to be created. Rather, another form of representative of the Crown could have been chosen by the State if it had so wanted. This was because Article 3 of the Treaty only provided that such a representative would be *appointed* like that of the Governor-General in Canada, and not that there had to *be* a Governor-General of the State, or one titled as a Governor-General, or even a Lieutenant Governor.

Nonetheless, the creation of an office of the Governor-General was what was chosen by the drafters of the Constitution, and the text of the Constitution appears to support a reading of some level of discretion on how the representative of the Crown was to exist. Article 60 of the Constitution provided that

> [t]he Representative of the Crown, *who shall be styled the Governor-General of the Irish Free State (Saorstát Eireann)*.[12]

Thus, the State interpreted the Treaty as a basis for choosing how to create a role for that representative, but merely chose to *style* that office, rather than deeply empower it beyond the necessities of what the Treaty demanded. Moreover, the title of the representative, was also significant. The chosen name was not that of a 'High Commissioner',[13] or some other form of representative role. Furthermore, in the Irish language version of the Constitution, the translation of the term of Governor-General was 'Seanascal Shaorstát Éireann', which approximately translates to 'high steward'.

The alternative view, however, was that any discretion conferred upon the State to create the office of the representative of the Crown as anything other than an office of a Governor-General might have been limited by other provisions in the Treaty. For example, Articles 1 and 2 of the Treaty undoubtedly placed the State in the British Empire, a feature replicated in the Constitution, with the self-assertion that the State would be a

[11] Article 3, Treaty.

[12] Article 60, Constitution, emphasis added.

[13] Laura Cahillane, *Drafting the Irish Free State Constitution* (Manchester: Manchester University Press, 2016), 60.

'co-equal member of the Community of Nations forming the British Commonwealth of Nations'.[14] Given that other states of the Commonwealth had Governors-General in office as the respective representative of the Crown in those states,[15] it would have been natural for a new office to be replicated in the State in the same way. The safe ground was adopted: a Governor-General of the Irish Free State was to be the chosen model.

The remuneration of the Governor-General was to be akin to that of the Governor-General of Australia, with Article 60 of the Constitution specifying that

> [h]is salary shall be of the like amount as that now payable to the Governor-General of the Commonwealth of Australia and shall be charged on the public funds of the Irish Free State (Saorstát Eireann) and suitable provision shall be made out of those funds for the maintenance of his official residence and establishment.

What followed to fulfil the obligation of the State under Article 60 of the Constitution was an Act of the Oireachtas,[16] which provided the Governor-General with an annual salary of £10,000.

The representative of the Crown in the Treaty, carried over into the Constitution with the creation of a new office of the Governor-General, was to be one of the key symbols which affirmed the new State's place in the British Empire. The other signs of the Crown were the oath of allegiance to be taken by members of the Oireachtas,[17] and the right of appeal to the Judicial Committee of the Privy Council.[18]

This trio of symbols had different levels of legal significance, with the representative of the Crown being, arguably—from a legal perspective and

[14] Article 1, Constitution.

[15] It should be noted that in some Canadian provinces and territories, the office was known, at the time, as merely the 'Governor'. See, for example, Newfoundland Act 1933, 24 Geo 5 ch. 2.

[16] Governor-General's Salary and Establishment Act 1923.

[17] Article 4, Treaty, referring to the 'Members of the Parliament of the Irish Free State', and Article 17 of the Constitution referring to the 'members of the Oireachtas'. See, Donal K. Coffey, 'The Commonwealth and the Oath of Allegiance Crisis: A Study in Inter-War Commonwealth Relations', *The Journal of Imperial and Commonwealth History* 44, no. 3 (2016): 492–512.

[18] See, Thomas Mohr, *Guardian of the Treaty: The Privy Council Appeal and Irish Sovereignty* (Dublin: Four Courts Press, 2016).

formal point of view—the most controversial. After all, without the representative of the Crown, there would arguably have been no need for an oath of allegiance of members of the Oireachtas to the King. Owing to the powers afforded to the Governor-General under the Constitution, it was more constitutionally significant than any superficial oath, that itself amounted to nothing more than a mere formality. That said, from a political perspective, it was the oath of allegiance that garnered the most attention and was ultimately a major contributory factor that led to the ensuing civil war.

The Powers and Terms of the Governor-General

In 1922 at the creation of the office, what was known about Governors-General had some aspects of what could be broadly understood as some level of legal custom,[19] but not amounting to anything that could be considered as settled law. It was clarified later, at the Imperial Conference of 1926, what the supposed function of Governors-General was to be, how they acted, and on the advice of whom they operated. In other words, in 1922, the 'corpus' of what a Governor-General was to be was not fully settled, and thus, the situation of the State in 1922 was rather different from the other states within the Empire with older offices of respective Governors-General. Therefore, the actual role and powers of the Governor-General of the State might have differed from those elsewhere.

For instance, despite some clarity on the place of Governors-General with the Imperial Conference of 1926, it could even be claimed that the Governor-General to the State was the 'personal representative' of the Crown.[20] Moreover, in theory, the Governor-General exercised all the same powers as that of the Crown, as his representative. At the same time, the representative of the Crown had to act within the described legal framework through the exercise of given powers under the Constitution.

It has been argued that Hugh Kennedy, first Attorney General of the State between 1922 and 1924, and later Chief Justice between 1924 and 1936, had an influential role in ensuring the powers of the Governor-General, in textual terms, and use of the associated powers, were designed in such a way that they departed from the practices of other

[19] For early analysis, see, Arthur Berriedale Keith, *Responsible Government in the Dominions* (Oxford: Oxford University Press, 1912).

[20] Barra Ó Briain, *The Irish Constitution* (Dublin: The Talbot Press, 1929), 96.

Governors-General in the Empire.[21] For example, the power of the office of the Governor-General was such that it was not empowered to play any role whatsoever in the formation of a government after a general election to Dáil Éireann, or in the midst of a Dáil term when a new government needed forming. This position of the Governor-General made it different to other dominions in the British Empire. Such government formation was solely a prerogative of the members of the Dáil—a practice which has continued after the entering into force of the Constitution of Ireland of 1937 as regards the President of Ireland and his or her non-role in negotiating government formation.

While the office of the Governor-General was mainly a ceremonial office, this was not entirely clear at the time the Constitution was drafted since there were certain provisions which could be read as giving power to the Governor-General. The Constitution, read as a whole, meant that the representative of the Crown did possess potential power and prerogatives reserved for him. For instance, the King, as the Crown, was to be part of the Oireachtas. Article 12 of the Treaty stated that

> [a] [l]egislature is hereby created, to be known as the Oireachtas. *It shall consist of the King and two Houses*, the Chamber of Deputies (otherwise called and herein generally referred to as 'Dáil Eireann') and the Senate (otherwise called and herein generally referred to as 'Seanad Eireann'). The sole and exclusive power of making laws for the peace, order and good government of the Irish Free State (Saorstát Eireann) is vested in the Oireachtas.[22]

Whilst various other provisions of the Treaty varied between the use of the 'King', 'His Majesty', and 'representative' in the text, what was important was the executive power. Article 51 of the Constitution provided that

> [t]he *Executive Authority* of the Irish Free State (Saorstát Eireann) *is hereby declared to be vested in the King, and shall be exercisable*, in accordance with the law, practice and constitutional usage governing the exercise of the Executive Authority in the case of the Dominion of Canada, *by the Representative of the Crown*.[23]

[21] See, Thomas Towey, 'Hugh Kennedy and the Constitutional Development of the Irish Free State, 1922–1923', *Irish Jurist* 12, no. 2 (1977): 355–70.

[22] Article 12, Treaty, emphasis added.

[23] Article 51, Constitution, emphasis added.

Thus, the Governor-General was the mechanism whereby key appointments to the institutions of the new State would be made. This included members of the Executive Council, who would be appointed by the Governor-General on the advice of the President of the Executive Council,[24] and members of the judiciary, also on the advice of the Executive Council.[25] The representative of the Crown was also empowered to summon and dissolve Dáil Éireann,[26] and Dáil Éireann could not appropriate money in any way unless the representative of the Crown had 'recommended by message', again, acting on the advice of the Executive Council.[27] Of course this did not involve any actual power since the decisions were made by the Executive Council, and it was through the Governor-General by which the decisions were made official.

The area where the Governor-General had the most potential power, however, was that of the royal prerogative, with specific regard to legislation. The Governor-General never had any formal consultees of a domestic kind like the contemporary Council of State for the President of Ireland. Instead, it was merely that of the Crown itself. This was, in turn, the power of the Governor-General to refuse to give royal assent to legislation passed by the Oireachtas. This power in Article 41 of the Constitution theoretically allowed the Governor-General to reserve bills from the Oireachtas, and thereby withhold royal assent to legislation passed by the Oireachtas. Article 41 of the Constitution stated, *inter alia*,

> So soon as any Bill shall have been passed or deemed to have been passed by both Houses, the Executive Council shall present the same to the Representative of the Crown for the signification by him, in the King's name, of the King's assent, and *such Representative may withhold the King's assent or reserve the Bill for the signification of the King's pleasure.*[28]

The same paragraph qualified this power to withhold royal assent. It went on to provide that such withholding was possible

> [p]rovided that the Representative of the Crown shall in the withholding of such assent to or the reservation of any Bill, *act in accordance with the law,*

[24] Article 51, Constitution.
[25] Article 68, Constitution.
[26] Article 24, Constitution.
[27] Article 37, Constitution.
[28] Article 51, Constitution, emphasis added.

> *practice, and constitutional usage governing the like withholding of assent or reservation in the Dominion of Canada.*[29]

In other words, it was merely convention from elsewhere in the Empire, beyond the Treaty and the Constitution, that dictated the procedure under which the Governor-General could withhold consent.[30] Given this, the British government and the Crown was likely of the view that the Governor-General could indeed be told to not to give royal assent to such legislation when so asked.[31] Yet, that is likely not the position held by the Executive Council. No formal conflict ever arose in this regard, as each Governor-General who was presented with legislation to sign did so. However, the first officeholder, Governor-General Healy, would have been under some pressure to consider his powers if the Oireachtas ever did anything during his tenure that might have violated the Treaty.

The Treaty and Constitution both stated that the actual nomination of the representative of the Crown, 'shall be appointed in like manner as the Governor-General of Canada and in accordance with the practice observed in the making of such appointments.'[32] The Canadian practice at the time, in respect of the process of the nomination of a person to serve as Governor-General, was that the British government made a recommendation, following liaison with the Canadian government, and the Crown made the appointment.[33]

It has been claimed that said that the British gave verbal assurances that the Executive Council of the State would have a greater-than-usual say in the nomination of the person to be chosen.[34] This in practice meant that the Executive Council of the State put forth its nomination of who was to be Governor-General to the Crown through the appropriate channels.

[29] Ibid.

[30] On the powers of the Governor-General of Canada, see, Jeremy Webber, *The Constitution of Canada: A Contextual Analysis* (Oxford: Hart Publishing, 2021), 83–101.

[31] When the government considered trying to put legislation in place before a Governor-General was appointed, the then Attorney General Hugh Kennedy advised that the British might take issue with this. See Enright, Chap. 12 in this collection.

[32] Article 3, Treaty; and Article 60, Constitution.

[33] Note, this practice continued only until 1931, when Letters Patent by the Crown changed the process, under which the government making the nomination Crown changed from the British government to the Canadian government.

[34] D. W. Harkness, *The Restless Dominion: The Irish Free State and the British Commonwealth of Nations, 1921–31* (London: Macmillan, 1969), 22.

The actual persons chosen to be Governor-General appear to confirm this view.[35]

Through the eyes of the British government and the Crown, it is difficult to know whom they ideally had in mind to become the Governor-General. It would be most unlikely that the Executive Council would have put forth anyone of the type that occupied the office of the Lord Lieutenant,[36] or another member of the British gentry. It was equally unlikely that the British would have wanted a person who was an ardent Irish nationalist or republican either.[37]

Instead, a more favourable officeholder, in the eyes of the British establishment, would have been someone that was able to ensure that the Executive Council of the State, and the wider institutions of the new State, were acting within the scope of the Treaty. For instance, though there was no textual prohibition in either the Treaty or the Constitution prohibiting the representative of the Crown also being the President of the Executive Council, though such a prohibition might have been implied, as it would have been unlikely that the Crown would have ever accepted a recommendation from the Executive Council for the Crown to appoint the President of the Executive Council to also be the Governor-General.[38]

An obvious flaw in the Constitution was what to do in the event of there being no Governor-General in place. There was no anointed person or officeholder who was authorised to deputise in place of the Governor-General, nor any committee or Commission that could act in the

[35] See, Sexton, *Ireland and the Crown 1922–1936: The Governor-Generalship of the Irish Free State*.

[36] On the Lords Lieutenant, see, Peter Gray and Olwen Purdue, eds., *The Irish Lord Lieutenancy c. 1541–1922* (Dublin: UCD Press, 2012).

[37] Note, for example, the appointment of Isaac Isaacs as Governor-General of Australia in 1930/1931, who was the first Australian to accede to that office, and the concerns expressed at the time about the appointment of a 'local'. See, L. F. Crisp, 'The Appointment of Sir Isaac Isaacs as Governor-general of Australia, 1930.: J. H. Scullin's Account of the Buckingham Palace Interviews', *Historical Studies: Australia and New Zealand* 11, no. 42 (1964): 253–57; John Waugh, 'An Australian in the Palace of the King-Emperor: James Scullin, George V and the Appointment of the First Australian-Born Governor-General', *Federal Law Review* 39, no. 2 (2011): 235–54.

[38] Compare, for instance, Article 12.6.3 of the subsequent Constitution of Ireland 1937 that replaced the 1922 Constitution, which provides that the head of state, the President 'shall not hold any other office or position of emolument'.

Governor-General's shoes.[39] With there being no Governor-General for most of the month of November 1932, the President of the Executive Council, Éamon de Valera, had wanted the Chief Justice, Hugh Kennedy, to act as Governor-General, following Governor-General MacNeill leaving office. Kennedy refused,[40] given that the Constitution would have appeared to inhibit him from accepting the invitation, without otherwise resigning from the Supreme Court. This is because Article 69 of the Constitution provided that '[a]ll judges shall be independent in the exercise of their functions, and subject only to the Constitution and the law. A judge shall not be eligible to sit in the Oireachtas, and *shall not hold any other office* or position of emolument'.[41] This idea to have the office of the Governor-General, effectively merged with a judicial office, was never formally attempted, but it was an indication of what was to come in terms of a diminished office.[42]

Lastly, the Constitution did not limit the number of terms that a person could serve as Governor-General. Only analogies to the office of the Governor-General in Canada could be realistically drawn, where office-holders ordinarily served terms of anywhere between four and six years, though formally serving at the pleasure of the Crown, and thus, dismissible at any given time.

The Abolition of the Governor-General

The straight abolition of the office of the Governor-General after the entering into force of the Constitution would have been too drastic a step for the Executive Council and the Oireachtas to try to undertake in the 1920s. First, it would have conflicted with the Treaty, and second, the Governor-General could have withheld royal assent to any such Bill passed by the Oireachtas. The initial position of the State was that the office of

[39] Indeed, this precisely occurred in November 1932 between second-serving Governor-General and the nomination and appointment of Governor-General Ua Buachalla. See, Donal K. Coffey, *Constitutionalism in Ireland, 1932–1938: National, Commonwealth, and International Perspectives*, Palgrave Modern Legal History (Palgrave Macmillan, 2018), 35–36.

[40] Deirdre McMahon, 'The Chief Justice and the Governor General Controversy in 1932', *Irish Jurist* 17, no. 1 (1982): 159. p. 159; Donal K. Coffey, 'The Need for a New Constitution: Irish Constitutional Change 1932–1935', *Irish Jurist* 48 (2012): 286–87.

[41] Article 69, Constitution, emphasis added.

[42] See "The Abolition of the Governor-General" section.

the Governor-General was, to some eyes, 'safeguarded'.[43] Hence, an alternative strategy arose in the State, to gently demote the relevance of the office to obscurity, before the legal possibility arose to abolish it.

Formally, the office of the Governor-General was abolished through constitutional amendment in 1936 (and subsequent legislation of the Oireachtas in 1937) before the 1922 Constitution itself was replaced by the Constitution of Ireland of 1937. The events that led to this development have proven that the British government, in their dealings with the Irish plenipotentiaries negotiating the Treaty, did not sufficiently embed the office of the Governor-General in the Treaty. Rather, given that it left the manifestation of the 'representative of the Crown'[44] to the internal development of what became the Constitution by the State, it proved possible for the State to diminish the office following developments in the United Kingdom, before lawfully abolishing it after just fifteen years.

The Oireachtas, whilst possessing powers to amend the Constitution, did not have the power to amend the Constitution in a manner inconsistent with the Treaty, as it was understood at the time that the Treaty was negotiated in 1921. For the British, the view was that the Treaty was static, whilst for the State, a more dynamic view was held. In other words, the State could indeed substantively amend the Constitution, as provided for by the Constitution, except for the provisions that were giving effect to the demands of the Treaty.

Yet even so, during this fifteen-year period between 1922 and 1936, the office of the Governor-General did indeed evolve within the boundaries of what was possible by the Treaty and the Constitution. This is not a post-factual reflection, but in fact, it was recognised, even at the time when the office of the Governor-General still existed, that 'the position ... had been modified' since its creation.[45] Therefore, developments between 1922 and the office's ultimate abolition years later can be traced to no single development, or any singular individual, but rather, a confluence of factors that contributed towards constitutional change.

The first major development that contributed towards the eventual abolition of the office of the Governor-General was a two-part event, with

[43] See, for example, J. G. Swift MacNeill, *Studies in the Constitutional of the Irish Free State* (Dublin: The Talbot Press, 1925), 28.

[44] Article 3, Treaty.

[45] Nicholas Mansergh, *The Irish Free State: Its Government and Politics* (London: George Allen & Unwin, 1934), 148.

the Imperial Conference of 1926, and then the Statute of Westminster of 1931 giving effect to it, *inter alia*. The latter, passed by the British Parliament, increased the possibility for parts of the Empire to exercise more sovereign powers in their own right. Though the State was not the reason for the Statute, recalling that the State was a mere small part of the Empire, the Statute of Westminster had a remarkable impact on the State.[46] Suddenly, what became apparent to the State, or rather, the Executive Council and the Oireachtas, was that it all of a sudden had the possibility to amend the Constitution, in line with the procedural requirements, on substantive matters that *may* indeed deviate from the Treaty.

The second major development was that of a change of government of the State in 1932, with Cumann na nGaedheal under the leadership of W.T. Cosgrave leaving the Executive Council, and Fianna Fáil under the leadership of Éamon de Valera taking over, marking the first transfer of power in the State. The new Executive Council in 1932 undertook its interpreted mandate to break with the Treaty through amendment to the Constitution that was not previously possible before the passing of the Statute of Westminster the year previous. At this time, Fianna Fáil was open, realistic, and honest about its intent concerning the role of the Governor-General.[47] Whilst the office of the Governor-General would initially remain for legal reasons, the party was of the view it must change (and be abolished) with time.

The third major development was a decision of the Judicial Committee of the Privy Council. Whether amendments to the Constitution that conflicted with the Treaty was lawful or not was soon to be tested following the enactment of the Constitution (Removal of Oath) Act 1933, which deleted Article 17 of the 1922 Constitution. In *Moore v Attorney General*, one of the rare examples of a case reaching the Privy Council in London, having already been decided by the Supreme Court in Dublin, the Privy Council ruled that amendments made to the Constitution by the State, in conflict with the Treaty, were indeed lawful. As per Sankey LC:

> The simplest way of stating the situation is to say that the Statute of Westminster gave to the Irish Free State a power under which they could

[46] See, Thomas Mohr, 'The Statute of Westminster, 1931: An Irish Perspective', *Law and History Review* 31, no. 4 (2013): 749–91.

[47] Coffey, *Constitutionalism in Ireland, 1932–1938: National, Commonwealth, and International Perspectives*, 16.

abrogate the Treaty, and that, as a matter of law, they have availed themselves of that power.[48]

Whilst the new Executive Council will have lauded this part of the judgment, but not others,[49] the ruling dramatically increased the powers of the State to engage in constitutional change that was previously not possible. In other words, the link between the Treaty and the Constitution could be broken and formally severed by the State. And although it has been stated there was a conflict between the decision of the Privy Council in *Moore v Attorney General*, and the decision of the Supreme Court in *Ryan v Lennon*,[50] the outcome of the two decisions, side by side, was nonetheless interpreted as being open-season for amendments to the Constitution to be made by the newly envigoured Executive Council, without regard to the Treaty.

The fourth major development was the abdication of King Edward VIII in December 1936, after acceding to the throne only eleven months previous, following the death of King George V in January 1936. In principle, the Governor-General's position in the State was unaffected, given the Crown was always *in situ*. Given the unexpected abdication of King Edward VIII however—and the newly constituted powers of the State following the Statute of Westminster, the newly formed Executive Council, and the ruling in *Moore v Attorney General* of the Privy Council—the power of the Oireachtas was thus immense, as it 'possessed power to regulate the [s]uccession to the Throne'.[51] Discussions on abolishing the office of the Governor-General were openly underway beforehand,[52] but the abdication and the happenstance of timing propelled the Executive

[48] *Moore and Other Appellants; and the Attorney General for the Irish Free State and Other Respondents* [1935] I.R. 472, 486–87 and [1935] A.C. 484, 499, Sankey LC.

[49] See, Thomas Mohr, 'Law Without Loyalty – the Abolition of the Irish Appeal to the Privy Council', *Irish Jurist* 37 (2002): 187–226.

[50] *State (Ryan) v Lennon* [1935] I.R. 170. See also, Gerard Hogan, 'A Desert Island Case Set In The Silver Sea: The State (Ryan) v. Lennon (1934)', in *Leading Cases of the Twentieth Century*, ed. Eoin O'Dell (Dublin: Round Hall Sweet & Maxwell, 2000), 80–103.

[51] K. C. Wheare, *The Statute of Westminster and Dominion Status*, Fifth Edition (Oxford: Oxford University Press, 1953), 263. On the wider responses to the 1936 abdication, see, Donal K. Coffey, 'British, Commonwealth, and Irish Responses to the Abdication of King Edward VIII', *Irish Jurist* 44 (2009): 95–122.

[52] Coffey, 'British, Commonwealth, and Irish Responses to the Abdication of King Edward VIII', 111–12.

Council into moving legislation in the Oireachtas to abolish the office of the Governor-General.

Step by step through these developments, the Executive Council went about denigrating the Governor-General through amendments to the Constitution. For example, the Oireachtas passed amendments that transferred the power of recommending the appropriation of money from the Governor-General to the Executive Council,[53] and removed the power of the royal prerogative on Bills on the Oireachtas that the Governor-General could be used by withholding assent.[54]

The ultimate amendment, however, was the Constitution (Amendment no. 27) Act 1936, which amended ten Articles in the Constitution to further root out the powers of the Governor-General. Ironically, it was Governor-General Ua Buachalla who signed all such legislation, including the one that abolished his office. This omnibus amendment meant the functions of the Governor-General were transferred to the Chairman of Dáil Éireann, the Ceann Comhairle, for internal matters. Indeed, it was considered whether, instead of the Ceann Comhairle, the powers could have passed to the Chief Justice, or the President of the Executive Council himself. Both would have been problematic for different reasons. For the former, having a Chief Justice wear two hats, as a *de facto* acting head of state, whilst also a judge sitting in cases of constitutional significance in the Supreme Court, would have raised partiality questions, and not least, whether the Constitution permitted the possibility.[55] For the latter, this would have been a merging of the head of government and head of state role, which, even for Europe of the time during the inter-war years, would have been misplaced.

The formal removal of the Governor-General from the Constitution, however, was not enough to actually *abolish* the office of the Governor-General. Two subsequent pieces of ordinary legislation through the Oireachtas were necessary: the External Authority (External Relations) Act 1936, and the Executive Powers (Consequential Provisions) Act 1937.[56]

[53] Constitution (Amendment no. 20) Act 1933.

[54] Constitution (Amendment no. 21) Act 1933.

[55] See "The Powers and Terms of the Governor-General" section.

[56] For insight into the considerations at this juncture, see, Gerard Hogan, *Origins of the Irish Constitution 1928–1941* (Dublin: Royal Irish Academy, 2012), 259–69.

Whereas the former of the two tried to clear-up how the foreign relations of the State were to be formally managed given that Ireland remained 'associated' with other parts of the British Empire[57]; the latter was also a tidy-up exercise to clarify the void that had to be filled in the absence of the office of the Governor-General. Notwithstanding that the Constitution (Amendment no. 27) Act 1936 had rooted out much of the office, the Executive Powers (Consequential Provisions) Act 1937 prescribed that

> [e]very power, function, duty, and jurisdiction which, ... was, by any means whatsoever, capable of being exercised or required to be performed by the King or by the Representative of the Crown (whether on advice, nomination, appeal, or other communication or without any such communication) shall be and be deemed to have been,...transferred to and (as the case may be) capable of being exercised by or required to be performed by the Executive Council.[58]

The Executive Powers (Consequential Provisions) Act 1937 also clarified that the Constitution (Amendment no. 27) Act 1936 did in fact abolish the office of the Governor-General, along with applicable secondary law applied to it, in that it 'shall be deemed for all purposes to have ceased on that date to have effect'.[59] Thus, retrospectively, the office of the Governor-General was formally abolished, and the constitutional experiment with the office of the Governor-General as the representative of the Crown was over.[60]

Conclusion

The Governor-General, as the representative of the Crown, could be said to have merely had symbolic existence in the State, but in fact, it was more than that, as the text of the Constitution set out some potentially significant powers, however moot those powers might have proved to be in reality. Accordingly, the office of the Governor-General should not be

[57] Article 3, Executive Authority (External Relations) Act 1936.

[58] Article 2, Executive Powers (Consequential Provisions) Act 1937.

[59] Article 4, Executive Powers (Consequential Provisions) Act 1937.

[60] Not all aspects of the abolition, however, were dealt with. For example, the costs of the rented residence at Gortleitragh were one point of contention over who was to foot the bill. See further, O Súilleabháin, *Domhnall Ua Buachalla: Rebellious Nationalist, Reluctant Governor*.

dismissed as a mere minor piece of history, and a set of political incidents of minor historical relevance.[61] In fact, many other states in the world still possess a Governor-General, as a representative of the British Monarch to this day,[62] and thus, the fact that the office of the Governor-General of the State only had a short-lived existence makes it worthy of deeper analysis.

The fall of the Governor-General is a textbook example of how to dismantle a constitutional office. The fact that the Governor-General as an officeholder, and representative of the Crown, only enjoyed formal protection under the Constitution, and not the Treaty, put the office in a constitutionally weak and vulnerable position. Through that lens, to some eyes, it could have been subjected to the internal powers of the State alone, and not the UK. But it is inaccurate to say President de Valera or anyone else simply abolished the office, as popularly understood. The more accurate truth is that the eventual abolition was as a result of both political *and* legal acts, including judicial decisions. As illustrated, whilst there was Irish developments in the form of the 1932 general election, there were numerous British developments in the form of the Statute of Westminster 1931, the decision of the Privy Council in *Moore v Attorney General*, and the abdication of King Edward VIII, which factored into the amendments to the Constitution that British developments made possible. Without these three British developments, and merely just one Irish development, the State would not have lawfully been able to abolish the office of the Governor-General.

The office also provided an example in terms of the creation of a head of state role in the new Constitution. If the office of the Governor-General had never existed, it is anyone's guess how the powers of the President of Ireland would be today, notwithstanding that the office of the President of Ireland possesses influences from a variety of sources. The link between the Governor-General and the subsequent Presidency is undeniable, and the use of the office to represent the permanent authority of the State in making important appointments was retained, and even the same form of language is used whereby according to Article 35.1, the President appoints judges, but in Article 13.9, it is specified that this is 'on the advice of the Government'. In *Attorney General v Crawford*, following the adoption of

[61] See, for example, Ewan Morris, '"God Save the King" versus "The Soldier's Song": The 1929 Trinity College National Anthem Dispute and the Politics of the Irish Free State', *Irish Historical Studies* 31, no. 121 (1998): 72–90.

[62] There are still Governors-General of Australia, Canada, and New Zealand, amongst others.

the Constitution of Ireland of 1937, Hanna J noted that 'the Crown, as such, has no place in our Constitution, but has been replaced by the President'.[63] Some traits of the office of the President of Ireland have great resemblance to many ceremonial heads of state in other republics in Europe,[64] which puts Ireland in-line with a strong continental tradition. In fact, many of the constitutional features of the Presidency in the Constitution of Ireland of 1937 have been linked to that of the President of Germany,[65] as well as the features of the President of the Weimar Republic, as contained in the Weimar Constitution of 1919.[66] But retaining the mainly ceremonial role held by the Governor-General in the new office of the President of Ireland may have been key to acceptance of the new office, since initially, there were fears that the presidency could evolve into a type of dictatorship.[67]

The Governor-General role changed markedly in such a short space of time. Such events occurring 100 years later, in the present, would most certainly be seen as a rule of law issue. After all, the office was slowly being 'deprived of dignity',[68] and the last Governor-General, to some, 'demean[ed] the office'.[69] Indeed, in the midst of the inter-war years of the 1930s, as noted above, there was genuine fear that a strong presidential role in the new Constitution could lead to a dictatorship.[70] As a result of these fears, the office was made primarily ceremonial and nothing of the kind has occurred, and notwithstanding the potential for rule of law backsliding to occur,[71] the checks-and-balances within the Constitution of Ireland of 1937 make this possibility unlikely to occur any time soon, though the possibility can never be totally ruled out.

[63] *Attorney General v Crawford* [1940] I.R. 335; 74 I.L.T.R. 140, Hanna J.

[64] See, Donal K. Coffey, *Drafting the Irish Constitution, 1935–1937: Transnational Influences in Interwar Europe*, Palgrave Modern Legal History (Palgrave Macmillan, 2018), 83–143.

[65] J. M. Kelly, *The Irish Constitution*, Second Edition (Dublin: Jurist Publishing, 1984), 68.

[66] See, for wider and deeper analysis, Hogan, *Origins of the Irish Constitution 1928–1941*.

[67] See Dáil Éireann Debates vol. 67 col. 1237, 28 May 1937.

[68] Nicholas Mansergh, *Survey of British Commonwealth Affairs: Problems of External Policy 1931–1939* (Oxford: Oxford University Press, 1952), 289.

[69] Lee, *Ireland 1912–1985*, 177.

[70] Kelly, *The Irish Constitution*, 57.

[71] See, Paul Gallagher, 'Challenges to the Rule of Law in twenty-first Century Ireland', in *Judicial Power in Ireland*, ed. Eoin Carolan (Dublin: Institute of Public Administration, 2018), 273–303.

Acknowledgement The author wishes to thank to the editors of this volume, Laura Cahillane and Donal K. Coffey, for their comments. All views remain those of the author alone.

References

Cahillane, Laura. *Drafting the Irish Free State Constitution*. Manchester: Manchester University Press, 2016.

Callanan, Frank. *T. M. Healy*. Cork: Cork University Press, 1996.

Coffey, Donal K. "The Commonwealth and the Oath of Allegiance Crisis: A Study in Inter-War Commonwealth Relations." *The Journal of Imperial and Commonwealth History* 44, no. 3 (2016): 492.

Coffey, Donal K. *Constitutionalism in Ireland, 1932–1938: National, Commonwealth, and International Perspectives*. Palgrave Macmillan, 2018a.

Coffey, Donal K. *Drafting the Irish Constitution, 1935–1937: Transnational Influences in Interwar Europe*. Palgrave Macmillan, 2018b.

Coffey, Donal K. "British, Commonwealth, and Irish Responses to the Abdication of King Edward VIII." *Irish Jurist* 44 (2009): 95.

Coffey, Donal K. "The Need for a New Constitution: Irish Constitutional Change 1932-1935." *Irish Jurist* 48 (2012): 286.

Crisp, L. F. "The Appointment of Sir Isaac Isaacs as Governor-general of Australia, 1930.: J. H. Scullin's Account of the Buckingham Palace Interviews." *Historical Studies: Australia and New Zealand* 11, no. 42 (1964): 253.

Gallagher, Paul. "Challenges to the Rule of Law in 21st Century Ireland." In *Judicial Power in Ireland*, edited Eoin Carolan, Dublin: Institute of Public Administration, 2018.

Gray, Peter, and Olwen Purdue (eds). *The Irish Lord Lieutenancy c. 1541-1922*. Dublin: UCD Press, 2012.

Harkness, D. W. *The Restless Dominion: The Irish Free State and the British Commonwealth of Nations, 1921-31*. London: Macmillan, 1969.

Hogan, Gerard. "A Desert Island Case Set In The Silver Sea: The State (Ryan) v. Lennon (1934)." In *Leading Cases of the Twentieth Century*, edited by Eoin O'Dell, Dublin: Round Hall Sweet & Maxwell, 2000.

Hogan, Gerard. *Origins of the Irish Constitution 1928-1941*. Dublin: Royal Irish Academy, 2012.

Keith, Arthur Berriedale. *Responsible Government in the Dominions*. Oxford: Oxford University Press, 1912.

Kelly, J. M. *The Irish Constitution*. Dublin: Jurist Publishing, 1984.

Kennedy, W. P. M. "Significance of the Irish Free State." *The North American Review* 218, no. 814 (1923): 320.

Lee, John Joseph. *Ireland 1912-1985*. Cambridge: Cambridge University Press, 1989.

Mair, Peter. "The Break-up of the United Kingdom: The Irish Experience of Regime Change, 1918–1949." *Journal of Commonwealth & Comparative Politics* 16, no. 3 (1978): 296.

Mansergh, Nicholas. *Survey of British Commonwealth Affairs: Problems of External Policy 1931-1939*. Oxford: Oxford University Press, 1952.

Mansergh, Nicholas. *The Irish Free State: Its Government and Politics*. London: George Allen & Unwin, 1934.

McDunphy, Michael. *The President of Ireland: His Powers, Functions and Duties*. Dublin: Browne and Nolan, 1945.

McMahon, Deirdre. "The Chief Justice and the Governor General Controversy in 1932." *Irish Jurist* 17, no. 1 (1982): 159.

Mohr, Thomas. "The Irish Media and the Foundation of the Irish State on 6 December 1922." *Irish Studies Review* 31, no. 2 (2023): 217.

Mohr, Thomas. *Guardian of the Treaty: The Privy Council Appeal and Irish Sovereignty*. Dublin: Four Courts Press, 2016.

Mohr, Thomas. "The Statute of Westminster, 1931: An Irish Perspective." *Law and History Review* 31, no. 4 (2013): 749.

Mohr, Thomas. "Law Without Loyalty – the Abolition of the Irish Appeal to the Privy Council." *Irish Jurist* 37 (2002): 187.

Morris, Ewan. "'God Save the King' versus 'The Soldier's Song': The 1929 Trinity College National Anthem Dispute and the Politics of the Irish Free State." *Irish Historical Studies* 31, no. 121 (1998): 72.

Ó Briain, Barra. *The Irish Constitution*. Dublin: The Talbot Press, 1929.

O Súilleabháin, Adhamhnán. *Domhnall Ua Buachalla: Rebellious Nationalist, Reluctant Governor.* Dublin: Merrion Press, 2015.

Sexton, Brendan. *Ireland and the Crown 1922-1936: The Governor-Generalship of the Irish Free State*. Dublin: Irish Academic Press, 1989.

Swift MacNeill, J. G. *Studies in the Constitutional of the Irish Free State*. Dublin: The Talbot Press, 1925.

Towey, Thomas. "Hugh Kennedy and the Constitutional Development of the Irish Free State, 1922-1923." *Irish Jurist* 12, no. 2 (1977): 355.

Twomey, Anne. *The Veiled Sceptre: Reserve Powers of Heads of State in Westminster Systems*. Cambridge: Cambridge University Press, 2018.

Waugh, John. "An Australian in the Palace of the King-Emperor: James Scullin, George V and the Appointment of the First Australian-Born Governor-General." *Federal Law Review* 39, no. 2 (2011): 235.

Webber, Jeremy. *The Constitution of Canada: A Contextual Analysis*. Oxford: Hart Publishing, 2021.

Wheare, K. C. *The Statute of Westminster and Dominion Status*. Oxford: Oxford University Press, 1953.

CHAPTER 7

The National Language and Article 4 of the 1922 Constitution

Róisín Á. Costello BL

> ... while the policy of the Constitution as regards the National language is being actively implemented ... the *Oireachtas* has at the same time recognised the facts as they were and must for a time continue to be, as regards adults and those beyond school age who have been deprived of the vernacular use of the National language.
> *Kennedy CJ*

Introduction

Kelly has observed that the portions of the Irish Constitution of 1937 which were most dwelled on at the time of drafting, and which continued to attract the most attention in subsequent years, were its "demonstrative

R. Á. Costello BL (✉)
School of Law, Trinity College Dublin, Dublin, Ireland
e-mail: roisin.acostello@tcd.ie

L. Cahillane, D. K. Coffey (eds.), *The Centenary of the Irish Free State Constitution*, Palgrave Modern Legal History,
https://doi.org/10.1007/978-3-031-46181-1_7

externals rather than in its legal core."[1] In the case of language rights in the text of the 1922 Constitution—and the position of the Irish language under the Constitution more broadly—Kelly's characterisation is particularly apt.

The 1922 Constitution mentions Irish only twice—grouping the national language and flag together in Article 4, which, in its final version, reads,

> The national language of Saorstát Éireann is the Irish language, but the English language shall be equally recognised as an official language. Nothing in this Article shall prevent special provisions being made by the Oireachtas for districts or areas in which only one language is in use.

and providing in Article 42 that

> [a]s soon as may be after any law has received the King's assent, the clerk, or such officer as Dáil Éireann may appoint for the purpose, shall cause two fair copies of such law to be made, one being in the Irish language and the other in the English language (one of which copies shall be signed by the Representative of the Crown to be enrolled for record in the office of such officer of the Supreme Court or Dáil Éireann may determine), and such copies shall be conclusive evidence as to the provisions of every such law, and in case of conflict between the two copies so deposited, that signed by the Representative of the Crown shall prevail.

The result of this framing of Irish was to relegate the language to a position of demonstrative symbolism.[2] It was a position which, whether it was intentional or not, continued to characterise the official view of the language for much of the State's first 100 years.[3] The stated intention of Article 4 was to bring Irish speakers in from the cold in institutional and legal terms—Irish became, in Kelly's words, part of the "legal core" of the new nation. And yet, the lack of any specific provision for the promotion or protection of the Irish language under the 1922 Constitution also led to a general failure to engage in any debate as to whether the language was

[1] J.M. Kelly, "The Constitution: Law and Manifesto," in *The Constitution of Ireland 1937–1987* ed. Frank Litton (Dublin: Dublin Institute of Advanced Studies, 1988), 208.

[2] On the link of Article 4 with the affirmation of popular sovereignty under Article 2 see Laura Cahillane, 'Constituting a Polity', Chapter 2 in this volume.

[3] See generally, Daithí Mac Cárthaigh, *An Ghaeilge Sa Dlí* (Contae na Gallimhe (Galway): Leabhar Breac, 2020).

intended as anything more than a "demonstrative external," symbol of identity and what, if any, *de facto* commitment had been made by the drafters to the creation or maintenance of a bilingual state. The constitutional status of Irish then, from the outset, was as a language whose existence was both highly visible and under-determined.

In exploring the origins of Article 4, I focus, in this chapter, on how the text of Article 4 (and, in turn, Article 8 of the 1937 Constitution) evolved, and how different the constitutional story of the Irish language might have been, had earlier—or alternative—drafts of the provision prevailed. The chapter then turns to explore how legislative and judicial applications of Article 4 can inform our understanding of how the scope of Article 4 was determined—both in its drafting and in its execution. Finally, the chapter considers Irish language policy in the period following the introduction of the 1922 draft, and in light of which the influence of Article 4 may be further determined.

The Historical Context and Drafting of Article 4

Various estimates have been given of the number of Irish speakers in Ireland by the eighteenth century. While no official and complete records are available, contemporaneous accounts by amateur linguists and private individuals recount that, as late as 1731, roughly two thirds of the whole community used Irish as their daily language.[4] More conservative estimates some sixty years later put the number of Irish monoglots as at least 800,000, with at least twice that number being bilingual but speaking Irish by preference.[5] Crucially, this population of speakers was not confined to what are now considered "Gaeltacht" areas but was widely distributed, including bilingual populations in Dublin and the area surrounding it and whose linguistic abilities were evidenced by their trade with monoglot communities.

It is only in the 1800s that information on Irish speakers is available on a specific and regional basis, though the evidence remains partial. Early in

[4] John Windele writing in 1851 and giving a total of 1.34 million speakers of an estimated population of just over two million, cited in Brian Ó Cuív, *Irish Dialects and Irish Speaking Districts* (Dublin: Dublin Institute for Advanced Studies, 1951), 19.

[5] Dr. Whitley Stokes in 1799 said that would it give a total of 2.4 million of a population of roughly 4 million. Cited in ibid., 20. See also the estimates provided by Garret FitzGerald, "Estimates for Baronies of Minimum Level of Irish-Speaking Amongst Successive Decennial Cohorts: 1771–1781 to 1861–1871," ed. Royal Irish Academy (1984).

the century, the Royal Dublin Society carried out a statistical survey of the counties of Ireland as part of which they inquired into the use of English. The results of the RDS survey are inconsistent but—when supplemented by parochial surveys based on Protestant church records from 1814 to 1819; accounts by individual scholars; as well as the numbers of Irish speakers collected by the 1851 census—a general picture of prevalence and distribution is attainable if not wholly reliable.[6]

Irish-speaking communities by the mid nineteenth century were focused most densely along the Western coast. The highest number of Irish-speaking monoglots recorded was consistently in Kerry, while in North Tipperary, Cork, and Limerick, both individual accounts and the statistical information show a decline in Irish and a rise in English-speaking communities from the 1750s.[7] On the Eastern coast, in places such as Dublin, Wicklow and Kildare there appear to have been pockets of Irish speakers scattered in intertidal areas bordering more fully Irish-speaking and bilingual counties.[8] Taking the available sources as a whole, Ó Cuív has suggested that we should understand that, in broad terms, more than half the population was Irish-speaking by the mid-1850s, with a smaller subset of only Irish-speaking citizens and perhaps a broader pool who understood but did not speak or write Irish.[9] Ireland was, in summary, a country characterised by a diversity of linguistic capacity, and a population whose majority was, if not Irish-speaking, then competently bilingual.

An accelerated language shift from the later 1850s onwards changed this pattern as English-medium education, continued population collapse in, and displacement from, densely monolingual and bilingual areas, as well as a continued hostility to Irish in official and institutional settings, fuelled a growing sense that progress (and survival) required the adoption of English, and the abandonment of Irish.[10] The recorded shifts are stark.

[6] Brian Ó Cuív, *Irish Dialects and Irish Speaking Districts* (Dublin: Dublin Institute for Advanced Studies, 1951)., 19–22.

[7] See the descriptive overview offered by Nicholas M Wolf, *An Irish Speaking Island: State, Religion, Community and the Linguistic Landscape in Ireland 1770–1870* (Wisconsin: University of Wisconsin Press, 2014).

[8] Ibid.

[9] Ibid., 26–27.

[10] See generally, Niall Ó Ciosáin, "Gaelic Culture and Language Shift," in *Nineteenth Century Ireland: A Guide to Recent Research*, ed. Laurence M Geary and Margaret Kelleher (Dublin: UCD Press, 2005); Gearóid Ó Tuathaigh, *I Mbéal an Bháis: The Great Famine and the Language Shift in Nineteenth Century Ireland* (Quinnipiac University Press, 2015).

By the 1870s, roughly 77 in every 100 individuals in Ireland were recorded as being unable to speak Irish, with only 5 in every 100 unable to speak English.[11]

The Legal Status of Irish Prior to Independence

The use of Irish in legal contexts prior to independence was governed primarily by the Administration of Justice (Language) Act (Ireland) 1737, which required the business of the courts to be conducted in English only. [12] Irish was thus afforded no official or legal recognition. As a result, English was the sole official language of the State—and of justice—in Ireland, a position that was to continue until Irish independence. The particular institutional view of the language during this period is typified by the judgment delivered by the King's Bench in Dublin in the 1906 decision in *Mac Giolla Bhríde v Mac Gamhna* (*McBride v McGovern*).[13]

The appeal in *Mac Giolla Bhríde* centred on an (ultimately unsuccessful) attempt to overturn a number of convictions of Irish speakers pursuant to the Summary Jurisdiction (Ireland) Act 1851 for failing to display their names and addresses in legible characters on their carts (as required by Section 11(3)) of the Act.[14] The ultimate appellant in *Mac Giolla Bhríde* had been arrested and subsequently fined for displaying his name and address on his cart using the Irish language and (crucially) in traditional Irish script. The appeal was rejected by then Lord Chief Justice O'Brien on the grounds that

[11] See, Ó Cuív, *Irish Dialects and Irish Speaking Districts*, 26–28.

[12] Which followed on earlier efforts effected through the Statutes of Kilkenny and the 1537 Act for the English order, habite, and language. For a brief overview of this history see, ibid., 12–13 and Tony Crowley, "Language, Politics and Identity in Ireland: A Historical Overview," in *Sociolinguistics in Ireland*, ed. Ray Hickey (Basingstoke: Palgrave Macmillan, 2016); *The Politics of Language in Ireland 1366–1922: A Sourcebook* (Dublin: Routledge, 2000). For an examination of the provision actually made for language rights in court, see Mary Phelan, *Irish Speakers, Interpreters and the Courts 1754–1921* (Dublin: Four Courts Press, 2019).

[13] *Mac Giolla Bhríde v Mac Gamhna* (*McBride v McGovern*) [1906] 1 IR 181. This was, incidentally, one of only two cases in which Pádraig Pearse appeared as counsel, the other being *Buckley v Finnegan* (1906) ILTR 76. See Ruairí Ó hAnluain, "Tuairiscí Speicialta 1980–1998," in *Tuairiscí Éireann/ The Irish Reports* (1999).

[14] On the litigation see, Mary Phelan, "A Trifling Matter? Names in Irish on Carts: The Dublin Castle Files," *Studia Hibernica* 46, no. 48 (2022). On the surrounding context see, hAnluain, "Tuairiscí Speicialta 1980–1998."

> [t]he characters were not the characters of the language which the Crown and Legislature recognise as the language of the United Kingdom for all legal and official and public purposes. Parliament conducts its debates in English, and legislates in English. The enacting body expresses itself, and the enactment which contains the relevant provision is expressed, in English. English is the language of the Crown; of, as I have said, the Legislature both in debate and enactment; of all the Government administrative and public departments; of the Courts, of the Supreme Court; of the Courts of Summary Jurisdiction, where the very offence under consideration is to be investigated; and, in the eyes of the law, of the Constabulary who, under the 14th Section of the Act, are to take cognisance of the offence. An Englishman … if knocked down by an Irish cart in any part of the country, whether Connemara or elsewhere, is entitled to have the name and address of the offender in characters that he can read, if Irish letters are used he may be powerless to identify.[15]

This then was the official view of the status of Irish prior to independence—namely, that it was an extra-judicial, and non-legal language, which—though not expressly prohibited—was neither tolerated nor utilised in institutional, legal or legislative settings. Despite this, Irish had remained the first language of the majority of the population nationally until the early 1800s and remained in general use by majorities of the populations in Western counties well into the nineteenth century. It was nevertheless, into the twentieth century, a language whose voice (and whose speakers) were not heard in the official record.

Drafting Article 4

Little can be said definitively about the change to this institutional status which accompanied early nationalist attempts to establish parallel systems of governance during the War of Independence. For example, the use of Irish in the oppositional judicial settings of the Sinn Féin, or the later Dáil, courts is not particularly clear. However, given their framing as deliberate rejections of the model of English administered law, as well as their more parochial and local structures, it is reasonable to presume that the courts

[15] [1906] 1 IR 181, 185.

at least permitted Irish, and potentially operated more or less through Irish, in Irish-speaking areas.[16]

Certainly, the earliest drafts of the 1922 Constitution and the minutes of the Drafting Committee do not aver to any preceding basis on which to recognise a Constitutional right for Irish speakers to use their language, or indeed of the existence of such a right at all. The minutes of the Committee, in particular, make only passing references to the language. Thus, in meeting seventeen of the Committee, the minutes record that it was decided

> that the Article dealing with the Language should be omitted subject to later consideration if a completely satisfactory form of words could be devised.[17]

Subsequent minutes make a reference to the Chairman having requested that the journalist and Irish language activist Risteard Ó Foghludha consider and provide to the Committee a list of Irish titles for use in naming certain bodies and officers referred to in the Constitution.[18] Ultimately, Ó Foghludha, in co-operation with three others, furnished an agreed list of such titles.[19]

The substantive consideration of the language itself, however, is relatively minimal. In their 22nd meeting, the Committee discussed the "the language question" once more and a draft of an Article was proposed, which would read,

[16] See generally, Mary Kotsonouris, *Retreat from Revolution: The Dáil Courts, 1920–24* (Dublin: Irish Academic Press, 2020).

[17] DE/9/12/2 (National Archives), meeting 17, minute 3, page 34.

[18] DE/9/12/2 (National Archives), meeting 19, minute 6, page 39. See, in this volume and the use of Irish titles, Graham Butler, 'The Representative of the Crown and the Governor-General of the Irish Free State: Text and Context' page 4.

[19] DE/9/12/2 (National Archives), meeting 23, minute 2, page 46, para 4, noting that the list of Irish titles agreed furnished to the Committee was agreed upon between Ó Foghludha, Tadg O'Donnchadh, an tAthair Ó Duinnín and Padhraic Ó Domhnalladh. The effort did not meet with universal approval, however, the titles later being referred to in the Morning Post as 'interpolated bastard Irishisms' (17 June 1922) and, as Cahillane notes, questions were also raised concerning the use of 'Erse' terminology in the draft (CAB 43/7 at 177). See, Laura Cahillane, 'Drafting the Irish Free State Constitution' (Manchester University Press, 2016), 61.

> The Irish and English languages shall have equal freedom, rights, and privileges, and all Bills, Acts and Notices of general public importance shall be made in both languages.

Despite this proposal, "no decision on the wording was reached"[20] but the revised Article concerning the Irish language was still inserted.[21] The tangible outcomes of these scant references provide some colour to the arid record provided by the minutes.

What has subsequently been referred to as "Draft A", provides in Article 4 that

> [t]he national language of Saorstát Éireann is the Irish language, but the English language shall be equally recognized as an official language. All records and proceedings of the Oireachtas may be kept in the Irish or in the English language, or in both, and all Acts and public announcements shall be issued in both languages. Nothing in this Article shall prevent special provisions being made by the Oireachtas for districts or areas in which only one language is in use.

Draft A is interesting for its imposition of specific, positive, obligations in respect of integrating Irish into the institutional activities of the executive and legislature, while preserving the power to make "special" provision for Irish in Gaeltacht areas. However, "Draft B" includes deletions which may indicate the source of the disagreement which the minutes of the Committee allude to, with a portion of the draft text struck through such that Draft B of Article 4 read,

> The national language of Saorstát Éireann is the Irish language, but the English language shall be equally recognized as an official language. ~~All reports and proceedings of the Oireachtas shall be kept in the Irish or in the English language, or in both and all acts and public announcements shall be issued in both languages.~~ Nothing in this article shall prevent special provision being made by the Oireachtas for districts or areas in which only one language is in use.

In "Draft C" the Article retained this form,

[20] DE/9/12/2 (National Archives), meeting 22, Minute 7, page 44.
[21] DE/9/12/2 (National Archives), meeting 23, Minute 2 page 46.

> The National language of the Irish Free State (Saorstát Eireann) is the Irish language, but the English language shall be equally recognised as an official language. Nothing in this Article shall prevent special provisions being made by the Parliament of the Irish Free State (otherwise called and herein generally referred to as the "Oireachtas") for districts or areas in which only one language is in general use.

However, the initial text of Draft C also included a proposed Article 26 which provided,

> 1. All records, journals and proceedings of [Parliament] ~~Congress~~ may be kept in the Irish or the English language or in both; all Bills, note and notices of general public importance issued by the government shall be in both languages,
> 2. The Irish and English language shall possess equal freedom, rights, and privileges; without prejudice to the attribution of a large measure of linguistic autonomy to uni-lingual minorities or areas, whether Irish or English speaking.

This proposed text hints at an alternative history which the constitutional status of Irish might have enjoyed—that is, the language could have been protected in a manner that compelled specific provision for its use in legislative and executive actions in Article 26.1 and implying that a rights regime for minority speakers might be provided in legislation or perhaps through judicial action in Article 26.2. It is difficult not to read the text of this draft, arriving late in the Committee's considerations, as revealing the measures they saw as following from the Constitution's recognition of the national language. It is difficult, also, to ignore the indication the text provides that the drafters saw the text as grounding those further, necessary measures which would be required to secure the future of Irish as the national language. The references to freedoms, rights *and* privileges clearly indicate that the Committee envisioned the development (whether gradual or not) of a comprehensive system of language rights and national language policy which was, on the basis of the Constitutional text, presumptively bi-lingual, with accommodations made for uni-lingual areas.[22]

[22] On the realities of Irish language policy in the first century of the Irish state see John Walsh, *One Hundred Years of Irish Language Policy 1922–2022*, ed. Eamon Maher, vol. 112, Reimagining Ireland (Oxford: Peter Lang, 2022). On the policy in respect of the Gaeltacht specifically see, *Díchoimisiúnú Teanga: Coimisiún Na Gaeltachta 1926* (Baile Átha Cliath: Cois Life, 2002).; and Caitríóna Ó Torna, *Cruthú Na Gaeltachta 1893–1922* (Baile Átha Cliath: Cois Life, 2005).

The language of Draft C is particularly striking for those familiar with more recent efforts to promote the use of, and protect, the Irish language through official languages legislation and EU law, which in both cases require efforts which Article 26.1 (a century before) envisioned as being necessary.[23]

However, in its final form, Draft C, omitted Article 26 and having made deletions, provided instead, only for the minimal text of Article 4 on which a consensus had emerged:

> The national language of Saorstát Éireann is the Irish language, but the English language shall be equally recognized as an official language. Nothing in this Article shall prevent special provisions being made by the Oireachtas for districts or areas in which only one language is in use.

This was augmented somewhat by Article 42 which provided that following the passage of any Bill by the Oireachtas and the royal assent to that Bill, two copies—one in Irish and one in English—would be made, with one signed by the Governor-General, that version having precedence in cases of conflict. The provision did not go as far as the initial text of Draft C, and Mac Cárthaigh has noted that, in this respect, the provision exposes the underlying tension which the drafters were forced to confront on an ongoing basis, namely, the need to broadcast a new era while struggling to break away from a unilingual tradition.[24] The result, he argues, was that while the Constitution textually committed itself to the idea of a bilingual state, at a practical level, it continued on a monolingual basis with Irish relegated to a symbolically strong but practically *leathoifigiúl*[25] or semi-official status.

While indicative, once more, of a desire for a bilingual state, Article 42 enjoyed a strange half-life, given that the Governor General was not required to have any knowledge of Irish and thus would (and did) decline

[23] See the Official Languages Act 2003 as repealed and replaced by the Official Languages Act 2021. On the provision in EU law for the recognition and use of Irish see Cárthaigh, *An Ghaeilge Sa Dlí.*, 81 *et seq*. It is also notable that the framing of the Article very much echoes the framing in terms of rights, and rights balancing adopted some ninety years later by the Council of Europe in its European Charter on Regional and Minority Languages. Council of Europe: Secretariat of the Framework Convention for the Protection of National Minorities, *European Charter for Regional and Minority Languages: Application of the Charter in the Slovak Republic*, 18 November 2009, ECRML (2009) 8.

[24] Ibid., 47.

[25] Ibid., 47.

to sign a text into law which he could not scrutinise, the reality was that the English versions of legislation had precedence in practice.[26] Indeed, Kohn noted that only the English versions of bills were ever presented, and that Irish translations were only subsequently made.[27]

The resulting text of Article 4, despite the slightly ambivalent phrasing on the status of English, did seek to establish the Saorstát as a bilingual state. Kohn has observed that Article 4 made Ireland unique among Crown dominions in that it granted an elevated status to a language other than English under the law. He contended further that, in as much as the final part of the provision appeared to limit any bilingual state, this was included as a contingency to "preclude apprehensions of a bilingual fanaticism, which might impede" a desired reunification of the island in future.[28] And yet, there is little to indicate this was indeed the case from the records of the drafters. The sparse consideration afforded to the Irish language provision in the records of the Committee's drafting process does not allude to such concerns and the text of Article 26 in Draft C as first proposed is clearly framed in a manner that provides—and indeed envisions—the potential for an island in which there were unilingually English-speaking areas, and which placed all speakers on an equal legal footing.

Ó Tuathail has taken a more charitable view of what the text of the 1922 Constitution sought to achieve, arguing that the aim of the text was, as Article 42 illustrates, to ensure that translations of all enacted measures were publicly available in the expectation that the courts would use and operate in both languages.[29] And yet, even this hopeful position was undermined by the omissions which are evident in the final text of the Constitution as compared to earlier, proposed, wordings.

Legislative and Judicial Applications of Article 4

To some extent, the scope of Article 4 as it was intended by the Committee can be pieced together from the passage of legislation and decisions of the Supreme Court during the operation of the Saorstát Constitution—in particular in judicial comments made by Hugh Kennedy, a former

[26] Ibid., 46–47.

[27] Leo Kohn, *The Constitution of the Irish Free State* (London: G Allen & Unwin, 1932), 210–212.

[28] Ibid.

[29] Séamas Ó Tuathail, *Gaeilge Agus Bunreacht* (Baile Átha Cliath: Coscéim, 2002), 10–12.

member of the drafting Committee, who subsequently became Attorney General and, ultimately, Chief Justice of the fledgling State. Kennedy was a fluent Irish speaker and, having been taught the language by his father—himself a native speaker from County Donegal—maintained a lifelong love of the language.[30]

The Courts of Justice Act 1924

As Attorney General from 1922 to 1924, Kennedy's time in office coincided with the development and subsequent passage of the Courts of Justice Act 1924, on which it is likely he provided significant advice to the State, and whose provisions are often identified as forming the basis for much of the practical standing afforded to Irish in courtroom settings. Indeed, the Act remains the source of much Irish language litigation to this day.[31]

Section 44 of the 1924 Act provides that

> [s]o far as may be practicable having regard to all relevant circumstances, the Circuit Judge assigned to any Circuit which includes a district where the Irish language is in general use shall possess such a knowledge of the Irish language as would enable him to dispense with the assistance of an interpreter when evidence is given in that language.

Section 71 contained identical provisions for District Court Judges and similar provisions applied in respect of Peace Commissioners (under section 81). The effect of these provisions, read in light of Article 4, was to ground a practical accommodation of Irish speakers in courtroom settings. In addition, as Kohn notes, the practice during the period was that, pursuant to Order XXIX of the Rules of the High Court and Supreme Court, official interpreters for both courts could be appointed, and summonses and notices served in the Gaeltacht were to be provided in Irish translation if the original was in English. Conversely, summonses and notices served elsewhere were to be provided in English translation if the

[30] Ronan Keane, 'Hugh Kennedy' *Dictionary of Irish Biography* (Cambridge: Cambridge University Press, 2012).

[31] On the litigation of such cases under the 1924 Act see the compilation of some the most relevant Irish language related cases provided in hAnluain, "Tuairiscí Speicialta 1980–1998".

original was in Irish.[32] Affidavits filed in the Central Office were also to be translated into either language at the request of the other party to proceedings where the latter filed a declaration that they did not understand the language which had been used in the original. Order 1 Rule 4 of the Circuit Court Rules similarly provided that "either the National Language or the English Language may be used in the proceedings in the Court."

This combination of statute and rules which, at the very least, possess a quasi-legislative character, would seem to indicate a desire to perpetuate a portion of the implied promise of Article 4 and to ensure a State in which Irish was, not only officially recognised, but also incorporated within institutional settings—in particular in those areas where Irish remained the quotidian language of the community and its members. However, no provision was made in law or policy requiring that any proportion of the judges of lower courts, much less members of the High or Supreme Courts, be able to speak or understand Irish. There was, then, a commitment in the 1924 Act which could not, in practice, hope to be realised consistently absent an institutional commitment to building the resources necessary for its effective provision. Indeed, the limitation of sections 44 and 71 of the Act by reference to efforts being made "so far as may be practicable having regard to all relevant circumstances" could be read as a recognition of this failure, and have continued to limit the capacity of courts, including in Gaeltacht areas, to operate in a manner that facilitates Irish speakers.

More puzzling, perhaps, is the endurance of the Administration of Justice (Language) Act (Ireland) 1737, which remained in force (though evidently void for unconstitutionality—as outlined above, it mandated that court proceedings be conducted only through English) until the reforms introduced by the Statute Law Revision Act 1962. While it is unlikely that this endurance is either indicative or revelatory, what is particularly evident from the text of the 1924 Act is a reluctance to wholeheartedly engage in the institutional or individual capacity building which would enable progressively improved compliance with the obligations outlined in the statute.

This reading of the 1924 Act is not contradicted by the small body of legal decisions in which the Courts of the Saorstát considered Article 4.

[32] Kohn, *The Constitution of the Irish Free State*, 25.

Article 4 Before the Courts

In *R (Ó Coileáin) v Crotty*,[33] the appellant had been charged in the Circuit Court with an offence contrary to the Finance (New Duties) Act 1916 and sought to give his evidence in defence and to conduct all cross-examination of witnesses through Irish. At the Circuit Court hearing before Crotty J, none of those appearing in support of the prosecution spoke Irish, and while it appeared the judge himself could speak and understand Irish, he did not consider it proper to act as interpreter. The accused declined to conduct his defence in English, contended that he had a right pursuant to Article 4 of the Constitution to do so and, having been being denied such right, did not present a defence. As a result, he was subject to a fine of £50 which he appealed.

On appeal, O'Sullivan P in the High Court quashed the decision of the lower court, noting they were satisfied that the constitutional right of the defendant to conduct his case in Irish under Article 4 had been disregarded by the trial Judge.[34] While the decision does not cast any great light on the scope of Article 4 as interpreted by the courts, it does, perhaps, offer us an insight into the position of Irish speakers in the Saorstát, as a group whose language was now afforded high symbolic importance in Constitutional terms, but little accommodation in practice.

A gradually more considered engagement with the meaning of Article 4 is evident in *Attorney General v Joyce*.[35] There, two defendants were tried jointly on a murder charge in the Central Criminal Court. During the trial, nine witnesses—as well as the defendants—gave evidence through Irish. A court appointed translator as well as one English-speaking and one Irish-speaking stenographer were present. As a result of some miscommunication, however, the Irish-speaking stenographer present in court made no record of the Irish testimony and only the record of the interpreter's English translations was recorded. The result was that the jury (as well as the Court of Criminal Appeal in due course) was provided only with an English translation of the appellants' testimony, which the appellants argued was poor in quality and did not accurately reproduce, nor adequately convey, the content of the testimony which had been given at trial.

[33] *R (Ó Coileáin) v Crotty* (1927) 61 ILTR 81.

[34] "Sequel to Bandon Concert. Conductor's Appeal. Costs Against Judge and District Justice' Irish Examiner, 30 March 1927, p.8.

[35] *Attorney General v Joyce and Walsh* [1929] IR 526.

Kennedy CJ in the Court of Criminal Appeal nevertheless declined to overturn the decision of the lower court noting that no objection had been raised at the trial or indeed subsequently on behalf of either the prosecution or the defendants regarding the accuracy of the interpreter's translations of the Irish evidence. He nevertheless observed,

> It would seem to me to be a requirement of natural justice, particularly in a criminal trial, that a witness should be allowed to give evidence in the language which is his or her vernacular, whether that language be Irish or English, or any foreign language.[36]

The Chief Justice freely acknowledged that the Constitution recognised the particular status of Irish in Article 4 and found that it followed that whether a citizen's vernacular was Irish or not, he was entitled to use the language. In the instant case he noted that the appellants, in giving their testimony through Irish,

> had, as it were, a double right to do so: first on general principles of natural justice as their vernacular language, and secondly as a matter of Constitutional right.[37]

And yet Kennedy CJ was reluctant, given the absence of objections to the work of the interpreter in the case, to find that any right of the defendants—whether pursuant to Article 4 or the requirements of natural and Constitutional justice—could ground an overturning of the defendants' conviction.[38]

Two things are particularly relevant in respect of the judgment in *Joyce*. The first is Kennedy CJ's use of the Constitutional status of Irish to secure a right to participate in legal proceedings in Irish, despite the absence of any particular right to that effect in the text of Article 4 or in statute. The second is the Chief Justice's recognition of the right to use Irish not only as a right derived from Article 4 but also secured by the requirements of natural and Constitutional justice. Both findings, while they did not assist the defendants, were positive in respect of Irish language rights more generally and seem to bear out a view of Article 4 as securing some of the

[36] Ibid., 581.
[37] Ibid.
[38] This approach is in contrast to the more recent approach taken by the Court of Appeal in the case of *DPP v HM and BO* [2021] IECA 315.

long-deleted "freedoms, rights, and privileges" of the proposed Article 26 in Draft C.

The 1934 decision of *Ó Foghluadha v McClean*[39] is perhaps the most well-known case dealing with language rights in Irish Constitutional law—and is certainly the most significant case in respect of Article 4. The case arose as a result of a tenancy dispute between Conradh na Gaeilge, an organisation co-founded by Dubhghlas de hÍde in 1893 which devoted itself to the promotion of the Irish language, and a tenant of the organisation who had ceased paying rent and from whom the organisation subsequently sought to recover the unpaid monies. The Conradh served the defendants with papers in Irish and, having received no response from them, brought an application seeking judgment in default of defence before the Master of the High Court. That application was denied, on the basis that the applicants had served the other party through Irish without providing a translation as required under Order XXIX Rule 3 of the Rules of the High Court and Supreme Court 1926. O'Sullivan P noted in the High Court that

> Article 4 declares that the national language of the Irish Free State is the Irish language, but that the English language shall be equally recognised as an official language. This can only mean that both languages are official languages and, as such, entitled to equal recognition.[40]

What this meant, however, was:

> ... no more than this—that every person shall be entitled at his option to use either language in transacting legal business, and he shall not suffer any impediment ... by reason of the language he uses where such use did not impose upon the affected parties any additional expense or burden, where it facilitated the progress of the litigation and did not place an obstacle in the way of those who desire to conduct their legal business in the Irish language.[41]

Hanna J, concurring, noted that what Article 4 permitted was that, when read in conjunction with section 36 of the Courts of Justice Act, a

[39] *Ó Foghluadha v McClean* [1934] IR 469.
[40] Ibid., 471.
[41] Ibid.

person was free to use the English language if they wished to do so, but that the Irish language was to be used subject to the Rules of Court.[42]

The Conradh appealed against this decision, arguing that any rule of court which sought to require the use of English, rather than Irish, discriminated against the Irish language and constituted a derogation from the status of Irish as the national language such that any rule of that kind would be invalid.[43] The Supreme Court, however, agreed with the analysis of O'Sullivan P, with Kennedy CJ noting:

> The declaration by the Constitution that the National language of the Saorstát is the Irish language does not mean that the Irish language is, or was at that historical moment, universally spoken by the people of the Saorstát, which would be untrue in fact, but it did mean that it is the historic distinctive speech of the Irish people, that it is to rank as such in the nation, and, by implication, that the State is bound to do everything within its sphere of action (as for instance in State-provided education) to establish and maintain it in its status as the National language and to recognise it for all official purposes as the National language. There is no doubt in my mind but that the term "National" in the Article is wider than, but includes, "official," in which respect only the English language is accorded Constitutional equality. None of the organs of the State, legislative, executive or judicial, may derogate from the pre-eminent status of the Irish language as the National language of the State without offending against the Constitutional provisions of Art. 4.[44]

The Chief Justice went on to note that Article 4's requirements were nevertheless contextualised by reference to the linguistic disability of a significant portion of the population as reflected in legislation including the Legal Practitioners (Qualification) Act 1929, and the Housing Act 1929 among others.[45] While the judge did not think the obligations which Article 4 imposed were stayed or otherwise waived by this context, he did find that the primary duty of the courts was, subject to the Constitution, to do justice between the parties and that this aim might require adopting a pragmatic approach (as reflected in the Rules) which

[42] Ibid., 472. See also the concurring comments of Byrne J to the same effect, ibid., 473.
[43] Ibid., 481.
[44] Ibid., 493.
[45] Ibid., 484.

> while rendering full pride of status [to the national language] ... the hard fact remains, and must of stern necessity remain at least for a generation, that of the adult population a number, decreasing as time goes on but even still perhaps a majority, not because of perversity nor of their own fault (because they did not prescribe the course of their own education), is unable to read or understand a summons or notice written only in the Irish language.[46]

In those circumstances, Kennedy CJ found that the rules requiring that documents served in Irish be accompanied by an English translation were not in breach of Article 4. Interestingly, the Chief Justice also took the opportunity to make *obiter* comments in respect of both the lack of an agreed vocabulary of Irish terms in legal rules[47] and the Oireachtas' implementation of the spirit of Article 4 (and indeed Article 42). He also remarked that since the enactment of Article 4 the Oireachtas had passed "not one Act" except in English and that while it was "not for me here and now to express any opinion as to whether each Act should not have been enacted at the same time in the Irish language (as seems to be suggested by Art. 42 of the Constitution) ... legislation in two official languages concurrently is the settled practice elsewhere."[48]

Once again, *Ó Foghluadha* perhaps offers some insight into the conflict, and indeed contradictions, with which the Drafting Committee struggled—namely how to adopt both the policies and the practices of a bilingual state when a significant proportion of the population would be placed at a disadvantage by doing so. The approach adopted in response to this difficulty—to require the minority of the population to accommodate the linguistic majority, and to permit the development of a *de facto* monolingually English state to continue pending the emergence of a sufficient share of Irish speakers would ultimately prove self-defeating.

In 1936, a year before the arrival of the new Constitution, the High Court considered Article 4 for the final time. In *The State v Coyne*[49] the appellant was charged with a criminal offence in the District Court, and the Garda testifying for the prosecution gave his evidence in Irish. Despite the solicitor for the defendant indicating that neither he nor his client understood Irish, the District Judge declined to order the evidence to be

[46] Ibid., 486

[47] Ibid., 488–489.

[48] Ibid., 483–484.

[49] *The State v Coyne* (1936) 70 ILTR 185.

heard in English or translated and subsequently delivered his ruling in Irish also. The defendant discovered his conviction only when a bystander informed him and subsequently appealed against the conviction. The High Court quashed the conviction, finding that a fundamental principle of the administration of justice had been disregarded in circumstances where the defendant could not understand the allegations made, the evidence presented, or respond to either.

Tongue Tied: Navigating Symbolism and Substance

The result of Article 4 then, was a Constitutional provision rich with symbolism but tongue-tied by the practical realities of how to create a bilingual state given the linguistic capacities, and institutional legacies, on the ground. This is not to say that the recognition of Irish as a national language was only symbolic, but it was the case that the commitment it sounded (and which was reflected by Article 42) did not succeed in compelling the Oireachtas, or in permitting the judiciary, to elaborate a more complete architecture of language rights or policies.

In a state which sought to ground its legitimacy on difference, language became a crucial identifier of that difference, and a principal means of articulating it. In this sense, the elevation of Irish to a constitutional footing was a manifesto moment—an important symbolic action in constructing the Saorstát's desired identity. And yet, as the vacillation evident in the various drafts of the constitutional text (and the later dicta of Kennedy CJ in particular show) there was significant concern to ensure that the language did not retreat to being a symbol only. That this was not accomplished is partly a fault of the text which was adopted but is also, as the Chief Justice's decision in *Ó Foghluadha v McClean* is at pains to point out, the fault of a legislature and executive reluctant to accept the invitation to action which Articles 4 and 42 presented.

Fifteen years after the entry into force of the 1922 Constitution, then Taoiseach Éamon de Valera justified the retention of Irish as a national language in the text of the 1937 draft, and the promotion of Irish to a "first" language on the basis that it was the "language that is most associated with the nation" and was the language of "the traditions of our people."[50] But it would be another seventy-seven years before concrete

[50] Éamon de Valera, 'Bunreacht na hÉireann (Dréacht) – Coiste' Dáil Éireann debate, 25 May 1937, Vol 67, No. 8.

rights of speakers to conduct business with the State (as had been envisioned by the discarded text of Article 26 of Draft C) were provided through official languages legislation. Other crucial components necessary for a bilingual state—including Irish-speaking juries, rights of Irish speakers to control land sales in Gaeltacht communities, continue to remain absent.[51]

We could, in many respects, consider ourselves the inheritors of the spirit of the 1922 document which presumes that symbolic commitment is sufficient to discharge the State's duties to the protection of the national language but does not delve deeper into the policies required to bring into being the bilingual state which the 1922 Constitution first dared to hope for. In this respect the 1937 document would carry forward a commitment to Irish which, for all its symbolic importance to the new State, remained, and may still remain, under-determined.

Acknowledgement My sincerest thanks to the editors for comments on an early draft of this chapter and to Amanda Morse, PhD Candidate, School of History and Geography, Dublin City University for her archival research assistance in preparing the final draft of this chapter.

References

Butler, Graham. "The Representative of the Crown and the Governor-General of the Irish Free State: Text and Context."

Cahillane, Laura. "Constituting a Polity." Chapter 2 in this volume.

Cahillane, Laura. *Drafting the Irish Free State Constitution*. Manchester University Press, 2016.

Crowley, Tony. "Language, Politics and Identity in Ireland: A Historical Overview." In Sociolinguistics in Ireland, edited by Ray Hickey, Dublin: Routledge, 2000.

Crowley, Tony. *The Politics of Language in Ireland 1366-1922: A Sourcebook*. Dublin: Routledge, 2000.

FitzGerald, Garret. "Estimates for Baronies of Minimum Level of Irish-Speaking Amongst Successive Decennial Cohorts: 1771-1781 to 1861-1871." *Royal Irish Academy* (1984).

Keane, Ronan. "Hugh Kennedy" *Dictionary of Irish Biography*. Cambridge: Cambridge University Press, 2012.

[51] See, for example, *Ó Maicín v Éire* [2010] IEHC 179; *Glann Mór Céibh Teo v An tAire Tithíochta* [2022] IESC 40; *Ní Cheallagh v An tAire Comhshaoil* [1980] Special Reports 52; *An Blascaod Mór Teo v Commissioner of Public Works* [2000] 1 IR 6.

Kelly, J.M. "The Constitution: Law and Manifesto." In *The Constitution of Ireland 1937-1987*, edited by Frank Litton, Dublin: Dublin Institute of Advanced Studies, 1988.

Kohn, Leo. *The Constitution of the Irish Free State*. London: G Allen & Unwin, 1932.

Kotsonouris, Mary. *Retreat from Revolution: The Dáil Courts, 1920-24*. Dublin: Irish Academic Press, 2020.

Mac Cárthaigh, Daithí. *An Ghaeilge Sa Dlí*. Galway: Leabhar Breac, 2020.

Ó Ciosáin, Niall. "Gaelic Culture and Language Shift." In Nineteenth Century Ireland: A Guide to Recent Research, edited by Laurence Geary and Margaret Kelleher, Dublin: UCD Press, 2005.

Ó Cuív, Brian. *Irish Dialects and Irish Speaking Districts*. Dublin: Dublin Institute for Advanced Studies, 1951.

Ó Torna, Caitríona. *Cruthú Na Gaeltachta 1893-1922*. Baile Átha Cliath: Cois Life, 2005.

Ó Tuathaigh, Gearóid. *I Mbéal an Bháis: The Great Famine and the Language Shift in Nineteenth Century Ireland*. Quinnipiac University Press, 2015.

Ó Tuathail, Séamas. *Gaeilge Agus Bunreacht*. Baile Átha Cliath: Coscéim, 2002.

Phelan, Mary. "A Trifling Matter? Names in Irish on Carts: The Dublin Castle Files." *Studia Hibernica* 46, no. 48 (2022).

Phelan, Mary. *Irish Speakers, Interpreters and the Courts 1754-1921*. Dublin: Four Courts Press, 2019.

Walsh, John. *Díchoimisiúnú Teanga: Coimisiún Na Gaeltachta 1926*. Baile Átha Cliath: Cois Life, 2002.

Walsh, John. *One Hundred Years of Irish Language Policy 1922-2022*. In *Reimagining Ireland*, edited by Eamon Maher, Oxford: Peter Lang, 2022.

Wolf, Nicholas. *An Irish Speaking Island: State, Religion, Community and the Linguistic Landscape in Ireland 1770-1870*. Wisconsin: University of Wisconsin Press, 2014.

CHAPTER 8

A New Constitution; a New Language? How the New Courts Talked About the Free State Constitution 1922

Maurice Collins

Introduction

The enactment of the Constitution of the Irish Free State (Saorstát Éireann) Act 1922 on 6 December 1922 involved (or, at least, appeared to involve) a radical rupturing of the established legal order in the State. The new Constitution gave new rights and freedoms, including the right to liberty and freedom of conscience, expression, assembly and association, and provided for a new and independent court system to enforce those rights, with the judicial power notably extending to "the question of the validity of any law having regard to the provisions of the Constitution" (Article 65).

Much has been written about the 1922 Constitution. The view of Donal K. Coffey, that it was "an experiment which ended in failure", is

M. Collins (✉)
Supreme Court of Ireland, Dublin, Ireland

L. Cahillane, D. K. Coffey (eds.), *The Centenary of the Irish Free State Constitution*, Palgrave Modern Legal History,
https://doi.org/10.1007/978-3-031-46181-1_8

widely held and difficult to dispute.[1] That is not simply the judgment of hindsight. The 1922 Constitution failed in real time and in plain sight. Hugh Kennedy's foreword to Kohn, *The Constitution of the Irish Free State*, should perhaps be read as part early obituary and part pathologist's report both recording, and offering an explanation for, the demise of (as Kennedy characterised it) "the first legislative act and fundamental instrument of the new State".[2] Two years later, in December 1934, the Supreme Court gave judgment in *State (Ryan) v Lennon*[3] and the unravelling of the new settlement was effectively complete. I will discuss *State (Ryan) v Lennon* in more detail later, but I would here venture to suggest that the judgments of Kennedy CJ and Fitzgibbon J, so opposed in so many ways, may be seen as howls of rage that, almost 90 years later, continue to reverberate like radio pulses from a dead star.

It did not, of course, start out that way. The Constitution enacted by Dáil Éireann on 6 December 1922—*qua* Constituent Assembly and not, as Kennedy CJ stressed in his judgment in *State (Ryan) v Lennon, qua* Oireachtas—appeared to establish a modern constitutional democracy, with significant protection for fundamental rights (though it did not characterise them as such, a point to which both Fitzgibbon J and Murnaghan J were to attach significance in *State (Ryan) v Lennon*). According to Hanna J (in *The State (O' Duffy) v Bennett*)[4] the Constitution "expressly conferred on the citizens of the State every fundamental constitutional right as known and embodied in the common law against autocratic or military power" adding that "no constitutional lawyer could have asked for more protection to the citizens, save that these rights should be permanent and that they should be sufficiently safeguarded".[5] That, of course, was a critically important saver. The vulnerability of the 1922 Constitution

[1] Donal K. Coffey, "The Judiciary of the Irish Free State" *Dublin University Law Journal* 33 (2011): 61.

[2] Leo Kohn, *The Constitution of the Irish Free State* (London: G Allen & Unwin, 1932).

[3] [1935] IR 170.

[4] [1935] IR 70.

[5] Ibid. at 95.

was, of course, apparent for all to see by the time of the decision in *O' Duffy*.[6]

The Constitution as adopted also contained innovative provisions providing for the referral of legislation to the people by way of referendum in certain circumstances (Article 47), as well as provision for the initiation by the people of proposals for laws or constitutional amendments (Article 48). Article 47 featured significantly in Kennedy CJ's analysis in *State (Ryan) v Lennon*. Those provisions did not "stick", however.

The Constitution has been characterised—aptly in my view—as "austere" in its drafting, avoiding the sort of rhetorical flourishes that may be found in Bunreacht na hÉireann.[7] It was also notably secular in tone, with the sole reference to God occurring not in the Constitution itself but in the recital in the Constitution of the Irish Free State (Saorstát Éireann) Act 1922 (subsequently the foundation—however fragile—for the Natural Law arguments made by Kennedy CJ in *State (Ryan) v Lennon*).[8]

As a matter of *Irish* constitutional theory, the 1922 Constitution derived its authority from the 1922 Act enacted by the Dáil: that was the view stated by Kennedy CJ in *State (Ryan) v Lennon*[9] and, on that point

[6] In later April 1934, John A Costello SC (who had represented Mr. O' Duffy in the proceedings) was among a number of TDs who proposed an amendment to Article 50 which would have provided that no ordinary law amending the Constitution enacted by the Oireachtas in respect of certain articles (including the rights provisions in Articles 6–9 and the provisions entrenching the independence and jurisdiction of the judiciary) would become law until after the holding of a general election and subject to the new Dáil resolving to approve of such amendment. The amendment, which took the form of an amendment to the Constitution (Amendment no. 24) Bill 1934, which proposed the abolition of the Seanad, was opposed by the Fianna Fáil Government and comfortably defeated. The debate is nonetheless of considerable interest. Shortly afterwards, on 24 May 1934, the 1934 Constitution Committee was appointed and it reported to the President of the Executive Council on 23 July 1934. Its Report recommended that certain specified Articles (including all of the Articles the subject of the failed amendment) should "be regarded as fundamental and should … be rendered immune from easy alteration" (Report, para 3). While the Committee's recommendations for the amendment of the 1922 Constitution (which also addressed emergency provisions and powers) were not implemented, they had a significant influence on the structure and content of the 1937 Constitution: see generally Gerard Hogan, *The Origins of the Irish Constitution, 1928–1941* (Dublin: Royal Irish Academy, 2012), Chapter 11.

[7] Thomas Mohr, "Natural Law in Early Twentieth Century Ireland – *State (Ryan) v Lennon* and its aftermath", *Journal of Legal History* 43(1) (2021): 1–34.

[8] For the circumstances in which the reference to God came to be inserted into the 1922 Act, see Mohr, "Natural Law".

[9] [1935] IR 170 at 203.

at least, Fitzgibbon J agreed with him.[10] A contrary view was subsequently expressed by the Judicial Committee of the Privy Council in *Moore v Attorney General of the Irish Free State*.[11] However, the decision of the Supreme Court in *The Criminal Law (Jurisdiction) Bill, 1975* leaves no room for doubt as to what the position is as a matter of Irish law.[12] In that case it was held that the "Constitution of 1922 derived its authority not from the Act of the imperial parliament passed on the 5th December, 1922, or from the proclamation made on the 6th December, 1922, but from the Act of Dáil Éireann sitting as a constituent assembly passed on the 25th October, 1922".[13]

That, in Article 50, the amendment provision, the 1922 Constitution contained the seeds of its own destruction is clear. The arc of its destruction that culminated in *The State (Ryan) v Lennon* can be traced back as far as the decision of the Court of Appeal in *R (Cooney) v Clinton* which, although decided on 23 May 1924, was not reported until 1935.[14] More of *R (Cooney) v Clinton anon.*

But in this chapter I am not seeking to review how the 1922 Constitution operated in practice. Rather, I want to say something about the way in which the courts spoke of the Constitution during its lifetime. Does the language used by the courts suggest an enthusiastic embrace of it as "the fundamental instrument of the new State" constituting an entirely new legal order? Or did the courts effectively approach the Constitution from a positivistic perspective? Was "the voice of the Gael"[15] liberated from the spectral "thraldom" referred to by Kennedy CJ in his foreword to Kohn?

[10] Ibid. at 232.

[11] [1935] IR 472, 484–485.

[12] *Re The Criminal Law (Jurisdiction) Bill, 1975* [1977] IR 129. The Court also referred to the decision of the former Supreme Court in *The State (Ryan) v. Lennon* and, in particular, the judgment of Kennedy C.J. at p. 203 and the judgment of Fitzgibbon J. at p. 225 of the report.

[13] Ibid. at 146–147.

[14] [1935] IR 245. The Constitution had, of course, made detailed provision for a new court system but the legislation required to give effect to those provisions was not enacted until 1924, when the Courts of Justice Act 1924 established (*inter alia*) the new High Court of Justice and the new Supreme Court of Justice. Judges were appointed to those courts only in June 1924. Until then, the existing courts continued to exercise jurisdiction under the transitional provisions in Article 75 of the Constitution.

[15] Ronan Keane, "The Voice of the Gael: Chief Justice Kennedy and the Emergence of the New Irish Court System 1921–1936" *Irish Jurist* 31 (1996): 205.

In truth, the position revealed by a review of the *Irish Reports* is untidy and difficult to interpret. The data-set is small and Article 50 throws a long shadow over what is there. The reality is that, at least as regards judicial review, the 1922 Constitution was effectively still-born.

R(O' Brien) v Military Gov NDU Internment Camp

That said, there was no lack of recognition of the new constitutional dispensation. The decision of the old Court of Appeal in *R(O' Brien) v Military Gov NDU Internment Camp*[16] provides an early and striking example. In a decision handed down on 31 July 1923 that court had held that a state of war no longer existed in Dublin and accordingly issued a writ of *habeas corpus* to the military authorities who held the prisoner. In its return to the writ, the Government certified that the prisoner was detained under an order made under the Public Safety (Emergency Powers) Act 1923 which had purportedly been enacted on 1 August 1923. The validity of that return was, however, challenged on the basis that the manner in which the Act had been enacted was in breach of Article 47 of the Constitution. Article 47 provided that any Bill passed or deemed to have passed by both Houses might be suspended for a period of 90 days on the written demand of two-fifths of the members of the Dáil Eireann or a majority of the members of Seanad Eireann presented to the President of the Executive Council not later than seven days from the day on which the Bill was passed or deemed to have been passed. Such a Bill might then be submitted by Referendum to the people. Article 47 did not apply to Money Bills or to Bills declared by both Houses to be "necessary for the immediate preservation of the public peace, health or safety".[17]

The prisoner argued that, in the absence of any such declaration, the Public Safety (Emergency Powers) Bill could not validly have been sent to the Governor General for his assent until the expiry of seven days from its passing. In response, the Government relied on the fact that the Governor General had indeed given his assent and submitted that such assent could not be impeached. Presumably, it did so in reliance on the "enrolled bill rule", a well-established common law principle precluding any form of

[16] [1924] 1 IR 32.

[17] Article 47 was deleted from the Constitution by the Constitution (Amendment no. 10) Act 1928, which also deleted Article 48.

procedural challenge to the validity of an Act of Parliament once passed by both Houses and given royal assent.

That argument was rejected by the Court of Appeal, in judgments of notable robustness whose language seems to anticipate the language later used by the Supreme Court in *McKenna v An Taoiseach (No. 2)* [1995] 2 IR 10.[18] According to Ronan LJ, Article 47 was "a very important Article of the Constitution", "the essence and substance" of which was the creation of a referendum. "A referendum is a most important element in a democratic Constitution and the substance of a referendum is that in certain cases and in certain circumstances the people themselves are to have a vote to determine whether a law shall be passed or not – that the law shall be finally submitted, in the words of this Article 'to the decision of the people'".[19] The arguments made by the Government—in essence that whether there should be a referendum or not was a matter for the President of the Executive Council—made "a farce of the entire thing". The giving of Royal assent to a Bill without a few hours of its passing the two Houses "would be an absolute fraud on the Constitution" and accepting the construction of Article 47 contended for by the Government "would sweep the referendum out of the Constitution".[20] Similarly, Molony LCJ (formerly the Lord Chief Justice of Ireland and, after the coming into operation of the Government of Ireland Act 1920, the Lord Chief Justice of Southern Ireland, though he sought and was granted permission to continue to use his former title) considered that the approach advocated by the Government would render Article 47 "nugatory". The prisoner was accordingly released.

In *Attorney General v McBride*,[21] the High Court (Hanna J) suggested that *R(O' Brien) v Military Governor* had declared the Public Safety (Emergency Powers) Act 1923 null and void. That may well have been the logical consequence of the Court's decision but the only order expressly referred to by Molony LCJ was an order releasing the prisoner. Even so, it is a remarkable decision, not least because the judges who gave it were stalwarts of the pre-1922 legal regime. It appears to be the only instance in which legislation enacted by the Oireachtas was successfully judicially reviewed under the 1922 Constitution.

[18] [1995] 2 IR 10.
[19] [1924] 1 IR 32.
[20] Ibid.
[21] [1928] IR 451.

In retrospect, *R(O' Brien) v Military Gov NDU Internment Camp* can plausibly be regarded as the highwater mark of constitutional activism under the 1922 Constitution. That it was a decision of the former Court of Appeal, rather than the High Court or Supreme Court to be established as constitutional courts under Articles 64–70, is a sharp and painful irony.

The forceful and expansive language in *R(O' Brien) v Military Gov NDU Internment Camp* was notably absent from *R (O' Connell) v Military Governor*,[22] a decision of the King's Bench Division on a *habeas corpus* application. The prisoner was in detention on foot of an order made under the Public Safety (Powers of Arrest and Detention) Temporary Act, 1924 and it was argued on his behalf (by *inter alia*, George Gavan Duffy) that the Act contravened Articles 6, 64, 70, and 72 of the Constitution by permitting detention without a criminal trial before a court. Those arguments were given short shrift by the Court, with all its members emphasising the broad scope of the legislative powers of the Oireachtas. According to Molony LCJ, "within the whole area of the Irish Free State it is a free and unfettered legislature and ... there is nothing in the Treaty or the Constitution or the statutes confirming same, which limits the power of the Oireachtas to make such a provision as is here impugned".[23] According to Dodd J, the policy of the Act was a matter for the Oireachtas and not any concern of the Court and the Court had to be careful not to overstep the powers conferred on it.[24] A notably formalistic approach was taken to Article 6's prescription that "no person shall be deprived of his liberty except in accordance with law" and to Article 70s requirement that "no one shall be tried save in due course of law". That was a feature of the subsequent jurisprudence also, including the majority judgments in *State (Ryan) v Lennon*.[25] It should be said, however, that Pim J did allow that a permanent law that gave the Executive power to deprive any citizen of his liberty without trial would be "contrary to the spirit of Article 6 and therefore a violation of the Constitution" but that was "a very different thing

[22] [1924] 2 IR 104.

[23] At 111.

[24] At 117.

[25] Bunreacht na hÉireann contains equivalent guarantees in Article 40.4.1 and Article 38.1. After some uncertainty, it is now well-established the references to "in accordance with law" and "in due course of law" import something more than simply a law enacted by the Oireachtas (see Gerard Hogan et al., Kelly: *The Irish Constitution* (Dublin: 5th ed., Butterworths, 2018) at chapter 7.4 (Article 40.4.1) and chapter 6.5 (Article 38.1).

form from a temporary law made in abnormal times and for a temporary purpose".[26]

That decision was appealed to the Court of Appeal. The appeal was heard and decided along with *R (Cooney) v Clinton.*

R (Cooney) v Clinton

In *R (Cooney) v Clinton*,[27] the State relied on section 3 of the Indemnity Act 1923 as having the effect of validating a sentence of imprisonment that had previously been imposed on the prisoner by a special military tribunal. In turn, the prisoner argued that section 3 violated Articles 6, 70, and 72 of the Constitution. Nothing in section 3 or in the 1923 Act purported to amend any provision of the Constitution.

O' Connor MR (who had, of course, given the celebrated decision in *Egan v Macready*[28] and who had also ruled against the *habeas corpus* application of Erskine Childers *in R(Childers) v Adjutant-General of the Provisional Forces*[29] and who was appointed a member of the Supreme Court on its establishment in June 1924) allowed that the argument "may raise a grave constitutional question" though he was "far from saying that the Constitution as it stood at the date of the passing of the Indemnity Act there was not power in the Oireachtas to pass such an Act without any amendment of the Constitution". However, it was in his view "quite unnecessary" to consider that question further, having regard to the terms in which the power of amendment conferred by Article 50 of the Constitution was framed. He stated: "It is difficult to see how, during the period of eight years, any Act passed by the Oireachtas can be impeached as ultra vires so long as it is within the terms of the Scheduled Treaty."[30]

As for the argument that legislation purporting to amend the Constitution should declare that it was so intended, the Master of the Rolls was dismissive: "I cannot accede to that argument in view of the express provision that any amendment made within the period may be made by ordinary legislation."[31]

[26] At 118.
[27] [1935] IR 245.
[28] [1921] 1 IR 265.
[29] [1923] 1 IR 5.
[30] [1935] IR 245 at 247.
[31] At 247.

Ronan LJ (who gave the judgment in O′ Brien cited above) and O′ Connor LJ agreed with the Master of the Rolls.

The appeal in *R(O′ Connell) v Military Governor* failed on the same basis. The Government relied on section 4 of the Public Safety (Powers of Arrest and Detention) Temporary Act 1924 which was "no doubt drastic legislation" but was clear in its meaning and had to be regarded as "intra vires and binding".[32]

If *R(O′ Brien) v Military Gov NDU Internment Camp* was a highwater mark, *R (Cooney) v Clinton* indicated that the tide was rapidly receding. Its holding had major implications for the status and effect of the 1922 Constitution and it appears to have been raised in the Dáil shortly afterwards—only to be dismissed by the President of the Executive Council as the product of a court that was not competent to interpret the Constitution.[33] Whether because it was overlooked or otherwise, the decision in *R (Cooney) v Clinton* was not referred to in *Attorney General v McBride*.[34]

It cannot be gainsaid that, having regard to the terms of Article 50, the 1922 Constitution could, during the period of eight years from the date it came into operation on 6 December 1922, be amended by ordinary legislation enacted by the Oireachtas (though, of course, the issue of whether certain Articles were immune to amendment, at least by ordinary legislation, was a significant element of the dispute in *State (Ryan) v Lennon*). But the argument that any such amendment had to be presented and adopted expressly as such an amendment unquestionably deserved closer and more anxious consideration than it received from the Master of the Rolls in *R (Cooney) v Clinton*. It required little judicial creativity or ingenuity to conclude that the status of the 1922 Constitution as such at least required that amendments to it should be formulated and debated in express terms and that it ought to be protected from alteration by a sidewind. *R (Cooney) v Clinton* (and *Attorney General v McBride* after it) represent a significant failure of constitutional imagination.

[32] [1924] 2 IR 104.

[33] Laura Cahillane, *Drafting the Free State Constitution* (Manchester: Manchester University Press, 2016) at 158–159.

[34] [1928] IR 451.

Attorney General v McBride

The arguments for reading such a restriction into Article 50 were rehearsed by Hanna J in *Attorney General v McBride.*[35] *McBride* concerned another piece of emergency legislation, the Public Safety Act 1927, which had been enacted in the aftermath of the assassination of Kevin O' Higgins. Section 16 of the Act provided for the detention for up to three months (initially on the order of a District Justice and then on the order of *an Executive Minister*) of persons suspected of being or having been engaged in the commission of a scheduled offence. The prisoner had been arrested on suspicion of conspiring to murder Mr. O' Higgins and an application was then made to the District Court for an order for his detention. The District Justice refused to make the order, on the basis (inter alia) that section 16 of the 1927 Act was an amendment of the rights of the subject guaranteed by Article 6 of the Constitution which had not complied with the formalities and was therefore null and void. The Attorney General sought certiorari of the refusal and *mandamus* to direct the Justice to make an order for detention.

Hanna J's judgment begins with a paean to the right to personal liberty which "we have inherited ... as the heirs of the ages of the common law" and which had been

> accentuated and emphasised in the Saorstát by its incorporation in this specific Article of the Constitution, which also in its terms proclaims that the High Court shall be its guardian ...The embodiment of this principle in the Constitution, while securing it more amply, and making it more difficult to suspend, efface or weaken, accentuates ... its importance in the Saorstát as a fundamental right of every citizen.[36]

There was, of course, a "but" and it was a significant one. Under Article 50 of the Constitution, amendments could be made by way of ordinary legislation. Section 3 of the 1927 Act provided that every provision of the Act which contravened any provision of the Constitution would, to that extent, operate and have effect as an amendment of such provision for as long as the Act continued in force (which was a period of 5 years). Thus the question was:

[35] [1928] IR 451.
[36] Ibid. at 454.

> Is it a sufficient compliance in law with Art. 50 to insert in an Act of Parliament, in vague and general terms, a clause such as this—a drag-net—without specifying either any Article, or part of an Article, of the Constitution that is to be amended or whether in fact any amendment is made?[37]

Hanna J then set out what might be thought to be a compelling argument that such an approach did not comply with Article 50:

> The Constitution is a sacred charter, not to be lightly, vaguely, or equivocally tampered with. But this sect. 3 leaves the subjects of the State, who have rights under the Constitution and rights to exercise against amendments of the Constitution, in the dark as to what is really altered in the Constitution, instead of enlightening them as to any change in their status. An "omnibus" amendment of this kind is contrary to the spirit of Art. 50, if not to the letter. The rights of the people should not be obscured by the facile pen of the parliamentary draftsman.[38]

However, while noting that the matter had not been fully argued before him, the Judge nonetheless concluded that

> having regard to the wording of Art. 50, that the amendment can be made "by way of ordinary legislation," I feel compelled, but with great hesitation, to come to the conclusion that this sect. 3 comes within that term; but it is a precedent that should not be followed.[39]

The decision of the Justice was quashed and *mandamus* issued to compel him to hear the application for a detention in accordance with the law "and thereupon make the order for detention applied for".

Again, one must be forgiven for questioning the adequacy of this analysis and the persuasiveness of the conclusion reached. If indeed the Constitution was "a sacred charter, not to be lightly, vaguely, or equivocally tampered with", it surely followed that there was a compelling argument that the Oireachtas, when exercising its power to amend the Constitution under Article 50, should at a minimum have been required to legislate in express and precise terms, so that the provisions of the Constitution could be at all times clearly identified? To impose such a

[37] Ibid. at 456.
[38] Ibid.
[39] Ibid.

requirement would not prevent the amendment of the Constitution but would at least have prevented its amendment by implication.

It hardly needs to be observed that the admonitory injunction that the precedent of the 1927 Act was one "that should not be followed ..." proved entirely impotent: the same drafting technique was the subject of adverse comment by Fitzgibbon J and Murnaghan J in their respective judgments in *State (Ryan)* v *Lennon*.[40]

State (O' Duffy) v Bennett

In *The State (O' Duffy) v Bennett*,[41] Hanna J offered an extended description of the "sacred charter". As adopted, it "expressly conferred on the citizens of the State every fundamental constitutional right as known and embodied in the common law against autocratic or military power" and its "object seemed to be to establish the predominant rule of law throughout the land".[42] He then summarised the constitutional rights given under the Constitution, observing that "no constitutional lawyer could have asked for more protection to the citizens, save that these rights should be permanent and that they should be sufficiently safeguarded".[43] But there was the rub. A yawning gap had opened up between constitutional language and constitutional reality which was brutally identified in *State (Ryan) v Lennon*.

The State (O' Duffy) v Bennett concerned the provisions of Article 2A of the Constitution, inserted by the Constitution (Amendment no. 17) Act 1931. By then, Article 50 had itself been amended so as to extend the period in which the Constitution could be amended by ordinary legislation enacted by the Oireachtas from 8 years to 16 years. The consequence was that the Constitution was amendable by ordinary legislation throughout its life. Article 2A provided for the establishment of a tribunal to be known as the Constitution (Special Powers) Tribunal, with far-reaching powers, including the power to impose the death sentence. Article 2A was, of course, the subject of *State (Ryan) v Lennon*. However, the decision in *The State (O' Duffy) v Bennett* was nevertheless an important one, in which the Divisional Court quite courageously sought to limit the scope

[40] At 229 (Fitzgibbon J) and at 238 and again at 245 (Murnaghan J).
[41] [1935] IR 70.
[42] Ibid. at 94.
[43] Ibid. at 95.

and effect of some of the more egregious provisions of Article 2A, insisting that the proceedings of Constitution (Special Powers) Tribunal were subject to judicial review, rejecting the Attorney General's argument that the Tribunal was itself a "Constitutional Court" which was not subject to the supervisory jurisdiction of the High Court and construing what appeared on its face to be a broad preclusion of the Court's jurisdiction as applicable only to acts done within the jurisdiction of the Tribunal and in the execution of their legitimate powers. The Court also insisted on strict compliance with all procedural requirements under Article 2A.

Lynham v Butler (No. 2)

Before coming to *State (Ryan) v Lennon*, there is the important decision of the Supreme Court in *Lynham v Butler (No. 2)*[44] concerning the separation of powers under Article 2 and the extent of the judicial power under Article 64 in the context of the functions of the Land Commission under the Land Commission Act 1923. Kennedy CJ was anxious to make it clear in his judgment that no argument had been made in *Lynham v Butler (No. 2)* that those provisions had been amended by implication by ordinary legislation.[45] Such a contention, he went on, "if ever it should come to be advanced for discussion, will raise considerations of profound importance as between the fundamental law of the State enacted by the Constituent Assembly and the method of amendment thereof by the Legislative Assembly during the period during which amendments may be made by the process of ordinary legislation".[46]

Even so, in his judgment Fitzgibbon J suggested that even on the assumption that the impugned provisions of the Land Law (Commission) Act 1923 were repugnant to the Constitution as infringing Article 64, "it is at least arguable" that they were valid as amendments under Article 50, adding:

> I am not prepared to accept without further argument the view that the Constitution cannot be amended unless the Statute containing the amendment is expressly described as "An Act to amend Article — of the

[44] [1933] IR 74.

[45] Ibid. at 92.

[46] At 93. The distinction drawn in this passage between the Constituent Assembly and the Legislative Assembly bore a lot of weight as far as Kennedy CJ was concerned, as is evident from his judgment in *State (Ryan) v Lennon*.

> Constitution", and in my opinion it may well be that, upon the principle leges posteriores priores abrogant, any enactment of the Oireachtas, clearly inconsistent with the Constitution, passed within the period during which amendment of the Constitution by ordinary legislation is permitted, should be construed as an amendment pro tanto, especially where, as in the present case, there is a direct reference to the material provisions of the Constitution, and it cannot be suggested that the Oireachtas had legislated with regard to them by inadvertence.[47]

The maxim *leges posteriores priores (contrarias) abrogant,* (later laws abrogate prior contrary laws) underpins the doctrine of implied repeal. Its invocation in this context is significant, reflecting Fitzgibbon J's background in the common law, in which unconstrained legislative sovereignty is vested in Parliament. His orthodoxy contrasts sharply with the rejection of another similar common law orthodoxy—the enrolled bill rule—by the Court of Appeal in *R(O' Brien) v Military Gov NDU Internment Camp.* In response, Kennedy CJ invokes the Dáil as Constituent Assembly adopting on the People's behalf a set of constitutional rules intended to be superior to positive law. They were effectively speaking different languages.

With that preliminary skirmish out of the way—which of course neatly set the scene for the confrontation to come in *State (Ryan) v Lennon*—the Supreme Court in *Lynham v Butler (No. 2)* addressed the substantive issue. Three judgments were delivered (the Supreme Court established by the Courts of Justice Act 1924 comprised only three judges, including the Chief Justice—the court was expanded to five only in 1936). The judgment given by the Chief Justice, which has been cited many times since—including extensive citation recently in *Zalewski v Adjudication Officer*[48]—certainly has its fair share of elevated rhetoric. The Judicial Power, he observed, was "one of the attributes of sovereignty" and

> one of the activities of the government of a civilised state by which it fulfils its purpose of social order and peace by determining in accordance with the

[47] At 112. As Kennedy CJ observed in his judgment, nothing in the 1923 Act purported to amend the Constitution. The "direct reference to the material provisions of the Constitution" referred to by Fitzgibbon J appears to have been a reference to section 3 of the Act which provided that, until the establishment of Courts pursuant to Article 64, section 28(5) of the Purchase of Land (Ireland) Act 1891 would apply to the Judicial Commissioner established by the Act and that, after the establishment of the new Courts, a High Court judge would be assigned to discharge the office of Judicial Commissioner.

[48] [2021] IESC 24.

> laws of the State all controversies of a justiciable nature arising within the territory of the State, and for that purpose exercising the authority of the State over person and property.[49]

The "exercise of the Judicial Power of this State has been entrusted by the Constitution exclusively to the Judges of the State, the manner of whose appointment is prescribed by the Constitution, which also declares their independence".[50] Johnston J notably observed that Article 64 "will undoubtedly be very useful in the future as a check on encroachments by the Legislature and the Executive upon popular rights".[51]

What "future" Johnston J may have had in mind is unclear but there is an unmistakable element of whistling past the graveyard in *Lynham v Butler (No. 2)* which was cruelly exposed in *State (Ryan) v Lennon*. Such was "the devastating effect of Article 50" (so Meredith J observed in his judgment in *State (Ryan) v Lennon*) that "the entire position of the judiciary, even their jurisdiction under Art 65"—the entrenched power of the High Court to review the constitutional validity of legislation— "might be changed".[52]

State (Ryan) v Lennon

Six judges gave judgments in *State (Ryan) v Lennon* (three judges sat in the High Court and, as already explained, the Supreme Court at the time was established as a court of three). All bar the Chief Justice firmly rejected the challenge to Article 2A. Of the five judgments that went the other way, that given by Fitzgibbon J undoubtedly exercises the greatest fascination. It is tempting—though perhaps unfair—to view the judgments of the Chief Justice and of Fitzgibbon J as reflecting a Manichean struggle for the soul of the Constitution. But, as I have said, it appears to me that each can be seen as a howl of rage, Kennedy CJ raging at the destruction of the Constitution he had helped to bring to creation first as a member of the drafting Committee and then as Attorney General and which, as Chief Justice, he had sworn to uphold (all flowing, it might be said, from drafting deficiencies in Article 50 that, it seems reasonable to assume, he had

[49] [1933] IR 74, 99.
[50] At 100.
[51] At 119.
[52] At 181.

failed to identify) and Fitzgibbon J, it appears, raging at everything that had occurred in the Free State since its establishment—raging indeed at the State itself. The conclusion of his judgment in *State (Ryan) v Lennon* is surely the most bitterly vituperative prose ever written by a judge in this—or, perhaps, any—jurisdiction. It is an extraordinary act of self-immolation, which shocks anew on every reading.

The judgment of the Chief Justice in *State (Ryan) v Lennon* has been the subject of much discussion and analysis and its powerful pull will no doubt continue to attract scholars in the future. Its natural law arguments have not weathered well (quite apart from the problem of their slender foundation in the preamble to the Act). The arguments based on implied limitations on the Oireachtas' power to amend cannot be so easily dismissed. There is, of course, an enormous literature in this area at this stage.[53] However, for all the judgment's very considerable rhetorical force and sincerity of conviction, its efforts to locate a limitation in the text and texture of the 1922 Constitution are, in my view, ultimately unpersuasive.

The central cleavage in *State (Ryan) v Lennon* can be (and has been) seen as a conflict between Austinian positivism on the one hand and the natural law on the other. That appears to me to be overly simplistic. There are, unsurprisingly, different views on that point and the debate continues.[54]

But Kennedy CJ was surely right to insist that, whatever its flaws, the 1922 Constitution should not have been seen as just another statute. Unlike the 1937 Constitution it was not approved directly by the people—that clearly would not have been practical in the midst of the Civil War and indeed it was not the practice of the time to hold such plebiscites. It was, however, solemnly enacted by the Dáil sitting as a Constituent Assembly. While it was, for (an extended) period, capable of amendment by ordinary legislation, that was because Article 50 specifically so provided (subject to the possibility of a referendum under Article 47).

It would not have been in any way inconsistent with the Oireachtas's power of amendment in Article 50 for the courts to have held that amendments to the Constitution were required to be expressly framed and

[53] See, for example, Richard Albert, "The Theory and Doctrine of Unconstitutional Constitutional Amendment in Canada" *Queens LJ* 41 (2015): 143 and Landau & Dixon, "Constraining Constitutional Change" *Wake Forest Law Review* 50 (2015): 859. The issue is also the subject of detailed discussion, with specific reference to *State (Ryan) v Lennon*, in A Kavanagh, "Unconstitutional Constitutional Amendments from Irish Free State to Irish Republic" in E Carolan (ed) *The Irish Constitution: Perspectives and Prospects* (2012).

[54] See Cahillane, *Drafting*, at 162–165.

enacted as such and had to specify precisely the manner in which the Constitution was to be amended. That is now expressly provided for in Article 46 of the 1937 Constitution but even in the absence of such an express provision, such a requirement could have been derived from the nature and purpose of the 1922 Constitution. That certainly was the view subsequently taken by Barrington J in the Supreme Court in *Laurentiu v Minister for Justice.*[55] The courts' refusal to take such an approach is certainly questionable and can plausibly be attributed, at least in part, to the legal positivist heritage of the judges concerned and their ingrained assumptions about parliamentary sovereignty, as well as a more general legal conservatism. There surely was no scope for the application of the doctrine of implied repeal—invoked in terms by Fitzgibbon J in *Lynham v Butler (No. 2)*—to a written constitution intended to protect fundamental rights.

The *State (Ryan) v Lennon* was not the last time that the 1922 Constitution came before the Courts but it is where I propose to stop. It embodies within it the very different ways that the courts spoke about the 1922 Constitution and reflects—through a mirror darkly—the disastrous effect of Article 50 on the constitutional conversation that might have been expected to develop following its enactment 100 years ago.

References

Albert, Richard. "The Theory and Doctrine of Unconstitutional Constitutional Amendment in Canada." *Queens LJ* 41 (2015): 143.

Cahillane, Laura. *Drafting the Free State Constitution.* Manchester: Manchester University Press, 2016.

Coffey, Donal K. "The Judiciary of the Irish Free State." *Dublin University Law Journal* 33 (2011): 61.

Hogan, Gerard et al. Kelly: *The Irish Constitution.* Dublin: 5 ed, Butterworths, 2018.

Hogan, Gerard. *The Origins of the Irish Constitution, 1928-1941.* Dublin: Royal Irish Academy, 2012.

Kavanagh, Aileen. "Unconstitutional Constitutional Amendments from Irish Free State to Irish Republic". In E. Carolan (ed.) The Irish Constitution: Perspectives and Prospects (Bloomsbury, 2012).

Keane, Ronan. "The Voice of the Gael: Chief Justice Kennedy and the Emergence of the New Irish Court System 1921-1936." *Irish Jurist* 31 (1996): 205.

[55] [1999] 4 IR 26, 69.

Kohn, Leo. *The Constitution of the Irish Free State*. London: G Allen & Unwin, 1932.
Landau, David and Rosalind Dixon. "Constraining Constitutional Change." *Wake Forest Law Review* 50 (2015): 859.
Mohr, Thomas. "Natural Law in Early Twentieth Century Ireland – *State (Ryan) v Lennon* and its aftermath." *Journal of Legal History* 43, no. 1 (2021): 1-34.

CHAPTER 9

'Environmental Stewardship' and Article 11 of the 1922 Constitution

Jamie McLoughlin

Introduction

The Irish Free State was ushered into being by the 1922 Constitution in circumstances of great adversity, including civil war and impecunity.[1] Over a hundred years later, Ireland, and indeed the World, is also faced with great adversity: this time in the form of the intertwined existential threats of climate breakdown, environmental degradation, and ecosystem collapse.[2] Human rights law and constitutional law have, in recent years,

[1] Laura Cahillane, "An Insight into the Irish Free State Constitution," *American Journal of Legal History* 54, no. 1 (2014): 1; Donal Corcoran, "Public policy in an emerging state: The Irish Free State 1922–25," *Irish Journal of Public Policy* 1, no. 1(2009): 66.

[2] IPCC, *Climate Change 2021: The Physical Science Basis* (Cambridge: CUP, 2021); IPBES, *Global Assessment Report on Biodiversity and Ecosystem Services* (Bonn: IPBES Secretariat, 2019).

J. McLoughlin (✉)
Sutherland School of Law, University College Dublin, Dublin, Ireland
e-mail: jamie.mc-loughlin@ucdconnect.ie

L. Cahillane, D. K. Coffey (eds.), *The Centenary of the Irish Free State Constitution*, Palgrave Modern Legal History,
https://doi.org/10.1007/978-3-031-46181-1_9

increasingly been mobilised in response to these threats. This has resulted in the emergence of climate change litigation (establishing the existence of state climate action duties[3]), the recognition of the rights of nature,[4] and the development of the idea of a human right to a healthy environment.[5] In 2020, Ireland had its own historic climate case, e.g. in which the Supreme Court invalidated the Government's insufficiently detailed plan for tackling climate change.[6] It is interesting to ponder, therefore, on its one hundredth anniversary, whether the 1922 Constitution of the Irish Free State has anything to say about the great ecological and climate crises of today. In that regard, this chapter contends that Article 11 of the 1922 Constitution can plausibly be read as creating a State duty of *environmental stewardship*.

Part I of the chapter briefly sketches the drafting of Article 11 of the 1922 Constitution, examines possible influences on its content, including the Brehon law, describes its main principles, and considers academic commentary on its content. In part II, the chapter analyses the case law interpreting Article 11. In this regard, judicial treatment of Article 11 has mostly featured in the case law on Article 10 of the 1937 Constitution which has looked back to Article 11 for guidance as to the meaning of Article 10. In particular, part II will consider the meaning of 'natural resources', the potential breadth of that concept, and the salience of the principle that the management and control of natural resources must be carried out pursuant to laws enacted by the Oireachtas. Part III of the chapter further interrogates the possible scope of 'natural resources', explains the concept of *environmental stewardship*, and shows how a State duty of environmental stewardship can be derived from the provisions of Article 11 (and Article 10).

[3] "Global Climate Change Litigation," Sabin Center for Climate Change Law, accessed March 10, 2023, http://climatecasechart.com/non-us-climate-change-litigation/

[4] For example, the Colombian Constitutional Court has recognised the Amazon Rainforest as a bearer of rights. See more generally David R. Boyd, *The Rights of Nature: A legal revolution that could save the world* (Canada: ECW Press, 2017).

[5] See generally, John H. Knox and Ramin Pejan, *The Human Right to a Healthy Environment* (Cambridge: CUP, 2018).

[6] *Friends of the Irish Environment v The Government of Ireland* [2020] IESC 49.

I – The Drafting of Article 11 of the 1922 Constitution

In 1912, a decade before the drafting of the 1922 Constitution, a local newspaper in New Zealand —the *Rodney and Otamatea Times*—published a short article entitled 'Coal Consumption Affecting Climate'.[7] This article documented how the combustion of fossil fuels releases greenhouse gas emissions which increase the Earth's temperature.[8] Unfortunately, however, anthropogenic climate change, despite being scientifically established, would not enter wider public consciousness or become a major legal or political issue, until much later in the twentieth century.[9] In contrast, the late nineteenth and early twentieth century witnessed the birth of the conservation movement in the United States which sought to protect nature from the commodity production-driven over-exploitation it had suffered throughout most of the nineteenth century and earlier.[10] Major legislation to safeguard various animal species, preserve habitats, create national parks, and provide for the more sustainable management and use of natural resources was passed during this period.[11] But it was not until the emergence of the modern environmental movement in the 1960s and thereafter that the idea of nature having rights and intrinsic value beyond its instrumental usefulness to humans started to become more widespread.[12] It is not surprising therefore that there is no evidence to suggest that concerns about climate change or biodiversity loss featured in the minds of the drafters of the 1922 Constitution. Nonetheless, a focus on the natural environment—'the nation's soil', its 'lands', 'water', 'air',

[7] Science Notes and News, "Coal Consumption Affecting Climate" *Rodney and Otamatea Times*, August 14, 1912, https://paperspast.natlib.govt.nz/newspapers/ROTWKG19120814.2.56.5

[8] Scientific awareness of climate change can be traced as far back as the 1820s. See Alexander Gillespie, *The Long Road to Sustainability: The Past, Present, and Future of International Environmental Law and Policy* (Oxford: OUP, 2017) 37–38.

[9] Jill Jager and Timothy O'Riordan, 'The History of Climate Change Science and Politics' in *The Politics of Climate Change*, ed. Jill Jager and Timothy O'Riordan (London: Routledge, 1996).

[10] Richard N. L. Andrews, *Managing the Environment, Managing Ourselves: A History of American Environmental Policy*, 2nd ed. (New Haven: Yale University Press, 2006) chapters 6 and 8.

[11] ibid.

[12] John McNeill, *Something New Under the Sun: An Environmental History of the Twentieth Century* (London: Allen Lane 2000).

and 'forces of nature'—can be seen in the drafting of the 1922 Constitution in those draft provisions concerning the ownership and control of the country's 'natural resources' which eventually crystallised into Article 11.

The drafting of the 1922 Constitution was overseen by a committee of nine individuals, including, Hugh Kennedy (the future Attorney General and Chief Justice), Darrell Figgis, author of a book on Brehon law and the ancient Gaelic state, and Clement J. France, a labour lawyer from the United States.[13] France was 'particularly concerned' that the country's 'natural endowments' should be constitutionally enshrined in State ownership to secure the economic development of the new State and to prevent the emergence of an 'economic autocracy' which he felt would result from the concentration of the country's resources in private ownership.[14] It appears that a memorandum presented to the committee by France on the natural resources of the State was influential in shaping its thinking in this regard.[15] The committee—owing to disagreement among its members—ultimately produced three different drafts—Draft A, Draft B, and Draft C—of a Constitution for the new State which were forwarded to the Provisional Government for its consideration.[16] Draft A was backed by Figgis, Draft B by Kennedy and France, and C by another committee member, Alfred O'Rahilly (a mathematics professor from UCC).[17] Drafts A and B contained Articles providing for unfettered public ownership of land and natural resources, while Draft C, by contrast, protected private property rights, though it also placed natural resources (including land) under the special supervision of the State.[18] Despite the 'left-wing thread' running through the various provisions on natural resources in the drafts, Cahillane argues that their origins lay, not in communism, but in the

[13] Laura Cahillane, *Drafting the Irish Free State Constitution* (Manchester: MUP, 2016) 4–5.

[14] Thomas Murray, "Socio-Economic Rights Versus Social Revolution? Constitution Making in Germany, Mexico and Ireland, 1917–1923," *Social & Legal Studies* 24, no. 4 (2015): 498; Document 24, Papers of E.M. Stephens, MSS 4234–41, Trinity College Dublin Archives.

[15] Cahillane (n 13) 22. ibid Document 24.

[16] ibid Cahillane 14.

[17] ibid.

[18] ibid 18–23. In Draft A, see Articles 1, 11, 12, 42, and 43; in Draft B, see Articles 1, 11, 12, 41, and 42; and in Draft C, see Articles 63, 64, and 65. Article 62 of Draft C protected private property rights. These provisions are set out in full in appendices in Cahillane (n 13). The three drafts are also available in Trinity College Dublin Archives, Papers of EM Stephens, MSS 4235.

ancient Gaelic state with its system of brehon law.[19] This state was said to be characterised by the public ownership of land and resources, held in common, for the good of the community as a whole.[20] As Cahillane puts it:

> The Gaelic state and its system of Brehon law ... was much more than a legal system—it was a way of life. The State was seen as one which placed people, life and nature above things like property.[21]

The presence of Articles in most of the post-war European constitutions—another key influence on the drafters—claiming ownership over natural resources such as forests, mineral wealth, and water, as well as the connection—in some conceptions—between 'popular sovereignty', the idea that the people were the font of all political authority—a 'leitmotif' of the entire 1922 Constitution—and the public ownership of land, also help to explain these radical provisions.[22] However, the nostalgia for the glorious ancient Gaelic utopia which existed prior to British rule seems to have been especially influential for the drafters as the 'ideal of a return to the ancient ways of the Gaelic state was seen as a sort of purification which would wipe out the pollution which was English rule.'[23]

Of course, in reality, the vision of the Gaelic state invoked by Figgis and others was a heavily romanticised one.[24] Although portrayed as 'upholding egalitarian values', including in relation to the status of women, in actuality, the brehon law divided society into social classes, with, e.g. the compensation a person was entitled to receive for suffering a legal wrong based on their 'honour price' or social standing.[25] Despite these 'terrible truths' about the reality of the Brehon law unearthed by modern scholarship,[26] it is arguable that the Brehon law did at least exhibit some recognition of the value of nature which was important materially and spiritually to the early

[19] ibid 23, 77–81, and 88–90.
[20] ibid.
[21] ibid 81.
[22] ibid 89–90.
[23] ibid 78.
[24] Thomas Mohr, 'Law in a Gaelic Utopia: Perceptions of Brehon Law in Nineteenth and early Twentieth Century Ireland' in *Remembering and Forgetting: Yearbook of Young Legal History*, ed. Oliver Brupbacher et al. (Martin Meidenbauer, 2007).
[25] ibid 264.
[26] ibid.

Irish.[27] The legal protection against injury accorded to trees under the Brehon law—which as Fields notes was not entirely dissimilar to the legal protection humans were entitled to—is a case in point. The Bretha Comaithchesa or 'judgments of neighbourhood'—a legal text dating from the eighth century CE—records a system whereby people had to make restitution (through the payment of a fine) for damaging any tree or shrub, belonging to their neighbour, on a list of protected species.[28] The more valuable the tree (a 'lord of the wood', like an oak, e.g.) in terms of the usefulness of what it could provide by way of food (for people and animals), or building material and so on, the higher the fine.[29] Fines (with payment in the form of livestock, usually cattle of some kind) were also increased if a tree was damaged during its growing season because of the heightened risk to the tree's survival from disease, evidencing a concern for sustainability.[30] Similarly, the Brehon law regulated the management of rivers and lakes with rules aimed at preventing overfishing by limiting the size of fish catches and the type of weirs that could be used in fishing.[31] While this falls short of modern conceptions of the rights of nature—an alternative paradigm in which nature has intrinsic worth and rights to exist independent of any instrumental value its exploitation holds for humans—it does suggest a certain level of respect for the natural world and a recognition of human dependence on nature.[32] Johnston has thus characterised the relationship of the early Irish with the natural environment as being one of 'reciprocity', i.e. a cognisance that in order to gain from the land, they also had to take care of it.[33]

Ultimately, the radical draft Articles on public ownership of natural resources, including land, were heavily watered-down to appease the

[27] Tina R Fields, "Trees in Early Irish Law and Lore: Respect for Other-Than-Human Life in Europe's History," *Ecopsychology* 12, no. 2 (2020): 131.

[28] Fergus Kelly, 'Trees in Early Ireland' (Augustine Henry Memorial Lecture, Dublin, March 1999).

[29] ibid.

[30] Fields (n 27).

[31] Dr. Elva Johnston, 'Brehon Law and Ireland's traditions looking to/after the Environment' (Address to the Citizens' Assembly on Biodiversity Loss, 15 October 2022) accessed November 28, 2022, https://www.youtube.com/watch?v=L08uT4fD5y4

[32] Ciara Brennan et al., 'Rights of Nature in Ireland: Towards a Living Island of Rights-Bearing Communities' (Environmental Justice Network Ireland, Submission to the Citizens' Assembly on Biodiversity Loss, September 2022) accessed November 28, 2022, https://ejni.net/rights-of-nature/

[33] Johnson (n 31).

wealthy sections of society (who the financially vulnerable fledgling Free State was dependent on to sure up its economy).[34] Nonetheless, the final version of Article 11 of the 1922 Constitution still holds potential from an environmental perspective. Article 11 provides as follows:

> All the lands and waters, mines and minerals, within the territory of the Irish Free State (Saorstát Éireann) hitherto vested in the State ... or held for the public use or benefit, and also all the natural resources of the same territory (including the air and all forms of potential energy), and also all royalties and franchises, within that territory shall, from and after the date of the coming into operation of this Constitution, belong to the Irish Free State (Saorstát Éireann), subject to any trusts, grants, leases or concessions then existing in respect thereof, or any valid private interest therein, and *shall* be controlled and administered by the Oireachtas, in accordance with such regulations and provisions as shall be from time to time approved by legislation, but the same shall not, nor shall any part thereof, be alienated, but may in the public interest be from time to time granted by way of lease or licence to be worked or enjoyed under the authority and subject to the control of the Oireachtas: Provided that no such lease or licence may be made for a term exceeding ninety-nine years, beginning from the date thereof, and no such lease or licence may be renewable by the terms thereof.

According to Kohn (writing during the lifetime of the 1922 Constitution), Article 11 was one of two (the other relating to primary education) 'programmatic declarations' in the 1922 Constitution.[35] He described Article 11's legal significance as being 'twofold', i.e. first, it entailed 'the legal succession of the Free State to all the rights in lands, waters, mines and minerals within the territory of the free State which were previously vested in the British Crown' and, second, it gave the Free State 'a general title to the control of all natural resources of the country' subject to valid existing private rights.[36] He noted that Article 11 vested the control and administration of these 'national trusts' in the legislature, rather than the Executive, and that the legislature was to regulate their use

[34] Cahillane (n 13) 89. However, the 1922 Constitution as ultimately adopted did not contain a guarantee of private property rights. For an analysis of this omission, see Rachael Walsh, chapter 11 in this volume.

[35] Leo Kohn, *The Constitution of the Irish Free State* (London: George Allen & Unwin Ltd, 1932) 172.

[36] ibid 173.

via legislation.[37] He also remarked on the fact that the Constitution limited parliamentary control by precluding the State from alienating any of its property held under Article 11; allowing only for it to be granted 'in the public interest' by way of lease or licence (for a period not exceeding ninety-nine years) under the supervision of the legislature.[38] Kohn stated that the 'practical effect of these provisions was to sanction the maintenance of existing forms of tenure, but to subject the terms on which they were held to a progressive measure of direct parliamentary control, to be exercised for the public benefit.'[39] Finally, Kohn traced the origin of Article 11 to the 'socialistic postulates' of the Democratic Programme of the First Dáil of 1919.[40] While he regarded Article 11 as 'a very incomplete realisation' of the Democratic Programme, he still felt its terms were 'wide enough to enable a progressive nationalisation of the natural resources of the country to be effected.'[41] However, as Murray has observed, such a path was not taken and 'successive governments would instead reproduce classic free market norms and practices.'[42] Mansergh, who was critical of Article 11, calling it 'alien to individualist democracy', identified a number of different ways it could be understood, including as envisaging a State duty 'to prevent a use of the property inconsistent with the public interest' or the idea of property being 'held in trust for the public welfare.'[43]

Despite the fact that the framers of Article 11 seem to have conceived of it in economic rather than ecological terms, it is possible to also interpret its provisions with a concern for the latter. The subject matter of Article 11—although treated as property—clearly addresses the constituent elements of the natural environment: land, water, minerals, air, and all 'natural resources'. It also places a duty to administer and control, through legislation, on the Oireachtas, a duty which Kohn and Mansergh say could be read as having to be carried out for the benefit of the People.[44] It is in the combination of these components that this chapter suggests lies a state

[37] ibid.

[38] ibid.

[39] ibid.

[40] ibid 172.

[41] ibid 172, 174.

[42] Thomas Murray, *Contesting Economic and Social Rights in Ireland Constitution, State and Society, 1848–2016* (Cambridge: CUP, 2016) 103.

[43] Nicholas Mansergh, *The Irish Free State – Its Government and Politics* (London: George Allen and Unwin 1934) 52–53.

[44] ibid and Kohn (n 35).

duty of *environmental stewardship*. But to develop the justification for this argument in greater depth, it is necessary to consider the jurisprudence interpreting Article 11 which has primarily arisen in relation to Article 10 of the 1937 Constitution—the successor provision to Article 11.[45]

II – Judicial Interpretation of Article 11 (and Article 10)

It is worth setting out here what Article 10 of the 1937 Constitution says to showcase its similarity to Article 11:

> 1 All natural resources, including the air and all forms of potential energy ... belong to the State subject to all estates and interests therein for the time being lawfully vested in any person or body.
> 2 All land and all mines, minerals and waters ... belong to the State to the same extent as they then belonged to Saorstát Éireann.
> 3 Provision may be made by law for the management of the property which belongs to the State by virtue of this Article and for the control of the alienation, whether temporary or permanent, of that property.
> 4 Provision may also be made by law for the management of land, mines, minerals and waters acquired by the State after the coming into operation of this Constitution and for the control of the alienation, whether temporary or permanent, of the land, mines, minerals and waters so acquired.

Again, the subject matter of the article refers to aspects of the natural environment: air, water, minerals, and 'All natural resources'. It also stipulates that the 'management' of State property, i.e. natural resources and so forth, and the control of the alienation of same, is to be carried out pursuant to 'law'. In the *Barlow* case (discussed below), O'Donnell J describes Article 11 as being the '*inspiration*' for Article 10, and he calls Article 10 a reworking or a recast of Article 11 using very similar language '*which seems to make it clear that the breadth of the State property* [in Article 10] *is*

[45] Litigation during the lifespan of the 1922 Constitution—*(Moore) v. O'Hanrahan* [1927] IR 416 and *Moore v Attorney General* [1929] IR 191 (the 'Erne fishery case')—e.g. involving disputes about fishing rights, mentioned Article 11 in passing, but its provisions did not impact the outcome of those cases.

at least as wide as captured by Article 11 of the 1922 Constitution.'[46] He goes on to say that the 'breadth' of the language used in both Article 11 and Article 10 is '*striking*'—a fact which he considers must inform how they are interpreted—and that both provisions '*can be understood as inserting the new State in place of the sovereign as the default owner of property.*'[47]

With regard to the drafting of Article 10, Coffey has documented that it was a 'source of some concern' for the Department of Finance which was keen to avoid replicating what it saw as the deficiencies of Article 11, namely, vesting State control of assets in the Oireachtas rather than the Executive, and restricting the State's ability to alienate such assets.[48] Thus, a notable difference between Articles 11 and 10 is that while the former proscribed the alienation by the State of property held under its provisions, the latter now expressly permits it. However, the principle that the management of natural resources should be carried out pursuant to laws enacted by the Oireachtas—as opposed to purely at the Executive's discretion—appears to have remained (at least based on the interpretation afforded to Article 10 in *Barlow* (discussed below)). Coffey also records the involvement of Arthur Matheson (parliamentary draftsman) with the drafting of Article 10.[49] Matheson stated that 'the theory underlying the old Article 11 and the new Article 10 is that all natural resources should belong to the State and should be exploited for the benefit of the people and not for the private profit of individuals.'[50]

A number of themes characterise the limited body of case law interpreting Article 11 (and Article 10): the 'sovereignty' of the State, the meaning of 'natural resources', and the principle of accountable or responsible State management of land and other resources. The expression 'all royalties' in Article 10 (also found in Article 11) was used in *Webb v Ireland*[51] by a majority of the Supreme Court to fill the gap left by the rejection of the

[46] *Barlow v Minister for Agriculture* [2017] 2 IR 440 (SC) 469, 479. O'Donnell J (at 471) discusses the origins of Article 11 as well, mentioning the socialist influence of the Democratic Programme of the First Dáil, but also, drawing on Hogan's work, the influence of Catholic social theory of the early twentieth century which shared with socialism 'a scepticism of unbridled rights of private property.' See Gerard Hogan, *The Origins of the Irish Constitution, 1928–1941* (Dublin: Royal Irish Academy 2012).

[47] [2017] 2 IR 440 (SC) 479.

[48] Donal K. Coffey, *Drafting the Irish Constitution, 1935–1937: Transnational Influences in Interwar Europe* (London: Palgrave 2018) 79.

[49] ibid 25–26.

[50] 1 March 1937 (UCDA: P150/2397). See Coffey (n 48) 81.

[51] [1988] IR 353 (SC).

continued existence of the royal prerogative in *Byrne v Ireland*.[52] The concept of 'treasure trove' was thus effectively replaced with the idea that objects of historical significance, like the Derrynaflan hoard, with no established owner, belonged to the State as an innate aspect of its sovereignty, an idea apparently captured by the expression 'all royalties'.[53] This reasoning was later adopted by Kearns J in *Murphy v Wicklow County Council*[54] who found that the ownership of land by the State was a reflection of the State's sovereignty, resulting in his conclusion in that case that State land could not be compulsorily acquired. Prior to its use as an indicium of the State's sovereignty, Article 10 was (and continues to be) cited to show that the State is a juristic person, capable of owning and disposing of property.[55] The latter ability is a point on which Article 10 is 'conspicuously' different from Article 11.[56]

Although *Webb* suggested Article 10's scope could extend to man-made artefacts, the Supreme Court in *Dunne v Minister for the Environment* (a case concerning the power of the Oireachtas to legislate in respect of national monuments) seemed to disagree.[57] It stated—albeit without directly commenting on *Webb's* interpretation of 'royalties'—that Article 10 applied only to natural resources like the air, and rivers, rather than to artificial structures or objects.[58] In doing so, the Court in *Dunne* appeared to be preferring the dissenting view of Walsh and McCarthy JJ in *Webb*.[59] Walsh J had in that case traced the philosophical origins of Article 10 and Article 11 to the Democratic Programme of the First Dáil.[60] However, he noted that while the Democratic Programme spoke of the people of Ireland owning all of the nation's material possessions and resources, Articles 10 and 11 specifically referred to 'natural resources'.[61] Thus, while historical artefacts 'the product of human art and workmanship' might be

[52] [1972] IR 241 (SC).

[53] Gerard Hogan et al., *Kelly: The Irish Constitution*, 5th ed. (Dublin: Bloomsbury Professional, 2018) 221–223.

[54] (HC, 19 March 1999).

[55] See, e.g., *Comyn v Attorney General* [1950] IR 142 (SC), *Re Irish Employers Mutual Insurance Association Ltd* [1955] IR 176 (SC), *Byrne v Ireland* [1972] IR 241 (SC), and *O'Donoghue v AIB* [2017] IECA 177.

[56] Hogan et al. (n 53) 224.

[57] [2007] 1 IR 194 (SC).

[58] ibid 211.

[59] Hogan et al. (n 53) 223.

[60] [1988] IR 353 (SC) 391.

[61] ibid 392.

described as 'national' resources, they could not be said to be 'natural' resources, and so were not covered by Article 10 (or by Article 11).[62] Walsh J also commented that even though they were mentioned separately, land and waters fell within the ambit of 'natural resources' [63]

As to whether 'natural resources' might encompass *flora* and *fauna*, the following might be said: traditionally, for the purposes of property law, 'all trees, shrubs, bushes, hedges and flowering plants whether cultivated or wild' are treated as part of the land on which they are growing, and all animals of a 'wild nature' (*ferae naturae*) were regarded as *nullius in bonis* or the property of no one as long as they remain free.[64] This would suggest, e.g. that the great oak forests of Killarney National Park—being trees on State land and therefore part of that land—are 'natural resources' within the meaning of Article 10, but iconic animal species living in the wild, such as red deer, are not. However, in a couple of cases, it has been held that certain animal species at least do constitute 'natural resources' under Article 10. In *McArdle v Minister for Communications*—a dispute over ministerial restrictions on eel fishing in the Shannon basin—Herbert J suggested that eels were a natural resource protected by Article 10 of the Constitution, and in *Barlow v Minister for Agriculture* it was held that mussel seed was a natural resource.[65] The *Barlow* and *McArdle* cases are of central importance to the core argument of this chapter, i.e. that Article 11 (and Article 10) can be read as creating a State duty of responsible management of natural resources, or framed another way, a duty of environmental stewardship. Accordingly, they will both now be considered in detail, starting with *Barlow*.[66]

Barlow concerned whether mussel seed was a 'natural resource', and if so, whether the authorisation of its harvesting from Irish territorial waters by Northern Irish registered fishing vessels, constituted the 'management' of a natural resource. The plaintiffs claimed that the plain meaning of the

[62] ibid. Walsh and McCarthy JJ located the right of the State to dominion over man-made objects forming part of the country's national heritage in the declaration that the State is 'sovereign' in Article 5 of Bunreacht na hÉireann.

[63] [1988] IR 353 (SC) 392.

[64] Andrew Lyall, *Land Law in Ireland* 3rd ed. (Dublin: Round Hall, 2010) 43–44.

[65] Also, in *Lough Swilly Shellfish Growers Cooperative Society Ltd v Bradley* [2010] IEHC 281 the Attorney General invoked Article 10 in a fisheries dispute suggesting that the State was of the view that fisheries are a natural resource for the purposes of Article 10.

[66] For an overview of the issues in *Barlow v Minister for Agriculture* [2017] 2 IR 440, see Estelle Feldman, "Constitutional Law," *Annual Review of Irish Law* 1, no. 1 (2016): 111.

term 'natural resources' encompassed mussel seed which was fished for and that it was regarded as such in a number of official publications. They also claimed, as a result, that mussel seed was the property of the State and that accordingly granting permission to harvest it was the management, control or even alienation of a natural resource which Article 10.3 stipulated had to be provided for by law, i.e. an Act of the Oireachtas. The defendants argued, *inter alia*, that mussel seed could not be treated as a natural resource and therefore State property under Article 10 because it was long-established that wild animals, including fish were *nullius in bonis*, or the property of no one. They argued further that finding mussel seed to be State property was inconsistent with ancient public fishing rights in territorial waters and that in any event the grant of permission to fish for mussel seed could not be regarded as an 'alienation' of property by the State. The plaintiffs contended in response that mussels should not be treated as *nullius in bonis* like other wild animals which roamed freely because they were largely sedentary creatures which attached themselves to rocks or the seabed and were therefore more analogous to seaweed, held not to be *nullius in bonis* in *Brew v. Haren*[67] they argued. In any event, they also argued that the principle of *nullius in bonis* had not survived the coming into effect of the 'clear terms' of Article 11 of the Free State Constitution or Article 10 of the 1937 Constitution which intended to secure the ownership of natural resources by the State on behalf of the People.

The High Court decided in favour of the State defendants.[68] Birmingham J held that while many wild animals, including marine species were valuable—whether as sources of food or tourism—it could not be said that the State actually owned them; rather they were capable of being managed by the State. As such mussel seed were found to be *nullius in bonis* and were not therefore a natural resource and the property of the State under Article 10. Moreover, Birmingham J was not convinced that the drafters or adopters of either the 1922 or 1937 Constitutions would have understood those Constitutions as making such far-reaching changes as abolishing the principle of *nullius in bonis* in respect of wild animals, or interfering with long-held and valuable public rights of fishing, by making marine species like mussel seed the property of the State.

[67] (1877) 11 I.R.C.L. 198.

[68] *Barlow v Minister for Agriculture* [2014] IEHC 471.

However, O'Donnell J, for a unanimous Supreme Court, overturned the High Court, and held that mussel seed (or the water from which it was harvested, or the capacity to extract it) could be regarded as a 'natural resource' and therefore State property under Article 10.1 of the Constitution. He highlighted the broad scope of the language used in Article 10—pointing to the repeated use of the word 'all' in conjunction with the extensive subject matter of the Article—something which was reinforced by the Irish language text—'Gach ábhar maoine nádúrtha' –literally meaning 'every natural source of wealth'.[69] And he concluded, that in accordance with the ordinary, everyday meaning of the wording in Article 10, that the harvesting of mussels from the sea could readily be understood as the management or control, of a natural resource. In relation to the defendants' arguments concerning the principle of *nullius in bonis* in respect of wild animals and related public fishing rights, O'Donnell J observed that they were not necessarily incompatible with a system of residual State ownership of natural resources, including fishing in territorial waters. He reasoned that the 1922 Constitution had endeavoured at every opportunity to replace the Crown as sovereign with the People and this included replacing the King as the ultimate default owner of all property with the State. As such, if the '*right of the sovereign prior to 1922 was not considered to be incompatible with either the public right of fishing in seas or tidal waters, or with the legal status of fish and other wild animals as nullius in bonis*', there was no reason why the same could not be true of the State.[70] Moreover, if public fishery rights had originated in the Monarch's decision to maintain and protect them, there was no reason to conclude that either the 1922 or 1937 Constitutions—both premised on popular sovereignty wherein all power rested with the People—would be any less protective of those rights, he concluded. He also pointed out in this regard, that the State's ownership of natural resources was made expressly subject to existing rights, trusts, grants and so on by Article 10. Finally, O'Donnell J explained that the status of mussel seed as a natural resource could be analogised to that of the air or water, i.e. even though no one could be said to own the wind or the waves, the capacity to generate energy from them clearly fell within the ambit of Article 10. Similarly, '*either the territorial waters in which the fish may swim or the mussel seed may*

[69] *Barlow v Minister for Agriculture* [2017] 2 IR 440 (SC) 469.
[70] ibid 480.

be found, or the right to fish in those waters, can be understood in the same terms' he held.[71]

Having established that mussel seed was a natural resource, and that therefore authorising foreign vessels to harvest it constituted the 'management' or 'control' of a natural resource, O'Donnell J turned to the requirement by Article 10.3 that such management be carried out 'by law'. This requirement was '*not merely a formal procedural provision*' he said, and in constitutional terms it meant that '*if State property, in particular natural resources, is to be sold, leased, managed or regulated, then that decision should be made in public by representatives who are accountable to the People who can accordingly make their views known.*'[72]Accordingly, the *voisinage* agreement, pursuant to which the Government purported to permit Northern Irish vessels to fish in Irish territorial waters, being an '*executive permission*', was, in constitutional terms, '*the antithesis of public legislation contemplated by Article 10.3 of the Constitution.*'[73]

It is argued here that O'Donnell J's remarks—stressing the importance of the democratic accountability of the State to the People in connection with the management of natural resources (which is achieved by carrying out that management through primary legislation)—evince the idea that the State is ultimately answerable to the People for *how* it manages the nation's natural resources. It might be said that this accountability requirement —which is present as a mechanism for the People to pass judgement on *how* the State is managing natural resources—implies that the State has a responsibility to manage natural resources on behalf of, or in the best interests of, the People, i.e. a State duty of responsible management of natural resources.[74] In *McArdle*, (the eel fishery case mentioned above) Herbert J seemed to suggest the existence of such a duty.[75] In that case, in response to evidence of a worrying decline of eel stocks, the Minister for Communications (acting under powers granted to him by the Oireachtas)

[71] ibid 481.

[72] ibid 482–483.

[73] ibid 485.

[74] In *Murphy v Wicklow County Council* (HC, 19 March 1999) Kearns J opined that the provisions of Article 11 of the Free State Constitution and Article 10 of Bunreacht na hÉireann suggest that '*State lands enjoy a special position under our Constitution*' and that this was '*hardly surprising as various State authorities do, in effect, ultimately hold these lands on behalf of the people of Ireland*.' Emphasis added.

[75] *McArdle v Minister for Communications, Energy and Natural Resources* [2012] IEHC 118.

imposed restrictions on fishing for eel in the Shannon basin.[76] These restrictions were challenged by affected fishermen; however, their challenge was rejected by the High Court on the basis that:

> *the respondent [Minister] was reasonably and rationally entitled to decide that to permit any commercial eel fishing to continue in the Shannon River Basin area pending mandatory review ... would amount to a failure on his part to properly manage this valuable resource of the State for which, as Minister, he was responsible by virtue of Article 10 of the Constitution.*[77]

The authors of 'Kelly: The Irish Constitution' interpret Herbert J's judgment as suggesting that in light of his constitutional responsibility, 'it would have been impermissible for the Minister, once faced with evidence of serious declines in eel stocks, to simply maintain the *status quo* pending confirmation of the cause(s) of such decline', i.e. the Minister had a duty to act to safeguard a natural resource when it was under threat.[78]

It is submitted that there are strong parallels between the idea of a State duty of responsible management of 'natural resources'—being the constituent elements of the natural environment—posited here, and the concept of 'environmental stewardship'. Accordingly, the literature on this topic is explored next and the potential it holds to provide a lens or paradigm through which the State's role in Article 10 and Article 11 may be understood, is analysed.

III – A State Duty of 'Environmental Stewardship'?

The concept of environmental stewardship has generally been employed to describe 'a responsibility or duty to treat a valuable or scarce resource with a certain degree of care through the use of control or dominion,

[76] This is an example of the management of natural resources being carried out 'by law' as the Minister acted pursuant to powers conferred on him by the Oireachtas via section 9(1) of the Fisheries (Consolidation) Act 1949 (as amended). O'Donnell J (at 463) in *Barlow* stressed that '*the distinction between the exercise of executive power under the Constitution and the exercise of functions or powers (even by a member of the Executive) under legislative authority*' was an important one to maintain.

[77] *McArdle v Minister for Communications, Energy and Natural Resources* [2012] IEHC 118 [30].

[78] Hogan et al. (n 53) 221.

based on some values for the benefit of someone.'[79] An example would be the management of common natural resources—rivers, forestry, fish and so on—by the State on behalf of the community.[80] For Hunter, stewardship reimagines 'the proprietary relationship with land', by looking at land through an ecological and not just an economic lens.[81] Worrell and Appleby, suggest environmental stewardship is 'the responsible use (including conservation) of natural resources in a way that takes full and balanced account of the interests of society, future generations, and other species, as well as private needs, and accepts significant answerability to society.'[82]

Barritt has identified four elements which she says are 'universal features' of the concept of stewardship: the object of the responsibility or the 'what', the duty holder or the 'who', the beneficiaries or 'for whom', and the values advanced or 'for what'.[83] It is the object of the responsibility, she argues, that reveals the nature of the Stewardship.[84] In the context of Article 11 (and Article 10) the stewardship can be said to be environmental in nature as it pertains to aspects of the natural environment, such as land, waters, and other natural resources. Moreover, the concept of 'natural resources' (as a matter of Irish law) encompasses things like forests, and indeed the *flora* of other habitat types as part of 'land', and at least some animals, including fish species, like pearl mussel and eel. Just how extensive the concept of 'natural resources' will prove to be, and whether it might be interpreted to include the climate and whole ecosystems remains to be decided. It is perfectly possible in that regard to see how a stable climate and healthy, functioning, bio-diverse ecosystems—upon which human survival depends—could be conceived of—even from a purely

[79] Tore Henriksen, "The Arctic Ocean, Environmental Stewardship, and the Law of the Sea," *UC Irvine Law Review* 6, no. 1 (January 2016): 63.

[80] ibid.

[81] David Hunter, "An Ecological Perspective on Property: A Call for Judicial Protection of the Public's Interest in Environmentally Critical Resources," *Harvard Environmental Law Review* 12, no. 2 (1988): 311

[82] Richard Worrell and Michael C. Appleby, "Stewardship of Natural Resources: Definition, Ethical and Practical Aspects," *Journal of Agricultural and Environmental Ethics* 12, no. 3 (2000): 269.

[83] Emily Barritt, "Conceptualising Stewardship in Environmental Law," *Journal of Environmental Law* 26 (2014): 3.

[84] ibid.

economic, let alone ecological perspective—as 'natural resources'.[85] Afterall, O'Donnell J in *Barlow* emphasised the '*striking*' scope of the language in both Article 11 and 10, citing in particular the Irish language phrase 'Gach ábhar maoine nádúrtha', meaning 'every natural source of wealth'. Healthy bio-diverse ecosystems (themselves contingent on a stable climate) and the ecosystem services, created from the interaction of living organisms with their environment, that they provide—'purifying air and water, detoxifying and decomposing waste, renewing soil fertility, … mitigating droughts and floods, controlling pests, and pollinating vegetation'—underpin human society, including wealth generating economic activity.[86]

The duty-bearer under Article 11 (and Article 10) is the State, or more specifically, the legislative arm of the State, i.e. the Oireachtas, which is tasked with the 'administration' or 'management' of natural resources. Duties of stewardship are often imposed on private landowners by the State, however in this instance, it is the State as landowner, or steward, which bears the burden of responsible management. This is especially pronounced in relation to Article 11 which prohibited the State from alienating property that came within the terms of that provision.[87]

The question of 'for whom' or for whose benefit the State manages the country's natural resources is perhaps more challenging. While the State, or to be exact, the Oireachtas, is answerable to 'the People' as a higher authority through the democratic process for the legislation it adopts to manage and control natural resources—an idea very much consonant with the popular sovereignty 'leitmotif' of both the 1922 and 1937 Constitutions—there is also the issue of whether the State owes a duty to future generations or other species for how it manages natural resources, as some of the definitions of stewardship canvassed above indicate. Whether or not the State's duty of stewardship is owed to nature in its own right, it can clearly benefit from wise management of natural resources

[85] J. B. Ruhl and James Salzman, "The Law and Policy Beginnings of Ecosystem Services," *Journal of Land Use & Environmental Law* 22, no. 2 (Spring 2007): 157.

[86] ibid.

[87] Although Article 10 now permits the State to alienate property that comes within its ambit, Kearns J in *Murphy v Wicklow County Council* (HC, 19 March 1999) stressed that '*[s]trict controls on the disposal for any purpose of State lands is the leitmotif of the constitutional provisions*', something which was mirrored by the requirement in the State Property Act 1954 to have the consent of two Government ministers for '*virtually every transaction to do with State lands*'.

designed to tackle the climate and biodiversity crises. It is difficult, as the Constitution stands, with its anthropocentric focus, to attempt to derive rights of nature from its provisions. There is some judicial support for the proposition that the 1937 Constitution is cognisant of the need to safeguard the interests of future generations.[88] Though the issue is beyond the scope of this Chapter, it may be noted that, as with nature, future generations will benefit, in the form of a habitable planet, from responsible management of natural resources by the present generation.

The final of Barritt's elements of stewardship—the 'for what'—denotes the values which the stewardship seeks to promote.[89] This is perhaps the point on which Article 11 (and Article 10) is most silent. Neither article expressly endorses the maximisation of economic growth as its lodestar, for instance; equally, nor does either provision explicitly direct that an ecological approach to the State's property and natural resources should be embraced. As such the 'for what' of the State's duty of stewardship is largely open to interpretation. Adopting an originalist—specifically framers' intent—interpretive approach, there is evidence from the drafting history of Article 11 that it was designed to facilitate the exploitation of natural resources such as fisheries, 'natural harbours' for trade and commerce, land, and sources of energy to power industry, to secure the independent economic development of the new Free State.[90] This was the thrust of the paper on 'natural endowments'—except for a brief mention of the power of the legislature to regulate fishing rights to prevent overfishing,[91] suggesting at least some ecological awareness—presented to the drafting committee by CJ France which appears to have influenced the content of Article 11.[92] However, given the open-textured nature of the language in Article 11, including the rather abstract concept of 'natural resources', it is possible, through a dynamic or evolutive approach to constitutional interpretation to (re)conceive its provisions in light of modern science in ecological and not just economic terms. Doing so would involve a recognition of human interconnectedness with and dependence on natural resources like land and the consequent need to protect and responsibly manage such resources. Moreover, economic and ecological perspectives

[88] *Brownfield Restoration Ireland Ltd v Wicklow County Council* [2017] IEHC 456 [307].
[89] Barritt (n 83).
[90] Document 24 (n 14).
[91] ibid 11.
[92] Cahillane (n 13) 5, 22, and 88.

do not necessarily have to be treated as being at odds with one another. Even if 'natural resources' are only understood from an economic standpoint as natural sources of wealth, a stable climate and bio-diverse ecosystems and the ecosystem services they provide could still be regarded as 'natural resources' because they are economically valuable insofar as they are pre-requisites to any kind of functioning economy. It can be argued, therefore, whether the lens is economic, ecological, or both, that the responsible management or *stewardship* of 'natural resources' under Article 11 entails their preservation, protection, conservation, and restoration, and not just their exploitation.

Conclusion

This chapter has sought to argue that Article 11 of the 1922 Constitution of the Irish Free State and its successor provision (Article 10 of the 1937 Constitution), creates a State duty of environmental stewardship, i.e. an obligation to responsibly manage the country's natural resources on behalf of the People of Ireland. It has suggested that this duty is derivable from the requirement—common to Article 11 and Article 10—that the management of natural resources must be carried out pursuant to primary legislation, thereby establishing a mechanism of democratic accountability through which the State is answerable to the People for *how* it manages natural resources. This chapter has also contended that the concept of 'natural resources' is capable of encompassing a stable climate, and healthy, functioning, bio-diverse ecosystems, which are both valuable to the State and society from an economic perspective, and essential from an ecological perspective for human existence. As a result, it has been argued that the State's duty of environmental stewardship can entail the promotion of ecological integrity, environmental protection, and climate stability, and not just the economic exploitation of 'natural resources'.

References

Andrews, Richard N. L. *Managing the Environment, Managing Ourselves : A History of American Environmental Policy* 2nd ed. New Haven: Yale University Press, 2006.

Barritt, Emily. "Conceptualising Stewardship in Environmental Law." *Journal of Environmental Law* 26 (2014): 3.

Boyd, David R. *The Rights of Nature: A legal revolution that could save the world.* Canada: ECW Press, 2017.

Brennan, Ciara et al. "Rights of Nature in Ireland: Towards a Living Island of Rights-Bearing Communities" (Environmental Justice Network Ireland, Submission to the Citizens" Assembly on Biodiversity Loss, September 2022) Accessed November 28, 2022. https://ejni.net/rights-of-nature/

Cahillane, Laura. "An Insight into the Irish Free State Constitution." *American Journal of Legal History* 54, no. 1 (2014): 1.

Cahillane, Laura. *Drafting the Irish Free State Constitution*. Manchester: MUP, 2016.

Coffey, Donal K. *Drafting the Irish Constitution, 1935-1937: Transnational Influences in Interwar Europe*. London: Palgrave 2018.

Corcoran, Donal. "Public policy in an emerging state: The Irish Free State 1922-25." *Irish Journal of Public Policy* 1, no. 1(2009): 66.

Feldman, Estelle. "Constitutional Law." *Annual Review of Irish Law* 1, no. 1 (2016): 111.

Fields, Tina. "Trees in Early Irish Law and Lore: Respect for Other-Than-Human Life in Europe's History." *Ecopsychology* 12, no. 2 (2020): 131.

Gillespie, Alexander. *The Long Road to Sustainability: The Past, Present, and Future of International Environmental Law and Policy.* Oxford: OUP, 2017.

Henriksen, Tore. "The Arctic Ocean, Environmental Stewardship, and the Law of the Sea." *UC Irvine Law Review* 6, no. 1 (January 2016): 63.

Hogan, Gerard. *The Origins of the Irish Constitution, 1928-1941*. Dublin: Royal Irish Academy 2012.

Hogan, Gerard et al. *Kelly: The Irish Constitution* 5th ed. Dublin: Bloomsbury Professional, 2018.

Hunter, David. "An Ecological Perspective on Property: A Call for Judicial Protection of the Public's Interest in Environmentally Critical Resources." *Harvard Environmental Law Review* 12, no. 2 (1988): 311.

IPCC. *Climate Change 2021: The Physical Science Basis.* Cambridge: CUP, 2021.

Jager, Jill, and Timothy O'Riordan. "The History of Climate Change Science and Politics." In *The Politics of Climate Change*, edited by Jill Jager and Timothy O'Riordan, London: Routledge, 1996.

Johnston, Elva. "Brehon Law and Ireland's traditions looking to/after the Environment." (Address to the Citizens' Assembly on Biodiversity Loss, 15 October 2022) Accessed November 28, 2022. https://www.youtube.com/watch?v=L08uT4fD5y4

Knox, John H., and Ramin Pejan. *The Human Right to a Healthy Environment.* Cambridge: CUP, 2018.

Kohn, Leo. *The Constitution of the Irish Free State*. London: George Allen & Unwin Ltd, 1932.

Lyall, Andrew. *Land Law in Ireland* 3rd ed. Dublin: Round Hall, 2010.

Mansergh, Nicholas. *The Irish Free State – Its Government and Politics.* London: George Allen and Unwin 1934.

McNeill, John. *Something New Under the Sun: An Environmental History of the Twentieth Century*. London: Allen Lane 2000.

Mohr, Thomas. "Law in a Gaelic Utopia: Perceptions of Brehon Law in Nineteenth and early Twentieth Century Ireland." In *Remembering and Forgetting: Yearbook of Young Legal History*, edited by Oliver Brupbacher et al, Martin Meidenbauer, 2007.

Murray, Thomas. "Socio-Economic Rights Versus Social Revolution? Constitution Making in Germany, Mexico and Ireland, 1917–1923." *Social & Legal Studies* 24, no. 4 (2015): 498.

Murray, Thomas. *Contesting Economic and Social Rights in Ireland Constitution, State and Society, 1848–2016*. Cambridge: CUP, 2016.

Ruhl, J. B. and James Salzman. "The Law and Policy Beginnings of Ecosystem Services." *Journal of Land Use & Environmental Law* 22, no. 2 (Spring 2007): 157.

Worrell, Richard, and Michael C. Appleby, "Stewardship of Natural Resources: Definition, Ethical and Practical Aspects." *Journal of Agricultural and Environmental Ethics* 12, no. 3 (2000): 269.

CHAPTER 10

The 1922 Constitution as a Failed Attempt to Break with Westminster Tradition

David Kenny

Introduction

Ireland under the 1937 Constitution has, in very many respects, a Westminster parliamentary model and its system of executive and parliamentary relations,[1] including its executive dominance and general sidelining of parliament.[2] While augmented in many respects—not least with

[1] No lesser commentator on British political arrangements than Meg Russell has queried if the term Westminster Model or Westminster systems is useful, and represents a coherent category. Meg Russell and Ruxandra Serban 'The Muddle of the 'Westminster Model': A Concept Stretched Beyond Repair' (2021) 56(4) *Government and Opposition* 744. I therefore use the term with some trepidation, and accept that it can be used to encompass a great many things, but I still think it is useful. See Matthew Flinders et al.,'"Stretched But Not Snapped": A Response to Russell and Serban on Retiring the "Westminster Model"' (2022) 57(2) *Government and Opposition* 353.

[2] See Conor Casey and David Kenny, 'The Resilience of Executive Dominance in Westminster Systems: Ireland 2016–2019' (2021) *Public Law* 355.

D. Kenny (✉)
Trinity College Dublin, Dublin, Ireland
e-mail: david.kenny@tcd.ie

L. Cahillane, D. K. Coffey (eds.), *The Centenary of the Irish Free State Constitution*, Palgrave Modern Legal History,
https://doi.org/10.1007/978-3-031-46181-1_10

a codified constitution and strong form judicial review of legislation—the operation of the parliament and the executive is very much in the manner of its London counterpart. This decision to cleave closely to Westminster practice is not only attributable to the drafters of the 1937 Constitution; very few aspects of the State's political institutions were radically changed in 1937, and much was carried over from its 1922 predecessor.

As such, the dominant narrative in Irish political and constitutional discourse is that the drafting of the 1922 Constitution involved a decision to stick closely to Westminster practice, and this was simply carried over in 1937.[3] This, however, is not the full story. While it is true that by the time of the drafting of 1937 Constitution, parliamentary practice under the 1922 Constitution very closely resembled Westminster practice, and that was carried over, the intention behind the 1922 Constitution was very different. Cahillane, Kissane and others have shown various different ways in which narratives about the 1922 Constitution and its drafting were oversimplified, or even incorrect.[4] The understanding of 1922 as simply continuing the Westminster tradition is an example of this.

When we think of the 1922 Constitution, some of its most interesting and important aspects are often overlooked. These are its unusual and inventive elements, its various facets and features that are unique to it. In big ways and small, the Constitution of 1922 was an experiment, as all life is an experiment. These elements generally did not thrive in practice, and the general malaise that beset the Constitution in its short history distracts from these features. But the creative and inventive spirit that animates the 1922 Constitution is, I think, one of its very best features.

One such element is its attempt to depart from the Westminster model of governance and parliamentary/executive relations. In its design, the

[3] Kissane highlights that the nuances of Irish constitutional tradition were 'completely obscured' by dominant constitutional history. Bill Kissane, 'The Constitutional Revolution That Never Was: Democratic Radicalism and the Sinn Féin Movement' (2009) 104 *Radical History Review* 77, 97, citing *inter alios,* Chubb's claim that Irish political thinking was 'wholly expressed in British categories'. See Basil Chubb, *The Government and Politics of Ireland*, 3rd ed. (Harlow, UK: Pearson, 1992).

[4] See Laura Cahillane, *Drafting the Free State Constitution* (Manchester: Manchester University Press, 2016); Kissane (n 3).

1922 Constitution envisaged a fairly radical departure from the Westminster tradition that never in fact took place. It was, as Kissane terms it, a revolution that never was.[5] Looking this attempted departure, and why it failed so completely, casts important light on the 1922 Constitution, gives us a new sense of its legacy, and gives us a different idea of what was inherited from it in 1937. In Part I, I discuss the 1922 Constitution and what it says about the model of parliamentary-executive relations, and how this fitted with Irish political thought at this time, including its suspicion of political parties and dedication to popular sovereignty. In Part II, I highlight the various experimental features that were supposed to effect a significant departure from the Westminster model: PRSTV, the Seanad, direct democracy, vocational councils, and external ministers. These, collectively, were to ensure the Irish Free State's Oireachtas did not succumb to the malaise that was seen to beset Westminster. In Part III, I discuss why these experiments failed so completely, and why it was probably inevitable that they would fail, and the ambitions of the drafters could not have been achieved.

Part I: The 1922 Constitution's Parliamentary Model and Irish Political Thought

The drafting of the Constitution was obviously done in the shadow of the Treaty that controlled and limited it, and would ultimately purport to restrict its future amendment. But the Treaty said only a small amount on the parliamentary model Ireland adopted. Article 1 of the Treaty said that Ireland's constitutional status would be the same as the Dominions 'with a Parliament having powers to make laws for the peace, order and good government of Ireland and an Executive responsible to that Parliament, and shall be styled and known as the Irish Free State'. While this is scant instruction, it does suggest something like a Westminster-style parliamentary system, as it requires an executive responsible to parliament. It does not specify any details of this relationship, so it hard to say that the Treaty dictates very much beyond this basic structure. But it would have prevented a very radical departure towards a presidential model or some vastly different conception of how the powers of state should be divided.

[5] Kissane (n 3). It should be noted that Bill Kissane, AJ Ward, and Laura Cahillane have all treated of this history in a much fuller way in pieces cited herein.

The 1922 Constitution's provisions on the Oireachtas, the parliament of the Free State, were fairly succinct. Article 12 read:

> A Legislature is hereby created, to be known as the Oireachtas. It shall consist of the King and two Houses, the Chamber of Deputies (otherwise called and herein generally referred to as "Dáil Éireann") and the Senate (otherwise called and herein generally referred to as "Seanad Éireann"). The sole and exclusive power of making laws for the peace, order and good government of the Irish Free State (Saorstát Éireann) is vested in the Oireachtas.

Further Articles dictated the Dáil's location;[6] eligibility for membership and for the electorate;[7] privilege in utterance and in coming to and from the Houses;[8] autonomy of the Houses to make rules and procedures;[9] basic rules for votes;[10] method of dissolution;[11] and a few other ancillary matters. It also famously set out the oath that members were to take.[12] There were similar provisions for the Seanad. These were in most cases formulations and formalisations of conventional practices or standing orders of Westminster. However, many elements of Westminster practice and convention were not formalised in these rules; they are far from comprehensive.

The powers of the executive, and its relationship to parliament, were set out in fairly scant detail. Responsibility of the executive to the Dáil was provided for,[13] along with appointment procedures[14] and collective responsibility for ministers in the executive council.[15] There was, however, little detail on what the powers of the executive were; how its functions were to be carried out; and what its relationship to the parliament would be in practice. It says nothing about political parties or party discipline in parliament. It seems like a reasonable inference that the expectation was these elements would follow Westminster, including strict party discipline

[6] Article 13, Constitution of the Irish Free State. See generally Leo Kohn, *The Constitution of the Irish Free State* (Allen & Unwin, 1932).

[7] Articles 14, 15, and 16, Constitution of the Irish Free State.

[8] Articles 18 and 19, Constitution of the Irish Free State.

[9] Articles 20, 21, and 23, Constitution of the Irish Free State.

[10] Article 22, Constitution of the Irish Free State.

[11] Article 24, Constitution of the Irish Free State.

[12] Article 17, Constitution of the Irish Free State.

[13] Article 51, Constitution of the Irish Free State.

[14] Article 53, Constitution of the Irish Free State.

[15] Article 54, Constitution of the Irish Free State.

and dominance of the legislature by cabinet leading to *de facto* executive governance. This is, in fact, largely what developed in practice as well.

It would have been understandable if—as the dominant narrative about the 1922 Constitution suggests—the drafters of the Constitution simply defaulted to the Westminster tradition rather than trying to reinvent the wheel. The pressures the drafting Committee were under were very substantial, with their time short and the matters tasked to them numerous. One could hardly blame the members of the committee if they did not feel they had the luxury of rethinking parliamentary governance and opted instead to stick closely to what they were familiar with. It is easy to see how this became a popular narrative, given the seemingly Westminster-style institutional design, and the fact, in practice, these institutions took on a Westminster mode of operation.

But if the drafters had intended this, it would have been a surprising departure from some of the ideological underpinnings of the Irish independence movement. This movement was deeply critical of the Westminster model of governance. This model was already under pressure in the UK and elsewhere, with the House of Lords Veto Crisis still in recent memory. Kissane argues at length that the Irish nationalist movement had been 'at the forefront of an emerging critique of the Westminster model' leading up to 1916.[16] The core of this critique, from the Irish nationalist point of view, was that Westminster was blighted by corruption, and that Parliament was improperly side-lined in London in favour of improper dominance by the executive. Irish nationalists identified the underlying problem as the dominance of political parties.[17] They were far from alone in this: it was a common charge by even the late 1890s that it was the parliamentary parties, not the parliament itself, that held the real power in Westminster.[18] Irish nationalist thought held that it was the evils of party caused Westminster's rigidity; excessive discipline and the side-lining of individual representatives; reward for loyal service to government and party; and the

[16] See Kissane (n 3) 77.

[17] Cahillane (n 4) 120 et seq; Kissane (n 3) 77 et seq. There was a certain irony in this, since the Irish Parliamentary Party had, at one point, practiced extremely strict party discipline. See Martin O'Donoghue, *The Legacy of the Irish Parliamentary Party in Independent Ireland, 1922–1949* (Oxford University Press, 2020).

[18] AJ Ward 'Challenging the British Constitution: The Irish Free State Constitution and the External Minister' (1990) 9(1) *Parliamentary History* 116, 117.

overall diminution of parliament and aggrandisement of the executive.[19] A core tenet of Irish nationalist political thought in the early 1920s was to 'avoid party domination'.[20]

Another major aspect of Irish nationalist constitutional thought was popular sovereignty.[21] The people, not a parliament or a king, were sovereign, and this was the core foundational principle undergirding the revolutionary and post-revolutionary period. This was not just an abstract commitment; it had tangible, real-world instantiations. As discussed below, direct democracy was one aspect of this. But the idea went further: the people had to be involved in a deep way in governance, and this would mean changing the way that parliament functioned, as Westminster did not embody this. Indeed, Westminster seemed against it: as Kissane notes, for Irish nationalist thought, '[a]s in classic republican theory, the virtue of a state based on popular sovereignty was contrasted to the existing parliamentary system.'[22] Popular sovereignty was seen as a radical and subversive idea,[23] and Irish politicians did not just want to pay lip service to this value, but to 'think of institutions to give expression to it'.[24]

Therefore, if the dominant narrative was correct, and the 1922 Constitution had just embraced the Westminster system, this would have disregarded two central tenets of Irish nationalist thought of the era—the suspicion of parties and popular sovereignty—and their attendant rejection of the Westminster norm. The fact that the 1922 Constitution 'substantially accepted'[25] the British model is thus surprising, and Farrell famously called it one of the paradoxes of Irish politics.[26] But this

[19] See Andrew Malone, 'Party Government in the Irish Free State' (1929) 44(3) Political Science Quarterly 363; Kissane (n 3) 77; Cahillane (n 4) 120–153; Laura Cahillane, 'Anti-Party Politics in the Irish Free State Constitution' (2012) 35 Dublin University Law Journal 34.

[20] Malone (n 19) 364.

[21] Kissane (n 3) 77, 88.

[22] Ibid 89.

[23] Ibid 89–90.

[24] Ibid.

[25] Ward (n 18) 117.

[26] Brian Farrell, "The Paradox of Irish Politics," in Farrell (ed.) *The Irish Parliamentary Tradition* (Gill and MacMillan, 1973).

acceptance was in fact highly qualified.[27] As Cahillane puts it, the constitutional drafters wanted to conduct 'experiments which attempted to bring politics closer to the people'.[28] In short, the 1922 Constitution's oft-overlooked experimental elements envisaged a quite stark break with the Westminster tradition, attempting to offset the executive dominance and party dominance of the Westminster model in favour of empowering parliament and the people. This was the clear aspiration, even if it was not the reality.

Part II: Experimental Elements of the 1922 Constitution

There were several elements of the 1922 Constitution that represented a break with the Westminster model.[29] The most obvious of these is judicial review of legislation for rights compliance. The story of how this revolution in principle was not a revolution in practice—epitomised by *State (Ryan) v Lennon*[30] but far from confined to that case[31]—is well known and it is not necessary to dwell on it here. But even if this feature of the Constitution had flourished in the manner that its 1937 successor did, this would probably not have had a very significant effect on the parliamentary-executive relationship. Judicial review of this sort is focused primarily on the *fruits* of the legislative and governance processes rather than their process. Even when process can be reviewed, as noted above the 1922 Constitution had few provisions about legislative-executive relations that

[27] Ward (n 18) 117. Farrell stresses that the 1922 Constitution 'sought to create a more direct and active role for the people in public affairs and tried to erect some safeguards against executive dominance. Brian Farrell, 'The First Dáil and After' in Farrell (ed.) *The Irish Parliamentary Tradition* (Gill and MacMillan, 1973) 122.

[28] Cahillane (n 4) 81.

[29] There is an extent to which, as Ward suggests, the 1922 Constitution was the first attempt to articulate the British cabinet model in a codified constitution; in the other dominions, the crown was the executive, and the de facto executive was regulated almost entirely by convention. Ward (n 18) 116. Kissane (n 3) makes a similar assessment.

[30] [1935] I.R. 170; see Gerard Hogan, 'A Desert Island Case set in the Silver Sea: *The State (Ryan) v. Lennon*' in O'Dell (ed.), *Leading Cases of the Twentieth Century* (Sweet & Maxwell, 2000).

[31] See Gerard Hogan, Gerry Whyte, David Kenny, Rachael Walsh, *Kelly: The Irish Constitution* (Bloomsbury Professional, 2018) [1.1.02]-[1.1.08]; Gerard Hogan, The Origins of the Irish Constitution 1928–1941 (RIA, 2012), 1–20.

could have been enforced by the courts. Other features of the Constitution, however, were designed to radically alter and augment the Westminster model.

A. Proportional Representation by Single Transferable Vote

A significant departure from Westminster elections at the time was the move from First Past the Post to Proportional Reputation by Single Transferable Vote (PRSTV). In changing the electoral dynamics very significantly, and making it far more possible for smaller parties or independent candidates to be elected to the Dáil, this had clear potential to change executive-parliamentary relations in a major way. This was not the primary purpose of introducing this system; the drive behind STV related to ensuring minority representation in parliament. Alongside the structure of the Seanad, it was hoped that this structural measure would ensure enough parliamentary representation for the southern Protestant community.[32] However, a secondary or ancillary purpose of this approach was—alongside other measures discussed below—to lessen the centrality of political parties. Preventing the dominance of parties, it was thought, would solve many of Westminster's most grievous faults, and the architects of the Free State Constitution genuinely (if perhaps naively) believed that they could avoid parties playing anything like the role that they did in London.[33]

PRSTV was expected to produce a parliament of many parties or independent representatives,[34] which would mean that independent judgement, compromise, negotiation, and coalition building would have to be a feature of Free State politics. This electoral system, the drafters believed, was incompatible with the British model of parliamentary governance, and would produce very different results.[35] This did not prove to be the case, however. The 1923 election produced two major parties—Cumann na nGaedheal and the Republican Party—that took 70% of the seats, 107 of 153. Two parties—the Farmers' Party and the Labour Party—received about 9% of the vote each. Though their 41% of seat share did not give Cumann na nGaedheal an absolute majority, de Valera's Republican Party refusing to take their seats allowed that party to govern without coalition.

[32] Cahillane (n 4) 124.
[33] See Ward (n 18) 118.
[34] Cahillane (n 4) 128.
[35] Ibid 130.

By 1932, the two main parties took more than 84% of the vote, though the Labour party's small number of seats were essential to electing several subsequent Fianna Fáil governments. It cannot be said, therefore, that PRSTV, in the early years of the State, led to the flourishing of a multi-party system that had been envisaged.

B. The Seanad

The Seanad of the Irish Free State has been treated of at length elsewhere,[36] so I will not dwell on it here. It suffices to say that the Seanad had an interesting set of features that could have potentially offset the tendency for executive and party dominance in Westminster. Its unusual electoral process—with senators elected for twelve years from a single, nationwide constituency, with elections for a portion of the house staggered every three years—attempted to provide a differently constituted upper house.[37] In theory, this should have returned representatives very different to the Dáil, so that even if the lower house were dominated by the executive, the Seanad could have provided a forum for significant opposition and independent thought and comment. A part of this was the Seanad had a significant potential role in the 1922 Constitution's direct democratic procedures which will be discussed below.[38] This obviously represented a potentially major change in parliamentary dynamics.

In the end, the Seanad did not make any significant impact on the reality of executive dominance. As with so much of the 1922 Constitution, it was subject to a great many constitutional amendments in its short lifespan. The electoral system proved difficult from its first use; its direct election system was replaced by an indirect electoral system; the terms of senators were reduced; its direct democratic elements were never used; and it was finally abolished in 1936. Even within its lifespan, while at first it did represent a less party-dominated house, party politics gradually took it over.[39]

[36] Donal O'Sullivan, *The Irish Free State and its Senate* (Faber, 1940).

[37] Cahillane (n 4) 145; O'Sullivan (n 36) 94–95.

[38] The Seanad could, with a three-fifths majority, trigger a binding referendum on a contested Bill.

[39] Cahillane (n 4) 150–151; Bjørn Sircar and Indraneel Hoyland, 'Get The Party Started: Development of Political Party Legislative Dynamics in the Irish Free State Seanad (1922–36)' (2010) 16(1) Party Politics 89; Nicholas Mansergh, *The Irish Free State: Its Government and Politics* (Allan & Unwin, 1934); Tom Garvin *The Irish Senate* (IPA, 1969) 9.

C. Direct Democracy

The direct democratic elements of the 1922 Constitution are one of its better known experimental features, and are discussed further elsewhere in this volume.[40] These elements were an instantiation of the Constitution's commitment to popular sovereignty.[41] Kissane stresses that it is a mistake to think that this idea 'had no radical potential.'[42] It envisaged a potentially significant role for the people, through a referendum process, to intervene in governance in a way that was not a core part of Westminster tradition. This was in addition to popular involvement in constitutional change in Article 50.

Article 47 provided that any Bill, other than a Money Bill or emergency bill, could be suspended for 90 days at the request of two fifths of the Dáil, or a majority of the Seanad. Within this 90 day period, if three fifths of the Seanad requested it or it was supported by a petition signed by one twentieth of registered voters, a referendum on the Bill would be held, and a majority of voters would determine if it should enter into force or be nullified. Article 48 provided for popular initiative referendums for laws or constitutional changes. It envisaged[43] 50,000 voters being able to petition for such an initiative, and either the initiative being acted upon or the matter being put to referendum for resolution.

Both of these procedures were very significant in principle. The former allowed the Seanad, or a minority in the Dáil, to delay legislation coming into force, and ultimately, with enough support, to have the people determine this question. There is no equivalent to this in the Westminster model, and it could have resulted in a very different legislative dynamic in the Oireachtas. Similarly, the idea of a semi-binding petition system, with unanswered petitions put to referendum, was a huge departure from Westminster practice. It empowered the people to a very great degree, and created a significant alternative power of legislative initiative, something

[40] See for example, William Quill, Chap. 13 in this volume.

[41] See Kissane (n 3) 89; Cahillane (n 4) 112; Laura Cahillane, 'The Origins of Popular Sovereignty in Ireland: Theory and Reality' in Maria Cahill, Colm Ó Cinnéide, Seán Ó Conaill, & Conor O'Mahony, *Constitutional Change and Popular Sovereignty* (Routledge, 2021).

[42] Kissane (n 3) 90.

[43] This was somewhat complicated, as a law was necessary to put the scheme into place, but the Constitution set out the 50,000 signature threshold that had to be in the law, and included a mechanism for triggering the enactment of such a law by petition with 75,000 signatures.

that in practice is controlled by the executive in Westminster systems. One could imagine this resulting in a very significantly different legislative process than the one seen in London. As Kissane puts it, the provisions 'give the people a veto on unjust legislation and allowed the public to initiate a referendum on issues ignored by the parliamentary elite.'[44]

It is well known that the referendum process for constitutional change never took hold because of the controversial use of—and then extension of—8 years of amendment of the Constitution by ordinary legislation.[45] The other uses of referendums were no more successful. The fact that so much legislation was emergency legislation—and thus exempt from referendum—was part of this.[46] The provisions lay dormant for years. An attempt was made to use Article 47 in respect of the Electoral (Amendment) (No. 2) Act 1927, but the required number of signatures to trigger a referendum was not obtained.[47] In 1928, Fianna Fáil, in opposition, attempted to use the initiative procedure in Article 48 to initiate a vote on removal of the parliamentary oath, and secured the requisite number of signatures.[48] While the proper procedure to follow in a case such as this was still being debated, the government introduced a constitutional amendment removing Article 47 and 48 entirely. Defending this move, the government said these procedures undermined representative government and could be used in an obstructionist manner.[49] Thus ended the 1922 Constitution's experiment in direct democracy, and its revolutionary potential was never fulfilled.

D. Functional/Vocational Councils

Another experimental element of the 1922 Constitution that is often overlooked is the provision, in Article 45, that allowed the setting up of functional or vocational councils.[50] These were envisaged as being legislative-adjacent and policy-relevant councils for various social and

[44] Kissane (n 3) 89.
[45] See Hogan (n 31).
[46] Cahillane (n 4) 114–5.
[47] Ibid 115.
[48] Ibid 117.
[49] Ibid 118.
[50] Functional and vocational representation was also considered in the context of design of the electoral system and the executive. See Cahillane (n 4) 26.

economic interests.[51] The exacts powers and duties of such councils was to be determined by law, and the Constitution was light on the detail of how they would work. The idea was again to make popular sovereignty real; to empower the people in politics and policymaking; to change executive governance and party dominance.[52] It was seen as another tool by which party politics could be countered.[53] This was also linked to the external ministers scheme, discussed below, as Article 56 of the Constitution envisaged that such ministers might be drawn from these councils or recommended by them.[54] This mechanism could ensure that government did not lose touch with the people.[55]

Nothing came of these provisions; they were never activated. There were few existing organisations that could take on these roles, and preparation was needed for them to take a place in national life.[56] It was perhaps not a priority in the relatively short life of the Free State to set up and maintain a complex system of this sort. Interest in vocationalism generally remained for some time, as seen in later experiments in vocationalism in the 1937 Constitution which had provisions for similar councils and a Seanad electoral system based on vocationalism.[57] However, within a decade of the 1937 Constitution's enactment, it was clear that vocationalism was not going to be developed in Ireland.[58]

[51] Ibid 138. One of the drafters, Darrell Figgis, had in earlier work proposed that functional or vocational representation could be used as a way to solve some of the weaknesses or parliaments and achieve better representation. See Darrell Figgis, *The Gaelic State in the Past and Future* (Maunsel, 1917).

[52] Ward (n 18) 131.

[53] Cahillane (n 4) 138 et seq.

[54] See Ward (n 18) 121.

[55] Cahillane (n 4) 140

[56] Ibid 142.

[57] On the Seanad's composition, see David Kenny, 'The Failed Referendum to Abolish the Ireland's Senate: Rejecting Unicameralism in a Small and Relatively Homogenous Country' in Albert, Baraggia, Fasone (eds.), *Constitutional Reform of National Legislatures Bicameralism under Pressure* (Edward Elgar, 2019) 163.

[58] See Donal K. Coffey, '"The union makes us strong": National Union of Railwaymen v Sullivan and the demise of vocationalism in Ireland' in Cahillane, Gallen and Hickey (eds.), *Judges, Politics, and the Irish Constitution* (Manchester University Press, 2017).

E. External Ministers

The most important feature of the 1922 Constitution, from the point of view of breaking from the Westminster model, was the external ministers scheme. This—rather than any change to the legislature—was the means by which the drafters hoped to radically depart from this model and its party domination. Cahillane calls it the 'principal weapon in the fight against party politics'.[59] The indirectness of this approach to break from Westminster—combined with the swift failure of the experiment—means its radical nature is often overlooked.

The motivations behind the external minister scheme, which was inspired by the Swiss model,[60] were several. One early hope was that it could allow representation of anti-treaty figures as ministers if they could be external to the parliament and thus not take the oath. However, the British government made it clear that every minister would have to take the oath, and so this part of the plan fell away.[61] It was, in any event, never the primary purpose of the scheme, which was to overcome the perceived evils of party and whip that stopped the parliament having real influence and authority by providing real parliamentary accountability. External ministers would be directly answerable to parliament, which would thus be empowered, and this would diminish the centralisation of power in the executive. They could also potentially be people with genuine expertise in certain technical areas that parliamentarians may not have.

Throughout the constitutional drafting process, there were various suggestions as to how this scheme could work.[62] Some proposals had the ministers as totally external to houses, with very long terms—up to 10 years—that would not be linked to the term or continuance in office of the government. Various proposals envisaged fully technocratic ministries, and direct exceptions to collective responsibility for external ministers. The core element that all these proposals had in common was the idea of direct responsibility of these ministers to parliament. The goal of this was to undermine party and executive dominance and bring ministerial government closer to the people.

The radical nature of this idea should not be underestimated. It was an attempt to rethink what it is to wield executive and administrative power;

[59] Cahillane (n 4) 127.
[60] Ibid 128.
[61] Ibid 128–9; Ward (n 18) 121–122.
[62] See Cahillane (n 4) 127 et seq.

to create entirely new lines of accountability between the executive and parliament; to substantially augment the relationship between parliament and (certain) ministers. It is a major deviation from the core ideas of collectively responsible government that undergird the Westminster model. Ward rightly called the scheme a 'direct attack' on the British model of government, and a 'contradiction' of that model.[63]

The British government was not enamoured of this plan, but other than insisting that all ministers would have to take the oath, they ultimately decided to acquiesce in it.[64] The Dáil, sitting as a constituent assembly, however, was sceptical of the proposal, perhaps not understanding its complexities. After a period of negotiation, a compromise (or compromised) version of the scheme was passed: a core executive of five to seven ministers would maintain responsibility for all departments they oversaw, and all resign in the event of a lack of confidence in the government. Another group of up to 7 (with a total number of ministers not to exceed 12) could oversee only the department assigned to them, and not be collectively responsible, but individually, directly responsible to the Dáil. They could be removed by a vote of the Dáil, which would not otherwise affect the government, and would serve the term of the House if not removed.[65]

This compromise was not necessarily particularly coherent; it did not fully encompass any of the proposals made along the way. As Kohn puts it, the ministerial scheme that resulted 'retained the complexity of the scheme of the Draft Constitution, but it lacked the inspiration.'[66] As a result, few external ministers were appointed; none were from outside the party of government[67]; and the government party apparently packed the Dáil committee to select their preferred candidates, making the nominal selection process a 'farce'.[68] It is thus unsurprising that the scheme failed to take off.

The flaws in the scheme ran even deeper, however. Underlying the whole idea of the scheme was a naïve view that there were certain 'technocratic' ministries that could be run by people with expertise without

[63] Ibid 116.

[64] Ibid 129.

[65] Articles 55 and 56, Constitution of the Irish Free State.

[66] Kohn (n 6) 133.

[67] Four were appointed after the 1923 election—in Post, Fisheries, Agriculture, and Local Government—and all were from the party of government. See Ward (n 18) 118.

[68] Ibid 126, quoting the Labour Party leader at that time.

political controversy, as opposed to core, political ministries.[69] While there is something of a spectrum in this respect, all ministries have control over some import aspect of public life that can (and often will) be the subject of political contest and controversy. This was graphically illustrated in the early years of the Free State, when significant controversy arose over whether or not agriculture and education should be technical ministries of this sort, with good arguments made for either independent oversight or core governmental accountability.[70] As Ward puts it, '[w]hat some regard as non-political, others see as nothing but.'[71] Moreover, all departments had to spend money, and so external ministers had to provide estimates that were then proposed to the House by the government, seemingly making the government collectively responsible for the decisions underlying these estimates.[72] This was a complication that had not been grappled with in the design of the scheme. By 1925, the idea had fallen out of favour, and it was removed by constitutional amendment in the years following.[73] It did not revolutionise the practice of parliamentary governance in Ireland.

Part III: A Failed Experiment

From the foregoing discussion, it is clear that the 1922 Constitution, far from simply replicating the structure and politics of Westminster, was a great experiment, and attempt to see how it might be changed. It is important to acknowledge the radical nature of this experiment in its political context. Speaking about the external ministers plan, Ward called it 'a much more ambitious experiment with the executive than any other self-governing colonies or dominions in the British Commonwealth had ever dared attempt' and stressed that it was a 'serious attempt' to do something different.[74] Kissane says that the 'immediate failure to convert these [radical] ideals into enduring structures does not mean that a constitutional

[69] Ibid 120, 125, 127.

[70] Ibid 124–125; Cahillane (n 4) 134–135. Some objected that education was not made external, as it should be technocratic. Agriculture was made external in the first government, which caused some dissatisfaction.

[71] Ward (n 18) 125.

[72] Kohn (n 6) 280. See discussion in Ward (n 18) 126.

[73] Cahillane (n 4) 137.

[74] Ward (n 18) 127.

revolution was never conceived of.'[75] This ambitious and even radical experiment was a failure, however, and it is interesting and important to consider why it 'not amount to a constitutional revolution'.[76] The lines of attack that were chosen in the 1922 Constitution to assail the Westminster system were not direct, but oblique. These ambitious but indirect approaches were not the most apt, though it might not have been readily foreseeable that this would be so, and there may have been little else that could have been done.

The first reason for failure was the need to cleave to certain aspects of the Westminster system by virtue of the Treaty, or British opposition to more radical measures in the 1922 Constitution, limiting what could be done. As noted above, the treaty did not dictate the specifics of the governmental and parliamentary model that the Free State was to have. However, it did clearly envisage the core of the Westminster model—a government responsible to parliament—would form the basis of governance in the Free State. Moreover, the British government were not at all laissez faire about the constitutional choices that were made by the drafters. There was close scrutiny of the document for compliance with the Treaty, and substantial negotiation and rewriting of the Constitution in response to the British government's concerns.[77] The British government insisted on the maintenance of a strong idea of the King in Parliament, and removed an attempt to fetter the dissolution powers of the monarch.[78]

It is somewhat surprising that the more radical experimental elements, like external ministers, did not attract more opposition from the British government. But acquiescence on this point was not endorsement; it was a function of the scale and extent of their other objections and rewrites, causing them to let this matter go.[79] It is reasonable to think that more overt departures from the Westminster model—any model that broke from the idea of a cabinet responsible to a popularly elected house—would have attracted further and stronger opposition, and would have been seen as inconsistent with Treaty commitments. It is not clear that the drafters sought to break more radically or directly from the Westminster system, but it is obvious that in any event no more overt departure was realistic.

[75] Kissane (n 3) 92.

[76] Ibid 83.

[77] Cahillane (n 4) Ch. 4.

[78] Ibid 51–62.

[79] See Thomas Mohr, 'British Involvement in the Creation of the Constitution of the Irish Free State' (2008) 30(1) Dublin University Law Journal 166.

The second reason for the failure of this experiment is that it entirely relied on, and tried to create the conditions for, non-party politics in the Free State. Ironically, if not unpredictably, the politics of the Free State was immediately dominated by two strongly opposed parties and very quickly party discipline 'had reached a high level'.[80] The Constitution did not address parties directly at all. It did not regulate them, or limit their power. It made no rules about party discipline or use of the whip that would have practically limited the power of parties and perhaps secured the independence for parliament from strict government control (though if this had been done, it might have presented practical challenges, or been amended out of existence like other constitutional fetters). It was instead expected that PRSTV would create a flourishing of parties and a pluralistic parliament, which it did not. Opposition to the Treaty and then the Civil War created and entrenched a major party divide.[81] de Valera and his supporters not taking their seats in parliament further allowed governance by one party in the early years of the State, even where it lacked a parliamentary majority, reducing the need for coalition and compromise. In another irony, external ministers—a core weapon against the evils of party—were immediately selected entirely on party lines.[82] This experiment relied on parties not dominating Free State politics, and they immediately did. As one commentator puts it, 'the constitution of 1922 was repeatedly punctured by the moves of party strategy'.[83]

Thirdly, the pressures of governance in a divided society probably prevented the flourishing of the experimental elements of the Constitution. Governing a newly independent state during a civil war is challenging, and it is understandable that strong cabinet governance and party discipline might be seen as essential to ensure effective governance in that era.[84] This might explain why truly external ministers were never appointed, and why party politics was so quickly accepted. As discussed above, the

[80] AW Bromage, 'Constitutional Developments in Saorstát Éireann' (1937) 31(6) American Political Science Review 1050, 1053. Cf Bill Kissane, *New Beginnings: Constitutionalism and Democracy in Modern Ireland* (UCD Press, 2011) 47.

[81] The anti-Treaty members of Sinn Féin were very against party politics, and this may have made the prospect of opposition parties forming around this cleavage seem more remote. Cahillane (n 4) 122.

[82] Ibid 137; Mansergh (n 39) 56.

[83] Bromage (n 80) 1054.

[84] See Kissane (n 3) 94–95, who says that the commitment to cabinet government that developed was forged in the 'crucible' of the civil war.

petition/referendums procedure was never facilitated; it was formally removed as soon as there was any real attempt to use it by the opposition, as this showed the mechanism was 'too frightening'.[85] Setting up novel vocational councils to revolutionise the process of policy- and law-making was not top of anyone's list of priorities in the early years of the Free State; far more important elements of the constitutional framework—fundamental rights and basic constitutional integrity—were seen as dispensable due to the exigencies of the period. All this is to say that if there was a period in which a daring experiment to break from the Westminster model using these techniques could have worked, this was not it. Cahillane documents in her book the 'many examples of the political context of the time leading to failures in implementing the true spirit of the Constitution.'[86] As Brian Farrell suggests, Irish politicians mentally reverted to the 'familiar and acceptable' Westminster model to make governance work in a deeply troubled period [87]

Fourthly, linking these elements together is a kind of political naivety amongst Irish politicians of the early 1920s. It is not clear that many of these ideas would have worked, or would have solved more problems than they caused. The drafters and political supporters of the 1922 Constitution were people that, for all their insight and talent, did not have much experience of government or legislating, in Westminster or anywhere else. As Kissane puts it, beautifully and charitably, their ideals 'had the virtue of being uncompromised by office'.[88] They believed that committing to the ideals of popular sovereignty and government linked closely to the people would, of itself, produce very different results from the Westminster parliament. They did not rethink the functioning of representative governance in practice very much, but assumed that this functioning would adapt to their different ideals. This, of course, ignores the reality that institutions are very hard to change because they have huge inertia and pragmatic path dependency, and that, in times of difficulty, institutions revert to type. Believing that political parties can be avoided is a common belief shared by many young democracies, but it is extremely hard to do, and it may be that it is antithetical to the stability to which new states aspire.

[85] Cahillane (n 4) 118.

[86] Ibid 115.

[87] Farrell (n 26) 40. Cf Kissane (n 3) 95: 'political life was recast in a British mold'.

[88] Kissane (n 3) 83.

This naivety meant that they accomplished much less than they might have if they had gone about this task more directly. Their 'organic', popular alternatives to responsible government were always going to be extremely challenging to make work, and all the more so in the divided society that was forming at the time of the Constitution's drafting. In short, their ambitions were so lofty, and their means so obtuse, that when their measures did not work, their failure was almost total. It was easy, almost natural, to revert to the Westminster system, and very little in the Constitution created any friction in this transition. If they had more experience of governing or legislating, they might have realised the scale of the challenge that faced them, and acted differently.

Fourthly, and closely related to this, a facet of this naivety was possibly a misunderstanding, as Ward puts it, of the 'imperatives inherent in the British model of government'; when it comes down to it, 'British government is party government'.[89] That is, without party and the models of responsibility that goes with it, the British model does not work. Since the fundamentals of that model were accepted and embraced in the 1922 Constitution, there was no escaping these elements of it. Kohn perceptively noted this when he talked about 'the inevitability of the structural design of the British system of parliamentary government once its fundamental framework has been accepted.'[90] Since, as noted above, there was almost certainly no way to depart from this fundamental framework within the term of the Treaty, this probably means that all efforts in this direction were doomed to fail.

Finally, and relatedly, it is possible that experiencing government under the Westminster system in practice, as Irish politicians did in the 1920s and 1930s, they came to appreciate it. 1937, after all, presented an opportunity to depart from model, but nothing along these lines was attempted. As Kissane puts it, it was understandable that 'politicians traumatised by the experience of civil war would reject this idealism' that underwrote former efforts.[91] But it might, rather than trauma, have been happy acquiescence in a system that had broadly worked for them. Having experienced government, perhaps Irish politicians no longer saw party politics and executive dominance as the great vices they had once thought them to be, and saw the functionality of the system as enough of a virtue to

[89] Ward (n 18) 128.
[90] Kohn (n 6) 271.
[91] Kissane (n 3) 93.

maintain it. Kissane describes at length the dichotomy in Irish nationalist constitutional thought between idealism and pragmatism.[92] Perhaps, in the end, pragmatism won out.

Conclusion

Revisiting the narrative about Westminster politics and structure in Ireland is important, because the 1922 Constitution deserves to be seen and framed correctly: it was a novel and daring experiment that attempted to radically reform the Westminster model of governance, albeit in a manner that was probably doomed to fail. This is an important part of the history of the Free State, and of the history of our present State, and it should not be forgotten.

While this history is important in and of itself, it can also inform our present situation, one hundred years on. The framers of the 1922 Constitution saw significant problems in the party—and executive-dominance that characterises the Westminster model. Some of these problems might have been somewhat lessened—though not solved and avoided as they imagined—by more direct constitutional means than the ones they chose. By the time of the 1937 Constitution, the zeal for constitutional experiment—at least along this axis—was no longer present. Perhaps not coincidentally, those making these decisions in 1937 were the beneficiaries of party dominance in a way that the architects of the 1922 Constitution were not (yet). The problems that they identified, however, have not gone away. The Dáil as a house of parliament is entirely dominated by the executive. We have a party whip that is strong even by the standards of other Westminster systems. In a recent period of minority government, the government kept essentially full control of the legislative process despite not having a majority of votes, so strong is the cultural supposition of executive dominance in our political system.[93] Political parties and executive governance are perhaps not the arch evils that Irish nationalists believed in the early years of the twentieth century. But taken to excess, they distort parliamentary governance. I wonder, then, if we could still learn something from the ingenuity and zeal—if not the methods—of the architects of the 1922 Constitution.

[92] Ibid 94–95; Kissane (n 80).

[93] For an extended account of this, and an argument about its cultural origins, see Casey and Kenny (n 2).

Acknowledgement I am grateful to the editors for very helpful comments and suggestions.

References

Bromage, AW. "Constitutional Developments in Saorstát Éireann." American Political Science Review 31, no. 6 (1937) 1050.

Cahillane, Laura. "Anti-Party Politics in the Irish Free State Constitution." Dublin University Law Journal 35 (2012): 34.

Cahillane, Laura. "The Origins of Popular Sovereignty in Ireland: Theory and Reality." In *Constitutional Change and Popular Sovereignty,* edited by Maria Cahill, Colm Ó Cinnéide, Seán Ó Conaill, & Conor O'Mahony, Routledge, 2021.

Cahillane, Laura. *Drafting the Free State Constitution.* Manchester: Manchester University Press, 2016.

Casey, Conor, and David Kenny. "The Resilience of Executive Dominance in Westminster Systems: Ireland 2016-2019." *Public Law* (2021): 355.

Chubb, Basil. *The Government and Politics of Ireland* 3rd ed. Harlow, UK: Pearson, 1992.

Coffey, Donal K. "'The union makes us strong': National Union of Railwaymen v Sullivan and the demise of vocationalism in Ireland." In *Judges, Politics, and the Irish Constitution,* edited by Cahillane, Gallen and Hickey, Manchester University Press, 2017.

Farrell, Brian. "The Paradox of Irish Politics." In *The Irish Parliamentary Tradition,* edited by Farrell, Gill and MacMillan, 1973.

Figgis, Darrell. *The Gaelic State in the Past and Future.* Maunsel, 1917.

Garvin, Tom. *The Irish Senate.* IPA, 1969.

Hogan, Gerard. "A Desert Island Case set in the Silver Sea: *The State (Ryan) v. Lennon.*" In *Leading Cases of the Twentieth Century,* edited by O'Dell, Sweet & Maxwell, 2000.

Hogan, Gerard. *The Origins of the Irish Constitution 1928-1941.* RIA, 2012.

Hogan, Gerard et al. *Kelly: The Irish Constitution.* Bloomsbury Professional, 2018.

Kenny, David. "The Failed Referendum to Abolish the Ireland's Senate: Rejecting Unicameralism in a Small and Relatively Homogenous Country." In *Constitutional Reform of National Legislatures Bicameralism under Pressure,* edited by Albert, Baraggia, Fasone, Edward Elgar, 2019.

Kissane, Bill. "The Constitutional Revolution That Never Was: Democratic Radicalism and the Sinn Féin Movement." *Radical History Review* 104 (2009): 77.

Kissane, Bill. *New Beginnings: Constitutionalism and Democracy in Modern Ireland.* UCD Press, 2011.

Kohn, Leo. *The Constitution of the Irish Free State.* Allen & Unwin, 1932.

Malone, Andrew. "Party Government in the Irish Free State." Political Science Quarterly 44, no. 3 (1929): 363.

Mansergh, Nicholas. *The Irish Free State: Its Government and Politics*. Allan & Unwin, 1934.

Matthew Flinders et al. "'Stretched But Not Snapped': A Response to Russell and Serban on Retiring the 'Westminster Model.'" *Government and Opposition* 57, no. 2 (2022): 353.

Mohr, Thomas. "British Involvement in the Creation of the Constitution of the Irish Free State." *Dublin University Law Journal* 30, no. 1 (2008): 166.

O'Donoghue, Martin. *The Legacy of the Irish Parliamentary Party in Independent Ireland, 1922-1949*. Oxford University Press, 2020.

O'Sullivan, Donal. *The Irish Free State and its Senate*. Faber, 1940.

Russell, Meg, and Ruxandra Serban. "The Muddle of the 'Westminster Model': A Concept Stretched Beyond Repair." *Government and Opposition* 56, no. 4 (2021): 744.

Sircar, Bjørn, and Indraneel Hoyland. "Get The Party Started: Development of Political Party Legislative Dynamics in the Irish Free State Seanad (1922–36)." *Party Politics* 16, no. 1 (2010): 89.

Ward, AJ. "Challenging the British Constitution: The Irish Free State Constitution and the External Minister." *Parliamentary History* 9, no. 1 (1990): 116.

CHAPTER 11

Property Rights and Democratic Decision-Making: Lessons from the 1922 Constitution

Rachael Walsh

Introduction

The relationship between constitutional property rights protection and respect for democratic decision-making on social and economic issues has been complex under the 1937 Constitution. There has been judicial oscillation over time on the appropriate balance to be struck, with periods of variously weak and strong interpretations of the constraining effect of the Constitution's guarantees for private property rights on legislative freedom.

Initially, the delimiting principles specified in Article 43.2—the 'exigencies of the common good' and the 'principles of social justice'—were treated as non-justiciable constitutional concepts. For example, in *Pigs Marketing Board v Donnelly*, Hanna J determined that the Oireachtas

R. Walsh (✉)
School of Law, Trinity College Dublin, Dublin, Ireland
e-mail: rachael.walsh@tcd.ie

L. Cahillane, D. K. Coffey (eds.), *The Centenary of the Irish Free State Constitution*, Palgrave Modern Legal History,
https://doi.org/10.1007/978-3-031-46181-1_11

should have the exclusive power to decide how property rights could be delimited to secure collective interests.[1] He commented in relation to the phrase 'social justice':

> I cannot define that phrase as a matter of law. It cannot be the old standard of the greatest good of the greatest number, for, at the present day, it may be considered proper that the claim of a minority be made paramount on some topic ... I cannot conceive social justice as being a constant quality, either with individuals or in different states. What is social justice in one State may be the negation of what is considered social justice in another State. In a Court of law it seems to me to be a nebulous phrase, involving no questions of law for the Court, but questions of ethics, morals, economics, and sociology which are, in my opinion, beyond the determination of a Court of law, but which may be, in their various aspects, within the consideration of the Oireachtas, as representing the people, when framing the law.[2]

Beginning with *Buckley v Attorney General*, the Irish courts asserted power to review political determinations in respect of 'the exigencies of the common good' and 'the principles of social justice', reasoning that if the drafters of the 1937 Constitution had intended those principles to be non-justiciable, they would have placed them in the 'Directive Principles of Social Policy' in Article 45.[3] This assertion of judicial authority in respect of Article 43.2 reached its zenith in three cases in the 1980s and 1990s wherein the Supreme Court ruled on the basis that the Constitution did not permit targeted burdening of some property owners as a means of securing benefits for other groups in society.[4] The 2000s onwards saw a further shift in approach, with a greater judicial focus on procedural issues in respect of property rights protection.[5] A renewed judicial interest in the protection of the dwelling in Article 40.5 of the Constitution, and its relationship with Article 43, emerged in the following two decades.[6]

[1] [1939] IR 413.

[2] *Ibid*, 418.

[3] [1950] IR 67 at 83.

[4] *Blake v Attorney General* [1982] IR 117, *Re Article 26 and the Housing (Private Rented Dwellings) Bill 1981* [1983] IR 181, *Re Article 26 and the Employment Equality Bill* [1997] 2 IR 321.

[5] On this trend, see Gerard Hogan, David Kenny, and Rachael Walsh, "An Anthology of Declarations of Unconstitutionality," *Irish Jurist* 54 (2015): 27.

[6] See e.g. *County Council of Meath v Murray* [2017] IESC 25, *Clare County Council v McDonagh* [2022] IESC 2.

Now, the housing crisis has refocused the political and legal spotlight in Ireland on the constitutional calibration of property rights and the common good, and on the impact of that calibration on the scope for legislative change. Many calls for a constitutional referendum on housing cite the need for an express right to housing to off-set the existing protection for property rights.[7] The global climate crisis, and Ireland's response to it, is also shaped by the balance struck between property rights and the common good in legal orders, including at a constitutional level. For example, important climate change mitigation measures such as compulsory retrofitting obligations for home-owners impact adversely upon property rights.[8] These pressing policy challenges prompt renewed reflection on the appropriate relationship between constitutional property rights and the decision-making power of the elected branches of government under the Irish constitutional framework.

The 1922 Constitution of the Irish Free State offers useful insights into how to structure and mediate that relationship. It does so by casting into sharp relief alternative approaches to that adopted in the 1937 Constitution. In stark contrast to the 1937 Constitution, the 1922 Constitution emerged with no protection for private property rights, although provision was made in respect of State property in Article 11.[9] Overall, property rights protection was left in 1922 to be secured through the democratic process and existing private law protections. This highlights a different way to

[7] See e.g. the amendment proposal from the civil society group, Home for Good, arguing: '[i]nserting a right to housing in our Constitution will eliminate any doubt that property rights can be appropriately restricted to allow access to decent, affordable, and secure housing for all.' See https://www.homeforgood.ie/referendum/ (last visited 27th February 2023). See also the argument of housing organisation Threshold, contending '[a] stand-alone right would resolve the tension between private property rights and the common good, by allowing the right to private property and that to housing to be balanced against each other.' See https://threshold.ie/advocacy-campaign/right-to-housing/ (last visited 27th February 2023).

[8] Rachael Walsh, "Climate Action and Constitutional Property Rights - Partners or Adversaries?" *DULJ* 42 (2019): 131.

[9] Article 11: 'All the lands and waters, mines and minerals, within the territory of the Irish Free State (Saorstát Eireann) hitherto vested in the State, or any department thereof, or held for the public use or benefit, and also all the natural resources of the same territory ... shall ... belong to the Irish Free State (Saorstát Eireann), subject to any trusts, grants, leases or concessions then existing in respect thereof, or any valid private interest therein ... [and] shall not, nor shall any part thereof, be alienated, but may in the public interest be from time to time granted by way of lease or licence to be worked or enjoyed under the authority and subject to the control of the Oireachtas'.

relate and connect property rights and democratic power, namely allowing the democratic process full control over the scope of legal protection afforded to such rights on an evolving basis. On this approach, property rights are not constitutionally entrenched, meaning that the distribution of resources reflected in such rights is equally not entrenched, paving the way for flexibility in respect of policy changes. In addition, other options were explored in the drafting process in 1922 that prompted the Constitution Committee to debate property issues that remain contentious to this day, notably how to deal with 'unearned increments' in land values and the circumstances in which compensation should be paid to expropriated landowners.

In these ways, the 'property moment' that was triggered by the drafting process in 1922 offers perspectives that are worthy of reconsideration today, as legislators, judges and administrators continue to grapple with how much relative weight to give to property rights and the public interest.[10] Part 2 of this chapter will explore the options that were tabled in 1922 in respect of private property. Part 3 will examine internal debates within the 1922 Constitution's drafting committee on contentious property rights issues. Part 4 will synthesise lessons that can be taken from that historical experience for responding to current social and economic challenges that implicate, in various ways, constitutional property rights protection.

Options for Property Rights Protection in 1922

On 17 January 1922, the Provisional Government appointed a committee for the purpose of drafting a Constitution, which draft document was to be submitted to the Provisional Government for consideration. Three draft constitutions (Drafts A, B and C), signed by different members of the committee, were put forward on 7 March 1922.[11] Each of the three drafts made provision in respect of private property and its relationship with the interests of the common good. Drafts A and B addressed both of these questions in very similar terms, and accordingly they will be considered together.

[10] Nestor M. Davidson and Rashmi Dyal-Chand, "Property in Crisis," *Fordham L.R.* 73 (2010): 1607.

[11] See NAI Department of an Taoiseach File S/8953 and the National Archive Boxes on the Constitution Committee 1922 for details of this process.

Draft C took a radically different approach on property issues.[12] Draft A was signed by Darrel Figgis, James McNeill, and John O'Byrne. Draft B was signed by James Douglas, CJ France, and Hugh Kennedy. Draft C was signed by James Murnaghan and Alfred O'Rahilly.

The question of private property and its relationship with democratic power was foregrounded in Article 1 in Drafts A and B. Property was connected to sovereignty, reflecting the highly significant role of land questions in the Irish independence movement.[13] These two drafts provided in almost identical terms:

> [t]he Nation's sovereignty extends not only to all the men and women of the nation, but to all the material possessions of the nation, the nation's soil and all its resources and all the wealth and wealth-producing processes within the nation; and all right to private property is subordinated to the public right and welfare of the nation. It is the duty of every man and woman to give allegiance and service to the commonwealth, and it is the duty of the nation to ensure that every citizen shall have opportunity to spend his or her strength and faculties in the service of the people. In return for willing service it is the right of every citizen to receive an adequate share of the produce of the nation's labour.[14]

Therefore, these drafts articulated a clear view of private property rights as heavily limited by collective interests. Thomas Mohr suggests, '[b]y including this clause, the drafters had hoped to provide the Constitution of the Irish Free State with a link to the events of Easter 1916 and also to Dáil Éireann's "Democratic Programme" of 1919 which had also used these words.'[15] Articles 11, 12, 41 and 42 of these drafts dealt with State prop-

[12] Its terms were published in 1937 by Professor Alfred O'Rahilly as part of his critique of the draft 1937 Constitution and informed the debate on the drafting of the present property rights guarantees. Brian Farrell, "The Drafting of the Irish Free State Constitution: III," *Ir Jur* 6 (1971): 111-112.

[13] See Terence A. M. Dooley, *The Land for the People* (Dublin: University College Dublin Press, 2004), 32–39; Philip Bull, *Land, Politics and Nationalism: A Study of the Irish Land Question* (Dublin: Gill & Macmillan, 1996), 4.

[14] NAI Department of an Taoiseach File S/8953.

[15] Thomas Mohr, "British Involvement in the Creation of the First Irish Constitution," *DULJ* 30 (2008): 172. The "Democratic Programme" itself was directly influenced by Labour, with Thomas Johnson and William O'Brien of the Labour Party providing the initial draft, in part as a political concession from Sinn Féin in return for Labour's decision to withdraw candidates from the 1918 general election. See John A. Murphy, *Ireland in the Twentieth Century* (Dublin: Gill & Macmillan, 1989), 9-10.

erty and State claims over natural resources. In those draft articles, individual reward in respect of such resources was to be limited to circumstances of clear value-enhancing contribution or creativity.[16]

Draft C was more protective of private property rights, but at the same time set out a detailed scheme for public control of such rights. In this respect, it presaged the approach to property rights protection that was to come in 1937. Draft C addressed these issues in a number of inter-related articles in Part IX, entitled "Economic Life". This part contained principles of social policy, individual rights and duties over property, and State powers over private property and natural resources. Article 62 provided:

> The right to hold private property is guaranteed; its extent and limits are defined by law. The right to hold private property, like other rights, implies a correlative duty, and it must not be exercised to the detriment of the community.
>
> The right to alienation, bequest, and inheritance is guaranteed without prejudicing the fiscal claims of the State and its right to limit the alienability of the homestead, and to abolish entails and anti-social restrictions.
>
> Expropriation of private property may be effected only by legislation, for the benefit of the community, and with compensation.

[16] For example, Draft A provided:
Article 11 –
All estates and interests in the lands, waters, and natural resources of Ireland heretofore claimed to be vested in the King or Crown of Great Britain are reserved to and vested in Saorstát Éireann. The air of Ireland and all forms of potential energy and forces of nature which are unknown or not usable because of lack of scientific or technical knowledge are also reserved to and vested in Saorstát Éireann; Provided that the Oireachtas may make provisions for rewarding any person making a scientific or technical discovery of general public utility.
Article 12 –
All estates and interests in the lands, waters, and natural resources of Ireland formerly claimed to be vested in the King or Crown of Great Britain but alienated prior to the adoption of this Constitution to individuals or corporations, which at the date of the adoption hereof were not developed or were not the subject of a mineral or development lease, and all wealth below the surface of the soil which was unknown or undeveloped at the date hereof, may be acquired by Saorstát Éireann acting on behalf of the people in such manner and on such basis of compensation as may be prescribed by law: Provided that in awarding compensation therefor account shall not be taken of the value accruing after the date of the adoption of this Constitution from any cause other than the industry of the individuals or corporations from whom they were acquired, or their predecessors in title.
(See NAI Box B 2 on these draft articles).

Draft C addressed further property issues in Articles 63 and 64. Article 63 limited rights of private property over natural resources in the public interest and asserted a claim of State ownership over all unappropriated natural resources. Article 64 specified the *obligations* of landowners and the scope of the wider community's claims in respect of private property:

> Ownership, inheritance, distribution and use of land are superintended by the State, so as to ensure to every citizen a healthy residence, and to secure an efficient exploitation of the soil and in the interests of the community.
>
> The land holder is bound, in duty to the community, to secure a reasonably efficient working or utilisation of the land.
>
> Increase in the value of land, arising without expenditure of labour or capital thereon shall accrue to the community.

The key architect of Draft C, Professor Alfred O'Rahilly, acknowledged the relatively radical nature of Part IX, saying it outlined 'a very drastic economic programme,' reflecting '... some fundamental Christian concepts concerning the duty of service, the right of work, the personality of the worker, the right to hold private property.'[17] Furthermore, he noted, '[t]he claims of the community not only to rectify maldistribution, but to supervise all natural resources, to appropriate all future 'unearned increment' and all resources not yet effectively appropriated by individuals, are rather vigorously asserted.'[18] However, O'Rahilly did not regard all of the provisions in Part IX dealing with "Economic Life" as judicially enforceable rights, providing an early example of the use of the kind of distinction employed in Article 45 of the 1937 Constitution. Article 45 of Draft C stated:

> The enumeration, in this Constitution, of personal, social, economic and religious rights and duties, shall not be construed to deny or disparage other rights and duties. In so far as these enumerated rights do not merely express

[17] These comments are contained in a document entitled "Notes of Draft 'C' of the Constitution for the Members of the Provisional Government", dated 12 April 1922, filed in the National Archives Boxes, at B6. Brian Farrell describes O'Rahilly as combining 'a passionate attachment to Catholic principles and values (as he saw them) with a special interest and relationship with Labour.' Brian Farrell, "The Drafting of the Irish Free State Constitution: I" *Irish Jurist* 5 (1970): 119.

[18] *Ibid.*

an ideal requiring to be elaborated, determined and applied by future legislation, they shall have immediate juridical effect from the date of enactment of this Constitution.

O'Rahilly commented:

Article 45 ... enables us to distinguish between two different things in the Constitution: (a) a definite statement of right having immediate juridical validity when the Constitution is passed, and (b) the expression of a guiding ideal to direct and inspire future legislation.

This statement indicates that Part IX on Economic Life contained a mixture of judicially enforceable rights and "guiding ideals" for legislators.[19] The idea behind this division of labour reflects the split that was eventually made in the drafting of the 1937 Constitution between the judicially enforceable right to private property and the unenforceable Directive Principles of Social Policy, a split that severed property's 'individual' and 'social' aspects in the Irish constitutional context.[20]

The terms of Draft C were published in 1937 by O'Rahilly as part of his critique of the draft Constitution. Brian Farrell suggests that while Draft C was not influential in 1922, there is evidence of Draft C's influence in the text of the 1937 Constitution, particularly in relation to the separation of social principles from judicially enforceable rights.[21] He also points to influence on Article 43's treatment of property, in particular its dual function of both protecting and delimiting private property rights.[22] Another notable connection between the texts of Draft C and the property rights provisions in the 1937 Constitution concerns the protection of particular 'incidents'

[19] Eoin Mac Neill criticised Draft C on precisely this basis in a memorandum dated 21 March 1922. He said it was '... largely a statement of national and social principles', which he felt should not be included in a Constitution but should be separately considered and adopted if approved, and he questioned whether such declaratory statements in other Constitutions had any real significance. NAI Department of an Taoiseach File S/8953.

[20] On the historical development of this split, see Rachael Walsh, "Private Property Rights in the Drafting of the Irish Constitution: A Communitarian Compromise" *DULJ* 33 (2011): 86.

[21] Brian Farrell, "The Drafting of the Irish Free State Constitution: III" *Irish Jurist* 6 (1971): 112.

[22] *Ibid.*

of private ownership.[23] As noted above, Draft C singled out alienation, bequest, and inheritance for protection, a distinction that also features in Article 43.1 of the 1937 Constitution.[24] This, in comparative terms, is an unusual drafting feature in a constitutional property clause, with the closest comparator being Article 14 (1) of the German Basic Law, which states '[p]roperty *and the right of inheritance* shall be guaranteed.'[25] Given the limited sources of international inspiration for this approach available to the constitutional drafting team in 1937, it is likely to have been another instance where Draft C was influential.

Draft B was ultimately selected by the Constitution Committee, but its terms were significantly modified in respect of property following consultation with the British Government.[26] Against the backdrop of a rising Labour movement in Britain and wider international developments in respect of socialism, the British Government expressed discomfort with the treatment of property in Article 1.[27] This led to the removal of property issues from Article 1 and the subsequent adoption of a Constitution for the Free State that did not directly address the relationship between private property rights and democratic power. Kennedy's strategic sacrifice of draft Article 1 to secure self-determination objectives provides a striking echo of

[23] On the 'incidents of private ownership', see Anthony M. Honoré, "Ownership", in *Oxford Essays in Jurisprudence*, ed. A. G. Guest (Oxford: Oxford University Press, 1961), 144-5.

[24] Article 43.1.2° of the 1937 Constitution provides: 'The State accordingly guarantees to pass no law attempting to abolish the right of private ownership or the general right to transfer, bequeath, and inherit property.'

[25] Emphasis added.

[26] Leo Kohn notes, '[t]he Irish Government, as was expressly admitted by the British Colonial Secretary in the House of Commons, was under no obligation to consult the British Cabinet. Inasmuch, however, as the Constitution represented an implementation of the Treaty and would, therefore, require to be confirmed by the British Parliament, it was obviously expedient prior to the publication of the Draft to secure an assurance from the British Government that it was regarded by Great Britain as conforming to the terms of the Treaty.' Leo Kohn, *The Constitution of the Irish Free State* (George Allen & Unwin Ltd., 1932), 78.

[27] Mohr notes, '[a]side from the sustained emphasis on Irish sovereignty, the British were shocked by what Austen Chamberlain, then Lord Privy Seal, called the "Soviet character" of these articles.' Mohr, "British Involvement", 172. I am grateful to Donal K. Coffey for pointing out the correspondence with the rise of Labour, with Ramsey MacDonald assuming the role of British Prime Minister in 1924.

Labour's decision to not contest the 1918 Irish General Election to avoid diverting focus from the independence movement.[28]

Noting the ease with which Hugh Kennedy conceded that aspect of Article 1 on the first day of the negotiation process with the British government, Mohr suggests that Kennedy may in fact have shared the British government's reservations on this issue.[29] This suggestion is plausible when considered against the background property dynamics in Ireland in 1922. The work of the Land Commission was well advanced by 1922, with two thirds of tenants having acquired their holdings by the time independence was achieved.[30] As Frederick Aalen puts it, 'Ireland, unlike Britain, became essentially a nation of farm proprietors'.[31] In that context, Kennedy might well have been readily persuaded to relinquish the socialist features of Article 1 in Draft B, and with them, the connection between the draft Constitution and the earlier Democratic Programme. Cahillane observes that in fact all the drafts considered by the Committee were 'left-leaning', particularly on property issues.[32] Given the extent to which a wider Irish land-owning class had already emerged by 1922, the left-leaning tendencies of all three of the draft constitutions may well have proved contentious amongst the Irish public, as well as with the British government.[33] Secrecy surrounding the detail of the 1922 drafts continued right through to the 1970s, which has generally been attributed to the political risks connected with the extent to which the drafts went beyond the Treaty and the extent of British influence on the agreed text.[34] However, the left-leaning tenor of

[28] On this political compromise, see William P. Ryan *The Irish Labour Movement* (Dublin: Talbot Press) 259.

[29] *Ibid.*

[30] Frederick H. Aalen, "Constructive Unionism and the Shaping of Rural Ireland, c 1880–1921" *Rural History* 4 (2) (1993): 141.

[31] *Ibid.*

[32] Laura Cahillane, *Drafting the Irish Free State Constitution* (Manchester University Press, 2016) 22, Francis S. L. Lyons, *Ireland Since the Famine* (London: Morrison& Gibb, 1971) 405.

[33] Murphy observes: '[i]t is very doubtful if revolutionary social doctrines would have found any real sympathy in the rural Ireland of the period. The conservativism bred by peasant proprietorship and by Irish Catholicism was strengthened by the complacency deriving from the high prices of the wartime agricultural economy.' Murphy, *Ireland in the Twentieth Century*, 10.

[34] See Farrell, "Free State I", 115-116, Mohr, "British Involvement", 186.

all three 1922 drafts might also have proved politically compromising for politicians with property-owning constituents who were highly influential in Irish life by this period.[35]

Internal Property Debates

Although Cahillane suggests that the Committee reached agreement on most constitutional issues, agreement on precisely how to treat private property rights proved elusive.[36] The divide between Drafts A and B on the one hand, and Draft C on the other hand, was very significant in respect of property. Divergences emerged on at least two fundamental points of principle: the appropriate constitutional treatment of 'unearned increment' and the question of compensation for expropriation. These debates illustrate different views within the Committee on the degree to which private property rights should constrain the decision-making freedom of the elected branches of government.

Unearned Increment

The Constitution Committee diverged on how to treat the so-called unearned increment—namely the increase in value that accrues to a landowner in a rising land market, which may also be influenced by social and economic developments, such as improved infrastructure. Within the Committee, CJ France made a strong case for a constitutional provision that would expressly allow the State to claw-back some or all of that increment for the benefit of the wider community. He drew on a budgetary proposal from Lloyd George that land would be valued and upon transfer to a new holder, where any increase in the land's value arose not from individual efforts but from community input, a certain percentage of that increased value would be taken by the State. France argued:

> The most glaring inequalities in wealth which are found in the world to-day result from the fact that an individual purchases a piece of land that has great

[35] On this influence, see Tom Garvin, "The Anatomy of a Nationalist Revolution: Ireland, 1858–1928," *Comparative Studies in Society and History* 28 (1986): 469. See also Tom Garvin, *The Evolution of Irish Nationalist Politics* (Dublin: Gill & Macmillan, 1981).

[36] Laura Cahillane, "An Insight into the Irish Free State Constitution," *American Journal of Legal History* 54 (2014): 11.

> strategic value, and in course of years becomes extremely wealthy through no effort of his own, but merely from the value given to that land by the community at large.[37]

France's approach had a long intellectual lineage. It drew inspiration from Henry George's 'single tax' proposal in the U.S. context, which was described as '... a social project for ameliorating the evils of, without abolishing, private property in land'.[38] Eugene Debbs, founder of the American Railway Union and the Socialist Party of America and five-time presidential candidate (including lastly in 1920), advocated collective land ownership where possible. Where it was not, he favoured taxation to capture 'unearned increment.'[39] John S. Mill similarly argued against the privatisation of land value increases. He contended:

> Suppose that there is a kind of income which constantly tends to increase without any exertion or sacrifice on the part of the owners: those owners constituting a class in the community, whom the natural course of things progressively enriches, consistently with complete passiveness on their own part. In such a case it would be no violation of the principles on which private property is grounded, if the state should appropriate this increase of wealth, or part of it, as it arises. This would not properly be taking anything from anybody; it would merely be applying an accession of wealth, created by circumstances, to the benefit of society, instead of allowing it to become an unearned appendage to the riches of a particular class.[40]

France failed to persuade the whole Committee on this point, but as was seen above, Draft C contained a specific provision in respect of unearned increment. It asserted that an individual had no right to any increase in land values that he or she did not contribute to, thereby connecting property

[37] NAI Constitution Committee boxes, Box K1, Document 24, "Memorandum on the Natural Endowments of a State".

[38] Evans Woollen, "A Third View of the Single Tax", *The Atlantic*, April 1914, available at https://www.theatlantic.com/magazine/archive/1914/04/a-third-view-of-the-single-tax/541074/ (last visited, 27 February 2023.

[39] For critique of Debbs' position on these issues, see Charles Johnston, "Socialism and the American Farmer", *The North American Review* 196 (682) (1912): 305. For his expressed views on the issue in his famous 'Canton, Ohio' speech, see Chris J. Magoc and David Bernstein eds, *Imperialism and Expansionism in American History* (Vol. 3) (ABC-CLIO, 2015), 956.

[40] John Stuart Mill, *Principles of Political Economy* (Toronto, 1965), 819 (first published 1848).

rights to individual labour and recognising the distinctive nature of land as a necessarily limited resource.

Notably, this dimension of Draft C had no discernible influence on the drafting of the 1937 Constitution, which does not expressly address the State's power in respect of unearned increment. As a result, the Irish courts have had to work hard to find coherent justifications for legislative claw-backs of land-value increases resulting from regulatory decisions, perhaps most notably in *Re Article 26 and Part V of the Planning and Development Bill 1999*.[41] In that case, the Supreme Court justified a claw-back of unearned increment by connecting that increment to the planning code and to grants of development permission within the parameters set by that code. The Court reasoned:

> In the present case, as a condition of obtaining a planning permission for the development of lands for residential purposes, the owner may be required to cede some part of the enhanced value of the land deriving both from its zoning for residential purposes and the grant of permission in order to meet what is considered by the Oireachtas to be a desirable social objective, namely the provision of affordable housing and housing for persons in the special categories and of integrated housing.[42]

On that basis, it concluded (without detailed analysis) that the Bill was a proportionate interference with property rights. The reasoning of the Court was clearly motivated by a concern to avoid constitutional entrenchment of unearned increments in land values arising through planning decisions. However, the Court struggled to ground that intuition in the text of the Constitution's delimiting principles in Article 43.2.

Land-hoarding, which is often cited as a contributor to the current housing crisis in Ireland, can be explained in part by the fact that increases in land values accrue by default to the landowner under the 1937 Constitution's treatment of property rights.[43] In response, successive

[41] [2000] 2 IR 321.

[42] *Ibid*, 354.

[43] For recent commentary, see David McWilliams, 'The problem with 'land capture'' (Irish Times, 25 February 2023) https://www.irishtimes.com/opinion/2023/02/25/david-mcwilliams-land-capture-is-a-significant-problem-in-this-country/ (last visited 27 February 2023); Cantillon, 'Land hoarding adding unwelcome premium to the price of housing' (Irish Times, 22 December 2022) https://www.irishtimes.com/business/2022/12/22/land-hoarding-adding-unwelcome-premium-to-the-price-of-housing/ (last visited 27 February 2023).

legislatures have continued to grapple with unearned increments in the land context, crafting highly complex grandfathering clauses and consultative processes to support such claw-backs, most recently in respect of the taxation of residentially zoned land.[44] Draft C's approach to unearned increment signals an alternative way of addressing this problem, namely to assert the State's claim over such land value at a constitutional level, which then serves to justify specific regulatory measures through which increases are 'clawed back'.

Compensation for Expropriation

Another property schism within the Committee concerned whether to make express provision for the expropriation, upon payment of compensation, of private property by the State for public purposes. Douglas, France, and Kennedy argued against locking the State into a blanket compensation requirement at a constitutional level:

> To lay down as a constitutional stipulation that all expropriation requires compensation would impose an impossible limitation on legislation. It is the common experience of legislation that cases occur in which full compensation cannot be made or cannot be assessed; and therefore a limitation of this kind would simply prove obstructive in the future.[45]

This approach won out in Drafts A and B, despite strong external submissions on the importance of expressly addressing the compensation question. For example, George O'Brien, an economist, argued in a submission to the Committee, 'it ought to be made quite clear that no expropriation can take place except for pressing necessity, after full inquiry and with full compensation.'[46] In addition, many of the foreign constitutions that the Committee considered in the drafting process took the approach advocated by O'Brien. For example, the records of the work of the Committee contain copies of the constitutions of Greece, Denmark, and the

[44] The Residential Zoned Land Tax was introduced as part of the current Government's Housing For All Plan in the Finance Act 2021.

[45] NAI Constitution Committee boxes, Box E4, Committee's reply to criticisms of Dr. George O'Brien (13 April 1922).

[46] NAI Department of an Taoiseach File S/8953.

Netherlands, which each provided that expropriation of private property could only take place pursuant to law, in fulfilment of the demands of public utility and with the payment of compensation or indemnity.[47] However, Drafts A and B resisted this evidence, motivated by a concern to maximise the State's freedom in respect of compulsory acquisition. Even Draft C did not specify the *value* of the compensation that was required to be paid to expropriated owners, although it included a compensation requirement.

This shared desire for flexibility in respect of expropriation of private property amongst the members of the Constitution Committee is likely attributable to the experience of land redistribution in Ireland up to 1922. At that stage, legislative programmes for land redistribution were a well-established feature of the Irish policy landscape and the work of the Land Commission in administering those programmes was advanced. The purchase of land by former tenants, financed through government-guaranteed land bonds, was the complex administrative culmination of the Irish Land Wars, and of prior land agitation.[48] In 1903, Charles Johnston noted the remarkable nature of this land redistribution process, saying: '[t]hat a nation, having lost its land by invasion, conquest, and confiscation, should buy that land back again by instalments, is a thing unprecedented in history.'[49] He reported greatly increased land improvements following tenant purchase. However, this came at a significant cost to the fledgling Irish State, with the outstanding value of the land bonds representing approximately 40% of Irish GDP at the time of partition.[50]

Considered against this backdrop, the absence of a right to compensation in the 1922 Constitution appears to have been intentional and carefully considered, reflecting the new State's early experience of the complexity of land redistribution, and of the resulting need for administrative flexibility. It is perhaps a legacy of this decision that the 1937 Constitution also does not expressly provide a right to compensation for expropriation, at all or at market value. Such an entitlement has been read into the 1937

[47] NAI Constitution Committee Boxes, at M1, T1, and S2.

[48] On the Land Bonds, see Nathan Foley-Fisher and Eoin McLaughlin, 'Irish Land Bonds: 1891-1938' (eabh Papers, No. 14-01, January 2014, available at: https://bankinghistory.org/wp-content/uploads/eabhpapers14_01.pdf) (last visited 2 May 2023).

[49] Charles Johnston, 'Mr Wyndham's Land Act and the Future of Ireland', *The North American Review* 177 (563) (1903) 552, at 555.

[50] (n 48), at 2.

Constitution's property rights provisions by the courts, although some doubt persists about the scope for sub-market value compensation where deprivation of private property rights occurs pursuant to legislation that aims to secure a compelling social justice/common good objective.[51] Again, current pressures in respect of housing highlight the benefits of a constitutional mediation of property rights and democratic power that promotes flexibility and adaptability by avoiding budgetary constraints on the policy-making sphere flowing from rigid compensation provisions.

Conclusions

The significance of the 1922 Constitution has often been marginalised in scholarly reflection on the development of Irish constitutional law. [52] The risk of such marginalisation is particularly acute in respect of constitutional property law—it would be all too easy to discount the relevance of the 1922 Constitution on this issue given the absence of private property rights protection from the document ultimately adopted. However, that absence is in itself a telling and insightful statement about the appropriate relationship between property rights and democratic power that was envisaged by the drafters in 1922. Cahillane observes that while the 1922 Constitution aligned with other Dominion Constitutions in not including a right to private property, this alignment was a product of the overall absence of 'bill of rights' provisions in other Dominion Constitutions.[53] In contrast, the absence of a private ownership guarantee in the 1922 Constitution, when considered against the backdrop of the land and independence movements in Ireland and the drafting history analysed in this Chapter, can clearly be understood as an intentional de-prioritisation of private ownership vis-á-vis the common good. While the explicitly socialist draft Article 1 was not ultimately included in the 1922 Constitution, the pendulum did not swing to a constitutional protection for property rights.

In addition, the drafting process in 1922 explored and tested solutions to 'wicked' property problems that continue to pose challenges to

[51] *Rafferty v. Minister for Agriculture* [2014] IESC 61.

[52] Charles Townshed, "The Meaning of Irish Freedom Constitutionalism in the Irish Free State," *Transactions of the Royal Historical Society* 45 (7 March 1998), https://doi.org/10.2307/3679288; Farrell, "Free State I", 115.

[53] Cahillane, *Drafting the Free State Constitution*, 90.

legislators and administrators today.[54] How should we distribute the value that accrues to land in a rising market, and as a result of wider social and economic development? Should the State or the individual be empowered to claim the value that is increasingly embedded in regulatory permissions in respect of land-use? Should compensation always be payable to an owner who is deprived of their property to secure the public interest? If payable, what should the value of such compensation be? These difficult questions are central to any effective response to current challenges in areas such as housing and environmental protection. The internal debates examined in this chapter show that the Constitution Committee in 1922 was alive to these issues, addressing them in a direct manner and regarding them as worthy of consideration for treatment at a constitutional level. In contrast, the 1937 Constitution chose to address these issues obliquely, through the prism of the State's general delimiting powers as established in Article 43.2 of that document.[55] These issues continue to present challenges, suggesting that the more direct approach adopted in 1922 might have been helpful in setting clearer parameters for legislative action impacting upon private property rights.

Thus re-analysed, the 1922 Constitution and its drafting history have much to offer current, highly contentious, debates about property and the public interest in Ireland. While property rights remain in the social, political, and legal spotlight, our earliest experience of confronting these difficult distributive issues as a State shows us new ways of framing and imagining the relationship between public power and private rights, which may in turn create new constitutional space for ambitious policy responses to serious national and global problems.

[54] The term 'wicked problems' was coined by H.W.J. Rittel and M.M. Webber, 'Dilemmas in a General Theory of Planning' (1973) 4 *Pol'y Sciences* 155, wherein they identified 10 characteristics of such problems, including the lack of a definitive problem-formulation. See also Lorna Fox-O'Mahony and Marc Roark, 'Comparative Property Law and the Pandemic: Vulnerability Theory and Resilient Property in an Age of Crisis' (2022) 82 (3) *Louisiana Law Review* 789.

[55] Article 43.2 provides:

1° The State recognises, however, that the exercise of the rights mentioned in the foregoing provisions of this Article ought, in civil society, to be regulated by the principles of social justice.

2° The State, accordingly, may as occasion requires delimit by law the exercise of the said rights with a view to reconciling their exercise with the exigencies of the common good.

Acknowledgement Thanks to the participants at the Centenary of the 1922 Constitution Conference, 5th December 2022 for helpful comments on the ideas developed here, and to Donal K. Coffey and Laura Cahillane for very useful suggestions as editors. Research for this Chapter was carried out at the National Archives of Ireland (NAI) and the Archives Department at University College Dublin (UCDAD), and I am grateful for the assistance of the staff in both institutions.

References

Aalen, Frederick H. "Constructive Unionism and the Shaping of Rural Ireland, c 1880–1921." *Rural History* 4, no. 2 (1993): 141.

Bull, Philip. *Land, Politics and Nationalism: A Study of the Irish Land Question*. Dublin: Gill & Macmillan, 1996.

Cahillane, Laura. "An Insight into the Irish Free State Constitution." *American Journal of Legal History* 54 (2014): 11.

Cahillane, Laura. *Drafting the Irish Free State Constitution*. Manchester University Press, 2016.

Davidson, Nestor M, and Rashmi Dyal-Chand. "Property in Crisis." *Fordham L.R.* 73 (2010): 1607.

Dooley, Terence A. M. *The Land for the People*. Dublin: University College Dublin Press, 2004.

Farrell, Brian. "The Drafting of the Irish Free State Constitution: III." *Ir Jur* 6 (1971): 111.

Farrell, Brian. "The Drafting of the Irish Free State Constitution: I." *Irish Jurist* 5 (1970): 119.

Foley-Fisher, Nathan, and Eoin McLaughlin. "Irish Land Bonds: 1891-1938." eabh Papers, No. 14-01, January 2014. https://bankinghistory.org/wp-content/uploads/eabhpapers14_01.pdf)

Fox-O'Mahony, Lorna, and Marc Roark. "Comparative Property Law and the Pandemic: Vulnerability Theory and Resilient Property in an Age of Crisis." *Louisiana Law Review* 82, no. 3 (2022): 789.

Garvin, Tom. "The Anatomy of a Nationalist Revolution: Ireland, 1858–1928." *Comparative Studies in Society and History* 28 (1986): 469.

Garvin, Tom. *The Evolution of Irish Nationalist Politics*. Dublin: Gill & Macmillan, 1981.

Hogan, Gerard, David Kenny, and Rachael Walsh. "An Anthology of Declarations of Unconstitutionality." *Irish Jurist* 54 (2015): 27.

Honoré, Anthony M. "Ownership." In *Oxford Essays in Jurisprudence*, edited by A. G. Guest, Oxford: Oxford University Press, 1961.

Johnston, Charles. "Mr Wyndham's Land Act and the Future of Ireland." *The North American Review* 177, no. 563 (1903): 552.

Johnston, Charles. "Socialism and the American Farmer." *The North American Review* 196 (1912): 305.

Kohn, Leo. *The Constitution of the Irish Free State*. George Allen & Unwin Ltd, 1932.

Lyons, Francis S. L. *Ireland Since the Famine*. London: Morrison & Gibb, 1971.

Magoc, Chris J, and David Bernstein. *Imperialism and Expansionism in American History* Vol. 3. ABC-CLIO, 2015.

Mill, John Stuart. *Principles of Political Economy*. Toronto, 1965.

Mohr, Thomas. "British Involvement in the Creation of the First Irish Constitution." *DULJ* 30 (2008): 172.

Murphy, John A. *Ireland in the Twentieth Century*. Dublin: Gill & Macmillan, 1989.

Rittel, H.W.J, and M.M. Webber. "Dilemmas in a General Theory of Planning." *Pol'y Sciences* 4 (1973): 155.

Ryan, William P. *The Irish Labour Movement*. Dublin: Talbot Press.

Townshed, Charles. "The Meaning of Irish Freedom Constitutionalism in the Irish Free State." *Transactions of the Royal Historical Society* 45 (7th March 1998). https://doi.org/10.2307/3679288

Walsh, Rachael. "Climate Action and Constitutional Property Rights - Partners or Adversaries?" *DULJ* 42 (2019): 131.

Walsh, Rachael. "Private Property Rights in the Drafting of the Irish Constitution: A Communitarian Compromise." *DULJ* 33 (2011): 86.

Woollen, Evans. "A Third View of the Single Tax." *The Atlantic*, April 1914. https://www.theatlantic.com/magazine/archive/1914/04/a-third-view-of-the-single-tax/541074/

CHAPTER 12

The Civil War, the Constitution and the Collapse of the Rule of Law

Seán Enright

The autumn of 1922 witnessed two momentous and contradictory events. The first was the creation of the Irish Free State Constitution which guaranteed liberty, freedom of religion, expression and association. It also guaranteed what we now recognise as the rule of law, universal suffrage, separation of powers between the judiciary and government and trial by due process of law. The second event was the implementation of the Execution Policy which would result in 83 executions for carrying arms and or attacking the National Army.[1] The policy was not the product of legislation or other process of law, and after the war, the government

[1] The Irish Military Archive (IMA): IE/MA/CW/P/02/02/23 'List of Prisoners Tried by Military Court'. The List names 77. To this number should be added National Army Private Barney Winsley shot in September of 1922 for supplying arms to the anti-treaty faction. Also, Jack Lawlor, shot in Ballyheigue on 31 October 1922. In addition, the Mountjoy Executions December 8, 1922. Barrett, O'Connor, McKelvey and Mellows.

S. Enright (✉)
Dublin, Ireland
e-mail: seanenright58@icloud.com

L. Cahillane, D. K. Coffey (eds.), *The Centenary of the Irish Free State Constitution*, Palgrave Modern Legal History,
https://doi.org/10.1007/978-3-031-46181-1_12

passed an Act of Indemnity to protect those who had taken part in military courts.[2] It did not render what was done legal but it prevented any prosecutions and litigation.

A century later provides an opportunity to re-assess and reconcile those two events.

A starting point is to identify the central provision of the Constitution that guaranteed due process – Article 70:

> *No one shall be tried save in due course of law and extraordinary courts will not be established, save only such Military Tribunals as may be authorised by law for dealing with military offenders against military law. The jurisdiction of Military Tribunals shall not be extended to or exercised over the civil population save in time of war, or armed rebellion, and for acts committed in time of war or armed rebellion, and in accordance with the regulations to be prescribed by law*

As we shall see, the commitment to uphold democratic rights in this context, despite the seemingly strong protection in this Article, proved rather elusive.

The Execution Policy

The Committee charged with drafting the Constitution first convened in January 1922 but by the autumn the political landscape had changed dramatically. The Civil War began with the explosion at the Four Courts and the capture of many anti-treaty leaders, including Mellows, Barrett, O'Connor and McKelvey who went into custody at Mountjoy prison. The first phase of the Civil War was won by the national army by August. This gave rise to a guerrilla insurgency which the provisional government concluded could not be won by conventional military victories.

The task faced by the provisional government was a daunting one. The primary aim was to bring the Free State into being and here there was some tension between the aspirations for complete self-government, and the requirements of the Irish Free State (Agreement) Act to enact a constitution which reflected the terms of the Anglo-Irish Treaty.[3] On this, the

[2] Indemnity Act 1923.

[3] The Irish Free State (Agreement) Act 12 Geo V. C. 4.

British government demanded strict adherence.[4] There was also a very difficult military dimension: the national army faced ambush and assassination and sustained many casualties, including Michael Collins and a significant number of senior officers. In Dublin, anti-treaty fighters launched attacks which showed a singular lack of care for civilians and there were many non-combatant casualties. Out in the provinces there were ambushes and railway-engines were destroyed, and tracks degraded.

The Cabinet of the provisional government lived under armed guard in an upper floor apartment on Dawson Street; the threat of assassination was real. Each morning mattresses were rolled up and the business of government began. In the evenings, Ministers smoked and played bridge[5] and no doubt read the papers of events in Europe: Germany sliding into poverty, Mussolini's ascent to power, turmoil in Russia and war in Greece.

The provisional government also faced industrial unrest, a post office strike and a railway strike. The government's very survival rested on a loan from Westminster. One quarter of government income was being spent on maintaining the army and this figure would continue to rise.[6] The war was draining the slender resources of the state, and this gave rise to the great fear: that the money would run out, that the army, the civil service and other organs of the state would wither away, and that Britain might once again send in the troops. It was in this context that the execution policy came about.[7]

The decision to bring in military courts would be justified to the Dáil as a crisis which threatened the existence of the state. Civil law had broken down, and 'The Army' General Mulcahy, told the Dáil, needed 'to stand in the gap.' Mulcahy argued that internment without trial was not a sufficient deterrent to those inclined to fight for the anti- treaty cause and if

[4] For an insightful analysis: see Laura Cahillane, Drafting the Irish Free State Constitution, Manchester University Press, 2016. And also, the National Archives of Ireland, files series DE9 where much of the work of the Constitution Committee is preserved.

[5] Bureau of Military History (BMH), Witness Statement No 939, File s.66, Ernest Blythe, p168.

[6] Expenditure on the army amounted to £7 m and would rise to £10 m by the spring of 1923. See Dáil Éireann Debates, Vol 2, no. 46, (27th March 1923), (Dáil in Committee – Central Fund Bill (No. 1) Bill, 1923), available at https://www.oireachtas.ie/en/debates/debate/dail/1923-03-27/25/

[7] For an analysis of the origins of the execution policy see Seán Enright, The Irish Civil War. Law Atrocity and Execution (Merrion Press, Dublin 2022). Also, John Dorney, The Civil War in Dublin: The Fight for the Irish Capital 1922–24. (Merrion Press, 2017).

military courts were not introduced, his own men would likely seek retribution and revenge.[8]

This was already happening. Historians of this period are in broad agreement that in excess of 150 prisoners died in the custody of the state during the civil war. Some were killed at the point of capture, like Cathal Brugha, others like Noel Lemass, were kidnapped and shot. The inquests concerning the Red Cow and Yellow Lanes killings are notorious examples of this phenomenon.[9] In the inquests that followed each killing, lawyers for the state obfuscated and obstructed.[10] General Mulcahy publicly condemned unlawful killings, but other ministers were ambivalent or uncomfortably silent. In private, O'Higgins urged the abolition of inquests and would eventually argue that persons captured with arms should be summarily shot.[11] While these events were being played out, the Cabinet was also actively involved in drafting the Constitution with all the solemn commitments to personal liberties contained within it.

Against this backdrop, the Cabinet of the provisional government prepared to bring in military courts and began by asking whether the Treaty between Britain and Ireland permitted the provisional government to pass legislation, pending the creation of the Irish Free State. The question was put to Hugh Kennedy KC, the Attorney General. His written advice was cautiously positive, but he pointed out that a statute would require the royal assent and since no Governor General had been appointed, this would require the personal signature of the King. Kennedy advised that the British government would object to legislation without royal assent and remarked 'this question might give rise to much difficulty.'[12]

One of the difficulties in assessing the response of the provisional government is that so very little was written down in the Cabinet minutes, but the record shows that Kennedy and the other law officers attended on ministers the next day, 25 September.[13] Ultimately, events show that pending the creation of the new State, the provisional government proceeded

[8] Dáil Éireann Debates, vol 13 no.1, (27 September 1922), available at https://www.oireachtas.ie/en/debates/debate/dail/1922-09-27/8/

[9] For an analysis of inquests of this period see: Seán Enright, The Irish Civil War *Law Atrocity and Execution*. (Dublin, Merrion Press 2022). P14–23.

[10] See for instance, Irish Times, 12 August 1922, Report into the Death of Harry Boland. See also John Dorney, *The Civil War in Dublin* (Dublin: Merrion Press 2017) chapter 15.

[11] UCD Archives, Mulcahy Papers P/7/101/19.

[12] UCD Archives, Mulcahy Papers P/7/B/142.

[13] Provisional Government minutes, (Sept. 1922), N.A.I., TSCH/1/1/3.

by resolution not statute. In respect of the execution policy, it may reasonably be inferred that political considerations prevailed: to rely on the signature of the King of England to bring about the execution of anti-treaty prisoners would be embarrassing and might even risk losing the support of pro-treaty deputies.

It was in these circumstances that the Army (Special Powers) Resolution was formulated: it did not amount to legislation and would have no force of law. It envisaged the trial of offenders by military courts for arson, looting, destruction of property and attacking national army or carrying arms and explosives. As an adjunct to this process, the Judge Advocate General prepared detailed regulations governing trials by military courts. The regulations stipulated that military courts would be 'bound by the laws of evidence' and provided significant safeguards; advance notice of evidence to be called; time to prepare the defence and legal representation.[14]

On 28 September, after scrutiny and debate, the Dáil voted by a margin of 47–15 to allow the national army to try civilians. The Dáil also sanctioned the trial regulations. The vote was all but a foregone conclusion because most anti-treaty deputies were absent save for three who had already been killed (Brugha, Boland and Devans). Also absent, was Laurence Ginnell, who had been excluded from the Third Dáil for disruptive conduct on the first session.[15] Almost by chance, power had coalesced in the hands of a small group of men backed by the national army.

A Proclamation was published the following week giving notice that military courts would try offenders in respect of offences committed on or after 15 October.[16] There was then a short delay while the army readied itself for this new duty and here, we see some tension between the Cabinet and Mulcahy. Cosgrave wrote to Mulcahy inviting attendance at the next meeting of the Cabinet: 'your business is first on the agenda.'[17] Executions would soon take place.

[14] IMA: DOD A07/266, Departmental A files, 'The General Regulations as to the Trial of Civilians by Military Courts. Made by the Army Council on 2nd October 1922'. See also Iris Ofigiúil, 21 November 1922. The Regulations also provided that the courts should have regard to the Regulations governing the courts martial of national army soldiers (which provided generous safeguards for the accused).

[15] Dáil Debates vol 1 no.1, (9 September 1922), available at https://www.oireachtas.ie/en/debates/debate/dail/1922-09-09/3/

[16] Iris Oifigiúil 31 October 1922.

[17] UCD Archives, Mulcahy Papers P7/B/247/142.

Fisher, Gaffney, Twohig, and Cassidy

The first executions took place on 17 November. Four young men were tried and convicted of possession of revolvers. They were sentenced to death and executed at Kilmainham. A key question in understanding all that took place is why, of all the very many young men who were captured in arms at this time, were these men singled out for execution? The evidence suggests that they were suspected of being involved in a raid on Oriel House, which was the office of the Criminal Investigation Department which was then at the forefront in supressing anti-treaty activities in Dublin. Despite the paucity of records that survive, the evidence that this was so comes from a number of reliable sources. Some deputies raised concerns about the attack on Oriel House and we see in the Dáil a firm reassurance by O'Higgins, that the matter was in hand.[18]

Another strand of evidence comes from the man who organised the attack on Oriel House. Joe O'Connor later intimated that the executed men had been involved in that attack.[19] The final link derives from a directive from the Cabinet to Mulcahy: 'arrange for the immediate trial of the men arrested in connection with the attack on Oriel House.' On the day of the executions there was an anxious debate in the Dáil, and government ministers rallied to support the policy. Ernest Blythe reassured the Deputies that 'Every person who will be tried under the Resolution passed by the Dáil will have a full opportunity for conducting his defence.'[20] That guarantee would soon evaporate.

Erskine Childers

That same week, Erskine Childers was captured in possession of a pistol. He had become a hate figure for the Executive and also at Westminster, because of the part he had played in inciting opposition to the Treaty. Soon after capture, he was seen at Portobello barracks by his friend and counsel, Michael Comyn KC. Childers had been 'roughed up' and his

[18] Dáil Debates, Vol 1 no. 27, (1 November 1922), available at https://www.oireachtas.ie/en/debates/debate/dail/1922-11-01/31/. O'Higgins: 'The official resources at the disposal of the government are sufficient to deal with the matter. I have reports from Oriel House and the DMP and the Military'.

[19] IMA: BMH Witness Statement No 554, File s.425, Joe O'Connor.

[20] Dáil Debates, Vol 1 no. 30, (17 November 1922), available at https://www.oireachtas.ie/en/debates/debate/dail/1922-11-17/13/

cufflinks and personal possessions stolen but, Comyn recalled in an unpublished memoir, he was 'perfectly calm' and recognised there was no defence: 'I had a gun.'[21]

Childers was tried by military court at Portobello barracks for possession of a handgun. At his trial, Comyn objected to the legality of the military court on several grounds, the fundamental assertion being that the court was not lawfully established. Another objection was that there was power to try the prisoner for unlawful possession of a gun under the Firearms Act, which carried imprisonment, but not otherwise.[22] The objections were overruled, and Michael Comyn then walked out to seek a writ of habeas corpus. He assembled a formidable team, including Patrick Lynch KC and the young Conor Maguire (later Chief Justice). The next step was an evening visit to the home of the Master of the Rolls to seek an ex-parte order forbidding execution. There is a hint, here, of what modern lawyers call 'forum shopping.' Sir Charles had ruled for a prisoner in a similar case the year before under British rule.[23]

Legal argument began on the Monday. It is an indication of the slightly chaotic circumstances that there were now two separate habeas corpus applications being litigated before different judges of the High Court. One before Chief Justice Moloney, concerning the formidable widow Johnstone, a Donegal landowner, who had been arrested for arms offences.[24] The other, Childers, before Sir Charles who issued a stay of execution pending the completion of legal argument and judgment.[25]

All this generated a crisis in the Cabinet. If the court ruled for the prisoner, then the execution policy was unlawful; the four men already executed had been unlawfully killed and the thousands of prisoners interned without trial were not in lawful custody. Once again, the Cabinet records are silent as to what was said behind closed doors but a revealing memoir by Blythe described the tensions.[26] Some favoured simply shutting down the courts and at least one minister argued that if the court ruled against

[21] From an unpublished family memoir quoted by his nephew James Comyn in: *Their Friends at Court*, (London: Barry Rose Publishers, 1973), p75.

[22] The Firearms Act 10 & 11 Geo V., Ch 43.

[23] *Egan v Macready* [1921] IR 265.

[24] *Johnstone v O'Sullivan and Others* [1923] IR II 13.

[25] See Gerard Hogan, 'Hugh Kennedy, the Childers habeas corpus application and the return to the Four Courts', in C. Costello (ed), The Four Courts: 200 years. (Dublin: Four Courts, 1996).

[26] IMA: BMH Witness Statement 939, File s.66, Ernest Blythe, p192.

the government, the prisoner should be taken out and shot. Curiously it was General Mulcahy who argued most strongly against this proposition, but he was in a minority. Ireland hovered on the brink of rule by oligarchy.

In the case of the widow Johnstone, Chief Justice Moloney ruled for the government but stated that an appeal lay to the Court of Appeal. The real crisis centred around the high-profile case of Childers. On the final evening of exhausting legal argument, Sir Charles O'Connor delivered his judgment. With the Four Courts still in ruins, he sat by candlelight in the Hall at Kings' Inns under a guard of the national army:

> *I am sitting here in this temporary makeshift for a court of justice. Why? Because one of the noblest buildings in the country … is now a mass of crumbling ruins, the work of revolutionaries, who proclaim themselves soldiers of an Irish republic.*[27]

Sir Charles railed against the demolition of the Four Courts, the Public Record Office and the destruction of property, but his view on the central issue was clear: a state of war existed, and the court would not intervene. The civil law had failed, he ruled. Suprema Lex, salus populi must be the guiding principle: the safety and preservation of the people is the highest law.

According to Gerard Hogan, Sir Charles declined to grant a stay of execution.[28] The law report is silent on this issue, but a refusal to grant a stay would be consistent with the ruling of the court that there was no power to intervene. The habeas corpus ruling in the Johnstone case was already enroute to the Court of Appeal. It is inconceivable that Sir Charles was unaware of that fact, but he declined a stay.[29]

Childers was being held at Beggars Bush and just before dawn he was brought out for execution, a thin figure in a crumpled cream linen suit.

[27] *The King (Childers) v The Officer Commanding the Troops, Portobello Barracks, in the County of Dublin and the Adjutant General of the Forces of the Irish Provisional Government* [1923] IR 5 at page 13.

[28] Gerard Hogan, 'Should Judges be Neutral?' Northern Ireland Legal Quarterly Vol 72 (2021) p63–90. Gerard Hogan's account is supported by a memoir by Cahir Davitt, the Judge Advocate General. IMA: BMH Witness Statement no 1751, File 1637, Cahir Davitt, p45.

[29] *The King (Childers) v The Officer Commanding the Ardravan House Barracks Johnstone v O'Sullivan and Others* IR [1923] Vol II. P13. This case was decided the previous day and established there was an appeal to the Court of Appeal. Leading Counsel on both sides, Kennedy KC and Lynch KC were also in the Childers case.

Stubborn to the last, he complained that there was no Doctor as the regulations required. A Doctor was sent for. He also complained that was not sufficient light for the firing squad to see and the execution was deferred 'until mornings beam give him light to die.'[30] Childers smoked and talked with the Dean of Kildare and finally dawn broke. Cahir Davitt recalled that Childers 'chatted with the firing party, disclaimed any feeling of ill will, against anybody.'[31] There was time for a final cigarette.

His counsel, Michael Comyn discovered the news a few hours later as he attempted to get a listing before the Court of Appeal. Comyn was no stranger to capital trials; he had defended many prisoners during the war of independence, and some had been executed by firing squad. The execution of Childers, however, would always rankle: 'the complete negation of justice. The worst I have ever known.'[32] Sir Charles O'Connor was also profoundly affected in a way that has never been fully explained. He did not doubt his decision, but regretted refusing the stay, and he retired soon after, his composure permanently fractured.[33]

The outstanding habeas corpus ruling (Mrs Johnstone) failed in the Court of Appeal on a split vote.[34] This was a pivotal moment in the conflict: the courts had declined to intervene, and the crisis faced by the provisional government abated. The executions resumed.

Spooner, Farrelly, Murphy, and Mallin

These four men were captured with handguns and mills bombs, following an attack on an army convoy on the south circular road. They were plainly suspected of involvement but were never charged with attacking the national army, presumably because the offence could not be proved.

[30] IMA: BMH Witness Statement no 1751, File 1637, Cahir Davitt, p46. Davitt was re-writing a line from Thomas Moore's Battle of Aughrim where soldiers of the defeated army waited overnight, knowing that dawn would bring their death. 'While mute, they watched, while mornings beam should rise and give them light to die.'

[31] ibid., p. 45.

[32] From an unpublished Memoir quoted by James Comyn, *Their Friends at Court* (London: Barry Rose Publishers, 1973), p75. For an analysis of the case see Colm Campbell, *Emergency Law in Ireland, 1918–25*, (Oxford: Clarendon Press, 1994) P248–250.

[33] Gerard Hogan, 'Should Judges be Neutral?' Northern Ireland Law Quarterly, Vol 72 (2021), p63–90.

[34] The Court of Appeal was divided 2:1. Mrs. Johnstone and her daughter were in fact released soon after. Not because their claim was successful but because, it seems, they were not reckoned to be a threat to the new status quo.

They were all sentenced to death. Mallin was spared. A memoir written by the Judge Advocate General recalled that he had written a note to the Army Council arguing for a reprieve for this young man, but the only argument that weighed with the Army Council was that he was the son of the late Michael Mallin.[35] We see here, due process unravelling by degrees: even then, the law recognised that punishment depended on culpability, not the familial connections of the accused or the sympathy of the sentencing tribunal.

Mellows, O'Connor, Barrett, and McKelvey

The execution of anti-treaty prisoners had caused Liam Lynch to issue 'a shoot on sight' order in respect of those involved in the execution process. The assassination of Deputy Sean Hales was the first step in that process, although ironically, he had not voted on the Army (Special Powers) Resolution.

The killing of Deputy Hales took place the day after the creation of the Free State and the adoption of the Constitution. The Executive Council (formerly termed the Cabinet) met that evening and quickly fixed on a decision to execute four men as a reprisal. If minutes of that meeting were taken, they do not survive, but it seems all were agreed on this course of action.[36] The Dáil was not consulted, and it seems that power had completely coalesced in the hands of the seven ministers.

The men had been in custody since the Four Courts siege in the summer and it is plain they were not party to the campaign of assassination that was being conducted by Liam Lynch and there was therefore, no legal or moral basis for imputing responsibility for the death of Hales. Ernest Blythe wrote that 'lives of the men who had been at the Four Courts were forfeit, as rebels.' A trial, he wrote, would have been 'farcical.'[37] It is trite to point out that in even as the law then stood, guilt was established by trial, not by the views of government ministers. The Constitution, so recently passed into law, guaranteed trial or at least trial by military court in times of Cvil War.

Late that night the prisoners were woken, and each was given a short typed written note explaining what was to take place: 'You are hereby notified that being a person taken in arms against the government, you

[35] IMA: BMH Witness Statement no 1751, File 1637, Cahir Davitt, p46.
[36] IMA: BMH Witness Statement No 939, File s.66, Ernest Blythe, p190.
[37] ibid p190–192.

will be executed at 8 am on 8th December as a reprisal for the assassination of Brigadier Sean Hales TD.'[38] There was time to see a priest and write a few last letters home. Mellows wrote a hurried letter to his mother: '*time is short ... in such moments heart speaks to heart*'.[39]

Canon Pigott was then a young priest in Dublin and was called upon to provide comfort for the prisoners and witness the executions. He carried out this painful duty and decades later recalled that Mckelvey survived and spoke: '"give me another." A shot was fired into him.'[40]

Members of the Dáil learned the news from gossip or banner headlines in the late morning papers. The Dáil re-assembled later that day and Cosgrave expressed surprise that anyone would want to comment on the executions: 'is there not business on the agenda?' [41] The debate, angry and tempestuous, was opened by Tom Johnson, then leader of the opposition, who pointed out that new State and the Constitution had been in existence barely 48 hours and 'the first act is to utterly destroy in the public mind the association of the government with the idea of law.'[42]

George Gavan Duffy raised the central point: What is our constitution for, if not for this? Duffy's condemnation was absolute and resulted in this exchange on the floor of the Dáil:

Duffy: 'You stand condemned by your own constitution'
General Mulcahy: 'You had better keep it about you when moving around the town.'

Mulcahy's remark was a stark reminder that Dublin was a small city and pro-treaty deputies were well known. This exchange went to the heart of the debate. Was the Constitution just a piece of paper or did it confer inalienable rights? No other Cabinet Minister answered the point raised about the Constitution. Of the Committee charged with drafting the Constitution, only Darrell Figgis was a member of the Dáil. He had been

[38] See Colm Campbell, Emergency Law, p167. Also UCDA Archives, Mulcahy Papers P7/B/85, in which a first generation copy can be found.

[39] South Dublin County Libraries Archives, Letter from Liam Mellows, Mountjoy Prison, Dublin, to his mother shortly before his execution, 12-Aug-1922, available online at https://source.southdublinlibraries.ie/handle/10599/9022

[40] Canon John Pigot, 'Executions (1922) Recalled' The Athenry Journal 8 (1997).

[41] Dail Debates, vol 2 no. 3, (8 December 1922), available at https://www.oireachtas.ie/en/debates/debate/dail/1922-12-08/4/

[42] ibid.

deputy to Collins' chairmanship of the Committee and had steered the Committee with some skill. He was a pro- treaty deputy but spoke against the executions without reference to the Constitution.[43] Figgis instead chose to argue against the policy on a different ground—that it was antithetical to the rule of law, and therefore to 'the whole foundation of democratic government.' He pressed the point by claiming that, far from being necessitated in order to preserve democratic governance as claimed by the Government, the policy being pursued was likely to undermine the very thing which it sought to preserve.

Eoin MacNeill was next to speak and delivered an abrupt rebuke to 'the deputy who has just sat down.'[44] This was not a time for 'subtlety.' MacNeill also poured scorn on the 'timorous croakings' of others. His argument can be shortly stated: 'When emergencies of extreme necessity arise there is no limit. The question is whether the emergency that faces the state is one of extreme necessity or not.' Figgis, plainly stung, responded: 'I hold that we, who are the makers of the law, should be the most scrupulous observers'.[45]

The justification advanced by Ministers was framed in terms of 'meeting terror with terror.' O'Higgins latched onto the judgment of the Master of the Rolls in the Childers case: 'Salus populi, suprema lex.'[46] The safety of the people quickly became the catchphrase of government supporters and was used to justify evermore radical decisions. The crisis was weathered, and the next step was even more draconian.

Trial by Army Committee

On the night of Mountjoy Executions General Mulcahy announced his intention to bring in trial by army committee, for arms offences where there was no factual dispute. A proclamation was posted in the press the following morning.[47] A difficulty only later became apparent: although this process was intended for arms cases where there was no factual

[43] ibid.

[44] ibid.

[45] ibid.

[46] *The King (Childers) v The Officer Commanding the Troops, Portobello Barracks, in the County of Dublin and the Adjutant General of the Forces of the Irish Provisional Government.* [1923] IR 5 at page 14.

[47] Published in the Irish Times 8 December 1922 'Proclamation 7 December 1922'. See also, IMA: DOD/A/07266.

dispute, the proclamation did not say that. A more insidious difficulty was the decision as to whether there was a factual dispute was made by the national army officers investigating the case. This development facilitated swift trials without rules of evidence. And this was done without the sanction of the Dáil.

The trial regulations drafted by the Judge Advocate General and approved by the Dáil only weeks before, had laid down careful and specific safeguards for the trial of prisoners, but these were now swept away. Four weeks later, General Mulcahy extended the remit of army committees and further downgraded the trial procedures.[48] After this, many prisoners were tried without legal representation or the opportunity to call witnesses and as the war progressed some prisoners would be tried in absentia.[49]

It is stretching the language of Article 70 to equate 'Military Tribunals' with army committees sitting in private without recourse to rules. Even in time of Civil War, Article 70 did not permit military tribunals to function unless authorised by law and these tribunals were not. Article 70 also required that military tribunals be governed by 'regulations to be prescribed by law' and there were none. To the charge of illegality, there is no answer.

Post 1922

In January the execution process quickened: there were 35 executions.[50] The emerging policy favoured local executions rather than any examination of culpability of the offender or the objective gravity of the offence. This policy would soon be finessed: reprisal executions became the new policy in February. The policy was summarised in an internal Army Council order: 'In every case of outrage in any battalion area, three men will be executed.'[51] General Mulcahy's prose was not his strong point, but events

[48] Internal National Army order, issued by General Mulcahy and dated 27 January. IMA: IE-MA-CMA 216 "Proclamation by the Army Council", "Court-martial administration Civil War period".

[49] That this was so, is apparent from an account by Cahir Davitt, who was then Judge Advocate General. See IMA: BMH Witness Statement 1751, File 1637, p45, in which he recounts the trial of Martin Byrne, tried in his absence for the murder of Doctor Thomas Higgins.

[50] IMA: IE/MA/HS/A0770.

[51] UCD Archives, Mulcahy Papers P/7/B/178, 'Decision of Army Council 12 February 1923'.

show that the new policy was to meet any ambush by executing prisoners from the area which the ambush had taken place. The bank of prisoners under sentence of death soon rose to over four hundred and when ambushes took place, prisoners from that bank were chosen for execution.

While these events were being played out, unlawful deaths in the custody of the state continued and the government turned a blind eye to the Constitution and the protections it afforded. The most infamous consequences can be seen in the Kerry landmines massacres of March of 1923. At Ballyseedy Cross, Countess Bridge and Cahirciveen, 19 untried prisoners were tied to landmines which were detonated. The national army account was that the prisoners had been killed while clearing mines from barricades, but this narrative began to unravel when it transpired that two prisoners had escaped. One at Ballyseedy (Stephen Fuller) and one at Countess Bridge (Tadgh Coffey) and their accounts began to circulate.

Some weeks passed and the inquests required by law were still not held, but following concerns expressed in the Dáil, General Mulcahy directed that an army inquiry be held at Ballymullen army barracks at Tralee. The venue was not neutral: it was well known that anti-treaty prisoners were tortured at Ballymullen.[52] The tribunal was not neutral: the president of the tribunal was General O' Daly, who was the commanding officer of the soldiers said to have carried out the massacre.

The press was not invited and did not attend. The families of the dead were not informed or present. The only witnesses called were national army soldiers. The Inquiry found that the prisoners had lost their lives as a result of landmine explosions while removing barricades placed on the roads by Irregulars. The Inquiry exonerated all national army soldiers. The Executive Council, according to Ernest Blythe, were suspicious of all that had taken place but uninclined to intervene.[53]

[52] See for example, T. Ryle. Dwyer, "Tans, terror and troubles: Kerry's real fighting story, 1913–1923." (Cork: Mercier Press, 2001). P369 and Ernie O'Malley, "The Men Will Talk to Me: Kerry Interviews by Ernie O'Malley" in Cormac O'Malley and Tim Horgan (eds) (Cork: Mercier Press, 2012).

[53] IMA: BMH Witness Statement No 939, File s.66, Ernest Blythe, p178.

The Legacy

The Constitution was an early and brave attempt to embrace the rule of law. It offered guarantees of liberty, due process and freedoms that would take many decades to be fully realised.

It is submitted that one of the legacies of this time was that identified by deputy Tom Johnson: the Mountjoy Executions brought the law into disrepute. Second, each derogation from the rule of law facilitated another. The government's ambivalent attitude to the Constitution permeated the army and facilitated the landmines massacres and the cover up that followed. Covering up became a feature of ugly events in Ireland, as the Magdalene Laundries inquiry and the Ryan Commission demonstrate. However, the simple fact that these committees of inquiry were instituted, demonstrate a growing commitment to the rule of law and a determination to set a higher standard. The signatories of the 1916 rebellion aspired to a state committed to 'cherishing all ... equally.' We are not there yet and perhaps it may be naïve to think that will ever be the status quo. However, the institutions of the state are now imbued with the rule of law and the mechanisms now exist to ensure that the state respects the Constitution and the rights of the citizens.

References

Cahillane, Laura. *Drafting the Irish Free State Constitution.* Manchester University Press, 2016.

Campbell, Colm. *Emergency Law in Ireland, 1918 – 25.* Oxford: Clarendon Press, 1994.

Comyn, James. *Their Friends at Court.* London: Barry Rose Publishers, 1973.

Dorney, John. *The Civil War in Dublin: The Fight for the Irish Capital 1922-24.* Merrion Press, 2017.

Dwyer, T. Ryle. "Tans, terror and troubles: Kerry's real fighting story, 1913-1923." Cork: Mercier Press, 2001.

Enright, Seán. *The Irish Civil War. Law Atrocity and Execution.* Merrion Press, Dublin 2022.

Hogan, Gerard. "Hugh Kennedy, the Childers habeas corpus application and the return to the Four Courts." In *The Four Courts: 200 years*, edited by C. Costello, Dublin: Four Courts, 1996.

Hogan, Gerard. "Should Judges be Neutral?" *Northern Ireland Legal Quarterly* Vol 72 (2021): 63.

O'Malley, Ernie. "The Men Will Talk to Me: Kerry Interviews by Ernie O'Malley." In Cormac O'Malley and Tim Horgan, Cork: Mercier Press, 2012.

Pigot, John. "Executions (1922) Recalled." *The Athenry Journal* 8 (1997).

CHAPTER 13

Revisiting the Legacy of the Amendment Procedure

William Quill

Was the amendment procedure of the Constitution of the Irish Free State ("the 1922 Constitution") a fatal flaw? Or did the 15 years of its operation provide the new state with a valuable, albeit unintended, period of constitutional experimentation for the nascent Irish state? To mitigate the effect of an arduous amendment procedure, an exception was made to allow for amendment by ordinary means for a limited period, an exception which would end up being the only means of its amendment. In principle, a constitution should not be amended with the same ease as ordinary legislation; however, given the influence of the 1922 Constitution on its successor, the Constitution of Ireland ("the 1937 Constitution"), we can consider the practical effects of a having had, for a time, a constitution

William is an investigator for the Office of the Commissioner for Environmental Information. This chapter is written in a personal capacity and nothing in it is the view or opinion of the Office of the Commissioner for Environmental Information.

W. Quill (✉)
Dublin, Ireland

L. Cahillane, D. K. Coffey (eds.), *The Centenary of the Irish Free State Constitution*, Palgrave Modern Legal History,
https://doi.org/10.1007/978-3-031-46181-1_13

which was easy to amend, balancing what was lost during those years with what was embedded in stronger terms in 1937.

In proposing the 1937 Constitution, Éamon de Valera described the old Constitution as "a tattered and torn affair".[1] It suited de Valera's agenda to describe the text in such terms, but that was not sufficient grounds for a new text. In analysing why a new constitution was enacted in 1937, Coffey identified four strands of justification: the implementation of the constitutional republican project; the problem of the juristic basis of the state; the degradation of the rights provisions; and weaknesses in the drafting of the 1922 Constitution.[2] Although a critique of the drafting of the amendment procedure is merited,[3] given this multi-faceted motivation, a new constitution may in any case have been deemed necessary. The drafters could not have anticipated the greater freedom that could be achieved after the Statute of Westminster 1931. In truth, a rigid amendment process would have constrained the constitutional development between 1932 and 1937 that followed the freedom the Statute offered. A constitution difficult to amend, as it was when drafted, with thresholds of turnout and approval, could have impeded this constitutional development.

Elements of popular sovereignty inserted in the 1922 Constitution included provisions containing the initiative,[4] the referendum on legislation,[5] and the referendum on constitutional amendments.[6] None of these provisions were utilised, with the first popular vote on a matter of policy being that of the adoption of the 1937 Constitution. But the degree of popular sovereignty embedded within the 1922 Constitution may arguably have endangered the development of parliamentary governance. The government was initially slow to respond to the possible use of the democratic devices, but eventually decided to excise them from the text, as explored below. This took place as a result of the oath controversy. The removal of the oath was the first amendment proposed by Éamon de Valera, and is also considered below in more detail.

[1] Dáil Debates, Vol. 67 No. 1. 11 May 1937. Bunreacht na hEireann (Dréacht)—Dara Céim.

[2] Donal K. Coffey, "The Need for a New Constitution: Irish Constitutional Change 1932–1935" (2012) 48(2) Irish Jurist, 275–302.

[3] See Laura Cahillane, *Drafting the Irish Free State Constitution* (Manchester University Press, 2016), 47–64.

[4] Article 48 – this allowed for potential constitutional amendments and legislative proposals to be initiated by the citizens.

[5] Article 47 – this would have allowed for citizens voting in a referendum to veto legislation.

[6] Article 50.

In 1931, an amendment added a new Article 2A, giving detailed constitutional protection for military tribunals.[7] This amendment took place after the initial period of amendment by legislative means had been extended to 16 years. A challenge to the legitimacy of this amendment in *State (Ryan) v. Lennon*[8] brought scrutiny to the ease of amendment and brought its effect into disrepute. This chapter does not seek to defend any specific use of the procedure; however, we can, with hindsight, appreciate how it assisted in paving the path for a more stable Constitution that has lasted. Rather than a transitory period of eight years, the flexibility of amendments allowed for 15 years during which the state could develop, fulfilling the potential Michael Collins ascribed to the Treaty in December 1921 as "not the ultimate freedom that all nations desire and develop to, but the freedom to achieve it".[9] In December 1935, Éamon de Valera, then head of government, stated that he regarded "this whole period as a necessary period of transition".[10]

This chapter will consider (1) the amendment procedure adopted in the 1922 Constitution; (2) the initiative and referendum procedures and how they were removed from the text; (3) the amendment on the oath, and other changes proposed by Éamon de Valera which chipped away at the Treaty settlement; and (4) how the provisions on amendment and referendums were adapted for the 1937 Constitution.

Thresholds of Turnout and Approval

In the draft proposed to the Third Dáil, the 1922 Constitution could be amended only by a referendum.[11] To pass, it would have required both a majority of registered voters to turn out, ***and*** either a majority of registered voters or two-thirds of votes cast to approve it. This combination of a turnout threshold with an approval threshold would have made it quite difficult to amend.

[7] Constitution (Amendment No. 17) Act, 1931 (No. 37), enacted 17 October 1931.

[8] [1935] IR 170.

[9] Dáil debates, Vol. T No. 6. 19 December 1921. Debate on Treaty.

[10] Dáil debates, Vol. 59 No. 17. 12 December 1935. Constitution (Amendment No. 24) Bill, 1934. - Motion Under Article 38A of the Constitution.

[11] Laura Cahillane, *Drafting the Irish Free State Constitution* (Manchester University Press, 2016), 67; Bill to Enact Constitution. Dáil debates - Monday, 18 September 1922. Vol. 1 No. 6.

No amendment to the 1922 Constitution was put to a referendum; however, we can appreciate the high standard it set by comparing it to the referendums held to amend the 1937 Constitution. Since 1937, there have been 41 referendums; of these, 11 were rejected and 30 were approved. Among the 30 approved, 12 were on a turnout of less than 50%, which would have failed the first threshold. A further 7 did not have the approval of two-thirds of votes cast, including those on divorce (1995) and marriage equality (2015). The alternate threshold of a majority of voters on the register was only reached twice, on EEC Accession (1972) and the Good Friday Agreement (1998). Only 11 reached the threshold of the 1922 amendment procedure. The addition of the Court of Appeal required a referendum in 2013: it was approved by 65% of voters on a turnout of 39%. It is the type of institutional change that the high thresholds would have impeded.

Had such a constraint been in place, it is likely that even fewer would have been approved. A 2010 game theory study found that with an approval threshold, only those who are indifferent will not participate, but that with a participation threshold, "if an opponent of the proposal believes that there is a solid majority in favour of the proposal but there is a good chance the participation [threshold] is not met, then the best chance to defeat the proposal is not to vote at all".[12] For example, the Eighth Amendment was approved with the support of 66.9% of votes cast, narrowly passing the required approval of two-thirds of votes cast. However, turnout was 53.7% of the vote; had there been a turnout requirement, it could have easily been defeated by a campaign of abstention, perhaps advocated by the government which had failed to secure its own preferred wording for the amendment.[13] Whatever one's views of the 1983 amendment, it illustrates how turnout requirements can be manipulated by those seeking to defeat a proposal.

Without polling data, we cannot determine the popularity of any of the amendments to the 1922 Constitution, but even assuming a similar distribution, many of the amendments may have struggled with either the turnout or approval thresholds to an extent that would have impeded

[12] Luís Aguiar-Conraria and Pedro C. Magalhães, "Referendum design, quorum rules and turnout" *Public Choice* 144, No. 1/2 (July 2010): 67–68. https://doi.org/10.1007/s11127-009-9504-1

[13] For alternative wording proposed by the Minister for Justice see Dáil debates, Vol. 341 No. 10. 27 April 1983. Eighth Amendment of the Constitution Bill 1982: Committee Stage (Resumed) and Final Stages.

constitutional development. Certainly some of the amendments proposed were in the category of minor institutional changes that would have been unlikely to excite the public.[14] While the 1922 Constitution suffered the flaw of being too easy to amend, it could easily have suffered the opposite flaw of being too difficult to amend.

Transitory Period of Amendment by Legislative Means

When the Third Dáil considered the amendment procedure of the draft constitution, it recognised that it was a rigid system. Thomas Johnson, leader of the Labour Party, argued for an initial period of review without a need for a referendum.[15] Kevin O'Higgins, on behalf of the provisional government, agreed, ultimately allowing amendments by way of ordinary legislation for eight years. He justified this by reference to the "undue haste" with which they were proceeding, being required to complete ratification by December 1922. O'Higgins stated that this addition was to address "latent defects" and that it would be "awkward" where there was unanimity in both houses, and then would be necessary to hold a referendum and get a majority of voters on the register. He concluded that that would "be a cumbrous process … out of all proportion to the importance of the amendment we might wish to make".[16]

Article 50 as adopted provided[17]:

> Amendments of this Constitution within the terms of the Scheduled Treaty may be made by the Oireachtas, but no such amendment, passed by both Houses of the Oireachtas, after the expiration of a period of eight years from the date of the coming into operation of this Constitution, shall become

[14] For instance, the Constitution (Amendment No. 12) Act 1930 (No. 5) set the standing orders of the Committee of Privileges between the Houses and the Constitution (Amendment No. 11) Act 1929 (No. 34) extended the franchise for Seanad elections from the Seanad alone to the Dáil and the Seanad.

[15] Laura Cahillane, "Popular sovereignty under the 1922 Constitution: theory and reality", in *Constitutional Change and Popular Sovereignty: Populism, Politics and the Law in Ireland*, edited by Maria Cahill, Colm Ó Cinnéide, Seán Ó Conaill and Conor O'Mahony (Oxford: Routledge, 2021) 22–37, 29.

[16] Dáil debates, Vol. 1 No. 18. 5 October 1922. I gCoiste ar an mBille um Bunreacht Shaorstáit Eireann. (In Committee on the Constitution of Saorstát Eireann Bill.) - Article 49—Amendments of The Constitution.

[17] Dáil debates, Vol. 1 No. 24. 19 October 1922. Amendments to Article 50.

> law, unless the same shall, after it has been passed or deemed to have been passed by the said two Houses of the Oireachtas, have been submitted to a Referendum of the people, and unless a majority of the voters on the register shall have recorded their votes on such Referendum, and either the votes of a majority of the voters on the register, or two-thirds of the votes recorded, shall have been cast in favour of such amendment. Any such amendment may be made within the said period of eight years by way of ordinary legislation and as such shall be subject to the provisions of Article 47 hereof.

This approach considered only "latent defects" that would manifest themselves during the initial operation of the constitution, and not amendments after any transitory period where there would be a political consensus, but low levels of public interest. If a referendum with strict thresholds was cumbersome in cases of political unanimity, this would also be true after any transitory period. The stated purpose might have been better achieved by a requirement to hold referendums where a constitutional amendment failed to secure a certain parliamentary threshold. For example, the Danish constitution requires five-sixths of the Folketing to approve the delegation of powers to international authorities; where a Treaty fails to secure this threshold, it must be put to a referendum.[18] Governments since 1937 have often held referendums on the same day as another election; but even that is no guarantee of reaching the turnout threshold, as referendums held to coincide with the 1997 and 2018 presidential elections had a turnout of less than 50%. The lack of full consideration of options as to how to address the difficulty of this "cumbrous process", including addressing the thresholds, was itself an example of the "undue haste" O'Higgins was concerned about.

Although Johnson had been the one to suggest a period of amendment by ordinary means, his contributions to later debates indicate a regret at so easy a formula for constitutional change. The first bill to amend the Constitution, proposed in 1925, clarified the terms and dates of elections of the first senators; it might then be seen as very much what Thomas Johnson had in mind when proposing the period whereby a referendum would not be necessary. Interestingly, Johnson himself raised concern about this, though he did not ultimately impede its progress: "I cannot but think that the decision to introduce a Constitution (Amendment) Bill

[18] Constitution of Denmark, Section 20.2.

over a matter of small detail of this kind is the best way of proceeding".[19] He did oppose the second bill to amend the Constitution, proposed in 1926, which introduced the rule that the outgoing Ceann Comhairle be returned without being required to seek re-election. On this occasion, Johnson called a division, criticising what he saw as the government's easy manner with the Constitution: "the Constitution itself assumes that changes will not be made in the Constitution without very strong reason, and that after the eighth year of the Constitution there will be very great difficulty in changing it. The view of the Ministry seems to be that, having regard to the difficulty of future changes, we must go to the other extreme in the interim and make changes now as lightly and easily as possible".[20] This could have been avoided had the Third Dáil adopted a more precise formula during the debate he himself had participated in.

Risk of Extra-Parliamentary Politics

The 1922 Constitution included two means for direct popular participation in the legislative process: the initiative to propose legislation and the referendum to veto legislation. After the first serious attempt to use them, they were removed from the text in 1928. In his study of the 1922 Constitution, writing after the procedures on the initiative and referendum had been excised, Leo Kohn wrote of the risks they posed, considering them to be "subversive of the authority of parliament" and that they "destroyed the coherence of representative government".[21] Although introduced in a text proposed by the Cosgrave government in 1922, that administration would later regret them.

Article 47 provided that a sufficient blocking minority of either 40% of the Dáil or a majority of the Seanad could delay the enactment of legislation. A resolution of 60% of the Seanad or 5% of Dáil voters could require that the legislation be submitted to a referendum, requiring 50% of votes cast to secure the enactment of the legislation. The final clause of Article 47 qualified the matter, as this procedure could not be adopted for a

[19] Dáil debates, Vol. 12 No. 9. 16 June 1925. Constitution (Amendment) No. 1 Bill—Second Stage.

[20] Dáil debates, Vol. 17 No. 6. 1 December 1926. Constitution (Amendment No. 2) Bill, 1926—Second Stage.

[21] Leo Kohn, *Constitution of the Irish Free State* (1930), 244.

money bill or a bill deemed by both Dáil and Seanad "to be necessary for the immediate preservation of the public peace, health or safety".

Article 48 provided for "the initiation by the people of proposals for laws or constitutional amendments". Legislation proposed by the people could be initiated by 50,000 Dáil voters. If the Oireachtas rejected the proposal, it would be subject to a referendum under the terms of Article 47; if it enacted, the legislation would be subject to the ordinary provisions for amendment of legislation or constitutional amendments.

A 1924 cabinet sub-committee proposed the deletion of both Articles.[22] However, it was not until there was an attempt to use the Constitution to undermine the provisions on the oath that government began a process of excising them.

Article 17 of the 1922 Constitution provided an oath which included fidelity to the king, agreed in the Anglo-Irish Treaty, which was required of every member of the Oireachtas before taking their seats.[23] Initially, apart from standing for election, the abstentionist policy of the Anti-Treaty group amounted to full non-engagement with the Irish Free State. In 1926, Éamon de Valera sought to persuade this group that they should enter the Dáil in the absence of the oath. After failing to secure agreement on this, he formed Fianna Fáil, a new political party, later that year. The position of Fianna Fáil was that in the absence of the oath, they would take their seats.[24]

In January 1927, Dan Breen, who had been elected as a Republican TD in 1923, broke with his Anti-Treaty colleagues, took the oath, and entered the Dáil.[25] He was first to attempt to use the mechanisms within the Constitution to remove the oath. In April 1927, he sought leave to introduce a constitutional amendment to repeal Article 17, arguing that "there will be no political unity ... until such time as the test which debars one-third of our representatives from attending here is removed".[26] It was defeated at first stage, opposed by W. T. Cosgrave on two bases: the fact

[22] Alan J. Ward, *The Irish Constitutional Tradition: Responsible Government and Modern Ireland 1782–1992* (CUA Press, 1994), 222.

[23] Article 17, 1922 Constitution; Article 4, Anglo-Irish Treaty.

[24] Mell Farrell, *Party Politics in a New Democracy, 1922–37* (London: Palgrave, 2017), 160–167.

[25] Dáil debates, Vol. 18 No. 1. 25 January 1927. Deputy Takes His Seat.

[26] Dáil debates, Vol. 19 No. 10. 6 April 1927. Private Business. - Constitution (Amendment No. 6) Bill—First Stage.

that it had formed a key part of the Treaty to which the state was bound, and the endorsement at subsequent elections.

A general election took place in June 1927, with Fianna Fáil only three seats behind the government party, Cumann na nGaedheal.[27] In the continued absence of Fianna Fáil and Sinn Féin, Cosgrave comfortably formed a new government, with the support of the Farmers' Party and Independent TDs. Remaining outside the Dáil, Fianna Fáil used the mechanisms of the Constitution to act politically. By 30 June, it had collected the required number of 70,000 signatures under Article 48 seeking an end to the oath.[28]

On 10 July, Kevin O'Higgins was assassinated. On 20 July, Cosgrave introduced a series of legislative measures in response to the heightened political situation. The Constitution (Amendment No. 6) Bill 1927 was the first proposal by the government to weaken direct democracy in the Constitution: it would have repealed Article 48 on the initiative and restricted the ability of members of the Oireachtas to call a referendum under Article 47 to those who had taken the oath.[29] Curiously, he did not yet propose removing Article 47 entirely.

Cosgrave also proposed an amendment to the electoral law, requiring TDs to take the oath or their election would be declared void.[30] Cosgrave justified this as an effort "to put an end to the present anomalous condition of things in which persons avail of the electoral machinery which has been provided by the State for the selection of members of the Oireachtas to offer themselves for election without having any intention of taking their seats".[31] This bill passed its final stages on 10 August.[32] de Valera led his party into the Dáil on 12 August, declaring the oath to be an empty formula. On 16 August, the government narrowly won a confidence motion. Following two government by-election victories, Cosgrave sought a dissolution of the Dáil on 25 August, with a new election in September. After the election, Cosgrave formed a new government, with

[27] Farrell, 160–167.

[28] "75,000 signatures — Fianna Fáil's plans — Legal action and a referendum" (30 June 1927), *The Irish Times*, p. 7.

[29] Constitution (Amendment No. 6) Bill 1927 (No. 24).

[30] Electoral (Amendment) (No. 2) Bill 1927, s. 4 (No. 26).

[31] Dáil debates, Vol. 20 No. 15. 28 July 1927. Electoral (Amendment) (No. 2) Bill 1927—Second Stage.

[32] Seanad debates. Vol. 9 No. 9. 10 August 1927. Electoral (Amendment) (No. 2) Bill 1927—Final Stages.

a formal arrangement with the Farmers' Party and support from Independents.[33]

The constitutional amendment to remove the initiative lapsed on the dissolution of the Dáil. Cosgrave could have reintroduced it but failed to do so, retaining the mechanisms of direct popular legislation within the Constitution. This left it open to the opposition to take advantage of it. On 16 May 1928, de Valera sought leave to present a petition, purported to have 96,079 signatures, to replace the oath in Article 17 with a requirement to sign the roll of members. Beyond the publication of legislation, Cosgrave had not acted to remove popular legislative action from the Constitution; nevertheless, he appealed to parliamentary sovereignty: "This Dáil is a sovereign Dáil, and the majority in this Dáil can take whatever decisions it considers best ... This is a frivolous petition. It is frivolous inasmuch as it comes after a general election at which this was one of the issues."[34] He then proceeded with a fundamental critique of the initiative procedure: "Any 75,000 people—which figure represents about one-sixteenth of the electorate—can come forward here with proposals, week after week if they like, and present them to the Oireachtas". William Thrift, an Independent TD, proposed a delay in consideration of de Valera's proposal to introduce a petition until procedures had been put in place.[35] It is indicative of the government's failure to act that it fell to a backbencher not formally a member of the government party to propose the counter-motion, which was approved on 1 June.[36] Despite considering removal of the initiative procedure as early as 1924, and publishing a bill in July 1927, the government had failed to act after the September 1927 election.

On 7 June, the government introduced the Constitution (Amendment No. 10) Bill 1928 to repeal Article 47 and 48. It was followed in both the Dáil and the Seanad by a motion under Article 47 declaring it to be "necessary for the immediate preservation of the public peace and safety". de Valera alluded to the government's own delay in introducing the legislation in opposing this motion: "There was no question of reintroducing [the Constitution (Amendment No. 6) Bill 1927]. It was only when we,

[33] Farrell, 174–181.

[34] Dáil debates, Vol. 23 No. 13. 16 May 1928. Private Deputies' Business. - Petition to Amend the Constitution.

[35] Dáil debates, Vol. 23 No. 16. 23 May 1928. Private Deputies Business. - Petition Under Article 48 of the Constitution.

[36] Dáil debates, Vol. 23 No. 21. 1 June 1928. Private Deputies Business. - Petition Under Article 48 of the Constitution.

in accordance with that Article, produced in this House the 96,000 signatures ... to a Petition asking that that Article should be put into operation that there was a question of removing it". de Valera's suggestion that the government had not shown the urgency the motion under Article 47 suggests is borne out by its own delay. However, this change ensured that debates on the development of the Irish state, and in particular on the Oath, would occur within the arena of the Oireachtas and general election campaigns.

Sixteen amendments were made in the first eight years of the enactment of the 1922 Constitution. One of these amendments extended the transitional period of amendment by ordinary legislative means itself, from 8 to 16 years. It was indicative of the hasty drafting that it could be done so easily. This amendment was approved in 1929 with remarkably little comment, with just over 200 words spoken between the three main party leaders, including a comment from de Valera that "we hope to see it availed of to make changes which will make this Constitution one which will be more satisfactory to the Irish people, we will not object to it".[37] Having removed the initiative and referendum procedures on ordinary legislation, the government did not propose removing referendums on constitutional amendments, but merely postponing their necessity, indicating a residual commitment to popular oversight over the Constitution. Neither was it a short extension; although Cumann na nGaedheal would have hoped to continue in office beyond 1932, they had only narrowly retained office in 1927, and would therefore have been conscious that they were giving a tool to Fianna Fáil were they to enter government.

Amendments Towards Sovereignty

The Statute of Westminster 1931 removed the right of the Westminster Parliament to legislate for the Dominions without their consent to such an enactment.[38] After the 1932 general election, Fianna Fáil took office with Éamon de Valera as president of the Executive Council, although dependent for its Dáil majority on the Labour Party. de Valera would take full advantage of this Statute. On 20 April 1932, he introduced the Constitution

[37] Dáil debates, Vol. 28 No. 10. 13 March 1929. Constitution (Amendment No. 16) Bill, 1928—Second Stage.

[38] Statute of Westminster 1931 (22&23 Geo 5) c. 4, s. 4; Farrell, 244–245.

(Removal of Oath) Bill 1932.[39] It had two substantive clauses: the repeal of Article 17, on the oath, in its entirety (as opposed to its substitution in the proposed 1928 petition) and the repeal of section 2 of the Constitution of the Irish Free State (Saorstát Eireann) Act 1922, which required the Constitution to be construed with reference to the terms of the Anglo-Irish Treaty.

Cumann na nGaedheal opposed the Bill in defence of the Treaty and asserted that both the oath and construction clause were required by the Treaty, such that any change could not be done unilaterally by the Irish Free State. Patrick McGilligan, a former minister, proposed an amendment to the legislation to limit the repeal of construction clause, arguing that although de Valera might claim a mandate to attack the oath, he did not have a mandate to attack the Treaty as a whole.[40] The Bill faced no serious prospect of defeat in the Dáil; it was in the Seanad, however, that it faced effective opposition. It was there amended with a clause delaying its commencement until "an Agreement has been entered into between the Government of the Irish Free State and the British Government providing that Article 4 of the Treaty of 1921 shall cease to have effect and such Agreement has been ratified and approved by resolution of Dáil Éireann".[41] Joseph Connolly, a government minister sitting in the Seanad, observed at final stages there that it had been "amended and lacerated here and that it is not the intention of the Government to accept the Bill in its present form".[42]

de Valera called an early election in January 1933, dissolving the Dáil after less than ten months, seeking to end his reliance on the Labour Party.[43] Although he did not quite manage this, the summoning of a new Dáil had a constitutional implication. A bill which was passed with amendments by the Seanad to which the Dáil did not agree could be submitted to the Seanad for reconsideration either 18 months after it was sent from the Dáil or from the date of the reassembly of the Oireachtas after a

[39] Dáil debates, Vol. 41 No. 3. 20 April 1932. Constitution (Removal of Oath) Bill, 1932—First Stage.

[40] See David Harkness, "Patrick McGilligan: Man of commonwealth", *The Journal of Imperial and Commonwealth History*, (1979) 8:1, 117–135.

[41] Constitution (Removal of Oath) Bill 1932 (No. 2a), as passed by Seanad Éireann.

[42] Seanad debates, Vol. 15 No. 18. 28 June 1932. Constitution (Removal of Oath) Bill, 1932—Fifth Stage.

[43] Mel Farrell, *Party Politics in a New Democracy: The Irish Free State, 1922–37* (London: Palgrave, 2017), 257.

dissolution. On 1 March, de Valera proposed a motion to resubmit the Constitution (Removal of Oath) Bill to the Seanad; had there not been a dissolution and reassembly, it could not have been resubmitted until November 1933. The Seanad voted that it "declines further to consider the Constitution (Removal of Oath) Bill, 1933, until it has been made the subject of negotiation between the Executive Council and the British Government with a view to an amicable agreement".[44]

Competing views were seen in the attitudes of two former TDs then sitting in the Seanad: Seán Milroy of Cumann na nGaedheal asked whether "the Treaty, an international agreement solemnly entered into between two State entities, [was] to be honoured only until it is convenient to one of the State members to break it with impunity". Thomas Johnson, the former Labour leader, referred to the mandate which the government had received in the election to pursue the amendment, "the House is asked to flout the definite and clear decision of the electorate within a month after the electorate has spoken". Johnson anticipated the fate of the Seanad when commenting as follows: "I do not suppose that they are concerned very much with the consequences, the inevitable consequences as I think, to a second Chamber when that Chamber deliberately and defiantly ... the almost inevitable consequences of irresponsible action ... are that future parliamentary government of this country will be government by one Chamber".[45] On 3 May 1933, the Dáil carried a motion of enactment.[46] It was signed by the Governor-General that day.

As suggested by Johnson, the failure of the Seanad to ease its opposition after the election may have hastened its own demise. In June 1933, the government initiated a Bill to reduce the period of delay under Article 38A[47] from 18 months to 3 months. This Bill itself was stalled in the Seanad, which called for a joint committee of both houses to consider changes to the Constitution and powers of the second chamber.[48] In

[44] Seanad debates, Vol. 16 No. 12. 15 March 1933. Public Business. - Constitution (Removal of Oath) Bill, 1933—Second Stage.

[45] Seanad debates, Vol. 16 No. 12. 15 March 1933. Constitution (Removal of Oath) Bill, 1933—Second Stage.

[46] Dáil debates. Vol. 47 No. 4. 3 May 1933. Constitution (Removal of Oath) Bill, 1932—Motion of Enactment.

[47] An amendment which had already been made to reduce the time of the Seanad in considering bills.

[48] Seanad debates, Vol. 17 No. 1. 11 July 1933. Constitution (Amendment No. 19) Bill, 1933—Second Stage.

1934, de Valera proposed instead a constitutional amendment to abolish the Seanad. Following a similar pattern of delay by the Seanad, this legislation took effect in May 1936.

This left a single chamber to consider the final amendment to the 1922 Constitution.[49] On 11 December 1936, Edward VIII abdicated as king of the United Kingdom. The British statute which gave effect to this made no reference to the Irish Free State, where it required separate legislation.[50] The Executive Council had already considered constitutional amendments to remove the role of the Governor-General in relation to the appointment of judges, the appointment of the Executive Council, and the dissolution of the Dáil.[51] These amendments became superfluous; on 11 December, de Valera proposed a constitutional amendment to remove all mentions of the monarchy from the Constitution, making the Irish Free State a Republic for all internal purposes.[52] It passed through all stages in the Dáil that same day. This could not have occurred had there been a requirement for a referendum, and given the turnout and approval thresholds, there would have been no guarantee it would have passed. On the following day, 12 December, the Dáil enacted the Executive Authority (External Relations) Act 1936, which amongst other matters, ratified the abdication.[53]

Repeal of the 1922 Constitution

The 1937 Constitution repealed the 1922 Constitution. To the extent that there was no provision for its wholesale repeal, the adoption of a new Constitution might be considered revolutionary.[54] In the Dáil, de Valera justified it by the mandate which he hoped it would receive, "[no one] can tell us that this Draft Constitution is *ultra vires* for it is the people themselves who will enact it. They are the authority. The people have power to determine from time to time who their rulers will be and also what their

[49] For further, see Butler, "The Representative of the Crown and the Governor-General of the Irish Free State: Text and Context" [pp covering section 4].

[50] His Majesty's Declaration of Abdication Act 1936, (1 Edw. 8 & 1 Geo. 6, c. 3).

[51] NAI TSCH/3/S2793; NAI TSCH/3/S2794; and NAI TSCH/3/S2795.

[52] Dáil debates, Vol. 64 No. 9. 11 December 1936. Constitution (Amendment No. 27) Bill, 1936—Second Stage.

[53] Executive Authority (External Relations) Act 1936 (No. 58), s. 3(2),

[54] Bill Kissane, *New Beginnings: Constitutionalism and democracy in modern Ireland* (University College Dublin Press, 2011), xiv and xvi.

government will be".[55] It may also have been legally permissible because it was within the period when the 1922 Constitution could be amended by ordinary means. The courts had held, in assessing public safety legislation, that during the period that the Constitution could be amended without a referendum, ordinary legislation could be considered to have amended it, following the canon of statutory interpretation that a later law repeals an earlier law.[56] The Plebiscite (Draft Constitution) Act 1937 fell within this period, and therefore its mechanisms can be considered to have been permitted under the constitutional law of the time.[57] This Act provided that the Draft Constitution be submitted to a plebiscite at the general election following the next dissolution.[58] It would be the first vote on a matter of national policy.

Under Article 62, the Constitution was to come into operation after its "approval by the people signified by a majority of the votes cast at a plebiscite". This plebiscite was not subject to any threshold. Voters in July 1937 were noticeably more interested in the general election than the plebiscite; more than 10% cast an invalid vote on the Constitution. It received the support of 56.5% of the valid vote poll (or 38.6% of the electorate), and therefore would not have passed the approval threshold under Article 50 of the 1922 Constitution.[59]

The 1937 Constitution contains two methods of plebiscitary democracy. Article 27, like Article 47 of the 1922 Constitution, provides a mechanism for resolving a difference between the Houses of the Oireachtas. A majority of the Seanad and one-third of the Dáil may issue a petition to the president that a bill be referred to a referendum. The president may do so on making determining that it "contains a proposal of such national importance that the will of the people thereon ought to be ascertained". As noted by Bláthna Ruane, despite de Valera's enthusiasm for the

[55] Dáil Debates, Vol. 67 No. 1. 11 May 1937. Bunreacht na hEireann (Dréacht)—Dara Céim.

[56] *R. (Cooney) v. Clinton* [1935] I.R. 245 (1924) and *Attorney General v. McBride* [1928] I.R. 451.

[57] An application in this context was later rejected in *Laurentiu v. Minister for Justice* [1999] 4 I.R. 26.

[58] Plebiscite (Draft Constitution) Act 1937 (No. 16), ss. 1 and 2. Enacted on 2 June 1937, while debate on the Draft Constitution continued in the Dáil.

[59] *Referendum Results 1937–2019*, (2020: Department of Housing, Planning and Local Government), 19.

It was rejected in five constituencies: Dublin Townships, Cork West, Wicklow, Sligo, and Dublin County.

initiative procedure in 1928, he showed no interest in its inclusion in the 1937 Constitution.[60]

Article 46 provides that amendments to the constitution are be initiated in the Dáil as a bill and pass or deemed to have passed both houses, before being submitted to a referendum. They must be expressed to be "An Act to Amend the Constitution" and may not contain any other proposal.

Article 47 contains provisions for both constitutional referendums and referendums on ordinary legislation. Referendums on constitutional referendums require a majority of votes cast, with no turnout or approval thresholds.[61] If a referendum were ever to be proposed to veto ordinary legislation following a procedure under Article 27, it would require not just a majority of votes cast to be against the measure, but that this number be not less one-third of votes on the register. This contrasts with the simple requirement in the legislative referendum in the 1922 Constitution of a majority of votes recorded. de Valera justified the high threshold "to make sure that, if the normal procedure and the will of the Parliament [were] interfered with, there [would] be no uncertainty as regards the will of the electorate in the matter".[62] To date, no petition under Article 27 on legislation has been submitted.

As in 1922, the drafters of the 1937 Constitution anticipated that there could be latent defects that revealed themselves after its adoption. Article 51 allowed amendments by ordinary legislative means for a short period. Learning the lesson of the 1922 Constitution, it contained three measures to limit its scope: it was limited to a three-year period, with de Valera rejecting an eight-year period, as "only looking for trouble";[63] time ran from the commencement of the term of the first president, with Article 51.2 permitting the president, after consultation with the Council of State, to certify that the proposal was of "such a character and importance that the will of the people thereon ought to be ascertained by Referendum prior to its enactment by law"; and, in contrast with the 1922 Constitution,

[60] Bláthna Ruane, "Democratic control and constitutional referenda", *Law and Government: A Tribute to Rory Brady* (Dublin: Round Hall, 2014), 209.

[61] In 1979, two amendments were approved on a turnout of just 28.6%; in 1995, the amendment to allow divorce was approved with 50.3% of the vote.

[62] Dáil debates, Vol. 68 No. 3. 10 June 1937. Bunreacht na hEireann (Dréacht)—Ath-Chúrsa i gCoiste (D'Ath-Thógaint).

[63] Dáil debates, Vol. 68 No. 3. 10 June 1937. Bunreacht na hEireann (Dréacht)—Ath-Chúrsa i gCoiste (D'Ath-Thógaint).

both Article 46 and Article 51 were specifically excluded from amendment under this procedure.

The three years ran from 25 June 1938 to 24 June 1941. Two amendments were enacted under this procedure: the First Amendment in September 1939 allowed a state of emergency to be declared although the State was not a participant in a war, and the Second Amendment in May 1941 was an omnibus bill, with forty separate amendments, many of which were minor in substance, although expansive wording defining the "time of war" meant that the state of emergency (though not the emergency powers) declared in September 1939 did not elapse until in August 1976, which was promptly followed by a new emergency declared in the context of the armed conflict in Northern Ireland, which was not declared to have ended until February 1995.[64]

Conclusion

Since 1937, when the Constitution of Ireland was approved by the people, it has continued to develop in a dialogue between successive governments and the people in referendum. This did not occur with the 1922 Constitution. It was approved by the Third Dáil sitting as a constituent assembly, subject to ultimate ratification by the British parliament, rather than being approved in a referendum.[65] It was intended to be amended by referendum only, but with thresholds of both turnout and approval that could have impeded the institutional adjustments in the 1920s and slowed steps towards greater sovereignty in the 1930s. In response to the barriers of the proposed amendment system, the Third Dáil adopted one that was porous. However, the democratic principle of popular sovereignty in the Constitution had not been abandoned. Although the initiative and referendum on legislation were removed in 1928, the principle of referendum for constitutional amendment was not. It was due to be realised in 1938, 16 years after the adoption of the 1922 Constitution. It was in fact realised in 1937, when the new Constitution was approved by a simple majority of votes cast.

By 1937, Ireland's constitutional relationship with the United Kingdom had transformed. As acknowledged in the debate on the wording of the amendment procedure, the 1922 Constitution was drafted under pressure

[64] Dáil debates, Vol. 448, No. 6. 7 February 1995. Cessation of State of Emergency: Motion.

[65] Referendums were not used to approve constitutions at the time.

of time. There would certainly be need for change, whether to the legislative process or in redefining Ireland's external constitutional status. It was also fortunate timing for the Irish State that the abdication crisis occurred in December 1936, at a time when the Irish Free State could respond swiftly with a constitutional amendment to remove references to the monarchy.

Had Ireland's politics followed a different path in the 1930s, the open nature of the amendment clause could have been fatal to our democracy. The insertion of Article 2A itself and the risks it posed are evidence of this. On the other hand, the removal of the measures on the initiative and the referendum entrenched politics into the parliamentary rather than extra-parliamentary arena. The oath was removed following parliamentary procedures, including the mandate of an intervening general election.

How harshly should the easy amendment procedure be judged? It may have saved the early Irish state from the risks of a more rigid system than we have under our current Constitution. It set the framework for popular sovereignty to be fully realised in the first referendum we had, in adopting a Constitution drafted without the constraints of the Treaty and the oversight of the British parliament. While it was a flaw in the Constitution as adopted, it was one that shaped our constitutional development, and strengthened its successor through a legacy of a commitment to democratic principles and traditions.

References

Aguiar-Conraria, Luís, and Pedro C. Magalhães. "Referendum design, quorum rules and turnout." *Public Choice* 144, No. 1/2 (July 2010): 67–68. https://doi.org/10.1007/s11127-009-9504-1

Butler, Graham. "The Representative of the Crown and the Governor-General of the Irish Free State: Text and Context."

Cahillane, Laura. "Popular sovereignty under the 1922 Constitution: theory and reality." In *Constitutional Change and Popular Sovereignty: Populism, Politics and the Law in Ireland*, edited by Maria Cahill, Colm Ó Cinnéide, Seán Ó Conaill and Conor O'Mahony, 22-37. Oxford: Routledge, 2021.

Cahillane, Laura. *Drafting the Irish Free State Constitution*. Manchester University Press, 2016.

Coffey, Donal K. "The Need for a New Constitution: Irish Constitutional Change 1932–1935." Irish Jurist 48, no. 2 (2012): 275–302.

Farrell, Mel. *Party Politics in a New Democracy: The Irish Free State, 1922–37*. London: Palgrave, 2017a.
Farrell, Mell. *Party Politics in a New Democracy, 1922–37*. London: Palgrave, 2017b.
Harkness, David. "Patrick McGilligan: Man of commonwealth." *The Journal of Imperial and Commonwealth History* 8, no. 1 (1979): 117–135.
Kissane, Bill. *New Beginnings: Constitutionalism and democracy in modern Ireland*. University College Dublin Press, 2011.
Ruane, Bláthna. "Democratic control and constitutional referenda." In *Law and Government: A Tribute to Rory Brady*. Dublin: Round Hall, 2014.
Ward, Alan J. *The Irish Constitutional Tradition: Responsible Government and Modern Ireland 1782–1992*. CUA Press, 1994.

CHAPTER 14

What the Drafters Learnt in 1937 from the 1922 Experience

Gerard Hogan

I.

It is clear with the benefit of hindsight that the Constitution of the Irish Free State of 1922 was largely doomed from the start. There are several reasons for this, some of which I propose now to explore. The key difficulty was that the 1922 Constitution was itself shackled to the Anglo-Irish Treaty of 1921, so that s. 2 of the Irish Free State Constitution Act 1922 provided that any legislation which contravened this Treaty was "absolutely void and inoperative". Although the Treaty itself had been approved by Dáil Éireann in January 1922 by 64 votes to 57, there were, unfortunately, appreciable elements of that minority who were prepared to resort to violence in their opposition to the Treaty.

To my mind the Civil War should best be seen as an attempt by a small (but well-armed) minority to usurp the authority of Dáil Éireann. The elections for the third Dáil had been held on Friday 16 June 1922 and

G. Hogan (✉)
Supreme Court, Dublin, Ireland

L. Cahillane, D. K. Coffey (eds.), *The Centenary of the Irish Free State Constitution*, Palgrave Modern Legal History,
https://doi.org/10.1007/978-3-031-46181-1_14

they, for good measure, showed a comfortable victory for the Pro-Treaty parties.[1] I cannot help thinking that the fundamentally anti-democratic character of the revolt by the Anti-Treaty side is insufficiently emphasised—even today—by those who comment on the Civil War. It was in essence an attempt at an army *coup d'état*.[2] I can well understand the concerns of those who opposed the Treaty. But that did not entitle them to resort to violence when they lost the Dáil vote. The Second Dáil which voted for that Treaty was, after all, an all-island body and there was no oath of allegiance required. The resort to violence on the part of a disaffected minority had baneful consequences, both then and afterwards.

Why, then, is the Civil War not seen in this way as an attempt by disaffected elements of an army to repudiate the civil authority, even though this is in truth essentially what occurred? One may, I think, venture the following explanations. First, the bitterness of the conflict evoked a response from the nascent Provisional Government/Free State Government which at times seemed unyielding, brutal, and even cruel. Second, the staid, religiously conservative, and generally unexciting nature of the Cumann na nGaedheal Government which emerged victorious in the Civil War rather lacked, for example, the glamour and appeal of the Spanish Popular Front following its victory in the February 1936 Spanish general election. Third, the nature of the conflict between the majority in Dáil Éireann and elements of the Army was obscured by virtue of the confused constitutional arrangements—specifically, the absence of an effective judicial dispute mechanism and the lack of clarity as to what the *Grundnorm* of the Irish Republic during the period of 1919 to 1922 actually was–which obtained in Ireland in 1922. The subsequent Constitution of the Irish Free State 1922 only partially addressed these concerns, and it would take another Constitution in 1937 before these democratic *Grundnormen* were fully bedded down. As I have written elsewhere,[3] a confusion in the Irish Republic's own legal system between 1919–1922 and the manner in

[1] Made up of 94 Deputies supporting the Treaty, with 34 against: see Donal O'Sullivan, *The Irish Free State and its Senate* (London: Faber & Faber, 1940), pp. 62–63. O'Sullivan calculated the Anti-Treaty vote as approximately 22 per cent.

[2] Cf. the comments of Duggan, in Joseph M Curran, *The Birth of the Irish Free State 1922–1923* (Alabama: University of Alabama Press, 1980) at 290: "Whether the State was to be ruled by the people or by a revolutionary junta was the most important question confronting Ireland in 1922 and the underlying cause of the civil war."

[3] Gerard Hogan, "The Count Plunkett Habeas Corpus Application and the end of the Dáil Supreme Court" (2022) 68 *Irish Jurist* 25.

which this was to inter-act with the new constitutional arrangements in 1922 contributed to the outbreak of the Civil War. Certainly, long-lasting lessons were learnt as a result of this confusion, and I contend that this influenced not only the drafting of the Constitution of the Irish Free State in 1922 but perhaps even more particularly the Constitution in 1937.

You might say that the vote for the Treaty was ill-advised or that a better deal could have been done with the British. In a democracy, however, that is generally beside the point. And, of course, a fundamental aspect of democracy is that the use of force is reserved to the State itself: one cannot vote for private armies, and they do not make themselves accountable to Dáil Éireann. The wanton breach of this rule constituted a grave form of original sin on the part of the Anti-Treaty forces.

It is salutary to reflect on what might have happened to the Irish democratic system had a solemn Dáil vote for the Treaty been overthrown by military force. It is hard to see how it would have led to anything else other than a form of authoritarian military government, a development which would have had long-lasting negative implications for our democratic tradition. And if those who opposed the Treaty by violence in 1922–1923 could have seen ahead to the 1930s—by which stage all of their objections to that Treaty had been removed by democratic means, a process reaching its apotheosis with the enactment of the Constitution in 1937 and the return of the Treaty ports in April 1938—could they possibly have thought that resorting to violence was worth it? They might of course say in turn that there was still the issue of Northern Ireland. Yet apart from the fact that Northern Ireland was not the actual basis of the Civil War[4] – since both sides had (somewhat naively) hoped that the Boundary Commission would produce a favourable result [5]—the sad reality is that one hundred years later the two nations who make up the island of Ireland are still as far apart and the institutions created by the most comprehensive endeavour to reach agreement—the Belfast (Good Friday) Agreement of 1998—are still not working properly or in the manner which the drafters of that agreement had originally intended. Some form of partition was inevitable in 1922.

[4] "The border within Ireland scarcely figured in that [Treaty] debate" in Colum Kenny, "'It is notorious that a lawyer cannot draft his own will clearly'; Framing the Boundary Commission in the Anglo-Irish Treaty 1921'".

[5] See generally Kenny ibid.

In some ways, however, the lesson of the Civil War was that democracy ultimately prevailed on the battlefield. The commitment to democratic rule and the subjugation of the Army to the civil power was made clear by both the Constitution of the Irish Free State in 1922 and emphatically re-stated by the Constitution of Ireland in 1937. Article 15.6 of the Constitution reserves the raising of any military or armed force to the Oireachtas and Article 28.3 reserves the right to declare war to the Dáil.

One way or another, however, the Constitution of Ireland was designed to cut a further link between the actions of 1916 and the unilateral military action proposed by illegal organisations who claimed a line of apostolic succession directly from Tone, Emmet and Pearse. Indeed, when de Valera spoke in the Dáil on the Treason Bill 1939, he spoke of it "in symbolic terms, arguing that it gave further legitimacy to the Irish State":[6]

> The moment the Constitution was enacted by the People, treason had a new meaning ... To make it clear that treason must no longer be understood in terms of allegiance to foreign powers ... treason was defined as an act of treachery against this State, and nothing else.[7]

de Valera later added:

> We have here a democratic Constitution and a democratic State, and democratic States need to watch with far more care how any body or group, by violent means, should seek to overthrow them. There can be no democracy and no liberty such as is provided for in that Constitution unless violent methods by groups within the community are prevented, and it is to prevent

[6] Seosamh Ó Longaigh, *Emergency Law in Independent Ireland 1922–1948* (Dublin, 2006) at 228.

[7] 73 *Dáil Debates*, Cols. 966–967 (23 February 1939). In Fanning's words, in Ronan Fanning, "'The Rule of Order': Éamon de Valera and the IRA, 1923–1940" in O'Carroll and Murphy eds., *de Valera and his Times* (Cork, 1986) at 167:

> The baldness of de Valera's words contrasts starkly with the labyrinthine language of so many of his earlier utterances on the subject. The reason why ambiguities were at an end, of course, was that, after 1937, the state was no longer the Irish Free State detested by all republicans but de Valera's 'Ireland". The framework for the application of the 'rule of order' was now complete."

such violent action by any groups within the community, and to draw the attention of the community as a whole to their liberty and to the obligation which that liberty imposes upon them as citizens, and upon the public authority which they have set up, that we are at this time bringing in this Bill.[8]

Some five years later de Valera spoke openly admitted to the Dáil that the *Grundnorm* had been changed by the coming into force of the Constitution:

The Constitution is a free Constitution, made by the Irish people, and every section in the country will have to obey the laws. It is our business to see that that is done and, if we do not do so, we will have chaos.

I appeal to all Deputies to see the seriousness of this matter. I appeal to the people of the country to give no countenance to this organisation, no matter what may be the aims they say they have, no matter how much they may appeal to sentiments which are dear to us and have been dear to us in the past. There is a change of position in this country: the methods which were used to try to defeat a foreign Power in this country ought not to be used against an Irish Government freely elected here under a free Constitution.[9]

This was further reinforced by the fact that, as de Valera was always keen to stress, the Constitution was adopted by popular vote. In contrast to the situation in 1916, there were now democratic mechanisms—the Oireachtas and, in the final analysis, the referendum—whereby the authentic voice of the Irish people could be heard. It should be recalled—although it nowadays rarely is—that the 1916 leaders claimed only to be entitled to act in the manner in which they did pending the establishment

[8] 73 *Dáil Debates* at Col. 968.

[9] 95 *Dáil Debates* at Cols. 1460–1462 (1 December 1944). This was a debate concerning the death sentence which had been imposed on Charlie Kerins, the "Chief of Staff" of the IRA, for the murder of a special branch detective in 1942. Kerins had been hanged that morning.

of such institutions.[10] This sentiment is also reflected in Article 6(1) of the Constitution which provides that all powers of government derive from the People "whose right it is to designate the rulers of the State and, in final appeal, to decide all questions of national policy."

II.

In this piece, however, I seek in a sense to go beyond 1922 in order to explore the influence on the drafting of the 1937 Constitution in respect of what was a fine and immensely praiseworthy document. It represented a codified stand-alone constitution in contra-distinction to the British common law tradition. It further provided for the most un-British features of popular sovereignty, initiatives and referendums and a catalogue of fundamental rights protections. As Coffey and others have conclusively shown,[11] the drafters looked especially at continental constitutions, particularly the Weimar Constitution of Germany which had entered into force in 1919. You might think that it was remarkable that a person—namely Mr. de Valera—who was prepared to encourage and support those Anti-Treaty forces who resorted to arms against the Dáil in 1922 would later come to admire that Constitution. Yet it seems plain that he did—it was just that like many things which he did after 1922, he could not admit this publicly. In this regard one may point to the fact of this was that every member of the key drafting team for the new Constitution in 1936–1937- such as John Hearne,[12] Michael McDunphy and Philip

[10] Thus, in the words of the Proclamation:

> Until our arms have brought the opportune moment for the establishment of a permanent National Government, representative of the whole people of Ireland and elected by the suffrages of all her men and women, the Provisional Government, hereby constituted, will administer the civil and military affairs of the Republic in trust for the people.

[11] Donal K. Coffey, "The Influence of the Weimar Constitution on the Common Law World" (2019) 27 *Rechtsgeschichte* 222.

[12] Hearne had not even been a member of the (original) Sinn Féin, having instead supported the old Irish Party. He later served as Commandant in the legal division of the Free State Army for the entirety of the Civil War and yet faithfully served de Valera a mere ten years later: see generally Eugene Broderick, "John Hearne and the Making of the 1937 Constitution" (2013) 69 *Decies* 171 at 172–173.

O'Donoghue—had been a pro-Treaty supporter. Further evidence comes from the fact that so many individual provisions in 1937 replicate the language (sometimes with simply verbal changes) of the Constitution of 1922.

Much as I admire the Constitution of 1922, I think nevertheless that on the whole the 1937 Constitution is a better—perhaps it would be even more true to say, a far better—document, subject to certain qualifications I will address in a moment. This is certainly true so far as the organisation and drafting of the document is concerned. And, moreover, there was much that was new and novel in 1937 which is to be admired—enhanced judicial review, an extended catalogue of fundamental rights, provisions for international law, the Presidency etc. The qualification is that the 1937 document reflected more faithfully the Irish nationalist/Catholic *Zeitgeist* of the period in a way which was not true of 1922. In the last fifty years or so as that *Zeitgeist* began to change—often dramatically—the existence of these particular provisions—such as the original prohibition on divorce, the recognition of the "special position" of the Catholic Church as "guardian of the faith of the majority" etc.—tended to obscure the real achievements of 1937—which in turn had built on those of 1922. It is only as the process of what might be termed constitutional secularisation—which commenced in December 1972 with the referendum on the deletion of the "special position" clause and which has now (almost) run to completion got under way—that the real merits of 1937 were there for all to see.[13] We now have a document which at every turn reinforces democracy, the rule of law, fundamental rights, effective judicial protection and the ultimate *Grundnorm* of popular sovereignty. There is here much to admire.

But to return to 1922, the Constitution of the Irish Free State was saddled with two major handicaps. First, it was inextricably bound up with the Treaty, although this was an unavoidable feature of that political agreement of December 1921. By the 1930s, however, the circumstances

[13]Thus, Whyte speaking regarding the deletion of the "special position" clause in December 1972 commented that the "religious freedom and equality guaranteed by section 2 of Article 44 now stand out sharply, unobscured by the ambiguous terminology of adjacent clauses". See John Whyte, *Church and State in Modern Ireland* (Dublin: Gill and Macmillan 1980) at 389.

surrounding the birth of the Irish Free State, the bitterness generated by the Civil War and the terms of the Treaty itself meant that a Lincolnian "new birth of freedom" was required, even if this took the form of an entirely new Constitution. The second was that a last-minute change to Article 50 of the 1922 Constitution provided that amendments could be made other than by way of referendum for an initial eight year period.

The judicial review powers of the 1922 Constitution did not prove to be a success and these powers seem to have been exercised at most twice during the period of the Irish Free State between 1922 and 1937.[14] Part of the reason was political: the 1922 Constitution had embodied the Treaty and as that Treaty had essentially caused a Civil War and riven Irish politics, it meant that that Constitution could never really obtain widespread acceptance. The other reason was essentially a legal one: the 1922 Constitution contained essentially the same internal legal flaws as the Weimar Constitution of 1919—an uncertainty as to the ultimate *Grundnorm* and the lack of an effective body which could rule authoritatively on such questions.

Article 50 of the Irish Free State Constitution had originally provided in draft form that every amendment to the Constitution could only be made by way of a referendum. An amendment to Article 50 was, however, made at the last minute in the course of the Dáil Debates so that as a result the Constitution could be amended by ordinary legislation for an initial eight-year period.[15] This well-intentioned amendment ultimately proved disastrous for the long-term stability of the Constitution. The courts took their cue from this and reverted to traditional thinking, regarding the Constitution almost as a statute which could be implicitly amended by ordinary legislation. As O'Connor MR stated in the last judgment of the (old) Irish Court of Appeal in May 1924 in *R. (Cooney) v. Clinton*[16]:

> It is difficult to see how, during the period of eight years, any Act passed by the Oireachtas can be impeached as ultra vires so long as it is within the

[14] The two examples appear to be *R. (O'Brien) v. Military Governor of North Dublin Union (No.2)* [1924] 1 IR 46; *Irish Transport and General Workers Union v. Transport and General Workers Union* [1936] IR 471.

[15] See generally, Gerard Hogan, *The Origins of the Irish Constitution* (Dublin: Royal Irish Academy, 2012) at 4–8.

[16] Belatedly reported at [1935] IR 247.

> terms of the Scheduled Treaty. It was urged that any Act of Parliament purporting to amend the Constitution should declare that it was so intended, but I cannot accede to the argument in view of the express provision that any amendment made within the period may be made by ordinary legislation.[17]

This trend was to continue throughout the life of the Irish Free State, with judges ultimately accepting what came to be known as the "implicit amendment" theory, that is, that if there was a conflict between the Constitution and a statute, the Constitution must be taken to have been implicitly amended.[18] Article 50 was itself amended by the Constitution (Amendment No. 16) Act 1929 which extended the original eight years period for a further eight years to 1938. When the validity of this constitutional amendment was upheld by a majority of the Supreme Court in December 1934 in *The State (Ryan) v. Lennon*,[19] this had the consequence that during the entire period of its existence the Constitution of the Irish Free State was totally vulnerable to legislative change, thereby rendering totally ineffective the idea of judicial review of legislation.

The Constitution of 1922 failed because it had suffered the same kind of fundamental problem as what the German constitutional lawyers call

[17] [1935] IR 245 at 247. Note the comments of Ó Dálaigh C.J. in *McMahon v. Attorney General* [1972] IR 69 at 101 to the effect that "during the existence of Saorstát Eireann it was at no time possible to challenge, as being unconstitutional, any ordinary legislation passed by the Oireachtas of Saorstát Eireann." In his judgment in *Laurentiu v. Minister for Justice* [1999] 4 IR 26 at 65–66 Barrington J was unsparing in his criticisms:

> To derive … a doctrine that the Constitution could be amended by ordinary legislation which need not even be expressed to be a constitutional amendment showed scant respect to the Constitution. It also assumed that the Constitution had so little respect for the Constitution that they would amend it without thinking of what they were doing. It also had the practical disadvantage that one could not find out what the Constitution of the Irish Free State provided without reading the whole body of statute law passed since 1922.

[18] See, e.g., *Attorney General v. McBride* [1928] IR 451 at 456, per Hanna J.; *Lynham v. Butler (No.2)* [1933] IR 74 at 112 per FitzGibbon J. See generally, Laura Cahillane, *Drafting the Irish Free State Constitution* (Manchester: MUP, 2016) at 157–162 and Gerard Hogan, Gerry Whyte, David Kenny & Rachael Walsh, *J.M. Kelly: The Irish Constitution* (5th Ed, Dublin: Bloomsbury, 2018) at 2608–2610.

[19] [1935] IR 70.

Verfassungsdurchbruch (roughly the equivalent of our "implicit amendment" doctrine) and it was the same problem which had occurred in respect of the Weimar Constitution. Thus, for example, the term of the (then) German President Ebert's office had been extended by a qualified majority vote the Reichstag in 1922 even though Article 41 of the Weimar Constitution had also specified that this had required a direct election by the public. This was the equivalent of amending the Constitution by implication.

As is well known, exactly the same happened during the lifetime of the 1922 Constitution of the Irish Free State. Article 50 had required that every constitutional amendment had to be subjected to a referendum, but at the last moment this provision was amended to allow the Constitution to be amended by ordinary legislation for an eight-year period. That period was itself amended in 1929 so that it was extended for another eight years. This meant that during the entire lifetime of the 1922 Constitution it could be amended by ordinary legislation. The Irish courts—unused as they were to ideas of judicial review or the hierarchy of norms—held that this meant that if there was a conflict between the text of the Constitution on the one hand and ordinary legislation on the other, the Constitution was "implicitly amended" as a result.

It is interesting that the new Constitutions/Basic Law which replaced these documents both opted for precisely the same solution. Article 46.3 and Article 46.4 of the Constitution provide:

> 3. Every such Bill shall be expressed to be 'An Act to amend the Constitution'.
> 4. A Bill containing a proposal or proposals for the amendment of this Constitution shall not contain any other proposal

Article 79(1) of the German Basic Law 1949 is expressed to be in very similar terms, with the essentially the same solution of the implicit amendment problem which had ultimately destroyed the Weimar Constitution in that it provides that:

> The Basic Law can only be changed by a law that expressly changes or supplements the wording of the Basic Law.

What is perhaps just as interesting a question is why the drafters of the Constitution of 1937 not only continued with the experiment of judicial review of legislation, but actually took the opportunity to strengthen and copper-fasten these powers. Planning for a new constitution had commenced in earnest in 1934. This was not in itself a particular surprise as the new political party—Fianna Fáil—which had been formed in 1926 by Mr. de Valera and others who were opposed to the 1922 Treaty had come to power following the March 1932 general election. That period between 1932 to 1936 was notable for the enactment of various constitutional amendments designed to undo the Treaty settlement, not least the oath of allegiance,[20] the appeal to the Privy Council[21] and (later) the Governor General. The validity of these amendments was ultimately upheld by the Privy Council in June 1935 in *Moore v. Attorney General of the Irish Free State*[22] on the basis that the Statute of Westminster 1931 had given the Oireachtas (as a Dominion Parliament) the power to amend the Irish Free State Agreement Act 1922.[23]

Rather remarkably the Supreme Court had come to the opposite conclusion in *The State (Ryan) v. Lennon* in December 1934, reasoning that the third Dáil sitting qua constituent assembly had never given a power to amend the Treaty to the new Oireachtas.[24] It was perhaps just as well that this conflict between the Supreme Court and the Privy Council on this most fundamental of issues had never been put to the test during the lifetime of the 1922 Constitution. This very lack of certainty on the entire Treaty settlement was itself another reason why a new Constitution was necessary.

[20] Constitution (Removal of Oath) Act 1933. This Act had purported to amend Article 50 of the Irish Free State Constitution which had provided that the Oireachtas had no power to amend the Scheduled Treaty.

[21] Constitution (Amendment No. 22) Act 1933.

[22] [1935] IR 472.

[23] As Viscount Sankey LC put it ([1935] IR 472 at 486–487):

"The simplest way of stating the situation is to say that the Statute of Westminster gave to the Irish Free State a power under which they could abrogate the Treaty, and that, as a matter of law, they have availed themselves of that power."

[24] It has to be said that aspects of this reasoning are rather unclear and not very satisfactory: see generally Donal K. Coffey, *Constitutionalism in Ireland 1932–1938* (Palgrave, 2018) at 65–70. It seems to suggest that the third Dáil possessed powers to bind its successors which subsequent Dálaí (and Oireachtais) did not possess. But why should this be? The third Dáil sat until August 1923 (when the first post-Civil War general election took place). Why should the members of that Dáil have had powers in October 1922 to bind their successors and then lose them once the Constitution of the Irish Free State came into force on 6 December 1922? The normal rule, of course, is that where there is a conflict between parliamentary statutes the most recent prevails: see *McLoughlin v. Minister for Public Service* [1985] IR 631 at 635, per Henchy J.

Writing shortly afterwards, Hood Phillips thought that it followed from the *Ryan* case that the Oireachtas was free to repeal "*ex post facto* Article 65 and part of Article 66 of the Constitution which give the Courts their power to review legislation."[25] Yet unbeknownst to him, events were already moving decisively in the opposite direction. Mr. de Valera had no intention at all of removing these powers of judicial review: if anything, he went about strengthening it. To this end he had already established a Committee drawn from the senior echelons of the civil service whose task it was to examine the existing Constitution with a view:

> to ascertaining what Articles should be regarded as fundamental on the grounds that they safeguard democratic rights, and to make recommendations as to steps which should be taken to ensure that such Articles should not be capable of being altered by ordinary processes of legislation.[26]

The Committee duly reported to Mr. de Valera and its report ultimately paved the way for the introduction of a new Constitution. The draft was approved by a unicameral Oireachtas between May and June 1937, with the draft Constitution being approved by a plebiscite held in conjunction with the general election which was held on 2 July 1937. The Constitution itself came into force on 29 December 1937.

While an account of the complex drafting history of the Constitution in 1937 lies well beyond the parameters of this book, there are three striking features of that document's organisation which may be noted here. First, the drafters took great pains to ensure that, henceforth, it could not be easily amended. There were to be no further implicit amendments, as Article 46.3 stipulated that every Bill to amend the Constitution must expressly be so described and Article 46.4 states that a Bill containing a proposal to amend the Constitution "shall not contain any other proposal." Article 46.2 provided that the only way of amending the Constitution was by way of referendum.[27] In some ways, it was this change

[25] Owen Hood Phillips, "Ryan's Case "*Law Quarterly Review* 52 (1936): 241, 246.

[26] National Archives of Ireland, Department of the Taoiseach, S 2979. Hogan, *Origins* at 74–100.

[27] It is true that Article 51 allowed as a transitional measure the Constitution (other than Article 46 itself and Article 51) to be amended by ordinary legislation in certain circumstances for a period of three years from the date on which the first President took office. That period lapsed on 25 June 1941 so that henceforth the Constitution can only be amended by referendum: see *Kelly: The Irish Constitution* (n 18) at 2605–2610.

which was transformative. It was this stipulation—excluding constitutional amendments save by referendum—which perhaps more than anything else contributed to the long term success and survival of the 1937 Constitution just as it was the last-minute change to Article 50 of the 1922 Constitution which more than anything else contributed to the latter's ultimate demise.

The second striking feature was that the power of judicial review of legislation was actually strengthened. So far as judicial review powers are concerned, Article 34.3.2 expressly and unambiguously conferred the right of judicial review of legislation on the High Court and the Supreme Court.[28] Article 26 introduced the entirely new procedure of *ex ante* judicial review in that the President was enabled, following consultation with the Council of State, to refer Bills passed by both Houses of the Oireachtas to the Supreme Court so that their consistency with the Constitution may be determined. These powers of judicial review are reinforced by the prohibition on the enactment of unconstitutional litigation contained in Article 15.4[29] and by the statement contained in Article 28.2 that the executive power of the State may only be exercised in a manner which is consistent with the Constitution itself.[30] Neither Article 15.4 nor Article 28.2 had any counterpart in the 1922 Constitution. It might, of course, be said that both of these provisions did no more than expressly state a principle which is in any event inherent in a system of judicial review where legislative enactments and executive action are subjected to examination for consistency with the higher law contained in the Constitution itself.

Third, the list of enumerated fundamental rights was much extended, including for the first time guarantees as to equality before the law (Article 40.1), property rights (Article 40.3.2 and Article 43), family and education (Article 41 and Article 42). Critically, there was also a provision—Article 40.3.1 and Article 40.3.2—which imposed a general obligation on the State "as best it may" to defend and vindicate constitutional rights,

[28] And since the establishment of the Court of Appeal in October 2014, the Court of Appeal: see 33rd Amendment of the Constitution Act 2013.

[29] "1. The Oireachtas shall not enact any law which is in any respect repugnant to the Constitution or any provision thereof. 2. Every law enacted by the Oireachtas which is in any respect repugnant to this Constitution or to any provision thereof shall, but only to the extent of such repugnancy, be invalid."

[30] Article 28.2 provides that: "The executive power of the State shall, subject to the provisions of this Constitution, be exercised by or on the authority of the Government."

including in particular the right to life, person, good name, and property rights. The Preamble to the Constitution also sought to protect the "freedom and dignity of the individual."[31]

IV.

There were other changes as well. Article 50 of the 1922 Constitution had made the passage of a referendum depend on *either* a majority of the voters on the register *or* two thirds of the voters who actually turned out to vote at the referendum. This made the passage of a referendum depend on *either* the size of the electoral turn-out at the referendum *or* upon an artificially high majority of the voters.[32] This was (wisely) dropped in 1937 so far as constitutional amendments were concerned, but a version of it was (unwisely) retained so far as the Article 27 referendum whereby Bills can be referred to the People was concerned: see Article 47.2.1. It is small wonder that the Article 27 referendum/initiative procedure has never been used.

And in conclusion, some other representative examples can be mentioned briefly: the manner in which Article 38.3. dealt with the Special Criminal Court is a big improvement on Article 2A providing for military tribunals. Of course, Article 2A was itself inserted by ordinary legislation in 1931 by the Constitution (Amendment No. 19) Act 1931 and it supplemented the original Article 70 of the 1922 Constitution which had prohibited "extraordinary courts". Yet even by 1934 senior civil servants had acknowledged that although the form of Article 2A was "grotesque", it was necessary also to find a replacement which more readily accommodated itself to a rule of law-type model.[33] Article 38.3.3 by allowing for the

[31] See generally, Samuel Moyn, "The Secret History of Constitutional Dignity" (2014) 17 *Yale Human Rights and Development Law Journal* 39; Christopher McCrudden, "Where did Human Dignity come from? Drafting the Preamble to the Irish Constitution" (2020) 60 *American Journal of Legal History* 485.

[32] So, for example, in a 49% turn-out the referendum would not have passed unless it obtained a 66.6% majority of the actual voters.

[33] Hogan, *Origins*, at 35.

establishment by law of the Special Criminal Court is a clear improvement on its forerunner.[34]

And de Valera correctly challenged John A. Costello in the Dáil Debates on the drafting of the Constitution as to whether he would be happy with describing—as Article 6 of the 1922 Constitution did—personal liberty as "inviolable". Not surprisingly Costello was not.[35] Article 40.4.1 now protects personal liberty in an important and significant fashion, but without resorting to the elevated phrase "inviolable."

[34] As I explained in my judgment in *Dowdall v. Director of Public Prosecutions* [2022] IESC 36:

"Its predecessor was, of course, the Constitution (Special Powers) Tribunal first established under Article 2A of the Constitution of the Irish Free State (as inserted by Constitution (Amendment No. 17) Act 1931) in October 1931. That Tribunal consisted of three military officers from whom there was no right of appeal. The Tribunal was, moreover, at liberty to impose any sentence it thought appropriate (including the death penalty), even if such was not provided for under the ordinary law. It was no wonder that members of this Court considered that the "extreme rigour" of Article 2A was such that "its provisions pass far beyond anything having the semblance of legal procedure" and that the "judicial mind was staggered at the very complete departure from legal methods in use in these Courts": see *The State (Ryan) v. Lennon* [1935] IR 170 at 237–238, per Murnaghan J.

Much was changed by both Article 38.3.1 of the Constitution and the Offences against the State Act 1939: the Special Criminal Court had to be established by law. Article 38.3.2 further required that the "constitution, powers, jurisdiction and procedure of such special courts shall be prescribed by law." The Court as so established was, moreover, a statute-based court with no inherent jurisdiction: see, *e.g.*, *The People (Director of Public Prosecutions) v. Rice* [1979] IR 15 at 20, per Henchy J.

Precisely as required by Article 38.3.2, the jurisdiction of the Court was carefully prescribed by ss. 46 and 47 of the 1939 Act. Article 38.3.2 further requires that the procedure of the Court be prescribed by law. Section 41(4) of the 1939 Act accordingly gives effect to this constitutional requirement in that it provides that the practice and procedure and the rules of evidence applicable to a trial in the Central Criminal Court "shall apply to every trial by a Special Criminal Court". Provision is also now made for an unrestricted right of appeal by any convicted person to the Court of Appeal: see s.44 of the 1939 Act (as inserted by s. 32 of the Criminal Procedure Act 2010)."

[35] 67 *Dáil Debates* at Cols. 1524–1525.

V.

In the closing lines of Gore Vidal's great historical novel, *Lincoln*, the author attributes to John Hay—Lincoln's loyal young secretary—the view that Lincoln "in some mysterious fashion, had willed his own murder as a form of atonement for the great and terrible thing that he had done by giving so bloody and absolute a rebirth to his nation".[36] In much the same vein I have come to the conclusion that by giving us a elegantly drafted Constitution which, above all else, reinforced democracy and the rule of law at every level in our political system and which provided for the will of the People as its ultimate *Grundnorm* in a way that we as a society still perhaps do not fully value or appreciate, de Valera sought thereby to atone for his mendacity, narcissism and petulance by defying the will of Dáil Éireann in the course of 1922 and for failing at that time to acknowledge the merits of the 1922 Constitution. It was these failings which had fanned the flames of an unnecessary and destructive Civil War.

Yet in concluding let us adopt the spirit of forgiveness and generosity which was one of Lincoln's defining characteristics by acknowledging that by way of implicit atonement for his actions in 1922 de Valera opted decisively for democracy and the rule of law in 1937 and cemented it firmly in the fabric of society in a way in which the drafters in 1922 had sought to do but had not fully accomplished. Democracy is a fragile plant and let us be grateful that in both 1922 and 1937 there were people who were prepared to provide the warm earth and the adequate moisture which would enable it to grow and flourish.

References

Broderick, Eugene. "John Hearne and the Making of the 1937 Constitution." *Decies* 69 (2013): 171.

Cahillane, Laura. *Drafting the Irish Free State Constitution*. Manchester: MUP, 2016.

Coffey, Donal K. "The Influence of the Weimar Constitution on the Common Law World." *Rechtsgeschichte* 27 (2019): 222.

Coffey, Donal K. *Constitutionalism in Ireland 1932-1938*. Palgrave, 2018.

Curran, Joseph M. *The Birth of the Irish Free State 1922-1923*. Alabama: University of Alabama Press, 1980.

[36] Gore Vidal, *Lincoln* (New York: Random House, 1984) at 657.

Fanning, Ronan. "'The Rule of Order': Éamon de Valera and the IRA, 1923-1940." In *de Valera and his Times*, edited by O'Carroll and Murphy, Cork, 1986.

Hogan, Gerard et al. *J.M. Kelly: The Irish Constitution*. 5th Ed, Dublin: Bloomsbury, 2018.

Hogan, Gerard. "The Count Plunkett Habeas Corpus Application and the end of the Dáil Supreme Court." *Irish Jurist* 68 (2022): 25.

Hogan, Gerard. *The Origins of the Irish Constitution*. Dublin: Royal Irish Academy, 2012.

Kenny, Colum. "'It is notorious that a lawyer cannot draft his own will clearly'; Framing the Boundary Commission in the Anglo-Irish Treaty 1921." *Irish Jurist* 68 (2022): 1.

McCrudden, Christopher. "Where did Human Dignity come from? Drafting the Preamble to the Irish Constitution." *American Journal of Legal History* 60 (2020): 485.

Moyn, Samuel. "The Secret History of Constitutional Dignity." *Yale Human Rights and Development Law Journal* 17 (2014): 39.

Ó Longaigh, Seosamh. *Emergency Law in Independent Ireland 1922-1948*. Dublin, 2006.

O'Sullivan, Donal. *The Irish Free State and its Senate*. London: Faber & Faber, 1940.

Phillips, Owen Hood. "Ryan's Case." *Law Quarterly Review* 52 (1936): 241.

Vidal, Gore. *Lincoln*. New York: Random House, 1984.

Whyte, John. *Church and State in Modern Ireland*. Dublin: Gill and Macmillan 1980.

CHAPTER 15

The Afterlife of the Constitution of the Irish Free State: Constitutional Echoes in South Asia

Donal K. Coffey

The year 1922 marked the beginning of independent Ireland's constitutional journey. The innovations detailed in this volume did not go unmarked outside of the Irish Free State. The constitutional model drafted and developed in the context of the lifespan of the Free State was the subject of interest to other drafters and theorists, particularly those attempting to chart a course that would lead to the outer constitutional reaches of the British Empire/Commonwealth and beyond. The fact that the Irish constitutional structure could exist within the British Commonwealth of Nations meant that theorists considering what constitutional futures their

D. K. Coffey (✉)
Maynooth University, Maynooth, Ireland

Max Planck Institute for Legal History and Legal Theory,
Frankfurt am Main, Germany
e-mail: Donal.Coffey@mu.ie

L. Cahillane, D. K. Coffey (eds.), *The Centenary of the Irish Free State Constitution*, Palgrave Modern Legal History,
https://doi.org/10.1007/978-3-031-46181-1_15

countries might enjoy could draw on the ideas underpinning it confident that the British Government had already accepted the basic structure. This was in keeping with the Free State's position as, as Shonk puts it, the 'shadow metropole'[1] and also the interactions between Irish and other colonial subjects during the time,[2] where the Free State often provided a source of anti-colonial inspiration.

The decision by the Irish Constituent Assembly to publish some of its preparatory work as the volume 'Select Constitutions of the World'[3] was to prove particularly influential, as it allowed the Irish view of constitutional development to be inferred. In the introduction, the text noted that the material had been presented chronologically, with the following brief note:

> In the present place it will suffice to indicate that the earliest Constitutions, whether monarchical or republican, place the weight of power in the Executive; Constitutions of the nineteenth century place the weight of power in legislative organisations; whereas recent Constitutions tend to place the weight of power more and more in the intervention of the people themselves.[4]

This basis of the Constitution of the Irish Free State in popular sovereignty was, as we shall see, of considerable interest in South Asia. The publication of the volume increased the visibility of the Free State Constitution as a model to be studied, and the chronological ordering of the constitutions in the volume meant it was the first draft that a reader encountered. In 1934 the Free State Government provided permission to Benegal Shiva Rao to use that volume for his own title of the same name.[5] This new volume contained some interesting departures from the original text—it included the text of the Irish Constituent Act which gave the force of law to the 1922 Constitution, as well as amendments subsequent to 1922, the text of the Statute of Westminster, and of dispatches between

[1] Kenneth Shonk, 'The Shadow Metropole: The Varieties of Anticolonialims in Ireland, 1937–68' in *Ireland in an Imperial World: Citizenship, Opportunism, and Subversion*, eds. McMahon, Nie, Townend, (London: Palgrave Macmillan, 2017).

[2] See, e.g. Kate O'Malley, *Ireland, India and Empire: Indo-Irish Radical Connections, 1919–64* (Manchester: Manchester University Press, 2008).

[3] *Select Constitutions of the World* (Dublin: The Stationery Office, 1923).

[4] Ibid, iv.

[5] B. Shiva Rao (ed), *Select Constitutions of the World* (Madras: Madras Law Journal Press, 1934).

Éamon de Valera, President of the Executive Council of the Irish Free State, and J.H. Thomas, the British Secretary for Dominion Affairs, in relation to the contours of Dominion status in 1933.[6]

The influence of the Irish Free State Constitution can be clearly seen in constitutional drafts prepared during the time of its existence. Perhaps the clearest example can be seen in the Nehru Committee report of 1928 which drew heavily on the Free State as an example. The draft, one of the most significant early draft constitutions for an independent India,[7] provided in its first clause:

> India shall have the same constitutional status in the comity of nations known as the British Empire as the Dominion of Canada, the Commonwealth of Australia, the Dominion of New Zealand, the Union of South Africa and the Irish Free State, with a Parliament having powers to make laws for the peace, order and good government of India, and an executive responsible to that Parliament, and shall be styled and known as the Commonwealth of India.[8]

The model here was obviously the first Article of Agreement for a Treaty concluded between Irish and British negotiators in 1921. The report drew on other provisions of the Constitution in a similar manner. The importance of the report for subsequent drafts of Indian constitutions created one pathway for Irish constitutional ideas to be adopted in the final Constitution of India of 1950.

It's not possible to canvass the entirety of the influence of the Free State on other legal systems in one chapter, so it is proposed instead to give an impressionistic account of that influence by paying particular attention to those provisions which have been the subject of scholarly attention elsewhere in this volume.

[6] See, e.g., 1, 36–38. See further Donal K. Coffey, 'The Influence of the Weimar Constitution on the Common Law World' *Rechtsgeschichte/Legal History* 17 (2019): 222, 227.

[7] See Bhuwan Kumar Jha, 'Nehru Report, Muslim Demands and the Hindu Mahasabha: Elusive Consensus on Future Constitution' *Indian Journal of Public Administration* 66(4) (2020): 534, 535.

[8] *All Parties Conference 1928: Report of the Committee appointed by the Conference to determine the principles of the Constitution for India* (Allahabad: All India Congress Committee, 2nd ed) 100–101.

Partition and Citizenship

In his chapter in this volume, Colin Murray has drawn attention to the legally complex, and fraught, nature of the relationship between the Free State and Northern Ireland.[9] The fact that Northern Ireland was afforded the opportunity of opting out of the Free State, an opportunity swiftly seized, was a legal precedent in dealing with territorial issues in constitutional law. Murray's chapter draws specific attention to questions of citizenship that arose as a result of this complexity. It is perhaps unsurprising that the fact of partition should also feature prominently in relation to the Indian constitutional experience.

India faced similar difficulties to Ireland. The short, sharp, and bloody nature of Indian independence and partition meant that questions of territory remained unsolved. Readers will no doubt be familiar with the violence which was midwifed by Partition along the Pakistan/Indian border, but there remained issues in relation to the Princely States. These States were not part of British India and subject to direct rule, but were rather treaty signatories with the UK and subject to various forms of direct and indirect control, e.g. through the British Resident in the Princely States who represented British interests.[10] On independence, this meant that the question of Princely States was still unsettled. This is perhaps most widely known in relation to the Princely State of Hyderabad which had an immensely wealthy Muslim ruler.[11] The question of Hyderabad's accession to India famously ended up before the United Nations in May 1949.[12]

The issues relating to the Princely States became particularly problematic in relation to the vexed question of citizenship; how should the new Indian state deal with individuals who were outside of the jurisdiction of the new Dominion of India but might ultimately become citizens in short order after the accession of the relevant Princely States? In May 1947, when the matter was under consideration by Benegal Narsing Rau, the

[9] Chapter 3.

[10] On the history behind this, see Michael H. Fisher, 'Indirect Rule in the British Empire: The Foundations of the Residency System in India (1964–1858)' *Modern Asian Studies* 18(3) (1984): 393.

[11] See, e.g. Kavita Datla, 'Sovereignty and the End of Empire: The Transition to Independence in Colonial Hyderabad' *Ab Imperio* 3 (2018): 63.

[12] Priyasha Saksena, 'Building the Nation: Sovereignty and International Law in the Decolonisation of South Asia' *Journal of the History of International Law* 23 (2021): 52, 63–68.

legal advisor to the Indian Constituent Assembly, it was not yet clear how long this process might take; in fact it had been broadly completed by the time the new Republic Constitution came into effect in 1950.[13]

The model adopted by Rau drew on the insights of partition on the island of Ireland. Rau separated out the Union territories and territories subject to the jurisdiction of India; the latter covered the Princely States who might choose not to opt into the new State while the former embraced the Princely States.[14] His proposal was that citizenship would apply, subject to the qualification, to every person 'domiciled in the territories included within the Union and subject to its jurisdiction ...'[15] He argued that the draft was different from the Irish provision on the grounds that 'initially at least the Union may not exercise jurisdiction over the whole of India.'[16] This was obviously different to the situation in Northern Ireland. In the event, the final draft of the citizenship clause in the Indian Constitution as enacted omitted the jurisdictional qualification, and hewed more closely to the Free State example, stating baldly that the provisions applied to 'every person who has his domicile in the territory of India ...' subject, again, to qualification. It is perhaps worth noting here that the qualifications followed those of the Free State Constitution, with the exception that the period of ordinary residence was shortened from 7 to 5 years in the Indian Constitution.

Language

In her chapter for this volume, Róisín Á Costello analyses the constitutional position of the national language in Saorstát Éireann.[17] The question of languages was understandably amongst the most vexed amongst the polyglot entities that made up the British Empire. The Union of South Africa, for instance, had provided in section 137 for British and Dutch, and only British and Dutch, to be the 'official' languages of the Union. In 1925, after some controversy, the definition of Dutch was expanded to

[13] There were, of course, later accessions to the Union such as Sikkim.

[14] 'Memorandum on the Union Constitution and Draft Clauses Prepared by the Constitutional Adviser May 30, 1947' in *The Framing of India's Constitution: Select Documents Volume 2*, ed. B. Shiva Rao, (New Delhi: The Indian Institute of Public Administration, 1967) 470–474.

[15] Ibid, 472.

[16] Ibid, 473.

[17] Chapter 7.

include Afrikaans by the Official Languages of the Union Act 1925. The contrast between 'official' languages and a 'national' language, as provided for under the Irish Free State Constitution, was to prove a difficult line to negotiate in the period of decolonisation.

The provisions of the Indian Constitution in relation to languages were amongst the most controversial, and remain so to this day. The possibility of introducing a 'national' language, i.e. Hindi, exercised protagonists and antagonists for the position. It was inevitable that the Irish example would be included in this debate, and the constitutional provision for Irish as the national language was duly appealed to by Pandit Ravishankar Shukla in the Constituent Assembly on 12 September 1949.[18] He argued for the adoption of the Irish position, with Hindi as the national language of India, for the possibility of adopting regional languages, but also for the rule that if there was a conflict between the languages English was to give way, following the Irish model.

In the end, Article 343(1) provided for Hindi in Devanagari script as the 'official' rather than 'national' language. A similar formula was adopted in Article 216 of the Burmese Constitution of 1948, despite the provision in Article 215 for a 'National' flag. More tragically, the provision of the Official Language Act 1956 in Ceylon was an attempt to entrench Sinhalese as the language of the new State, with the abolition of English as an official language. The Act was clearly discriminatory to the Tamil minority, but the legislation was upheld by the Ceylonese courts in Attorney General v Kodeswaran, before being overtaken by the new Republican constitutional settlement.[19]

Article 11 of the Constitution of the Irish Free State

Article 11 of the 1922 Constitution is the subject of Jamie McLoughlin's chapter in this volume which concerns the provision relating to the governance of 'natural resources' in the Free State.[20] It's not well-known that this provision did in fact, travel, albeit to a constitutional model that was

[18] Constituent Assembly Debates volume IX (12 Sept 1949) accessed online at https://indiankanoon.org/doc/192004/

[19] See further Rehan Abeyratne, 'Uncertain Sovereignty: Ceylon as a Dominion 1948–1972' *International Journal of Constitutional Law* (2019): 1258, 1271–1273.

[20] Chapter 9.

ultimately unsuccessful. In 1944 Ceylon was engaged in a constitutional drafting exercise in anticipation of the grant of Dominion status.[21] The key national political grouping responsible at this point in time was the Ceylon National Congress (CNC). Ultimately, the CNC was sidelined in the drawing up of the final Constitution in favour of a closed drafting group involving D.S. Senanayake, Oliver Goonetilleke, and W. Ivor Jennings.[22] In November 1944, officials within the CNC were still engaged in this process, however. On 29 November, J.R. Jawyewardene wrote to S.W.R.D. Bandaranaike (both future Prime Ministers of Ceylon/Sri Lanka) to propose a new draft Constitution. In Article XII of this draft, one finds the clear influence of the Free State Constitution in relation to 'lands, waters, rivers, and minerals…'[23] The text has been modified, but there are direct textual links, specifically the use of the phrase 'All natural resources in Ceylon (including the air and all forms of potential energy)'. The Ceylonese draft also follows the 'lease or licence' model of Article 11 of the Free State Constitution, but here with a renewable term of 33 years (rather than a 99 year non-renewable lease) and crucially this clause is restricted to 'any foreign body'. The phrasing of the Ceylonese draft, in

[21] The leading text on this time in Ceylonese history is Benjamin Schonthal, *Buddhism, Politics and the Limits of Law: The Pyrrhic Constitutionalism of Sri Lanka* (Cambridge: Cambridge University Press, 2016) chapter 2.

[22] See Harshan Kumarasingham ed., *The Road to Temple Trees – Sir Ivor Jennings and the Constitutional Development of Ceylon – Selected Writings* (Colombo: Centre for Policy Alternatives, 2015).

[23] Michael Roberts (ed), *Documents of the Ceylon National Congress and Nationalist Politics in Ceylon 1929–1950 volume III* (Colombo: Department of National Archives, 1977) 2595:

> All lands, waters, rivers, and minerals which is not privately owned in Ceylon shall vest in the State or any department thereof according to law to be held for the benefit and use of the citizens of the Republic. All natural resources in Ceylon (including the air and all forms of potential energy) subject to any agreement, trust, grant, lease or concession or private interest granted shall vest in the Government according to such regulations and provisions as will be made by the Parliament from time to time. No lease or licence or monopoly of the natural resources of the Republic shall be granted to any foreign body, corporation, trust or company except with the prior sanction of the Parliament in the public interest for a period not more than thirty-three years and such lease or licence or grant may be renewable according to the public interest.

particular the 'lease or licence' section, make it clear that the draft is based on the Free State Constitution, rather than the Irish Constitution of 1937.

Ultimately, this draft was not adopted as part of the Ceylonese drafting process; as Senanyake's influence waxed, that of the CNC waned. The importance of the question of land may, however, be gauged by the relatively brief period of time taken to set in place the legal framework dealing with the central issue in the Crown Lands Ordinance 1949.

State (Ryan) v Lennon and Constitutional Autochthony

The most high-profile use of the constitutional theory of the Irish Free State, beyond those elements which recur in the Constitution of 1937, must surely be the case of *State (Ryan) v Lennon*,[24] considered in this volume by Alan Greene[25] and Maurice Collins.[26] It featured at some length in one of the most famous international constitutional cases in the twentieth century—the Indian Supreme Court case of *Kesavananda Bharati v State of Kerala*. This decision introduced the world to the idea of the 'basic structure' doctrine—the idea that there existed in the Indian Constitution certain features which could not be amended, India notably using the parliamentary amendment of the constitution model under Article 368. A significant discussion in the case was about the use of *State (Ryan) v Lennon* as a precedent, which was commented upon by David Gwynn Morgan at the time.[27] It must be admitted, however, that while the Free State case was cited, it was peripheral to the ultimate decision of the Indian court.[28]

Where *State (Ryan) v Lennon* was more successfully utilised abroad was in relation to the principle of constitutional autochthony. In Ireland, we

[24] [1935] IR 170. The case has been the subject of academic consideration for decades. Recently see, e.g., Tom Hickey, 'Revisiting *Ryan v Lennon* to make the case against Judicial Supremacy (and for a new model of Constitutionalism in Ireland' *Irish Jurist* 53 (2015): 125; Thomas Mohr, 'Natural Law in Early Twentieth Century Ireland – *State (Ryan) v Lennon* and its Aftermath' *The Journal of Legal History* 42(1) (2021): 1, 14–21; Donal K. Coffey, 'The Judiciary of the Irish Free State' *Dublin University Law Journal* 33 (2011): 61.

[25] Chapter 4.

[26] Chapter 8.

[27] (1973) 4 SCC 225; see David Gwynn Morgan, 'The Indian "Essential Features" Case' *The International and Comparative Law Quarterly* (1981): 307, 312 n 27, 320 n 57.

[28] See, e.g. ibid., Sikri CJ at [374].

are more familiar with the term as it relates to the enactment of the 1937 Constitution by plebiscite. Writing in 1960, however, K.C. Wheare adopted the idea of autochthony and applied it to the Irish Free State Constitution, indicating the ideological continuity of the idea in both of independent Ireland's constitutions, and specifically reviewed *State (Ryan) v Lennon* as part of the exegesis of the concept.[29] Similarly, in Ceylon/Sri Lanka, the term was traced backwards to the Free State Constitution and to *State (Ryan) v Lennon.* J.A.L. Cooray explained the relevance of the case as follows:

> The principle of autochthony had in fact been asserted by the Irish in 1922 and upheld by the Irish Courts. The view taken by the Courts was that the 1922 Constitution obtained its legal validity through its approval by the representatives of the people, sitting in the Irish Free State Legislature (Dail Eireann) as a Constituent Assembly. According to that view the Constitution was entirely derived from the sovereignty of the Irish people.[30]

Cooray explained that the British idea of the legal foundation of the State was different, resting as it did on a British statute. Cooray critiqued the 1946 Dominion Constitution of Ceylon on this basis, and advocated the adoption of an autochthonous Constitution which derived its sovereignty from the people of Sri Lanka. This idea was to be adopted in the Republican Constitution of Sri Lanka in 1972 when Cooray acted as a Constitutional Advisor.[31]

Constitutionalism

A final note may be pertinent outside of the parameters of legal transfers or transplants. This is in relation to matters which are not necessarily susceptible to the same process—the influence and understanding of

[29] K.C. Wheare, *The Constitutional Structure of the Commonwealth* (Oxford: Clarendon Press, 1960) chapter 4, particularly 92–93.

[30] J.A.L. Cooray, *Constitutional and Administrative Law of Sri Lanka* (Colombo: Sumathi Publishers, 1995) 88 (footnotes omitted).

[31] See further Asanga Welikala, 'The Failure of Jennings' Constitutional Experiment in Ceylon: How 'Procedural Entrenchment' led to Constitutional Revolution' in *The Sri Lankan Republic at 40: Reflections on Constitutional History, Theory and Practice*, ed. Welikala, (Colombo: Centre for Policy Alternatives, 2013).

constitutionalism within the Free State. This subject has been touched upon in the chapters by Seán Enright[32] and David Kenny[33] in this volume.

What was the perception outside of the jurisdiction of constitutionalism within the Free State? In the 1942 Northern Ireland Legal Quarterly, there is an anonymously authored article entitled 'Law in Eire'.[34] The article considered Irish constitutional developments during the Free State and under the new Constitution in 1937, with the preponderance of the analysis concerning legislature and executive action during the timespan of the Irish Free State.

The author was concerned with the development of constitutional law and theory during the Irish Free State. The article first canvassed the claims of the de Valera Government to be able to amend the Constituent Act containing the repugnancy clause before concluding that, under the Irish theory of the State, this was outside the powers of the Oireachtas under Article 50.[35] The author commented: 'A more lawless proposal can seldom have been made by the responsible head of any state, and yet Mr. de Valera knew what he was doing.'[36] This was followed with an analysis of the decision of the Supreme Court in *State (Ryan) v Lennon* which had thrown into doubt the constitutionality of the Oireachtas' actions in attempting to remove the Oath of Allegiance from the Irish Constitution under the Irish theory (although not the British theory).[37]

The argument then considered the habit that the Oireachtas had developed of legislating with the intention of reversing or preventing the adjudication of legal disputes, drawing attention to the passage of the Copyright (Preservation) Act 1929 (overturning *Performing Rights Society v Bray Urban District Council*) and the Land Purchase (Guarantee Fund) Act 1936 (which prevented legal action on foot of action that was arguably ultra vires). For the purposes of this chapter, it suffices to draw attention to the retrospective nature of the legislation. In the 1929 Act, section 4 provided that 'no remedy or relief' was recoverable by reason of a copyright infringement in the Free State 'before the passing of this Act'. In the 1936 Act, section provided that it was deemed to have come into effect on

[32] Chapter 12.
[33] Chapter 10.
[34] (1942) 5 NILQ 84.
[35] Ibid, 86.
[36] Ibid, 87.
[37] Ibid, 88–89. On the controversy, see further Donal K. Coffey, 'The Commonwealth and the Oath of Allegiance Crisis: A Study in Inter-War Commonwealth Relations' *The Journal of Imperial and Commonwealth History* 44(3) (2016): 492.

1st April 1932, and that anything done before the passing of the Act on 16th January 1936 but after 1st April 1932 which was 'in relation to or for the purposes' of the Act was lawful.[38]

The anonymous author did draw attention to the actions of the courts in cases where they prevented excessive executive jurisdictional claims in cases such as *Re Mountcharles' Estate* which quashed a decision of the Land Commission made without providing notification to affected parties.[39] Notwithstanding this praise for the judicial arm of the State, the commentator then went on to consider the manner in which this arm had been sidelined by the establishment of Military Tribunals through a succession of Public Safety Acts from 1923 to 1933.[40] The article argued that the powers of arrest, the lack of appeal, the provision for capital punishment, the fact that it could oust the jurisdiction of the ordinary courts, and the lack oflegislative review was analagous to the Star Chamber or Revolutionary Tribunal of the Terror and stated 'it seems almost ludicrous to examine laboriously breaches of constitutional law in the face of this tyranny.'[41]

The article concluded:

> Thus there is no rule of law in Eire, theoretically or in fact. The principle was broken with straight away. Then the fundamental law was flouted and when the Courts struggled to support it a new Constitution was issued. The Executive was given wide powers, but when these were not wide enough, they legislated to make legal prohibition ineffective. Finally, to ensure the ineffectiveness of law they established a Court of their own with powers to deal with 'any offence whatsoever.' Is there anything more that tyranny can do? So far these powers have been cautiously used, but the powers are there and the rule of law is gone.[42]

The tone struck is over wrought, but it is notable that there were similar, albeit more couched, criticisms from commentators such as Arthur Berriedale Keith, the pre-eminent constitutional theorist of the British

[38] The time was chosen to coincide with the outbreak of the Anglo-Irish Trade war as a result of the failure of the Free State Government to repay land annuities to the British Government. Coincidentally, the outbreak of that trade war also saw an Act with retrospective effect, with custom duties backdated from June 1932 to March 1932 by virtue of the Finance (Customs Duties) (No. 2) Act 1932.

[39] [1935] IR 163.

[40] Above note 22, 95.

[41] Ibid, 96.

[42] 96.

Empire in the inter-War period.[43] Two points are, however, worth noting. The first is that Ireland within the United Kingdom had never experienced the rule of law as conceived in Dicey's exposition of the British Constitution. Christopher Roberts terms the experience of British rule over Ireland 'repressive legality' and has noted the way in which legislation enforced in Ireland provided a template for the export of this repressive legality throughout the British Empire.[44] Second, Northern Ireland was after 1922 subject to the Civil Authorities (Special Powers) Act, and the tenor of the analysis may have been conditioned by an attempt to claim that the Free State, and latterly Ireland, were so much more lawless than what was experienced in Northern Ireland.

What cannot be gainsaid, however, is that the claims made were based on constitutional amendments, legislation, and constitutional practice in the Free State. The article also contains two points about the history of constitutionalism in Ireland which are worth noting. First, the actions of the judiciary in relation to constraints on governmental action ensured that there was always some check on the actions of the other branches. In particular, it is worth noting that even in the case of the Constitution (Special Powers) Tribunal, the High Court held that it was subject to review.[45] It is foreseeable, therefore, that this could later develop into a more robust consideration of the provisions of the 1937 Constitution. Indeed, our anonymous author would seem to concede something like this was inevitable, for in relation to the 1922 Constitution they argued that the courts' interpretation of constitutional provisions began in 1934 and '[t]his slow development is quite natural.'[46] It is noteworthy that with the exception of *The State (Burke) v Lennon* and *Re Article 26 and the School Attendance Bill*,[47] this was the trajectory that the 1937 Constitution also followed.[48]

[43] See, e.g., A.B. Keith, *An Introduction to British Constitutional Law* (Oxford: Oxford University Press, 1931) 145–146.

[44] Christopher N.J. Roberts, 'From State of Emergency to the Rule of Law: The Evolution of Repressive Legality in the Nineteenth Century British Empire' *Chicago Journal of International Law* 20(1) (2019): 1.

[45] [1935] IR 70. The limitation on what was achievable substantively may be seen in cases such as The State (McCarthy) v Lennon [1936] IR 485.

[46] Ibid, 85.

[47] [1943] IR 334.

[48] See Gerard Hogan, 'The Supreme Court and the Reference of the Offences against the State (Amendment) Bill 1940' *Irish Jurist* 35 (2000): 238 for the background and aftermath to the case.

Second, the fact that the powers conferred were 'cautiously used' demonstrated a core political limitation on the otherwise wide latitude that was granted. There was demonstrably less of a consideration of the legal niceties that modern constitutional theory would concern itself with, but there remained within Irish political circles a self-imposed limitation on more widespread use of these powers, perhaps conditioned by the essentially lawless actions of the State during the Civil War.

Conclusion

This chapter has sought to demonstrate that despite the fact that the Irish Free State only existed for 15 years, the constitutional ideas which it developed were influential in ways that are not always appreciated. The fact that the development of constitutionalism as a limiting force on the actions of the State was viewed with a critical eye in some quarters does not detract from the interest which these ideas attracted in other jurisdictions. In particular, this chapter has shown the deep interest in the ideas underpinning the Irish Free State in South Asia. These ideas were not accepted uncritically, but it is worth bearing in mind the international legacy of the Free State Constitution when considering its impact in the round.

It is also worth noting that the twenty-first century has demonstrated a greater willingness on the behalf of the Irish judiciary to consider constitutional developments outside of the United States and the old Settler Dominions of Canada and Australia in the exposition of Irish constitutional principles. The recent judgement of MacMenamin J in *Costello v Government of Ireland* is interesting as it inverts the histories we have considered here. In the context of his exposition of the Administration of Justice under the 1937 Constitution, he argued:

> Any court will be alive to the criticisms that, in speaking of the scope of Article 34 judicial power, it is engaging in special pleading. Judicial rhetoric on this issue is sometimes regarded with reserve. It is not coincidental that there are other constitutions which, through inheritance and adaptation, share some identity or constitutional "DNA" with ours. The Indian Constitution of 1950 is one such constitution. Courts sometimes resort to quotations from Madison or Jefferson. I refer instead to one of the great framers of the Indian constitution, a man who deserved to be referred to in the same breath as the American framers. Dr. Ambedkar referred to the power of the Indian Supreme Court contained in the constitution of the largest democracy in the world as being "the soul of the constitution, and

> the very heart of it". To Ambedkar, a member of the Dalit social caste, who were a sometimes described as "Untouchables", the constitutional provision had a particular importance. It provided the means whereby remedies could be provided for rights violations, oppression and discrimination, including those on caste. Article 32 of the Indian Constitution, dealing with the jurisdiction of that Supreme Court, was one, without which the Indian constitution would be nothing but a "nullity". It "made rights real" (Constitutional Assembly Debates, December 9, 1948). I would respectfully adopt the same phraseology with regard to Article 34 of our Constitution.[49]

This is noteworthy but also fitting, as core ideas were developed as transplants from the same tree. The twenty-first century may see a greater consideration, and where appropriate adoption, of the constitutional fruits of other legal systems that share a common constitutional hinterland.

References

Abeyratne, Rehan. "Uncertain Sovereignty: Ceylon as a Dominion 1948-1972." *International Journal of Constitutional Law* (2019): 1258.

Coffey, Donal K. "The Influence of the Weimar Constitution on the Common Law World." *Rechtsgeschichte/Legal History* 17 (2019): 222.

Coffey, Donal K. "The Judiciary of the Irish Free State." *Dublin University Law Journal* 33 (2011): 61.

Coffey, Donal K. "The Commonwealth and the Oath of Allegiance Crisis: A Study in Inter-War Commonwealth Relations." *The Journal of Imperial and Commonwealth History* 44, no. 3 (2016): 492.

Cooray, J.A.L. *Constitutional and Administrative Law of Sri Lanka*. Colombo: Sumathi Publishers, 1995.

Datla, Kavita. "Sovereignty and the End of Empire: The Transition to Independence in Colonial Hyderabad." *Ab Imperio* 3 (2018): 63.

Fisher, Michael H. "Indirect Rule in the British Empire: The Foundations of the Residency System in India (1964-1858)." *Modern Asian Studies* 18, no. 3 (1984): 393.

Hickey, Tom. "Revisiting *Ryan v Lennon* to make the case against Judicial Supremacy (and for a new model of Constitutionalism in Ireland." *Irish Jurist* 53 (2015): 125.

Hogan, Gerard. "The Supreme Court and the Reference of the Offences against the State (Amendment) Bill 1940." *Irish Jurist* 35 (2000): 238.

[49] [2022] IESC 44, at [177].

Jha, Bhuwan Kumar. "Nehru Report, Muslim Demands and the Hindu Mahasabha: Elusive Consensus on Future Constitution." *Indian Journal of Public Administration* 66, no. 4 (2020): 534.

Keith, A.B. *An Introduction to British Constitutional Law*. Oxford: Oxford University Press, 1931.

Kumarasingham, Harshan. *The Road to Temple Trees – Sir Ivor Jennings and the Constitutional Development of Ceylon – Selected Writings*. Colombo: Centre for Policy Alternatives, 2015.

Mohr, Thomas. "Natural Law in Early Twentieth Century Ireland – *State (Ryan) v Lennon* and its Aftermath." *The Journal of Legal History* 42, no. 1 (2021): 1.

Morgan, David Gwynn. "The Indian 'Essential Features' Case." *The International and Comparative Law Quarterly* (1981): 307.

O'Malley, Kate. *Ireland, India and Empire: Indo-Irish Radical Connections, 1919-64*. Manchester: Manchester University Press, 2008.

Rao, B. Shiva. *Select Constitutions of the World*. Madras: Madras Law Journal Press, 1934.

Roberts, Christopher N.J. "From State of Emergency to the Rule of Law: The Evolution of Repressive Legality in the Nineteenth Century British Empire." *Chicago Journal of International Law* 20, no. 1 (2019): 1.

Roberts, Michael. *Documents of the Ceylon National Congress and Nationalist Politics in Ceylon 1929-1950 volume III*. Colombo: Department of National Archives, 1977.

Saksena, Priyasha. "Building the Nation: Sovereignty and International Law in the Decolonisation of South Asia." *Journal of the History of International Law* 23 (2021): 52.

Schonthal, Benjamin. *Buddhism, Politics and the Limits of Law: The Pyrrhic Constitutionalism of Sri Lanka*. Cambridge: Cambridge University Press, 2016.

Select Constitutions of the World. Dublin: The Stationery Office, 1923.

Shonk, Kenneth. "The Shadow Metropole: The Varieties of Anticolonialims in Ireland, 1937-68." In *Ireland in an Imperial World: Citizenship, Opportunism, and Subversion*, edited by McMahon, Nie, Townend, London: Palgrave MacMillan, 2017.

Welikala, Asanga. "'The Failure of Jennings' Constitutional Experiment in Ceylon: How 'Procedural Entrenchment' led to Constitutional Revolution." In *The Sri Lankan Republic at 40: Reflections on Constitutional History, Theory and Practice*, edited by Welikala, Colombo: Centre for Policy Alternatives, 2013.

Wheare, K.C. *The Constitutional Structure of the Commonwealth*. Oxford: Clarendon Press, 1960.

Index[1]

A

Amendment of the Free State Constitution, 4, 13, 29, 31, 47, 48, 53–57, 55n28, 59, 61, 63–65, 67, 68, 70, 73, 75, 84, 89, 165, 182, 272, 275, 277–279, 283
Anglo-Irish Treaty 1921 (The Treaty), 4, 6, 53, 92, 218, 240, 244, 253
Anniversary, 10, 22, 37, 154
Anti-Party, 16
Anti-Treaty, 54, 63, 70, 78–81, 83, 83n47, 85–88, 89n78, 187, 191n81, 217n1, 218, 219, 221, 222, 226, 240, 254, 255, 258
Attorney General, 33, 97, 124, 144, 147, 149, 156, 164n65, 220

B

Border, 3, 7, 26, 28, 31–38, 41, 43, 44, 274
Boundary Commission, 31, 35, 38, 44, 78, 255
Brehon law, 154, 156–158
Britain, 14, 29, 42, 58, 74n1, 91, 202n16, 205, 205n26, 206, 219, 220
British parliament, 104, 205n26, 249, 250
Bunreacht na hÉireann, 5, 25, 44, 91, 137, 141n25, 164n62

C

Carson, Edward, 17, 28, 31, 39
Ceylon/Sri Lanka, 7, 277

[1] Note: Page numbers followed by 'n' refer to notes.

L. Cahillane, D. K. Coffey (eds.), *The Centenary of the Irish Free State Constitution*, Palgrave Modern Legal History, https://doi.org/10.1007/978-3-031-46181-1

Childers, Erskine, 80, 84, 86, 142, 222–225, 228
Churchill, Winston, 79, 81
Civil War, 2, 6, 16, 19, 22, 28, 79, 80, 80n32, 88, 97, 150, 153, 191, 193, 217–231, 253–256, 254n2, 258n12, 260, 268, 283
Collins, Michael, 2, 29, 32, 38, 219, 228, 235
Common Travel Area, 26
Commonwealth, 77, 96, 201, 271
Constituent Assembly, 13, 15, 18n33, 52–54, 58, 59, 62–65, 69, 75, 76, 80, 81, 85, 86, 136, 138, 148, 150, 188, 249, 263, 276, 279
Constituent power, 3–4, 47–71
Constitutionalism, 279–283
Constitution Committee, 14, 15, 137n6, 200, 205, 207, 211, 213
Cosgrave, W. T., 26, 30, 37, 38, 77, 104, 227, 239–242
Courts, 5, 6, 17–19, 30, 34, 56, 57, 59, 60, 86, 117, 118, 123–127, 129, 135–151, 163, 182, 198, 209, 212, 218–221, 221n14, 223–226, 247, 260, 262, 264, 267n34, 276, 278, 279, 281–283
Courts of Justice Act 1924, 124–125, 138n14, 148
Craig, James, 26, 27, 27n10, 30–33, 35–40, 35n49, 37n60, 40n78, 44
Crown, 4, 12, 86, 91–109, 114, 118, 123, 166, 181n29, 202n16
Cumman na nGaedheal, 104, 182, 241, 243–245, 254
Customs, 26–29, 34–36, 44, 97, 281n38

D

de Valera, Éamon, 30, 43, 44, 70, 80, 80n32, 87, 88, 88n72, 93, 102, 104, 108, 131, 182, 191, 234, 235, 240–248, 256–258, 256n7, 258n12, 263, 264, 267, 268, 273, 280
Decade of Commemorations, 22
Democracy, 2, 6, 7, 10–14, 19, 21, 51, 73, 75, 136, 160, 192, 247, 250, 255, 256, 259, 268, 283
Democratic programme, 82, 160, 163, 201, 206
Direct democracy, 5, 12, 177, 180, 184–185, 241
Dominion, x, xi, 11, 17, 27, 27n9, 27n10, 29–31, 34, 44n96, 54, 77, 92, 98, 123, 164n62, 168, 177, 181n29, 189, 243, 263, 273, 274, 277
Douglas, James, 14, 201, 210

E

Éireann, Dáil, 13, 75, 79–83, 87, 88, 89n78, 98, 99, 106, 114, 136, 139, 178, 201, 244, 253–255, 268, 279
Environmental rights, 213
Execution, 6, 115, 147, 217–230
Extern ministers, 74, 78, 78n17

F

Fianna Fáil, 2, 14n12, 17, 88, 104, 183, 185, 240, 241, 243, 263
Figgis, Darrell, 156, 157, 186n51, 201, 227, 228

France, Clement J., 156, 171, 201, 207, 208, 210
Functional/vocational councils, 5, 185–186

G
Gaelic state, 12, 156, 157
Gaeltacht, 115, 120, 124, 125, 132
Gavan Duffy, George, 75, 76, 141, 227
German Basic Law, 205, 262
Government of Ireland Act 1920, 25, 27, 31, 76, 140
Governor-General, 4, 20n38, 62–63, 91–109, 93n9, 122, 139, 220, 245, 246, 263
Griffith, Arthur, 28, 86
Grundnorm, 7, 254, 257, 259, 260, 268

H
Housing, 5, 199, 209, 212, 213

I
Independence, 5, 11, 18, 28, 31, 86, 117–118, 137n6, 149, 179, 191, 201, 206, 212, 225, 274
India, 7, 273–276
Initiative, 6, 12, 13, 14n12, 18, 184, 185, 234, 235, 239, 241–243, 248–250, 258, 266
Irish Free State, 1–3, 7, 9, 11, 12, 25–28, 31, 35–37, 40, 44, 47–71, 73–89, 91–109, 121, 128, 135, 137, 141, 153, 154, 159, 172, 177, 178, 183, 199, 199n9, 201, 218, 220, 233, 240, 244, 246, 250, 253–256, 256n7, 259–262, 261n17, 263n20, 263n24, 267n34, 271–284
Irish language, 18, 82, 95, 114, 115, 117, 119–124, 121n22, 124n31, 127–130, 166, 170
See also National language
Irish speakers/Irish-speaking, 114–117, 119, 124–126, 130, 132

J
Judicial review, 5, 7, 17–21, 75, 139, 147, 176, 181, 259–262, 264, 265
Judiciary, 6, 17, 18, 21, 99, 131, 137n6, 149, 217, 282, 283

K
Kennedy, Hugh, 2, 3, 17, 21, 29, 48, 57, 61–66, 68–70, 97, 102, 123, 124, 127, 129–131, 136–138, 138n12, 147–150, 147n46, 148n47, 156, 201, 205, 206, 210, 220
Kohn, Leo, 2, 18, 19n36, 84n53, 123, 124, 136, 138, 159, 160, 188, 193, 205n26, 239

L
Legacy, 3, 10, 19–22, 131, 177, 211, 231, 233–250, 283
Lloyd George, David, 27, 28, 31, 207

M
MacNeill, James, 102
Martial Law, 32

McNeill, James, 92, 93, 93n7, 201
Military courts, 6, 59, 218–221, 223, 226

N
National language, 4, 113–132, 275, 276
Natural resources, 5, 154–172, 164n65, 168n76, 199n9, 202, 202n16, 203, 276, 277, 277n23
1919 Constitution of Dáil Éireann, 81–83
Northern Ireland, 3, 25–27, 27n9, 27n10, 29–45, 32n34, 37n60, 40n78, 76, 77, 249, 255, 274, 275, 282

O
Oath of faithfulness/allegiance (parliamentary oath), 14n12, 28, 63, 66, 78, 96, 97, 185, 254, 263, 280
O'Higgins, Kevin, 13, 220, 222, 228, 237, 238, 241
Oireachtas, 13, 16, 55–67, 69, 88, 92, 96–100, 102–106, 114, 120–122, 130, 131, 136, 137n6, 140–143, 141n25, 145, 146, 148, 150, 154, 159, 160, 162, 163, 165, 167, 168n76, 170, 177, 178, 184, 197, 198, 199n9, 202n16, 209, 237, 238, 240–244, 247, 256, 257, 260, 263, 263n20, 264, 265n29, 280
O'Rahilly, Alfred, 156, 201, 203, 203n17, 204

P
Participatory democracy, 6
Partition, 3, 25–45, 54, 70, 211, 255, 274–275
Pearse, Padraig, 256
Popular sovereignty, 7, 10–13, 17–19, 21, 157, 166, 170, 177, 180, 184, 186, 192, 234, 249, 250, 258, 259, 272
Post-war European constitutions, 12, 157
President, 4, 13–15, 20n38, 91–93, 98, 99, 101, 101n38, 102, 106, 108, 109, 137n6, 139, 140, 143, 230, 247, 248, 264n27, 265, 273
Private property, 156, 197, 199–205, 207, 208, 210–213
Property rights, 5, 156, 156n18, 197–213, 265, 266
PR-STV, 16, 18

R
Referendum, 6, 12, 13, 14n12, 18, 52, 53, 55, 57, 59, 64, 70, 88, 137, 139, 140, 150, 183n38, 184, 185, 192, 199, 234–241, 234n5, 241n28, 243, 246–250, 249n65, 257–260, 262, 264–266, 264n27, 266n32
Republicanism, 11n6, 12, 54, 70, 77, 81, 87, 101, 180, 234, 256n7, 272, 276
Repugnancy clause, 84–85, 280
Rule of law, 6, 7, 56, 57, 109, 146, 217–231, 259, 266, 268, 281, 282

S
Seanad Éireann, 13, 42, 76, 98, 139, 178
Security, 32–35
State (Ryan) v Lennon, 3, 17, 19, 21, 48, 56–58, 136–138, 138n12, 141, 143, 146–151, 147n46, 181, 235, 261, 263, 278–280, 282
Stormont, 37, 44

U
Ua Buachalla, Donal, 92, 93, 93n9, 106
Unionist/Unionism, 4, 26, 36, 37, 37n60, 40, 43, 44, 74, 76–78
United Kingdom (UK), 6, 26, 28, 32, 33, 35, 36, 38, 39, 41, 42n90, 43, 48, 51–53, 55, 56, 59, 68, 76, 77, 91, 92, 92n2, 103, 108, 118, 179, 246, 249, 274, 282

W
Weimar, 109, 260, 262
Westminster, 5, 11, 20, 26–28, 27n9, 34, 39, 52, 54, 66, 68, 70, 81n36, 85, 86, 104, 105, 108, 175–194, 219, 222, 234, 243, 263

GPSR Compliance
The European Union's (EU) General Product Safety Regulation (GPSR) is a set of rules that requires consumer products to be safe and our obligations to ensure this.

If you have any concerns about our products, you can contact us on

ProductSafety@springernature.com

In case Publisher is established outside the EU, the EU authorized representative is:

Springer Nature Customer Service Center GmbH
Europaplatz 3
69115 Heidelberg, Germany

www.ingramcontent.com/pod-product-compliance
Ingram Content Group UK Ltd.
Pitfield, Milton Keynes, MK11 3LW, UK
UKHW020834290926
15470UKWH00004B/1346
9783031461804